THE CONDUCT OF LIFE

Lewis Mumford was born in Flushing, Long Island, in 1895, and was educated at the College of the City of New York, Columbia University, and the New School for Social Research. Though he has a specialist's reputation in the field of American literature and culture, architectural criticism, urban sociology, and technical history, he has been, from the beginning, a "generalist," a scholar in Emerson's original sense. Starting with *The Story of Utopias* (1922), almost half of his books have been in the fields of literature, education, politics, and philosophy; and it was as a representative of philosophy that Mr. Mumford was chosen to take part in the fiftieth-anniversary celebration of Stanford University, which made him an Honorary Fellow. From 1942 to 1944, he was Professor of Humanities at Stanford, and gave four courses that formed the core of the last two volumes in *The Renewal of Life* series. This series opened with *Technics and Civilization* (1934), followed by *The Culture of Cities* (1938) and *The Condition of Man* (1944). *The Conduct of Life,* published in 1951, was the final volume of the series. Mr. Mumford is a fellow of the American Academy of Arts and Sciences, a member of the National Institute of Arts and Letters, and a member of the American Philosophical Society.

THE CONDUCT OF LIFE

LEWIS MUMFORD

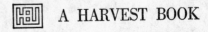 A HARVEST BOOK

HARCOURT BRACE JOVANOVICH, INC. • NEW YORK

Printed in the United States of America
ISBN 0-15-621600-0

F G H I J

PREFACE: 1970

With this book the series on which I began work in 1930 came to a close. In these volumes I sought to deal in a unified way with man's nature, his work, and his life-dramas, as revealed in the development of contemporary Western civilization. Though I reserved for The Conduct of Life—and my own further maturity—a discussion of the final problems of man's nature, destiny, and purpose, the present volume, so far from being an epilogue, served in fact as a preface to the earlier books. While each volume stands alone, they modify each other; and the full import of any one cannot be grasped without an understanding of the other three.

Yet because seven years elapsed between the publication of The Condition of Man and The Conduct of Life, the final book presented difficulties I found it hard to overcome; for the hopeful note that pervaded the earlier volumes, conceived as they were in 1930, no longer rang true; and the concrete richness of illustration, drawn from actual life in the earlier books, was too often missing. But if the impetus of the original conception was lost, and irrecoverable by any act of personal will, something was likewise gained. For as it turned out, The Conduct of Life outlined some of the major themes of the volumes that were to follow: Art and Technics, The Transformations of Man, The City in History, and The Myth of the Machine. None of these books could have opened up fresh territory without this preliminary examination of the nature of man, emphasizing the social importance of the dream, the formative role of language, and the dynamic offices of religion in molding both personality and culture.

That a generation filled with existential nausea, bent on inverting or subverting all traditional values, would reject The Conduct of Life goes without saying. Yet in spite of this the book has survived. As late as 1960, almost a decade after its publication, it became the first paperback in The Renewal of Life series; and the fact that a new edition is now called for shows that it has not indeed died of neglect, as such an unfashionable book, doggedly "waging contention with the times' decay," might be expected to die. In so far as The Conduct of Life helped to prepare the way for my later books, it belongs as much to the future as to the past. So I dare to leave these pages without any modifications and revisions; for they have in fact by now been made: not least in the latest volume, The Pentagon of Power (1970).

L. M.

CONTENTS

THE CONDUCT OF LIFE

CHAPTER I. THE CHALLENGE TO RENEWAL

1: THE PROMISE OF OUR AGE

The age that we live in threatens worldwide catastrophe; but it likewise holds forth unexpected hope and unexampled promise. Ours is no time for faint-hearted men. No matter how rugged the obstacles that confront us, we must push on, like Bunyan's Pilgrim, not heeding the Worldly Wisemen who are torpid to the danger and fearful of the promise. If we do not sink into the Slough of Despond, we may yet find our way to the Delectable Mountains and to that fair land where the sun shines night and day. The shadows that now fall across our path measure the height we have still to climb.

Perhaps never before have the peoples of the world been so close to losing the very core of their humanity; for of what use are cosmic energies, if they are handled by disoriented and demoralized men? But the very threat of general disintegration has also increased the possibility for a rapid and radical improvement in the condition of man. The most generous dreams of the past have now become immediate practical necessities: a worldwide co-operation of peoples, a more just distribution of all the goods of life; the use of knowledge and energy for the service of life, and the use of life itself for the extension of the human spirit to provinces where human values and purposes could not heretofore penetrate. If we awaken in time to overcome the automatisms and irrational compulsions that are now pushing the nations toward destruction, we shall create a universal community. Even if we awaken only belatedly, the fresh insight and the new philosophy that might have saved us in the first place will be needed to carry us through the dark days ahead.

The renewal of life is the burden and challenge of our time: its urgency lightens its risks and its difficulties. For the first time in history, the tribes and nations have the means of entering into an active partnership, as wide and unrestricted as the planet itself. Universal

fellowship, which the higher religions conceived for many millenniums as mankind's destiny, now has become technically feasible as
well as ideally conceivable: to seal that promise with acts of political
and economic co-operation on a worldwide scale has likewise become
a practical imperative.

Nothing short of such a transformation will keep the human race
from sliding back still further into barbarism: a barbarism whose
powers of destruction have been multiplied by the very scientific knowledge that most modern thinkers, up to our own age, believed a sure
guarantee of the continued advance of civilization. The rational conduct of life, plainly, demands something far different from the automatic extension of science and invention.

The age of the machine is already over. We cannot save our cunning inventions and our complicated apparatus of scientific research
unless we save man; and when we do so, the human person, not the
machine, will dominate the scene. The New World Symphony of exploration and conquest, and the Ballet Mécanique of modern industrialism, have both been performed to the point of exhaustion. The
next number on the program will be scored for a full orchestra and
a multitude of human voices, like Beethoven's Ninth Symphony: a
mass for the dead, a hymn for the living, a paean to the unborn: the
Oratorio of One World and of a new man capable of being at home
in that world.

For each of us, the moment of reorientation and renewal has come.
There is no mechanical device capable of effecting this transformation
in society: it must first take place in the minds and hearts of individual men, who have the courage to re-educate themselves to the realities
of the present human situation, and, step by step, take command of it.
Up to the limits of his capacities and insights, each one of us must
undertake his self-examination, re-appraise his standards and values,
alter his attitudes and expectations, and re-direct his interest. That
hour will demand a capacity for humility and sacrifice difficult under
any circumstances; but particularly difficult to a generation for whom
these words awaken only contempt or self-justifying resistance. Hence
the main purpose of this book is to assist in the necessary self-appraisal,
as the first means toward getting ready for playing a part in the new
drama of life.

If man were "just an animal" he would never have found that fact
out. If he were "just a machine" he could never have invented machines. If his existence were in fact purposeless, he might have sur-

vived without having a conscious purpose of his own; but he would never have been concerned with his own further development; and he would not have found it impossible to fulfill his animal needs without finding a place for them in some wider plan of life which transforms biological need into social ritual and social ritual into significant forms of communal and personal drama. For man existence is a continued process of self-fabrication and self-transcendence. Today, this act of self-understanding is the first step toward renewal: for each of us has a new part to master, a new role to enact, a new personality to shape, and new potentialities of life to fulfill.

The heroes of the old drama, proud, self-willed, formidable men, aggressive in action, isolationist in thought, will become the clowns and villains in the new; and those who were once cast for supernumerary parts will find themselves, because of their capacity for mutual aid, in the very center of the stage. For the renewal of life *is* the new drama of life. The main task of our time is to turn man himself, now a helpless mechanical puppet, into a wakeful and willing creator.

2: CANVASS OF POSSIBILITIES

The potentialities of the present age have often been childishly misconceived. Too readily, we extol our mistakes and miscarriages, and overlook our latent virtues. That is why it is important, at the beginning, to make a fresh tally of the new conditions that confront us and the new paths of development that lie ahead.

First of all, we must reject the popular Baconian notion that the "advancement of learning" and the progress of mechanical inventions will automatically bring about the improvement of man's estate, if man's own welfare and self-realization are included in that hope. The fact is that the inventions the twentieth century once innocently boasted, in Mr H. G. Wells' highly accurate "Anticipations," have proved, like the magical promises in a fairy tale, to have an unexpectedly wry or sinister outcome. The more godlike our powers have become, the more demonic our applications of this power have often turned out. At the beginning of this century, Dr Richard Bucke gave the approaching conquest of the air as one of the three changes that would transform mankind: he did not have the slightest foreboding that it might turn great cities into graveyards.

We can no longer naively believe, then, that human improvement will follow directly from man's conquest of nature: indeed, when that triumph is too thorough, when we remove too much of the forest cover, or extract too many elements from the soil, or activate too large a quantity of fissionable elements, it may have precisely the opposite effect.

"Knowledge comes but wisdom lingers." The fact that physical scientists have penetrated the interior of the atom and have begun to explore the outer edges of astronomical space does not in itself promise to better the general human condition, though it makes life more significant to astronomers and physicists. There is no hope for human salvation, or even mere relief from our present anxieties and obsessions, in the fact that we can shoot rockets into the stratosphere and already begin to dream of Magellan voyages around the solar system. Some of our mechanical inventions have been beneficent, many are trivial or life-harassing; but the only question is: What kind of culture and what manner of man do they tend to produce? Even an economy of abundance will not serve us if it is not directed toward the fulfillment of life: its utmost plenitude may only choke us or defile us, as similar wealth traditionally ruined so many great princes and emperors.

Our blessings and our promises are actually of a quite different order than those proclaimed by the older prophets of mechanical progress. One can condense most of them into the simple proposition that man, during the last century, has extended the possibilities of full human development to every member of his species. Up to the present age, all the advances brought about by civilized societies have rested mainly on slavery and forced labor, upon people too fully committed to the day's work ever to extract the spiritual benefit of their own efforts, too grossly exploited even to realize that alternatives might exist. Only small groups of people, aristocratic minorities, jealously guarding their privileges but rarely making full use of their advantages, have enjoyed the usufruct of civilization itself.

But today, for the first time, the human race as a whole commands resources that have hitherto been perverted or restricted, partly because of their original scarcity, for the benefit of a fortunate minority: in a fashion never so true before, we live by helping one another, and we shall live better by helping each other to the utmost. Now, at least potentially, every person has a claim to the highest goods of life: sensibility, intelligence, feeling, insight, all that goes toward the development of the person are no longer the property of a single ruling group or a chosen nation. This equalized potentiality for life and for development is the true promise of democracy: a promise so vivid and so impelling that even those who now practice tyranny and compulsion in the most wanton fashion must nevertheless do so under the slogan of establishing a "people's democracy."

Through five centuries of exploration and invention, Western man has opened up the globe and brought its peoples into direct contact with each other. Though the nineteenth century prophets of mechanical progress hoped for too much to come about automatically through the spread of the machine, it would be an equal error to underestimate these effects; for rapid flight and instantaneous communication and global commerce at least provide the technical facilities, hitherto lacking, for worldwide intercourse and co-operation. For the first time in history, man has achieved the basis for a unified world: the state foretold by Isaiah. In that unity, once it has been translated into daily practices, lies such an abundance of life as no commonwealth or empire, however powerful, ever possessed. But this transformation will be incomplete until it is directed primarily to the fulfillment of the human person: the desirable end-product is neither energy nor knowledge nor wealth but men.

Originally, people conceived themselves as living in a wholly self-contained world, designed for their private purposes. In overcoming his illusions about this world, modern man, since Copernicus, often also lost interest in himself, and in purposes and ends that both created and directed, but also transcended himself. Though he explored, with increasing success, both astronomical space and molecular space, he lost sight of his inner world and tended to defame the special capacities he exhibited: the capacity for detached evaluation, for rational interpretation, for purposeful anticipations and significant dreams. Today, fortunately, modern man has returned, by way of positive science, to the very attributes of personality he thought a few centuries ago he had dismissed forever.

Man finds himself involved in processes that reach beyond the development and fulfillment of his individual life, or even of mankind's historic existence: processes to which his own existence adds a new dimension of meaning. Both the creative and the destructive forces, once widely dispersed throughout nature, are now concentrated in man: in the domain of meaning his culture has the same order of magnitude as the phenomena it interprets. For better or worse, man's responsibilities, his anxieties, his potentialities, have all increased. Powers once crudely represented as angels, principalities, and thrones may yet, by man's untrammeled inventiveness, be brought into existence. Watching the birds soar through the air, man long dreamed of flight; observing the dream-images rising from his unconscious, modern man will again shape a new self and a new environment, as different from those of past cultures as Chartres Cathedral is from a dark empty cave. In this game, man is but at the beginning of his development.

Up to now, men have not found it easy to throw off their tribal selves and work within a more universal mold. Perhaps men will never completely overcome their self-love, with its regressive particularities and partialities: constant reminders of the closed society, with its limited "consciousness of kind," out of which wider associations and organizations eventually grew. But the proportion between self-love and mutual aid may be altered: only the other day, the mutual aid of the family was extended through UNRRA to hungry peoples on every continent. Today mankind is possibly on the brink of a large-scale reversal of the relation of the instinctual to the rational, of the tribal to the universal, of the habitual to the conscious, of closed to open forms of co-operation. Aided by the expansion of his technical facilities—but aided even more by deeper insight into the processes of human growth—the position of dominance for the primitive impulses and attitudes and subordination for the more highly developed ones may be reversed. The very ferocity with which men have sought to recover primitive and tribal ways—the return to "blood and soil," to isolationism, to terrorism and compulsion in government—may actually be a sign that their final breakup approaches.

Fortunately, periods of extreme disruption are often favorable to a wider integration: it was in such a period that Hebraism, Hellenism, Zoroastrianism, Mithraism, and many other partial religious insights detached themselves from the societies that had brought them forth and united in the Christian myth, which gave them a wider province. As long as hope and faith are possible, we may reasonably assume that such a transformation now opens before us. Like most great changes, this one has already begun in a preparatory reorientation of concepts and ideas; and our new philosophy makes it possible to bring back into rational discourse and into the domain of significant experience many of the insights of art and religion that were necessarily thrust to one side by the pragmatic ideology of the machine. In the course of this book, I shall examine some of these concepts and show how radically they affect our plans and actions.

Turning from the natural world to the specific realm of human culture, man finds a world as extensive and densely populated as the heavens themselves; indeed, without the aid of his words and symbols and patterns of culture, external nature would be inconceivable— almost invisible. Man stands at a busy crossroads where he directs the flow of traffic between the past and the future: his present, correctly viewed, is a composite of seen and unseen forces derived from the past, and anticipated or potential forces, directed back into the present from an ideal future. As Korzybski once put it, in a phrase that says as much as the whole book that contained it, man is a time-binding animal: he lives in three dimensions of time as well as space. Without that temporal depth, itself the product of human culture, the present would be so meaningless as to be non-existent.

But it is not alone through his deepened self-consciousness or through the agency of directed scientific thought that man finds himself on the brink of a decisive constructive change, as the alternative to further disintegration. Whereas other civilizations, in similar moments, were faced with a definite shrinkage of life, we behold quite different conditions and prospects. No Polybius can point to the worldwide falling of the birth rate; no Cyprian can say that Nature herself is ceasing to support life. In a single century, the population of the earth has doubled—the result of an increased food supply and the more hygienic care of the young. Despite reckless misuse, man's vital assets were never greater than now; and there is a fund of reserve vitality, visible today in countries whose net reproduction rate was once dwindling, ready to be released if occasion demands. Observe the rise of the birth rate in many Western countries during the last decade. Even with only our present knowledge of organic processes, we can reforest the earth and create such a plenitude of raw materials as will enable a keen and sinewy race to flourish in every part of the planet. So, too, with our command of energy: a new period of sun-power and electric power is at hand that will utilize current income, instead of dissipating our capital reserves of wood, coal, petroleum, or uranium. The output of our machines will rise, while the role of the machine in life itself will diminish; many instrumental processes that still remain uppermost in human consciousness, because of their imperfection, will presently be transferred to automata. Vitality and energy are the natural foundations of a higher life: never before did mankind have such an abundance of both to tap.

These benefits are plainly only of a preparatory nature; and they are small and insignificant compared to the approaching mobilization of man's greatest source of developments: the cultural heritage itself, now divided, dispersed, and very largely dissipated through lack of organs of communication. We now stand at the beginning of an age of cultural cross-fertilization, the meeting of the East and the West, the North and the South: the first true age of man. Even the most primitive of such interchanges has already had immense results on human life: witness the original transmission of printing from Korea and China to the Western World. It is only a few hundred years since the Chinese classics became available to the West, or Christian religion and Western science penetrated the Orient. Only a century and a half have passed since Sanskrit was first translated into English; and the human race is still only at the beginning of a new epoch, when all its national and racial possessions, once regarded as isolated and exclusive, shall be universally shared.

But the promise before us is plain: a planetary interchange, not merely of goods but of people, not merely of knowledge but of ideas, values, ideals, scientific discoveries, religious insights, patterns of life. These possibilities define the new goals of human development.

The Maitreyan Age, long prophesied by the Buddhists, the age of balance and organic symmetry, lies before us: the dialectic opposite of the age of specialism, division, and disintegration from which we must now emerge. Fullness, wholeness, exuberance, balance, mutual aid: these are the words that characterize the potentialities of our age and set it off from times of low vitality, dearth, miserliness, isolation, painful specialization, cultural regression. The greater number of men, in every historic civilization, have lived only partial, fragmentary lives, beset by anxiety, limited in understanding and action, confined mainly to the surface of their meager acres and the even narrower boundaries set by their own skins: lives not yet human except by promise and intention.

But here and there in history one notes a sudden concentration of energies, a more favorable constellation of social opportunities, an almost worldwide upsurge of prophetic anticipation, disclosing new possibilities for the race: so it was with the worldwide changes in the sixth century B.C. symbolized by Buddha, Solon, Zoroaster, Confucius, and their immediate successors, changes that gave common values and purposes to people too far separated physically for even Alexander the Great to unite them. Out of still deeper pressures, anxieties, insecurities, a corresponding renewal on an even wider scale now seems about to open for mankind.

Today man is like a mountain climber who must leap at his peril over a formidable crevasse, in order to continue his upward way; and to make the physical jump he will have to draw on all his personal resources. If he be too weak or cowardly to make the effort, he will freeze in his present position, unable to climb up or down, until cold or terror or fatigue, or some combination of all these, forces him to lose his grip and fall to his death. No small reluctant efforts will overcome the conditions that threaten not simply the advance, but the sheer animal survival, of the human race. True, man has never made this leap and there is no guarantee that he will reach the other side: but the upward ascent now beckons as it never beckoned before, and above the parting clouds we can now discern the nearest of the sunlit peaks. If we have faith, we shall reach the other side. But first, we must take the measure of our dangers; for a half-way leap will prove as mortal as no leap at all.

3: DIAGNOSIS OF OUR TIMES

Perhaps fortunately, there is a negative pressure toward the transformation of modern man: without it, the positive advantages and opportunities might not move him sufficiently to action. We have reached a point in history where man has become his own most dangerous enemy. At the moment he boasts of conquering nature, he surrenders his higher capacities, and he weakens his ability outside the limited framework of science for co-ordinated thought and disciplined action. Today it is man's higher functions that have become automatic and constricted and his lower ones that have become spontaneous and irrepressible. We arrest our inner creativity with external compulsions and irrelevant anxieties, at the mercy of constant interruptions by telephone and radio and insistent print, timing our lives to the movement of a production belt we do not control. At the same time, we give authority to the stomach, the muscles, the genitals—to animal reflexes that produce obedient consumers, whip-wielding man-trainers, slavish political subjects, push-button automatons.

The failure to respond to this situation is a symptom of the very disease that has brought it about. Unlike his electronic thinking machines, the civilization modern man has built is not so contrived that, when it goes wrong as a whole, it will issue a warning signal and halt in its operation. Indeed, our emotions and feelings, which would normally provide these signals, have in fact been deliberately extirpated, in order to make the machine work more smoothly. Worse than that: so habitually have our minds been committed to the specialized, the fragmentary, the particular, and so uncommon is the habit of viewing life as a dynamic inter-related system, that we cannot on our own premises recognize when civilization as a whole is in danger; nor can we readily accept the notion that no part of it will be safe or sound until the whole is reorganized. Hence the fatuous degree of optimism people continue to exhibit, though valuable areas of our civilization are already destroyed and even greater sectors, perhaps, have become meaningless.

The visible symptoms of our present state are numerous: if they are too well known to be repeated, they are also too generally neglected to be taken for granted. They range from the mass extermination of an estimated eighteen million people by the Nazis, some six million of these being Jews, extermination accompanied by every conceivable refinement of brutality and torture, to the cold genocide practiced by my own countrymen—the 180,000 Japanese civilians killed by fire bombs in Tokyo in one night, or the 200,000 people [final estimate] who were instantly incinerated, or mutilated and eventually doomed to die, in Hiroshima in the course of a few seconds.

During the last thirty years between forty and fifty million people, at a rough estimate, have met premature death through war and genocide alone. In such statistics one has the gross indications of the widespread miscarriage of all our humane intentions, so strenuously exerted in other departments. For every life we learn to save in childhood, through advances in hygiene, diet, and medical care, "civilized" governments, which still threaten each other's existence, are now prepared to take away indiscriminately a score of lives, in acts of planned genocide. These acts, by their very nature, will make impossible any rational settlement capable of promoting fellowship and mutual aid. In such a situation the only remedy for total insecurity would be total extermination.

Now there is no doubt that our recurrent world wars have brought to the surface more speedily many evils that might have remained latent for a longer period; but it would be foolish, I believe, to look to a single institution or a single set of events for the full explanation of our present condition. All social phenomena, almost without exception, are the result of a multitude of converging and interacting events; and therefore to single out any one of them—as Christian theologians did in their providential interpretation of history, or as Marxians now do in their economic interpretation of history—is by that very act to misread the nature of human society itself. Wars have indeed aggravated all our difficulties today; but we would do ill to attribute to war alone the breakdown that was already visible to penetrating observers from one to two generations earlier, in a period that now seems incredibly peaceful. War is both the product of an earlier corruption and a producer of new corruptions. The wars of our time have only brought out a destructiveness and a denial of life that were latent in this society: they were in a sense the negative alternatives to a general renewal that no ruling class was self-denying enough to sanction.

At all events, our present moral breakdown has long been under way. Wholly engrossed in the fabrication of machines and the exploitation of nature, we had neglected the proper education of man. Through our skill in invention, we had created a highly complicated and inter-related world community whose very existence depended upon religious and moral values we permitted to lapse. Western civilization has lived for more than a century under the sign of power: forgetting, in our pride, that uncontrolled power in any of its manifestations, as heat, as light, as physical force, as political compulsion, is inimical to life; for life flourishes only to the extent that it is able to regulate power, screening off its direct impact and reducing it to those amounts that are favorable to vital processes. By something closer than a mere figure of speech, what is true for the single organism is likewise true for the whole civilization. Our very will-to-survive is subject to destructive irrational turnings upon itself, as people lose the sense of a goal and a purpose beyond mere animal existence. Life proceeds by measure and balance: unlimited and undirected power is another name for suicide.

The deeper grounds for this relapse into nihilism have still to be adequately explored. The English poet, A. E. Housman, pictured himself "a stranger and afraid, in a world I never made." But the fact is that in the mechanistic world conceived and fabricated by science, man has become even more of a stranger, and has even more reason to be afraid.

Western culture no longer represents man: it is mainly outside him, and in no small measure hostile to his whole self: he cannot take it in. He is like a patient condemned in the interests of X-ray photography to live upon a diet of barium sulphate. Indeed, the more intense modern man's effort to take in this culture, the more pitiable his actual condition. There is no inner relation between man's organic and personal needs and the special institutions he has created for the expression of the power complex. The great city, with its drone of unceasing mechanical activities, is no longer man writ large: at best, to adapt himself to his environment, man has reduced himself to a minor mechanism: the machine writ small. The autonomous activities of the personality, choice, selection, self-regulation, self-direction, purposiveness, all the attributes of freedom and creativeness, have become progressively more constrained, as external pressures become more pervasive and overbearing. In the end, as Samuel Butler satirically prophesied, man may become just a machine's contrivance for reproducing another machine.

But something even more disastrous has happened within this machine culture: life itself, for the ordinary man, though protected and furthered by a hundred devices that increase his expectation of life, has become less interesting and less significant: it is at best a mild slavery, and at its worst, the slavery is not mild. Why should anyone give to the day's work the efforts and sacrifices it demands? By his very success in inventing labor-saving devices, modern man has manufactured an abyss of boredom that only the privileged classes in earlier civilizations have ever fathomed: the small variations, the minor initiatives and choices, the opportunity for using one's wits, the slightest expression of fantasy, have disappeared progressively from the daily tasks of the common man, caught in big organizations that do his thinking for him. The most deadly criticism one could make of modern civilization is that, apart from its man-made crises and catastrophes, it is not humanly *interesting*.

To alleviate his boredom modern man has invented an extravagantly complicated outer life, which fills up his leisure hours with forms of play that are hardly to be distinguished from his work. As man's inner life has shriveled, he has recovered a sense of vitality and purpose by giving release to the most primitive elements in his unconscious: the crimes and guilts of Electra, Orestes, Hamlet, Macbeth, are relatively human expressions compared to the calculated cruelties and infamies so-called civilized nations have introduced, both in fantasy and in deed.

Apart from these pathological results, our mechanized culture has produced a pervasive sense of frustration. No one can possibly know more than a fragment of all that might be known, see more than a passing glimpse of all that might be seen, do more than a few random, fitful acts, of all that might, with the energies we now command, be done: there is a constant disproportion between our powers and our satisfactions. The typical role of the personality today is an insignificant one: non-commanding, unpurposeful. The walls of the outer shell of our life have thickened, and the creature within has diminished in size in order to accommodate himself to this inimical overgrowth.

The contents of modern man's daydreams too closely resemble those of Bloom in Ulysses, filled with the dead tags of newspaper editorials, the undigested vomit of advertising slogans, greasy crumbs of irrelevant information, and the choking dust of purposeless activity. The duty to become part of this chaos, to keep up with it, to accept it internally, is the bitter duty of modern man—most adequately described and analyzed by Waldo Frank, in his description of The American Jungle, in The Rediscovery of America. Unfortunately, the more busy the mental traffic, the emptier becomes the resultant life: therefore the more abjectly dependent the individual atom in this society becomes upon the very stimuli which—though they have, in fact, caused his emptiness—divert his attention from his plight.

Such a mechanical routine results in a loss of self-confidence and self-respect that few primitive communities would countenance: indeed, the "machine-herd," as we should properly call this passive creature, is a poorer animal than the stolidest cow-herd, largely because he "knows so much that ain't so." Hence the current spread of quackery, superstition, fanaticism, comparable to that which marked the decline of the Hellenic and Roman order: a growing tendency to gamble and to believe in Chance as the supreme Goddess of human destiny: the erratic Wheel of Chance being the only possible happy alternative to the undeviating iron rails of Fate, on which a declining civilization helplessly rolls.

Unable to create a meaningful life for itself, the personality takes its own revenge: from the lower depths comes a regressive form of spontaneity: raw animality forms a counterpoise to the meaningless stimuli and the vicarious life to which the ordinary man is conditioned. Getting spiritual nourishment from this chaos of events, sensations, and devious interpretations is the equivalent of trying to pick through a garbage pile for food. Even those who have direct access to the kitchen do not get properly fed. Our leaders are themselves the victims of the very system they have helped to create. What Dr Sheldon has called "psychological overcrowding" is the typical mischief of Western civilization in its present aspect. As a result of our very ingenuity in inventing reproductive and manifolding devices, even the economy of a stable, abstract medium like print has been lessened; a clumsy concreteness retards the whole process of thought, and we are as much handicapped by an excess of data as by a lack of it. So instead of producing a new gain of time and energy for the consummations of life, our uncontrolled mechanization has made it necessary to spend a larger part of the day on the preparatory means. Final results: a surfeit of tasks, interests, stimuli, reactions: an absence of valuable order and purpose.

In the end, such a civilization can produce only a mass man: incapable of choice, incapable of spontaneous, self-directed activities: at best patient, docile, disciplined to monotonous work to an almost pathetic degree, but increasingly irresponsible as his choices become fewer and fewer: finally, a creature governed mainly by his conditioned reflexes—the ideal type desired, if never quite achieved, by the advertising agency and the sales organizations of modern business, or by the propaganda office and the planning bureaus of totalitarian and quasi-totalitarian governments. The handsomest encomium for such creatures is: "They do not make trouble." Their highest virtue is: "They do not stick their necks out." Ultimately, such a society produces only two groups of men: the conditioners and the conditioned; the active and the passive barbarians. The exposure of this web of falsehood, self-deception, and emptiness is perhaps what made Death of a Salesman so poignant to the metropolitan American audiences that witnessed it.

Now this mechanical chaos is plainly not self-perpetuating, for it affronts and humiliates the human spirit; and the tighter and more efficient it becomes as a mechanical system, the more stubborn will be the human reaction against it. Eventually, it must drive modern man to blind rebellion, to suicide, or to renewal: and so far it has worked in the first two ways. On this analysis, the crisis we now face would be inherent in our culture even if it had not, by some miracle, also unleashed the more active disintegrations that have taken place in recent history.

In his final state, on the highest levels of our society, modern man becomes a mixture of two prophetic nineteenth century heroes: Hawthorne's Ethan Brand and Melville's Captain Ahab—both fanatically concentrated upon a single end. Ethan Brand, pursuing his quest for truth, becomes entirely indifferent to the human results of his work; rigorously suppressing his emotions, he cuts himself off from the "magnetic chain of humanity." This dearth of feeling and emotion, this lack of human-heartedness, is the typical by-product of our traditional conceptions of science. In the same mood of withdrawal modern physicists concentrated on the development of atomic theory and on the perfection of instruments leading to the release of atomic energy, without the faintest concern—until they finally faced the results of their "disinterested" activity in a last moment of remorseful panic—about the social destination of their scientific experiments, though as early as 1914 H. G. Wells had prophetically outlined, in vivid detail, the consequences we now face. This monomaniac concentration on a limited order of truth, intensified by the withdrawal of human feeling, is, as Hawthorne saw, the unforgivable sin of modern man.

But there is another side to the modern personality, that of Captain Ahab: full of pride, anger, self-righteous aggression, conscious through little Pip of the claims of love, but brushing them aside in order to pursue his demonic hunt of the White Whale, taking on in his pursuit of the monster the very character of unreasoning aggression of which he himself had been the victim earlier. Brand throws himself into his charcoal furnace, as the physicist may yet consume himself in his atomic pile; Ahab throws overboard every scientific instrument that might guide him homeward in order to confine in still narrower channels his unqualified aggression. Both cases—one through passive withdrawal and through the drying up of feeling and emotion, the other through the active expression of the more aggressive and dominating sides of the personality—result in a fatal extinction of the human, and a final terminus to further development. Here, rather than in the Faust legend, are the true myths of modern man.

The conclusion should be plain. All the resources our society now possesses, all its present energies and vitalities, all its funded values and ideas, must be concentrated on the upbuilding and regenerative functions, in both the personality and the community. Where do these forces exist? By what method can we tap them and apply them? To what goals shall we direct them? What discipline must we establish for the daily life, and what system of thought, what body of ideals, must guide both the person and the community? These questions are now uppermost in all awakened minds.

But we shall not achieve a more adequate philosophy merely by rejecting wholesale our present way of life or by reverting to some simpler archaic scheme of life and thought. It is not enough to say, as Rousseau once did, that one has only to reverse all the current practices to be right. The cure for our over-concentration on the outer world is not a recoil into an equally sterile and shut-off inner world; the alternative to blindly conquering nature is not to neglect nature entirely and focus wholly on man. If our new philosophy is well grounded we shall not merely react against the "air-conditioned nightmare" of our present culture; we shall also carry into the future many of the elements of positive good that this culture actually embraces—its sense of impersonal truths that lie beyond mere wishful thinking, its technique for collective verification, its capacity for directed thought: indeed, we shall transfer its sense of order from the too-limited realm of science to life at large.

4: ALTERNATIVES TO CATASTROPHE

Logically speaking, three main courses are now open to modern man. First: All the existing institutions may continue to carry forward the methods and forms of the past, without any effort either to reconstitute the overall pattern or to re-orient any single institution. Since, dominated by our present purposes, these forces and institutions have already shown themselves capable of unparalleled destructiveness, there is no evidence whatever that the vital and upbuilding elements that are also at work will, without further effort, gain the upper hand again. On the contrary: the present indications are as clear today as they were to Augustine in the fourth century A.D. with regard to Rome. If we continue on our present downward course, at the accelerated rate that marks the last half-century, the end of Western civilization is in sight: very probably the end of all civilization for another millennium: possibly even the extinction of life in any form on this planet. For the first time in history, man has the means in his possession to commit collective genocide or suicide, on a scale sufficient to envelop the whole race. "The end of the world" is no longer an apocalyptic hyperbole, now that an atomic chain reaction might bring it to pass.

Second alternative: Western man may make a compulsive attempt at stabilization and fixation, without bringing about any radical renewal or reorientation. This was the method of totalitarian fascism as practiced in Nazi Germany: a deliberate regression to tribal ideals and infantile practices, an attempt to throw off the complex inter-relationships, the patient co-operations and accommodations of a developed society, and return to fixed custom, to a servile conditioning of responses, to untrammeled aggression on the part of the ruling classes. Though soviet communism began its revolution with a eutopian vision of freedom and brotherhood, it has in the course of a single generation descended to almost the same level of barbarism; and if the present tensions between "communist" (now actually fascist) Soviet Russia and the non-communist states continue for any length of time, there is now plenty of evidence at hand, particularly in the United States, to show that a similar retreat to barbarism will take place in the very effort to ward off Russian domination. In America the forces of reaction, already utilizing irresponsible slander and legal coercion to silence rational opposition, may easily, under the rabid leadership of privileged Senatorial demagogues, pass on to the stage of active violence—unless those who believe in freedom and democracy quickly recover the initiative. No new philosophy, no personal transformation, no untried mode of action is required for such stabilization by regression: all that is required is a release from civilized inhibitions and a cringing submission to the criminal and psychotic personalities who rise to the top in such a situation.

Fortunately, this second alternative is ultimately self-defeating. In their fear of dangerous thoughts the heads of such a regime tend to call all thoughts dangerous; so, given enough time, they must succumb, as the Nazis did, to the general stultification of science and common sense that results from the very effort to achieve protection. But unfortunately, the violence and quackery and fear, which cause totalitarian rulers to plunge into a succession of blunders as great as that which Stalin made in his treaty of collaboration with Hitler, may also wipe out society at large in the very act that causes barbarism's own downfall. What is worse, despite the fact that its ultimate fate is sealed, a totalitarian regime may well last for at least a century or two, as Russian Czarism did, before it is corrupted beyond repair by its evils.

Now history shows that even the most successful efforts at stabilization by fixation and compulsion, such as that begun under Constantine the Great in the Eastern Empire, or under the Papacy in the West, do not offer anything more hopeful than a long period of hibernation. Perhaps the happiest effort, since it re-trained many humane attributes, was that which took place in Rome under the Empire, from Augustus to Trajan. An even more successful effort was that which took place in the Roman Catholic Church, from the thirteenth century on, in its effort to preserve and perpetuate medieval civilization: the state that was ideologically crystallized in the Summa Theologia of Thomas Aquinas. Relying upon compulsion because it now lacked the power to conjure up faith or impel consent by more patient rational methods, the Inquisition became the typical organ of this kind of effort. In the end the Church saved itself, but only at the price of losing hold over the rest of Western society.

Third alternative: But today another course opens: this is comparable to that which opened in Rome in the fifth century A.D. when the Christian Church laid the basis in faith and thought and practice for a new society. Out of the immense vitalities of our present civilization, a dynamic integration and renewal may still take place. This will not come by following the path of least resistance; nor will it come by effecting a succession of small, unco-ordinated, day-to-day modifications and reforms: it involves nothing less than a change in the total pattern of life, working simultaneously throughout every institution, group, and person in society: not at first necessarily commanding a majority, but at least taking hold of a "saving remnant," whose new vision and new practices will in time be transfused through every part of the community. Such a change does not come about purely by rational decision: it will come, probably, only as the outcome of a crisis so threatening, so calamitous in its possibilities, so empty of easier alternatives, that something like a spontaneous collective decision will be possible— much like that which roused the British people after Dunkirk. At that point, the bounds of possibility will be widened: that which ordinarily could not be done will be done.

Even now, the fateful constellation of forces I have been describing has probably come about; and if we are not to bow passively to catastrophe or cower under the totalitarian compulsions that will, so to say, freeze catastrophe into the stable form of our society, we must make the personal decisions and undertake the heroic duties and efforts that will bring about a collective regeneration. To understand the nature of this situation, to extend the knowledge and to re-create the values necessary for our survival and our salvation, is in fact the main purpose of the present book.

Such, then, are the alternatives we face today. We may either follow the downward cycle of de-building, devaluation, and disintegration, till life is not either attractive or endurable, or we may achieve a brief, illusory reprieve by committing the latent forces of life to the process of fixation and stabilization: a negative kind of renewal, in which the lower forms of life will supplant the higher, in which mind and spirit will be sacrificed to power, in which organized criminality will become the established government.

By this second process we may outwardly arrest the present diseases of our civilization and keep them from spreading; but only by creating a kind of living death for everyone. And as the patient whose limbs are in a plaster cast may by his relief from pain have the illusion of improvement, before gangrene sets in, so a nation that has arrested the processes of decay by stabilizing on a low level, may have, as in Nazi Germany or in other totalitarian countries today, the sense of being the healthy exponents of a new form of life. This is but a momentary illusion. The totalitarian drug is as fatal as the infection it arrests.

Thus the inertia of "progress" today leads swiftly downhill; while the attempt to achieve stabilization by collective compulsion and social arrest likewise leads to the same destination—death. Only one road lies open to those who would remain human: the road of renewal. Each one of us must dedicate himself, at whatever effort, with whatever willing sacrifice, to such a transformation of himself and all the groups and associations in which he participates, as will lead to law and order, to peace and co-operation, to love and brotherhood, throughout the planet. Since the terms of this transformation are familiar ones, it is the situation itself and the method we bring to it, that will make the difference, changing the empty professions that have so long gone unheeded into operative principles and tangible goals.

CHAPTER II

1: POSTULATES OF SYNTHESIS

Plainly, a profound change in goals and purposes is an essential basis for the new life that must germinate, if the development of man is to go on. But this alone is not sufficient. Socialism, during the nineteenth century, projected far-reaching changes in society to introduce justice and humane co-operation at the expense of private property and privilege. Many of these changes have already been effected, even in nominally capitalist regimes. But socialism sought to effect these changes without transforming the psychological potentials of its adherents. Believing in the spontaneous goodness of man, it assumed that the evils in the body politic were wholly external to its members, that capitalism and militarism could be replaced without creating disciplines to transform greed, avarice, luxury, pride, aggression, and regimentation. As a result socialism in practice often shows characteristics uncomfortably like the system it has partly replaced.

But it would be equally faulty, in the light of our present knowledge, to seek merely an inner change: that was the mistake of the Greek philosophers after Plato: they sought only the salvation of enlightened individuals, capable of discourse at their own high level of abstraction. They had nothing to offer the mass of men, and no vision of the general renewal of society.

We need a doctrine which, because it aims at the transformation and development of the person, will be capable of guiding and re-directing the energies of men in groups and associations: an ethical discipline and an education capable of giving human institutions and organizations the potentials for freedom we so far find—and still only sporadically here—in individual persons. To this end, we must create a framework of more adequate concepts and ideas, capable of enclosing every dimension of life. This framework so far is not yet supplied by any single system of philosophy or religion. Above all, we need an ideology so profoundly organic that it will be capable of bringing together the severed halves of modern man, the private and the public, the inner and the outer, the domain of freedom, emergence, creativeness, and the domain of necessity. In short, before modern man can live a sane life he must escape his present ideological straitjackets.

Each one of us sees the world through a screen: the screen of his physical constitution and his temperament, his vocation and his varied social roles, his family relations and his other group affiliations, his personal philosophy and the total body of his culture. While each of these aspects is typical every actual experience is unique; so one might easily assume that their collective expression would lead mainly to hallucinations, cross-purposes, self-deceptive projections, and errors. But all these screens, apparently so different and divergent, are themselves the results of the continued transformations of life, the ceaseless interactions between organism and environment. Their very incongruities are the products of a common medium, a common process, common tasks and common ends: so that the world is not in fact a shattering chaos but a cosmos, in which error and illusion can be detected because they occur as erratic elements on a ground pattern of order. This underlying unity makes significant difference possible.

From one end of creation to another we must not merely posit a unifying process that underlies all variety and diversity: we must also posit a direction of change: a set toward life and mind and consciousness. Life occurs indeed at a very late stage in cosmic evolution: organized mind at a still later stage, and human beings, with consciousness, rational purposes, and free choices, last of all. Quantitatively speaking, life seems extremely rare and precious, even in the humblest, least sentient forms: the nearest solar system that might be disposed favorably toward life is, the astronomers tell us, about four and a half light years away. But the emergence of life and mind gives fresh significance to every preparatory activity. Values and purposes, so far from being trivial human interventions in cosmic events that deny them, exist as potentialities at the lowest levels and become increasingly evident, indeed increasingly dominant, at each upward stage.

In the world of nature it is becoming plain that physical events cannot be fully understood except with reference to the pattern of the whole in time and space. No analysis of the parts and no mere addition of analyses and abstractions will ever give any insight into the pattern or purposive configuration that endows them with a special significance: indeed, this organic relationship will not even be suspected when methods of abstraction and isolation are the sole ones employed.

What applies to the "physical world" applies even more to the person. Even the most primitive physical phenomena may be quite inadequately interpreted—as "merely" of a thermal or electrical nature—if the ultimate tendency of the evolutionary process is not kept in view. No definition of matter is complete unless one adds that certain elements have the potentiality for uniting in complex organic units which produce the phenomena of life. More than this: the philosophy of Lao-tse, the plays of Molière, the equations of Gauss, may all be unique events in the history of the universe: but they are still events, just as real in their uniqueness as mass phenomena that have been repeated a billion billion times. A philosophy that would dismiss these events as unreal or insignificant, in order to reduce matter to "nothing but" electrons or neutrons, violates the simplest canons of truth. What it dismisses as unreal is merely what discloses the limits of its system of interpretation.

Does it not follow, then, that the current speculations of the astrophysicists on the earliest shaking down of order in the universe, or the equally marvelous penetration by the nuclear physicist into the constitution of the atom, are still insufficient if they stop short of the unique and unpredictable events which begin to appear, in increasing number, with the development of man himself? The newer insights in physical science point to this fact. However blind and repetitive physical processes once seemed to be when living forms were left out of account, some initial taint of tendency and purpose and creativeness seems to have been present from the beginning: and in turn the destination casts a retrospective meaning over every earlier stage on the journey.

Many of man's latter-day inventions, products of his own evolving needs, have been anticipated in organic forms at far earlier stages: he took his paper-making from the hornets; he copied the soaring birds in his airplane; he re-invented organized society, based on the division of labor, about sixty million years after the ants had perfected their own. Part of man's own development consists in a conscious reconstruction and re-appraisal of nature's processes, so that he may make them serve ends that play no part in nature except in man himself. But if a philosophy of synthesis must emphasize the last stages of this long process, the attributes of freedom, uniqueness, self-direction, it cannot remain indifferent, like past forms of subjective idealism, to all that man owes to the energies and vitalities that preceded his own emergence. Continuity: emergence: creativity—these are the basic postulates of the new synthesis.

2: THE NATURE OF MAN

The world, according to a view that dates back to Democritus, is a random mixture of atoms: chance created solid aggregations out of endless atomic collisions, and man's nature was formed, essentially, by extraneous forces, likewise operating by necessity or chance. This view contrasts with the religious intuition that man is the object of a divine purpose: a rational soul with an eternity in which to realize and perfect his own development—whether that ends in non-being, as with Buddhism, or in everlasting beatitude, as in the Christian doctrines. These latter beliefs perhaps over-magnify man's self-sufficiency and make him a terminal point in a too-limited process: but the first view not merely demolishes the significance of human history but shuts its eyes to the evidence of order and purpose that even physical nature presents. Let us aim at a fuller and juster statement.

Before every attempt to describe the world and life and time there stands an unspoken prologue: human history itself. Without that prologue, the rest of the play would be an unintelligible buzz and blur. Neither history nor nature is given directly in contemporary experience, except in snatches that would be meaningless if they were not part of a long sequence of interpretations to which man has given his days and years. Each generation, each individual, can make but a minute sampling of the whole in its effort to reduce to intelligible order the collective experience upon which both knowledge and practice rest. What we know of the world comes to us mainly by interpretation, not by direct experience; and the very vehicle of interpretation itself is a product of that which must be explained: it implies man's organs and physiological aptitudes, his feelings and curiosities and sociabilities, his organized social relations and his means for transmitting and perfecting that unique agent of interpretation, language. History itself would remain indecipherable without the meanings and values that have emerged from it.

Man's basic data are not in the least simple or elemental: what is basic is the highly complex structure of meanings and values produced and transmitted in history. What man knows about the nature of the physical universe is only a subordinate part of his own process of self-discovery and self-revelation. In recent times, baffled by his own inner state, tormented by insoluble problems, Western man was in fact driven to postulate, almost as much for his peace of mind as for any more practical purpose, a highly simplified order, from which most of his own essential characteristics were excluded: a world free from desire and feeling and dream, a world divorced from human purposes and human hopes: a world in which mind was laid to sleep, in order to operate more efficiently on the body. But the fact is that complexity, contradictions, paradox, and mystery are original features of human experience; whereas simplicity and clarity and order are extremely sophisticated end-products. The classic scientific attempts to picture the world, from Thales onward, confuse conceptual simplicity with the primitive and basic.

When we take into account the unspoken prologue of human history we must demolish this misleading elementalism. Not sense data or atoms or electrons or packets of energy, but purposes, interests, and meanings, constitute the underlying facts of human experience. These values rise out of impenetrable historic depths, like a coral reef, by the heaping up of layer upon layer of life, with each visible event emerging out of a million events that have left their historic deposit and out of countless millions of lives that have never quite passed away. Whatever man knows about external nature is a by-product of man's culture, as revealed in history; and the dimensions of nature alter with every change in man's own development: our present views of the universe are no more ultimate than the cave man's. On every page of nature's opened book, man scrawls in the margin his own autobiography.

To understand the nature of man, accordingly, we must first of all understand this prologue; that is, we must take man as we now find him, in all his historic complexity: no bare animal shivering in his skin, groping in the dark, clawing for food, an alien in a hostile land, surrounded by enemies. Quite the contrary: we find man a creature born into a going society, which provides him with clothes, protects him from dangers, shelters him against the elements, offers him food, supplies him with speech, surrounds him with some degree of love, endows him with a score of gifts before he has even left the cradle. Starting out in such a world, we discover that friendliness and unfriendliness, good and bad, are more primordial elements of human experience than matter or motion. Tenderness appeared in man's mammalian ancestors eons before he learned to preserve fire or shape a stone.

Human life, in its historic manifoldness and purposefulness, is our starting point. No single being can embrace that life; no single lifetime contains it; no single culture can encompass all its potentialities. One cannot even partly understand the nature of man, unless one realizes that its roots lie buried in the debris of countless invisible lives and that its topmost branches must by their very frailty defy the most daring climber. Man lives in history; he lives through history; and in a certain sense, he lives for history, since no small part of his activities goes toward preparation for an undisclosed future. Without animal faith in the past that he helped to make and in the future he is still making, human life would shrink in all its dimensions.

3: THE BACKGROUND OF LIFE

In his own person, man represents every aspect of the cosmos. Reduced to his lowest terms, he is a lump of carbon and a puddle of water, mixed with a handful of equally common metals, minerals, and gases. But man is likewise a unit of organic life; he is a member of the animal world, and of a special order of the animal world, the vertebrates, with capacity for free movements, for selective intercourse with the environment, for specially canalized responses through a highly developed nervous system. Still further, man belongs to the family of warm-blooded animals, the mammals, whose females give milk to their young and so form a close and tender partnership, often fiercely protective, for the nurture of their offspring; and through his own internal development, his whole life is suffused with emotions and erotic responses which have persisted, like so many other traits of domestication—the cow's milk or the hen's eggs—in exaggerated form. Starting as an animal among the animals, man has stretched and intensified certain special organic capacities in order to develop more fully what is specifically human. In a fashion that has no rivals in other species he thinks: he plays: he loves: he dreams.

Before dealing at length with that part of man's heritage which accounts for his special creativeness let us examine for a moment the traits and propensities he shares with the whole world of life. Given the waters, rocks, soil, and solar energy out of which life originally emerged, one is struck at once by the immense fecundity of all living beings, the inexhaustible creativeness of nature herself.

Long before mind became dominant, life gave itself over to the endless magic of metamorphosis: its own self-transformation. To create scales or feathers or skin or fur, to transform a fin into an arm or a wing, to invent breathing apparatus for warm-blooded animals, venturing the radical experiment of living entirely out of water, to separate the cycles of growth and reproduction, as in the fern, to mimic leaves or twigs or more poisonous creatures—for countless eons these efforts sufficed to absorb the vital energies of every species.

Along with the most prudent kinds of adaptation go many other factors, not accounted for in terms of our dominant utilitarian ideology: sheer riotousness of imagination—sometimes verging on the comic—seems as common in nature as in human culture. By the very wealth and diversity of forms, life assured its own continuity and extension over every part of the planet: so that there is scarcely a depth of the sea or a height of mountain top to which life, in some form, has not penetrated.

This exuberance of life, this audacious inventiveness, cannot be reduced to an endless series of accidents. Reading nature's story, we observe organic equivalents of what, in human terms, we should call plan and plot. When "coincidences" multiply far beyond the bounds of probability one must call the result "purpose," and suspect that it shows likenesses with similar processes and patterns man discovers in his own life.

Every beginner in biology quickly learns the elementary properties of organisms: nutrition, growth, reproduction, repair, and so forth; but there are certain other attributes of life that must not be taken for granted. First of all, all organisms follow a life-plan peculiar to their species. Until death, the most radical changes that take place within an organism proceed in a directed orderly sequence, determined partly by its own nature: life-time is not reversible, nor is life itself a succession of random responses to an overpowering environment. Whereas one may identify an inorganic element by its phase, one must identify a higher organism not merely by its species and sex, but by its age, its stage of maturation, its plan of life, its partnerships and ecological associations.

One constant effort of the organism is to regulate the processes outside it, so that they come in the right succession as well as in the right quantities. "To everything," as The Preacher put it, "there is a season, and a time to every purpose under heaven: a time to be born and a time to die; a time to plant and a time to pluck that which is planted: a time to kill and a time to heal; a time to break down and a time to build up."

The fact that each species has a norm of growth, that successive stages in life are accompanied by the maturation and perfection of related organs, culminating usually in reproduction, is a specific quality of life. Life is self-limited in time and space; and each species has its own specific norm of growth, with a small margin of free play on either side of the line. In the physical world, considered apart from what man has made of it, there are no such regulations of quantity and no such definitive life-plan—though, according to astro-physicists, there may conceivably be some regular succession in the building up of the elements in cosmic evolution.

The maintenance of an underlying identity through all the processes of change, and the continued transformation of forms and functions in the passage from conception to death, are among the essential attributes of higher organisms. Continuity and emergence greet one everywhere. The shape of any living thing depends not merely upon outside pressure but upon inner, self-maintaining, self-restoring, and self-fulfilling processes. The blow of a hammer will leave a dent on a piece of lead: if the solid lump is melted, the liquid, on cooling, will show no trace of its original dent. But a blow on a living organism is not taken so passively, nor will it vanish at all, except from consciousness: the body at once mobilizes itself to take care of the injury, in a determined effort to restore its original state. Even when the effect of the blow has been repaired and the organism recovers its equilibrium, the blow will leave behind an impression, sometimes twofold—visibly, say, in the form of a scar, mentally as a memory.

This quality of preserving its identity and retaining impressions begins at the organic level and has in man been carried into an extra-sensory apparatus of culture. Organic experience is both cumulative and anticipatory. The organism enregisters and remembers: it remembers and reacts: it reacts and it anticipates: yes, it proposes and projects. All living behavior, even when seemingly blind, is forward-looking: without instructions or past observations a cat who is about to have kittens looks for a proper nest—a drawer of silk underwear will do—to receive her offspring. That will stand for a thousand other similar modes of anxiety and providential anticipation over what is still to come. No organism can be adequately described in terms of its immediate functions or its momentarily visible structure: above all, not man.

There are two other characteristics of organic life that must be reckoned with, as essential to a fuller understanding of man's creative make-up. One of these is common in some degree to all protoplasm, and is generally called irritability, but may, in a larger sense, be called responsiveness: a tendency to react to inner or outer stimuli by contraction, expansion, withdrawal, attack, by submission or protection, by lying low or coming forth to do battle. The other characteristic peculiar to life is the effort to maintain a dynamic equilibrium, balancing accounts between daily profits and losses, making good temporary deficits, putting aside reserves for use against an unexpected demand. At the lowest level, an alteration in the acid-alkaline balance in the blood leads to both internal changes and external adjustments. Long ago Claude Bernard pointed out that the sensitive maintenance of equable internal conditions was extremely important for man's higher development, since gross internal variations undermined, first of all, not the heart action or the muscles, but the ability to "concentrate, to think logically, to pay attention."

So far as man is an animal, then, he shares these characteristics of the organic world. But living forms, in their emergence from the lifeless and non-organic, still retain some of the inertia of matter: the temporary raising of the level of energy calls for continuous effort. There is indeed a sort of dialectic opposition, throughout all creation, between the tendency to fall into a state of stability and immobility, and the tendency to climb upward, to seize more energy than is needed for survival, taking risks, making adventurous leaps, placing the flag of life on some higher mountain top, before seeking safety once more—eventually death—in the valley below. However independent man may seem through his own proud intelligence and its creations, he still needs at every moment the constant co-operation of all the forces of nature and history, in order to hold his own. Without food man can survive for barely thirty days; without water for little more than three days; without air hardly for more than three minutes: but without hope he might destroy himself in an even shorter time.

The same vital impetus that flows through all nature flows through man and carries him onward: the forward movement of life, its insurgence and its expectancy, cannot be left out of any account of man's deepest nature. When he is disheartened and defeated by some immediate setback to his own plan of life, an inner voice still whispers: "Hold fast! Life is on your side; and in time you or your issue will continue your development and overcome the obstacles that now hold you back." Reason often has told man he was defeated: why should the prisoner, the slave, the corrupted and the deformed and the ailing all go on with so few exceptions to their dismal end? For even the healthy and the fortunate, does not death lie in wait, to cancel out each individual gain? Fortunately, the total effort of life in the past still wells through every living creature; and a sense of life-to-come—projected as heaven and eternity in the older forms of religion—still beckons man on. Here the tritest of proverbs utters the profoundest of truths: while there is life there is hope; and, one may add, while there is hope there is life.

Even when man surpasses his animal needs, he starts from the point where they leave off or become insufficient, and if sometimes he relapses into organic lethargy, his original impetus toward mind and love comes from that source too. In his blood, the salt of the original oceans in which life took rise still circulates; in the period of ovulation the lunar month repeats its cycle; in the noblest acts of self-sacrifice and love, he widens for the good of his race the impulse his animal ancestors achieved, even as far back as the fish, in their care of the young. I have seen that shy fish, the lake bass, attack with his teeth an intruder who stumbled near the nest he was guarding: as a father I understood his feelings and withdrew. The duties of parenthood were not discovered yesterday.

To recapitulate. Life, even at the lowest level, is a selective process: a process of choosing, restraining, promoting, taking from the environment just such sustenance as is helpful toward the creature's development, rejecting what is irrelevant. But life does not float on a timeless ocean of existence: it moves forward, impelled by an immanent purpose that in man becomes a conscious one. Every act of growth brings about a temporary upset in an organism's equilibrium; and the final phase of an organism's existence, death, marks the presence of a radical unbalance. Life is directional in tendency, goal-seeking, end-achieving, in short, purposive. But unlike inanimate matter, it brings into its present effort the memory of a past and the anticipation of a future: by that enlargement of the field of its operations it opens up the sphere of freedom.

The life-maintaining functions tend toward autonomy or self-direction. Nature's injunction to every organism, speaking mythically, is: "Be yourself. Fulfill yourself! Follow your destiny!" Within the limits of time and chance and necessitous circumstance, every organism seeks to be master of its own fate. What Patrick Geddes called the insurgent quality of life, its capacity for initiating new activities and going off in unexpected directions in order to overcome its inner limitations and external handicaps is almost as characteristic as the more tangible attribute of motility.

There is one final characteristic of organisms that enters into every higher form: the more developed a creature is, the more independent it seems, the more heavily does it rely upon the companionship and support of many other species. Life has flourished only by extending the area of mutual aid, reciprocal interplay, or symbiosis: every creature, voluntarily or blindly, is in an active give-and-take relationship, not merely with its bare physical environment, but with a multitude of other organisms. Living organisms, by the most complex and far-reaching operations, form food-chains and work-chains that extend from the bacteria in the soil and the air to the domesticated animals, indeed they constantly co-operate to remake the whole environment for the benefit of life. Even the most solitary and carnivorous eagle forms a link in a living chain and depends for his own life on the prosperity of his eventual victims.

Just as purpose in the human sense exists at a much lower unconscious stage as "function" and "mechanism" so does love, in the human sense, exist at a lower level as mutual aid and ecological partnership. Thus life maintains not merely an internal dynamic balance, so well described by Dr Walter Cannon in The Wisdom of the Body: it also maintains an equally dynamic external balance between all its constituent species, whose members live by acts of co-operation that, in the higher organisms, are called self-restraint and self-sacrifice. This is the fundamental morality of nature. Wherever this morality breaks down and creates an unbalance between the species that need one another or the men that need one another there is disintegration and disorganization. Even the absence of some inorganic element in this organic fabric of inter-relationship—as in a diet deficient in iron —may be sufficient to place life in danger.

Balance: autonomy: symbiosis: directional development—these are the fundamental concepts we extract from a study of living organisms at a pre-human level and apply further toward the understanding and development of man's life and destiny in society. Where these features are lacking, where life has become purposeless and unbalanced, we have reason to suspect that a profound miscarriage has taken place.

The relative complexity of man's external environment is matched by his internal environment; and here, if one may judge on the basis of his overt actions and fabrications, his departure from the norm of his biological companions is most marked; for though they share in the development of his higher nervous system, up to a point, they are held to the needs of survival by a shorter rope than man has contrived. Plainly, man is full of self-begotten urges, desires, interests, dreams, that have no visible and immediate relation to his biological prosperity. Unlike the animal's nicely adjusted reflexes, man's propensity to delay his responses and play with alternative modes of action sometimes brings about fruitless expenditures of energy and miscarriages of effort; but fortunately, out of this very propensity to exceed his animal limitations, to defy common sense and security, man has found new sources of creativeness. Man can through his adaptability survive in a crowded slum or a filthy trench, under conditions that would sicken many other creatures; but he is also capable of imagining and creating temples, palaces, gardens, houses, cities, which give him pleasures derived from orderly form and accomplished design. By a similar process he has created an endless variety of forms and patterns for social life.

On the basis of this organic existence the human personality emerges out of the matrix of communal functions and activities; and with it certain conditions, essential to all life, become intensified and heightened: for in man there is a sharpening of sensory equipment, a sensitizing of emotional reactions and feelings, a finer capacity to assimilate and recall events, even single experiences, an ability to project organic functions into extra-organic forms, a capacity to transfer experience into symbols and symbols into experience.

Now in a world only partly under its control, life always exists on a precarious basis, holding on from moment to moment, ever wakeful, ever anxious, since security and safety may, by their very presence, asphyxiate the sentinels on duty and bring about disintegration or death. For the individual member of a species, life is limited, contingent, perilous, and in the final measure, brief. In the highest realm of all—the realm of personality—life is even more delicately poised over the abyss of non-existence than it is on the organic level: for the balance is harder to maintain, and the very habits and rituals that help to conserve life in the human community may, by their prolongation, also undermine it. A blessing repeated once too often becomes a curse. Organic growth and repair have their counterpart in the personality in the process of renewal: a continued making over of ideas and attitudes, of sentiments and plans, so that the person will overcome the animal tendency to repetition, fixation, automatism.

4: ECONOMY OF THE SUPERFLUOUS

From the very beginning, it would appear, man has usually had a margin of energy not devoted wholly to the struggle for survival. This margin, observable in the most primitive culture, is also visible in man's physiological organization; and its existence there offers a key to no small part of his eventual creativity. Evolution itself, indeed, presumes that there are capacities and potentialities latent in life itself, in its most primitive manifestations, that impelled the organism to exert itself beyond the measure necessary to maintain itself or its species: how otherwise in fact could purposeful, directional change, with all the hazards and fatalities of untried experiments, come to characterize the complex world of living organisms?

Because of the impact of economic life on human thought during the last century, this margin has often been overlooked or misinterpreted: so long as man was viewed as a mere bundle of adaptive mechanisms, as narrowly contrived for work as a mechanical loom or a locomotive, his true character was overlooked. Nature, however, has gone about its work with a freer hand than man; it has patently not been so intent on the single goal of economy and efficiency. Not that economy is necessarily lacking in nature's plans: the grasses and grains form seeds, for example, with conspicuous economy; but it was an artist, rather than a mechanical engineer, who designed the orchid or the flowering magnolia: even the pitcher plant could have enticed its customers without presenting such an alluring show-window. The exuberance of life . . . exuberance and largess—these make all our rational standards of economy seem mean and restrictive.

In general, we may say that growth and development themselves represent the margin all creatures have, in the upward curve of their life, above the energy needed for bare survival; and in man's organs the role of superfluity is particularly conspicuous: Dr Walter Cannon pointed out that many organs of the body, as well as the body considered as a whole, have a "factor of safety" far above normal requirements. Thus most of the functions of the paired organs, like the lungs and kidneys, can be carried on quite effectively by single ones; and even a small part of the adrenal glands or the pancreas ensures life, while their complete extirpation causes death. Perhaps the greatest largess, the most luxuriant overgrowth of all, however, has taken place in the brain: Morley Roberts went so far as to call it tumorous. Comparative embryological studies, as Coghill points out, indicate that the higher the animal in the order of intelligence, the more the general overgrowth, as regards the immediate possibility of behavior, involves the conditioning mechanism. . . . "This means that in man at a stage of development when body movements are of the simplest order, that part of the mechanism of association which deals particularly with the highest mental and moral processes not only is relatively massive but has definitely begun to organize itself into the mechanical pattern that characterizes it in the adult."

This organic efflorescence was of critical importance to man: probably it is the foundation of all those playful impulses, those self-starting activities, those circuitous explorations and long-continued elaborations, which differentiate human behavior from the brutal directness of other animals—though even at lower levels, as in the nest-adorning habits of the bower bird, there may exist some faint early extra-organic premonition of this new order of activity. The quality we call playfulness depends upon an excess of energy: in the young it comes forth, at a physiological level, as random cries, gurglings, babblings, bubble-blowings, movements of arms and legs, closing and opening of hands—quite apart from any promptings of hunger, discomfort, or a friendly presence. Let these energies be dissipated in a fever, and the child's body immediately becomes droopy, inert, death-like. At a later stage of growth, idle associations, superfluous images, involved dreams, random explorations, play a part in development that could never be justified, in origin, on any principle of economy or by any direct expectation of usefulness. In a mechanistic culture like our own, these important activities have been either undervalued or overlooked.

Once we rid ourselves of the unconscious bias of mechanism, we must recognize that the "superfluous" is just as essential to human development as the economic: that beauty, for example, has played as large a part in evolution as use and cannot be explained, as Darwin sought to, merely as a practical device of courtship or fertilization. In short, it is just as permissible to conceive nature, mythologically, as a poet, working in metaphors and rhythms, as to think of nature as a cunning mechanic, trying to save material, make both ends meet, do the job efficiently and cheaply. The mechanistic interpretation is quite as subjective as the poetic one; and up to a point each is useful.

The species that have continued the upward climb, notably man himself, are the relatively imperfect, unspecialized, uncommitted, self willed, and even maladjusted ones. These species reject Spencer's one-sided passive definition of life, as "the continuous adjustment of internal relations to external ones"; they stubbornly seek to reverse this process, in order to bring external relations into harmony with their own life-plans. Man dominates the line of the brainy animals; and the over-development of the brain itself, with its thousands of still unused neurones, was the most critical step, possibly, in the emergence of manlike stocks. In man this change was probably accompanied by the expansion of the role of feelings already developed in the mammalian line. These further intensifications of feeling, which went with the increase of intelligence and modified it, were due, possibly, to the direct hormonic action of monthly ovulation and the prolonged activity of the mammary glands of the female and the overactive genitals of the male.

All the threats of arrested development, the threat of complete adaptation, the threat of parasitism, the threat of insensibility, were diminished or overcome by the development of organs that increased the range, vividness, and autonomy of human responses. Through the overgrowth of his brain, man had an agent capable of carrying creativeness from the organic realm, where it could only be slowly embodied in relatively stable animal structure to the super-organic realm, the specific domain of human culture. Instead of carving one's answer in flesh and blood, one could write the answer on the sand and erase it the next day, or perpetuate it in wood and stone, on papyrus or paper. Man is the unfinished animal. Unlike other organisms, the final stage of his growth is not determined by his biological past: it rests with himself and is partly determined by his own plans for the future.

With that change to the super-organic, the first age of man properly began. Very possibly, in the difficult days of the later glacial periods, this change had survival value, too: but that must be taken as an incidental gratuity. In the end, man paid for his creative exuberance by his increased consciousness of death; yet in facing death, he added a new dimension to his life, which no other animal, apparently, has even dimly sensed.

5: SOCIAL DISCOVERY AND FABRICATION

The human community, as Aristotle observed, is an association of people who need each other. And they need each other for two reasons: spiritually in order to find themselves in the full dimensions of the group: practically to take advantage of their differences. Unfortunately by perfecting their special aptitudes they become more helpless as they become more efficient, unless they constantly interchange their goods, their services, and above all their understanding. Had men remained as like unto one another as ox is to ox, men would have discovered only a small fragment of the potentialities of Man. No amount of inner probing could bring out the immense wealth of human nature: to find himself man had as it were to divide himself into a thousand strands or skeins, each one of which would isolate some special aptitude and interest, carrying it further, intensifying its quality by joining it to a similar aptitude or interest. It was through the social division of labor—a further transference to culture of the original division of labor between the sexes—that man unearthed many obscure inchoate capacities and brought them to perfection.

The old saying, that it takes nine tailors to make a man, is far too modest: it takes not merely many tailors but all the professions, all the vocations, all the castes and classes and families, all the primary communities and purposive associations to make a man. All men are, in some sense, fractional and incomplete: a complete man would have to incarnate a whole society. "Man" in that sense is purely a figment, for he would have to encompass future achievements as well as past ones. Thus human society, unlike animal societies, is an agency of self-consciousness and self-exploration and self-revelation. Man does not merely exist as an organic product: he makes something of himself, and the making of man is the meaning of history.

Had this process of self-transformation remained a purely biological one it would no doubt have been extremely slow and limited in all its possibilities. Suppose, for example, man had concentrated upon increasing his individual working capacity so little as two horsepower: along that line, he might have taken half a million years to effect, by selective breeding or otherwise, this tremendous change in his muscular capacity. And when he had done so, he would probably have been much nearer to a glorified gorilla than to his present self, thereby losing various other highly valuable attributes, like sensitivity, flexibility, mobility, intelligence, by the way.

By creating an extra-biological mode of inheritance, his "culture" or social heritage, man was able to produce extra horsepower first by his domestication of horses, and then, many times his original working capacity by inventing machines, without altering a single organ of his body. With his transmitted skill in making tools and machines, and passing on knowledge by symbolic means, man has created windmills, water mills, steam engines, transformers, atomic piles, in the short space of two thousand years: these instruments meet man's utmost needs for power far better than any conceivable organic adaptation.

Essentially, a culture is an extra-organic means of changing man's nature and his environment, without leaving indelible marks on his organism or curtailing his essential flexibility and plasticity. A heated house for winter living is the equivalent of the horse's trick of acquiring a shaggy winter coat of hair: an X-ray tube is the equivalent of acquiring a more penetrating form of vision—and so on. For thousands of years man's non-material culture, mainly verbal, esthetic, and ritualistic, outpaced his technical culture. His habit of projection, symbolization, detachment, has enabled man to make many experiments whose bad results, if encountered in organic form, would have been fatal to the species. At the same time, it has given a certain durability to insights and discoveries that would otherwise have vanished, perhaps, with the moment or the individual that produced them.

What Leibnitz said about the nature of the world itself, that it provided the maximum amount of freedom compatible with order, might be said even more truly of human culture. By means of his culture, man transforms his environment, attaches new values to natural processes, projects his own purposes on natural functions, and eventually fabricates a whole succession of new selves, interacting in highly individualized communities, without committing himself irremediably to any single way of life or any single type of personality.

Every human group, every human being, lives within a cultural matrix that is both immediate and remote, visible and invisible: and one of the most important statements one can make about man's present is how much of the past or the future it contains. Since culture must be extraneous, or at least detachable, to be transmitted—though the detachment may take the form of a remembered precept, transmitted by word of mouth, or a motor reaction, like bowing, passed on by direct imitation—even the most immaterial form of culture nevertheless has a physical aspect which cannot be wholly ignored, while every physical event that comes within human range has a symbolic aspect, which must be interpreted.

Without interpretation, there would be no distinction between a peasant's partaking of bread and wine at an inn and his having bread and wine in Holy Communion at Church. As physiological performances, both acts are the same: in meaning, value, and purpose, they are as distinct as vegetarianism and cannibalism. In the organic view of human development, any part of man's life or his environment may become an active element in his culture; and so of himself. By the same token, any part of himself may become operative in the external world: no single aspect of either personality or culture has any understandable existence except in terms of the total life in which it shares. "Mind and matter, soil, climate, flora, fauna, thought, language, and institutions [are] aspects of a single rounded whole, one total growth." That perception of Charles Horton Cooley's is fundamental to an understanding of the nature of man. Nature is nature as brought forth and interpreted by man's culture; and culture even in its most evanescent and ethereal aspects is still the culture of nature: the energies and vitalities man finds himself endowed with and supported by. Each is inconceivable except in terms of the other.

Man lives and learns by many devices; but the most important of all his adaptations, the one that differentiates him from the brutes and has given him a large measure of dominance over nature, is man's capacity for symbolic interpretation. That is not merely a key to knowledge and a key to self-fabrication: it is also a key to man's activities and actions. Karl Marx quarreled with idealism and older forms of materialism because they were content merely to interpret the world: whereas he understood that thought, being a process of life, must also help transform the world. But he overlooked, in his polemic, the extent to which interpretation itself produces change: primarily by transforming the potentialities of the interpreter.

6: THE MIRACLE OF LANGUAGE

The growth of conscious purpose and self-direction—all that is implied in the historic concepts of the soul and the person—was made possible by man's special skill in interpreting his own nature and working his experiences into a meaningful and valuable whole, upon which he could draw for future actions and operations. That skill rests upon a special aptitude, embedded in man's very physiology: the ability to form and transmit symbols. Man's most characteristic social trait, his possession of an extra-organic environment and a super-organic self, which he transmits from generation to generation without using the biological mechanism of heredity, is dependent upon his earlier conquest of the word.

During the last century this essential fact about man's nature has been obscured by the false assumption that man is primarily a "tool-using animal." Carlyle called him that long before Bergson suggested that the term Homo Faber, Man the Maker, should replace Homo Sapiens. But man is not essentially distinguished from his animal relatives either by the fact that he lives in groups or performs physical work with tools. Man is first and foremost the self-fabricating animal: the only creature who has not rested content with his biological form or with the dumb repetitions of his animal role. The chief source of this particular form of creativity was not fire, tools, weapons, machines, but two subjective instruments far older than any of these: the dream and the word.

Without dwelling on the function of symbolization, one cannot begin to describe the nature of man or plumb the deepest spring of his creativeness. That is why I pass over many other attributes, fully taken into account today by anthropology and psychology, to dwell on man's role as interpreter. Language, the greatest of all human inventions, is the most essential key to the truly human. When words fail him, as we find in the few authenticated cases of wild children reared without the benefit of human society, man is an animal without a specific life-plan, compelled to imitate the wolfish habits of the animal in whose brood he has been suckled and reared.

One can, of course, only speculate on the way in which man invented and perfected the various tools of symbolization. But in the primary instance of speech, the word was made possible by changes in the bodily organs including the larynx, the tongue, the teeth, and not least the creation of mobile lips: in the earliest skulls identifiable as man, the anatomists find the speech centers already relatively well developed. The enlargement of man's powers, through his quicker ability to learn by trial and correction, demanded a special instrument for dealing with the multitude of sensations and meanings, suggestions and demands, that impinged upon him. Every sensation, as Adelbert Ames has experimentally demonstrated, is a prognostic directive to action: hence even the simplest stimulus must be interpreted, for whether we accept it or reject it depends not only upon its own nature but upon our purposes and predispositions and proposals. Even the purest sensation must be translated and re-ordered, before the organism will in fact see it, hear it, or answer it. In that response, the entire organism co-operates; and what is actually seen or heard or felt is only what makes sense in terms of the organism's immediate purpose or its historic plan of development.

At every moment of his waking existence, man senses, interprets, proposes, acts in a single unified response: but between the starting point and the end, the intermediate steps of interpretation and planful reorganization are critical, for it is here that error, miscalculation, and frustration may intervene. With the development of language, man created an instrument of interpretation that gave him a way of traversing the largest possible field of life. What he took in of the world expressed his own nature: what he expressed of himself partook of the nature of the world; for it is only in thought that organism and environment can be separated.

Now other creatures than man respond to immediate signals: the snarl of a dog has meaning for another dog, and the upraised white tail of a doe tells the fawns, as plainly as words, "Follow me!" But man, at a critical moment in his development, began to invent signs, in the form of audible words, which represent an event or a situation even when they are not present. By this act of detachment and abstraction, man gained the power of dealing with the non-present, the unseen, the remote, and the internal: not merely his visible lair and his daily companions, but his ancestors and his descendants and the sun and the moon and the stars: eventually the concepts of eternity and infinity, of electron and universe: he reduced a thousand potential occasions in all their variety and flux to a single symbol that indicated what was common to all of them.

Similarly, by kindred means, man was able to give form to and project his inner world, otherwise hidden and private: by words, images, related sounds, it became part of the public world, and thus an "object." This extraordinary labor-saving device, for extracting, condensing, and preserving the most complicated kinds of events, was perhaps another manifestation of the creative uses of his exuberance and vital proliferation. Man's possession of a "useless instrument," his special voice-producing organs, with their wide range of tones, plus a love of repetition, which one observes in the fullest degree in infants, opened up playful possibilities. If man is an inventor or an artist, the first object of his interest is his own body: he falls in love with his own organs long before he seeks to master the outside world.

"We must never forget," the distinguished philologist Jespersen once observed, "that the organs of speech . . . are one of mankind's most treasured toys, and that not only children but also grown people in civilized as well as savage communities, find amusement in letting their vocal cords and tongue and lips play all sorts of games." Out of this original organic overflow, man found too a way to shape a meaningful, orderly world: the world realized in language, music, poesy, and directed thought. The gift of tongues is the greatest of all gifts: in the beginning was the Word.

Speech, human speech, affected a miraculous transformation in human society: by such magic Prospero tamed Caliban and released Ariel. Speech, at first probably inseparable from gesture, exclamatory, disjointed, structureless, purely emotive, laid the foundation for a more complex mechanism of abstractions, the independent structure of language itself; and with language, human culture as an extra-organic activity, no longer wholly dependent upon the stability and continuity of the physical body and its daily environment, became possible. This broke through the boundaries of time and place that limit animal associations.

In the behavior of that perpetual primitive, the human infant, we can follow the original transition from babble to the involuntary reproduction of facial movements, from private gurglings for self-satisfaction to public demands in which a particular tone will be evoked to bring forth a particular response from the mother: the offer of a breast, the production of a dry diaper, the removal of a pricking pin, the reassurance of human companionship. Much of the intercourse between mother and child is the expression, on both sides, of feeling: tenderness, joy, rage, anxiety. Beyond doubt, the introjection and projection of feeling were basic to the whole achievement of language: a point often overlooked by pragmatic or rationalist interpretations.

In the instances of wild children nurtured by animals, we can verify this interpretation: for the ability to form words seems to disappear altogether when the infant's earliest vocalizings are not encouraged by similar vocalizing on the part of those who look after him. With the loss of language man also loses the facility for more complex forms of human behavior: though some of his organic capacities become intensified to animal sharpness, in an extra-sensitive nose or in muscular endurance, the veritably human touch remains absent: above all, the wild child forfeits the capacity to understand or communicate human feeling, thus becoming inferior, not only to other human beings, but to the dog or cat, who have had the benefit of human association, and who have learned the gestures and tones by which human feelings are expressed. Negatively, there is still another way of understanding the specifically human role of language: for psychologists have found that deaf-mutism, even when combated with skillful care, is a greater handicap to intelligence than blindness. Speech, even though accompanied by blindness, opens the path of social co-operation.

In his attempt to associate intelligence with the special faculty for dealing with the geometrical, the mechanical, the non-living, Henri Bergson curiously underestimated the formative effect of language and over-stressed the part played by physical tools and mechanical aptitudes, for he perversely interpreted speech as being lamed by man's rational preoccupation with static objects. On the contrary, language developed far more rapidly and effectively than mechanical tools; and it was probably in origin primarily a means of representing labile feelings and attitudes, the least geometrical part of man's experience. The most important thing for a human being to know, from infancy onward, is whether he is welcome or unwelcome, whether he is being loved and cherished and protected or hated and feared; and the give-and-take of speech, with all its modulations of color and tone, provides these essential clues. Language was not invented by philosophers seeking truth or by scientists seeking to understand the processes of nature, nor yet by mechanics seeking to shape a more adequate tool; nor was it created by methodical bookkeepers seeking to make an inventory of the contents of the world. Language was the outcome of man's need to affirm solidarity with his own kind. Because it was a prime organ, not only of social co-operation, but of sympathetic and dramatic insight, it helped to control and direct all human behavior.

In time, no doubt, language lent itself to many other uses besides communion and fellowship: it gave rise to a sense of "thatness" as well as "we-ness" and furthered causal insight into processes and relationships. Not least, language was a means whereby subjective reactions became externalized, and objective facts became internalized: thus it favored constant intercourse and traffic between the public world and the private world. In every sense, then, speech was man's prime instrument for sharing his private world with his fellows and for bringing the public world home to himself, though in time it was supplemented by the symbols and significants of the other arts. He who could speak the language could be trusted: every word was a password, indicating friend or foe, in-group or out-group; and these practices linger on in establishing identity right down to our own day.

The practical and rational offices of language, which now seem to us all-important, must for long have been purely incidental.

The complicated structure, the grammatical and logical subtlety, and the immense variety of even primitive languages drive one to believe that a large part of man's creative activity, perhaps for hundreds of thousands of years, must have concerned itself almost exclusively with the development of intelligible speech, and with secondary means of symbolization through the visual arts; for painting, too, in the Aurignacian caves, shows an exquisite perfection that argues a prolonged period of unremitting effort. No machine that man invented before the twentieth century compares in complexity and refinement with the simplest of human languages. No wonder this superorganic structure transformed the terms of man's self-development.

Beavers can build dams: bees can construct efficient dwellings: the meanest bird has still a surer mechanism for flying and landing than man has yet achieved. But no other creature has come within sight of man in the arts of symbolic communication. Mainly through language man has created a second world, more durable and viable than the immediate flux of experience, more rich in possibilities than the purely material habitat of any other creature. By the same agent, he has reduced the vastness and overpowering multiplicity of his environment to human dimensions: abstracting from its totality just so much as he could handle and control. The very formal qualities of words served as an instrument for understanding and directing the everlasting flow of things: it is because the structure of language and logic is relatively static (Parmenides and Plato) that the unceasing changes and processes of the natural world (Heraclitus) can be interpreted. If meanings changed as quickly as events, no event would have a meaning.

Let us make no mistake then: language is far more basic than any other kind of tool or machine. Through man's overdeveloped forebrain and his overflowing sensory-emotional responses, he came into contact with an ever-enlarging field of action; and through language, he found an economic way of dealing with this complexity and turning every state and activity to the service of meaning. So essential is language to man's humanness, so deep a source is it of his own creativity, that it is by no means an accident in our time that those who have tried to degrade man and enslave him have first debased and misused language, arbitrarily turning meanings inside out. Civilization itself, from the most primitive stage onward, moves toward the continuous creation of a common social heritage, transcending all the peculiarities of race and environment and historic accident, shared over ever wider reaches of space and time. This heritage, apart from environmental modifications, such as roads, canals, and cities, is transmitted largely in symbolic form; and by far the greater part of its symbolization is in spoken and written language. Contrary to the proverb, words make a greater difference than sticks and stones: they are more durable, too.

7: THE INTERPRETATION OF DREAMS

In dwelling on the invention of speech, as the most universal form of symbolism and the most weighty vehicle of communion and communication, I have, for the sake of clearness, treated this form of symbolism as if it stood alone. But as a matter of fact, the symbol plays a much wider role in human life. From what we know of the present nature of man, we must infer that the spontaneous babblings out of which is shaped the word were accompanied by another primitive and unlearned trait, likewise welling up through that capacious, overexcitable organ, the brain: the habit of dreaming. Babble and dream imagery are perhaps the raw stuff out of which man fashioned all his symbols, and consequently, most of his meaningful life: music and mathematics and machines: social patterns of behavior and the culture of cities.

Civilized man tends to associate dreaming most definitely with sleep: a sort of interior drama that goes on in the darkened theater of consciousness. He is occasionally not a little abashed when he becomes aware of his own dream states in waking life, for they sometimes displace his immediate sense of the external world; but he slides easily from the half-wakeful state of revery into the inner recesses of sleep where the events he experiences often seem more realistic, more gripping, more intense than any actual life provides. Indeed, in certain cases he may live a dream progressively, from night to night, and become a little confused as to which has the more dominant role in his life—as in the famous instance of Chuang-Chou who dreamed that he was a butterfly and then asked himself whether, in waking life, he was not perhaps a butterfly dreaming that he was a man.

Even in the most highly organized and controlled personality, no little part of the working day is spent in acting an interior drama with snatches of dialogue and action surprisingly different from overt conduct: these spontaneous associations have many of the characteristics of a dream, as James Thurber showed, with hardly more than a touch of exaggeration, in The Secret Life of Walter Mitty. In daydreams mild men often become murderers and faithful husbands become libertines: perhaps half the sins and crimes men commit come about because they pass too easily, without prudent reflection, from that inner state to the public performance of their fantasy.

In childhood, perhaps even more in adolescence, daydreaming may occupy the larger part of an individual's waking hours, rivaling nightdreaming in its absorption and self-enclosure; and very probably in primitive man there was far less of a gap between waking consciousness and sleeping consciousness than there now is. Against the current tendency to over-value the externalized and the objective, John Butler Yeats' words are a fine corrective: ". . . My theory is that we are always dreaming—chairs, tables, women and children, our wives and sweethearts, the people in the streets, all in various ways and with various powers are the starting point of dreams. As we fall asleep we drift away from the control and correction of facts into the world of memory and hope. . . . Sleep is dreaming away from the facts and wakefulness is dreaming in closer contact with the facts and since facts excite our dreams and feed them, we get as close as possible to the facts if we have the cunning and the genius of poignant feeling."

In normal people, we think of the waking consciousness as being more rational, more directed, more rigorous, more conventional, than the imagined behavior that takes place in sleep: this is largely true. But the life of early man was not so definitely organized into rational and irrational compartments; and though a certain wakefulness and alertness was necessary for his survival and would impose many practical limitations on his behavior, the dream may well have occupied the greater part of his energies; and throughout much of his life fantasy perhaps had the upper hand over common sense. Possibly the primitive's tendency to regard what we call insanity with respect, indeed, with awe and reverence, is a survival of this fact.

At all events, the notion that man's days have been continually spent in the hard "struggle for existence" is probably only another one of those subjective interpretations derived from the grim state of life under nineteenth century industrialism. We do ill to transfer these interests into the life of primitive man. In mechanical invention man was for countless years almost an imbecile, as helpless as a baby; and after he had stayed his hunger, he did little to improve his general situation: his practical devices, his technical adaptations, his improvements of the environment were few and far between; indeed he was, on the evidence, incapable of sustained labor and easily diverted from his meager utilitarian pursuits except when hunger was pressing. All too quickly the primitive settles back into a dreamful lethargy; and his subjective world must often have loomed far larger than the visible environment.

Plainly, we know no more about the origin of the dream than we do of the origins of language. But we can speculate on the special role of the dream, in order to find perhaps a faint clue to later developments. Given what we know of man's organic equipment and present traits and aptitudes, there is some reason to think that the dream had two main sources. One was man's extreme impressionability to both externally and internally aroused stimuli, so that the bodily changes which take place in fear, anger, and sexual passion, pouring their hormones into his bloodstream, may well leave traces in the cortex long after the immediate occasion has passed. The other source, arising out of that very impressionability, would be—especially for primitive man—his constant anxiety. This anxiety was not solely of neurotic origin. With good reason, fear has left a deep mark on the human race, for as man emerged from his animalhood, he had many occasions, particularly at night, to be fearful. Until primitive man had invented weapons and the means of organized social co-operation, he was a relatively defenseless animal surviving only by his sharper wits: he had hard work to hold his own among savage creatures that had natural weapons: tusks, horns, teeth, coils, poisons, far superior to anything in his own natural armory: some of them capable of working in close packs like the wolf, the bison, or the elephant.

With man's highly evolved sensorium, the coming of darkness would redouble all the fears of the day instead of quieting them. Here the dream performed a special function: it maintained man's persistent state of anxious alertness, yet it alleviated it and counteracted it. In the dream the power he lacked in reality would come back to him in a highly magnified form: denied his prey in the hunt, he would seize it in his dream; and though he might relive the fear he was forced to suppress, he might also awaken from the dream—as many an inventor has awakened since—with some new plan of action. Released from the constraints of practical necessity, the dream freed man from the fear-constricted routines and compulsive rituals on which his security had been built: it was the sphere of spontaneity and untrammeled experiment. Much was possible in the dream that could not penetrate through the walls of daytime habit. So the dream was both a shock-absorber, cushioning man's anxieties, and an uninhibited expression of his inner self, releasing him from dull constraints and paralyzing compulsions.

Should we do man an injustice, then, to characterize him as essentially the neurotic animal, subjected, in his earliest phases, to constant hallucinations, like those that even highly rational people quickly develop, for example, in the eerie darkness of a medium's séance? We say that a person is "out of his mind" when he has, in fact, withdrawn completely into his mind; yet this over-valuation of the inner life may have been, in the end, the chief source of man's outer mastery. On this hypothesis, man's irrationality perhaps contributed as much to his departures from animal conformity as his mother-wit: it was man's nervous apprehensions that gave his mind its peculiar bent and set: a readiness to re-organize his sensory experience on the basis of more perfect dream-images that conformed to inner desire as well as outer necessity. In the dream his obsessions and fears, his desires and lusts, but likewise his gropings and his aspirations beyond his brutish daily existence, would take on new shapes, almost independent of his volition.

Escaping the restraints of practice, escaping also the inhibitions of his strict social code, the dream served as an agent of creative detachment. This special agent probably enabled man to surpass, not only his more torpid animal competitors, but also his own matter-of-fact self as it had been shaped to a degree by the conditions of organic life and physical survival. Man is the only creature who lives a twofold life, partly in the external world, partly in the symbolic world he has built up within it; and the dream vies with the word in emancipating him from a constricted here and now. By means of the dream man learned to think and act more daringly than other, more stable creatures, better aware of their limitations and better adjusted to their natural state.

More primitive, probably, than speech, dream imagery became the source and foundation of many other symbolic activities; for every man, while he is asleep, is an artist, creating shapes that his hand may not yet know how to execute; and dream-work may be the earliest form of work, in that it was perhaps the most simple way of re-making the environment and re-organizing purposive activity. The inventiveness and creativeness man displayed in the dream, first under pressure of anxiety and then more freely, in response to need, may

be the main source of man's more enduring activities in symbolization, indeed in his own humanization.

In short, this rich spontaneous outflow of psychic material, a river
of varying shallows and depths by day, a seething, spreading flood by
night, gave man an extra means of reconstituting his life. For if sleep
itself detaches man from the bodily events of waking life, the dream
divorces him from all other conditions: it brings him out of his immediate world, with its constant difficulties, frustrations, and anxieties, and shows him, in its more benign aspects, how the miseries of
life can be counterbalanced and overcome. To this end, the psyche
stows away material in the dark caverns of the unconscious, and delivers it up, in new combinations, for creatively recasting the future.
Because nothing is impossible in the dream, because nothing is incredible, the dream enlarges the domain of human potentialities: the
territory that is so reclaimed can in time be cultivated during the
waking life. The fact that dream-images normally recur with the
least relaxation of attention, the fact that they arrange themselves spontaneously into dramatic and often purposeful sequences, irrational perhaps in content but creative, may well offer a master clue to the development of human culture. Even the most disciplined and directed kind
of thought cannot do without the free associations of dream: Henri
Poincaré, the mathematician, has reminded us of this fact. Hence a
failure to cultivate the inner life, a failure to do homage to the function of dream or to permit its untrammeled exercise, may also explain
the lack of self-confidence and the imaginative paralysis that leads to
the death of a civilization. People in that state can conceive no alternative to their man-made catastrophes. They do not realize that the very
power of conceiving alternatives might block the fatal advent of disaster.

Dream, hallucination, illusion—these are some of the means by
which man was able to overcome his fears and to compensate for his
inferiorities: at the moment he abandoned his animal securities and
lost his organic connections with nature, the dream magnified his own
image and restored his faith in himself. Admittedly, these self-begotten images and symbols may muddy the few clear moments of man's
daylight consciousness: even worse, man's absorption in dream, precisely because it brings him so swiftly to his goal, may have long stood
in the way of his achieving that causal insight into non-personal nature which science, first in ancient astronomy, came to reveal. There
is some reason to think that man's exploitation and mastery of his

subjective medium may have even retarded his practical mastery of the external environment: the wish that could be fulfilled in fantasy seemed hardly worth the further trouble of working out in the more refractory materials of wood and stone and fiber. This would suggest that man's late achievement of mechanical invention rested upon his reluctance to suppress a good part of his dream life: Homo Faber, the tool-user, could not in fact develop until he was willing to give words and images an inferior role.

Though at the beginning man's skill in using symbols was responsible for emergence into a truly human state, in the end it sometimes constituted a grave handicap: for he would apply subjective symbols to matters where real mastery depended upon the use of objective tools: fire and earthquake and rain and crop growth cannot be controlled by runes and verbal formulae—though to a limited extent we know certain diseases can. No small part of man's rational development consists in freeing himself from the misleading suggestions and the devious commands of his own undirected dreaming. So retarding was man's dream consciousness, so easily did it lend itself to perversion, that Dr A. L. Kroeber has properly taken, as a definite indication of human progress, the transformation of the infantile irrationalities of primitive man into the relatively mature rationalities of modern man.

But after all these allowances are made, we can see that without the aid of dream and word mankind could never have escaped from the animal world of the here and now. For there is still another function of the dream that must be taken into account: its prophetic or anticipatory nature. The dream is an organ of man's inchoate desires; and no small part of these impulses must come to fruit in the future. Freudian interpretation has over-stressed, perhaps, the deviousness of the dream mechanism: its tortuous methods of concealing the impulses that it expresses. There is in addition a much closer connection between need and dream-satisfaction which operates continually at almost every level of waking existence; for the dream often represents the direct pressure of an unsatisfied impulse and points the way to an appropriate goal or to a line of action: sometimes to future alternatives of action. It is in the persistent recurrence of a particular human image during even his waking hours that a person may become conscious suddenly of the fact that he or she has fallen in love: just as an adolescent first becomes conscious of bodily changes through the sudden onslaught of thinly disguised erotic images in dreams. Such dream-images become dynamic promptings to future behavior: and they further prepare the way for it by enabling the subject to enact in fantasy the divergent possibilities that life presents. Psychodrama is the essence of the dream. In the dream one acts alternative roles and releases oneself from the momentum of the past and the steady drive of habit: where in real life one's practical intention may keep one pushing along a narrow track, looking neither to one side nor the other, in the dream one's anima may give one wiser counsel; to accept life in its wholeness and depth: above all, the life to come.

8: MAN AS INTERPRETER

Those who try to understand the nature of man mainly by emphasizing his continuities with other animal species, naturally neglect the organs and agents that set him off from those species: hence they underestimate his creativeness and originality. Their attitude is, no doubt, partly a reaction against the ancient misuse of the symbolic functions: the attempt to make words directly perform operations. In general modern man over-values the act and undervalues the word: did not Goethe himself, word-magician though he was, say: In the beginning was the Deed?

Now language, as the vehicle of social solidarity, emotion, feeling, and thought often produces potent results on other human beings: not merely gross changes in behavior like those brought about via words, in hypnosis and suggestion, but a large range of minor modifications, every day and hour of our lives. To overlook this fact in the spiritual economy of the organism is like overlooking breathing in its physiology. It is the very success of symbolic functions in transforming the attitudes and the behavior of other human beings that has tempted man to misuse this magic: he has foolishly thought that it is possible to apply verbal formulae to alter the behavior of physical bodies. If the experiments of Dr Rhine and his colleagues in psycho-kinesis prove correct, even this propensity may not rest on a complete hallucination; but it is obviously much easier to make one set of spots face upward in dice by placing them in that position than by using an extra-sensory factor to bring about this result: so man probably wasted on word magic much valuable effort that might, long ago, have gone into the invention of more appropriate methodology. Even the great Roman physician Galen supplemented his natural knowledge with spells and magic formulae.

But man's capacity for misusing verbalization is no reason for devaluing the function itself. The various contemporary reactions against the full employment of language, from da-daism to logical positivism, will not in the least save us from error and self-deception: they merely substitute for the small detectable errors of misused speech the colossal error of rejecting the greater part of man's subjectivity, because it comes to us primarily in symbols of a non-operational order: symbols that have as many meanings as there are contexts and internal states. Modern man's insulation against the poetic use of words as mere propaganda—irrespective of whether the attempt to persuade is based on truth or falsehood—can lead only to a general denial of the possibilities of growth or transformation in the self, except by a purely physiological process. But since medicine teaches us that there are no purely physiological processes, no part of the body that is not in some degree affected by mental states, that is, by images and symbols, this self-imposed immunization and impoverishment is also a self-deception. On this matter, the present argument sharply disagrees with all forms of behaviorism: it also differs radically from the analysis put forward by the late Dr Trigant Burrow, to whose works I cordially refer the reader. Where Dr Burrow sees in the use of language only division and distortion, I read mainly socialization and self-development.

If all the mechanical inventions of the last five thousand years were suddenly wiped away, there would be a catastrophic loss of life; but man would still remain human. But if one took away the function of interpretation, by destroying the capacity to use language, an earlier human invention, the whole round earth would fade away more swiftly than Prospero's vision: insubstantial and dreamlike, without the words that arrest it and order it into widening patches of significance and value. Worse than this: man would sink into a more helpless and brutish state than any animal: close to paralysis. In the case of brain injury through accident, or in senile decay, one gets final proof of the key place occupied by man's symbol-using functions. Where there is a breakdown of tissue in the brain, sufficient to wipe out large areas of memory, an aged person will sometimes say: "My sight is poor; I am getting blind." Actually, medical examination may prove that the eyesight remains excellent; so what the afflicted person means is: "I am losing the capacity to understand what I see: it no longer makes sense to me." Once a person ceases to function symbolically, a water tap would be merely a visible tube of brass, but would not indicate water, and the nearby glass on the shelf would not, however close the physical association, suggest a method of bringing water to the lips; while pictures or verbal texts that represented these objects would be even less effective in prompting the right actions in response to thirst. The researches of Dr Kurt Goldstein leave no doubt on this score.

Almost all meaning above the animal level of response comes through abstraction and symbolic reference: in fact, the symbolic medium—verbal, musical, graphic—is the very one in which man, as man, lives and moves and has his being. The invention of the symbol was not merely the first great step from the organic to the super-organic: it also led to the further development from the social to the personal. Without constant reference to essences, as represented by symbols, existence would become empty, meaningless, and absurd—which is, precisely, what it seems to the mere existentialist. But what the existentialist, in horror and despair, finds lacking in the world, is merely what is lacking in his philosophy. Once one throws over symbols and essences as Captain Ahab threw over compass and sextant in his effort to come to grips with Moby Dick, the empty malice of unfocused energy, taken into the soul as a paranoid impulse to destruction, is all that will be left. When one begins by defacing the word one ends by defaming life. That is part of the plight of modern man.

The symbol-making activities of man, speech and dream, have turned out, then, to be more than tools, and they have until now played a far larger part in human life than his technical mastery of the natural environment, through weapons and machines. Dreaming is the dynamic, forward-striving, goal-seeking complement to remembering. While man's organic and social memory, through monuments and books and buildings, opens up for him the large resources of his past, the dream pushes his life forward to a more varied future, not given in either nature or his own history: the next moment, the next lifetime, the next century first comes to him in images of foreboding and hope: he sees a future pre-formed by the self, obedient to man's emergent nature, capable of projecting into public forms the hidden soul. Through the dream, man offsets his sense of guilt and anxiety, caused by his willful departure from his animal destiny, by his effort to set himself up in rivalry with nature and to put forth an independent creation, more responsive to his nature and desires than the actual world. So it is not an accident, but the very essence of human life, that some of its best and its worst moments are lived exclusively in the mind: anxiety and anguish, joy and fulfillment, are never so pure as they are when represented in art: "emotion recollected in tranquillity."

But note: through the mechanism of the dream, both directly and as elaborated in the arts, man surpasses his simple biological self both ways: upward and downward, bettering and worsening his natural self, embellishing and yet often defiling his environment. Long ago he departed from his ancestral home, in order to spend most of his years in two resorts of his own devising: heaven and hell. Man's very deviltry is a product of the same imagination which first represented his own utmost potentialities in the image of an all-wise and infinitely loving God. On this interpretation, literature, music, religion, those artful by-products of man's subjective life, are no less integral a part of man's existence than the natural world and the ingenious instruments he has devised for mastering it.

In other words, the dream is no mere mechanism of escape, but the foundation of man's own specific mode of life: the life that emerges in the person out of his stolid animal limitations and his compulsive social controls. However much we admire, with Whitman, the contentment and aplomb of animals, our own life-course is a more defiant and daring one, defiant to the point of madness, but enlivened, in its contradictions, its disparities, its absurdities, by a sense of comedy, which recognizes, with a wry grimace, how far his godlike pretensions have fallen short: how impulse has hardened into habit, how gesture has frozen into tics and compulsions, how every leap upward has ended, at last, in a clownish fall. But out of man's very maladjustment, promoted by his concentration on his inner world, he has achieved a deeper consciousness of existence, and eventually an ampler sanity and balance than dumb animal existence could achieve. When mankind gave its days over to babbling and dreaming, life took a new path, at right angles to the horizontal plane of organic survival. For no promethean fire has ever burned so steadily or so brightly as the flame man first lighted within himself.

What holds of the dream holds in almost equal degree of the word. Every part of the "real" world, from the wooded mountain top to the towered city, has become material for man's symbolic activities, and gains in visibility, and usability, through man's capacity to interpret it and re-fashion it in his mind. Even the photographic image of the remotest star bears the imprint of man's subjectivity: this pin-point of white on a dark ground becomes more than that only through the operation of a complex structure of interpretation that man has built up since the time of the Chaldean star-gazers. As soon as any part of the external environment, natural or man-made, ceases to further man's purposes, it ceases to have meaning, and even when it remains in sight it falls out of mind: witness what happened to the Roman baths once the Christian fathers condemned the ritual of bodily care that they subserved. Once a structure ceases to have meaning, men will quarry it for stone, as readily as they would quarry into an open hillside: witness again the assault on Gothic buildings in eighteenth century France. So, too, a change in the direction of human interest, an interior subjective change, could wreck New York as destructively as an atom bomb. On the other hand, even a "worthless" natural object—a martyr's lock of hair or the fragment of Java man's skull—may acquire value through the projection of meaning upon it: in this case, it will be guarded tenderly from generation to generation, as if it were a precious work of art.

At every moment, thanks to our symbols, we are nourished by other lives that have flourished and faded, leaving behind only an apparently wraithlike deposit of words and images, on paper, stone, or celluloid: a story memorized, an observation recorded, a line skillfully drawn, a formula condensed in special signs. What man is and does passes away: what continues in existence is the ever-enlarging structure of interpretation derived from history, and stored, sifted, transmitted, from generation to generation: that is the capital fund that makes human productivity and creativity, indeed the very capacity to become human, possible. Since man not only lives his life but represents it to himself, since he not merely accepts the order of nature but re-fashions it in his mind, the very subjective elements that destroy his animal harmony contribute to his creativity. Man is happiest when he feels that all his frustrations and struggles, though often painful, may have significance: he is unhappy, on the contrary, when he believes that even his most pleasurable fulfillments may be meaningless. Whatever else man's social heritage has done for him, its chief function has been to lay a stable foundation of values, meanings, and purposes beneath his life-sustaining activities.

Against the long-prevalent view that man is but an insignificant speck in a sterile, depersonalized universe, the present philosophy holds that it is the physical universe that is insignificant until man emerges from it and takes possession of it and interprets it in terms of his own past and future. Apart from man's purposes and values, a grain of dirt is as important as a planetary system: without man both are in fact non-entities.

Man, in other words, is the agent through which natural events become intelligible and natural forces valuable, since events and forces may be increasingly directed, in accordance with man's own plan of life, to their human, and eventually their divine, destination. While this fact makes man an active mediator it does not turn him into a God. Apart from mind and spirit, word and dream, man's powers are in fact smaller than the forces acting upon him; and he is accordingly at their mercy: a change of a few degrees upward or downward in the body's temperature will bring about human death. This philosophy conceives the role played by man as interpreter as the apex of natural existence: the quintessence of all that has gone before, the embryonic vehicle of developments and fulfillments that lie far ahead. Man's ability to interpret the world truly, with insight into potentialities as well as causes, gives the measure of his ability to transform it.

Man, in his full historic dimensions, encloses the primitive and the sophisticated, the infantile and the mature: he takes into himself times past and times to come, places near and places distant, the seen and the unseen, the actual and the possible. What was once called the objective world is a sort of Rorschach ink blot, into which each culture, each system of science and religion, each type of personality, reads a meaning only remotely derived from the shape and color of the blot itself. Like Brahma, man himself is the slayer and the slain, the knower and the known, the creator and the creature of a world which, though it encloses him, he also transcends. Though he did not fabricate the world he has colored every part of it by his consciousness and reconstituted it by his intelligence.

If man has surpassed his animal destiny, it is because he has utilized the dream and the word to open up territory that cannot be reached on foot or opened up with ax or plow. He has learned to ask questions for which, in the limits of a single lifetime or a single epoch of culture, he will never find the answer. Each civilization treats that territory, boundless and almost impenetrable, as in some significant way the coeval of its familiar homeland: it represents the sum of things worth living for and worth dying for: the values and purposes that not merely evoke a higher life, but even justify death itself, through whose foreknowledge, applied to the affairs of the moment, man further overrides his animal limitations. As zero and infinity give him a sense of possibilities he cannot reckon with the aid of his ten digits, so his heavens and hells bring to light otherwise hidden potentialities of his earthly existence; and the ideal is accordingly the fourth dimension of every structure he builds.

This sphere is the realm of religion: the sphere beyond knowledge and certainty, where ultimate mystery itself adds a new dimension to meaning. Out of the silence of infinite space comes a sound: the birth cry of human consciousness. Against the enveloping darkness man throws the searchlight of his intelligence. As man projects further the cone of light, through his gifts of interpretation, he likewise widens the perimeter of the surrounding darkness. The ultimate gift of conscious life is a sense of the mystery that encompasses it.

CHAPTER III.   COSMOS AND PERSON

1: ON THE USE OF UNANSWERABLE QUESTIONS

If there were general agreement as to the nature of man and the purpose of life, it would have been unnecessary to attempt preliminary definitions. But unfortunately even the sciences that deal directly with man cannot, within their present framework, provide such agreement: for their conclusions assume the validity and sufficiency of their particular method of inquiry. In its quest for certainty, science keeps to the broad, visible, neatly edged paths and avoids the obscure thickets of subjectivism: this means that it rejects, as either indecipherable or negligible, a considerable part of mankind's experience. Because such science can predict future behavior only in terms of the known past, it must leave out many potentialities not so determined; and because it deals with statistical order, it has tended to reject the unique and the non-repeatable, though such events may powerfully affect the course of human development.

Up to now the sciences have sought limited answers to limited and isolated problems: they have not concerned themselves with the pattern of the whole. Religion historically preceded science in attempting to interpret the cosmos and man's part in its processes; and it has worked on a radically different set of assumptions, although at various points, in their early development, the paths of science and religion coincided. Because of its reliance on subjective revelation, religion has dared to include whole tracts of human experience that escape the scientific net, no matter how fine the mesh or how skillful the casting. "Purpose," "value," "free will," "potentiality," "ideal," and "final goal" have had, until today, no place in the scientific description of the physical world, whose special mode of interpretation was developed in the seventeenth century. But these concepts and categories are so essential for an account of human experience in its entirety that their absence from the original scientific world picture—an omission over which positivism once took pride—is enough to make one doubt either its accuracy or its sufficiency. That doubt is now confirmed in the most advanced departments of science.

Religion, as I shall here define it, is a body of intuitions and working beliefs that issue out of that part of man's nature and experience which science, deliberately seeking piecemeal knowledge of an immediately verifiable nature, rejects. For the questions that religion asks are not concerned with particulars but with the whole: not specific questions as to What and How? but questions of the widest generality and the most teasing elusiveness: Why? Wherefore? For what purpose? Toward what end? Religion seeks, in other words, not a detailed causal explanation of this or that aspect of life, but a reasonable account of the entire sum of things.

All the transient phenomena of life and civilization and the human personality religion sets against the cosmic perspectives of time and space. The concepts of infinity and eternity, which are not verifiable by piecemeal observation, have been the very core of the higher religious consciousness: so at a period in culture when the scientific mind was still bogged in the materialism of the four elements, earth, air, fire, and water, a Pythagoras or a Plato sought to deduce from harmonic mathematical relationships a clue to a deeper pattern of order. In its widest reaches, religion concerns itself with the impenetrable substratum of reality; with what, from the standpoint of science, is unknowable: the *mysterium tremendum*.

In terms of positive science, most of the questions religion puts are unanswerable questions; and for the conventional scientist, still imprisoned in a partial, mechanistic ideology, they represent illusory problems. The very vocabulary of religion is regarded by many scientists as nonsense, because it cannot be turned into the Basic English of operationalism. So much the worse, then, for the limitations of the scientific method: primitive tribes and little children, who dare ask the same unanswerable questions, are in practice wiser, for they are not inhibited in their concern with the whole, and are not embarrassed in the free utterance of their bafflements, their forebodings, their hopes.

Once man achieves consciousness, there is no way of casting off these questions or of evading a provisional answer, without repressing an essential quality in life itself. Even when men try to evade any concern with ultimate issues, by losing themselves in the day's work, filling their spiritual emptiness with excesses of food or drink, or with a surfeit of esthetic sensibility and abstract knowledge—for there are

gluttons and drunkards of the spirit, too—they are still haunted by
the specters of themselves and by their relation to the universe: the
selves that might have been: the selves that still may be.

Such people may, like the elder Karamazov in Dostoyevsky's novel,
seek to lose themselves in squalid love affairs, and may deliberately
scorn and mock those who seek to confront the mystery of their being,
as old Karamazov sniveled and grimaced before Father Zossima: yet
the very intensity of their reaction only shows, perhaps, the depth of
the human need. If human life has no purpose and meaning, then the
philosophy that proclaims this fact is even emptier than the situation
it describes. If, on the other hand, there is more to man's fate and history than meets the eye, if the process as a whole has significance,
then even the humblest life and the most insignificant organic function
will participate in that ultimate meaning.

We shall never get to the bottom of man's nature and his present
dilemmas, unless we realize that he is, to begin with, the kind of
creature who has persistently asked such ultimate questions about himself and the universe: indeed he is so thirsty for this order of truth
that he will swallow it in almost any degree of dilution or adulteration.
And so far, let us confess, those questions are wiser than all the answers. From the beginning man views life, above all his own life, with
a mixture of curiosity, humility, and wonder: he claims the Unknown
as his province and the Unknowable as his object, for the reason that
he realizes that the true condition of man is "beyond him," and that
the fate of man is not entirely in his own hands.

Man's answers to these mysteries were bound by the very terms of
his own finite nature to be inadequate. However penetrating his vision,
whatever man finds out about the all-enveloping world must be only
so much of it as he can encompass within his person and culture:
an infinitesimal sample in space and time. Almost certainly, his sense
of the whole came forth at only a late date in his evolution and is
plainly one of his most fragile and imperfect achievements. Yet each
one of us, in some degree, resonates to the world as a whole, and picks
up and transforms waves that come from distant transmitting stations:
we hear their noise in our receivers, perhaps, long before we have
learned the code or are able to spell out any part of the message. But
because man has sought to project himself beyond the here and now,
because he has been willing to traffic with the inactual, the unknown,
the mysterious, he has had a better grasp of cosmic processes than a
more limited, down-to-earth attitude would have given him. The little

questions, for which there are definite answers, have an important practical function: yet it is only within the larger frame that they are fully significant. Nothing can be settled until everything is settled. The first step in the re-education of man is for him to come to terms with his ultimate destiny.

Each culture has developed its own way of putting these ultimate questions about man's nature and fate; and has assigned special values to the experiences symbolized as God, eternity, immortality, being and non-being. The answers to these questions differ in innumerable details; yet they all point to a common substratum of human experience which is none the less real because language is so inept and ineffectual in coping with it. Most of the more naive conceits of theology are, to a great degree, impatient attempts to picture, in familiar terms, more obvious forms of continuity between the known and the unknown, between the immediate and the whole, the manifest and the mysterious, than the facts warrant. Yet without some recognition of the whole, the part played by earthly life would be almost as meaningless as the severed hand, in Aristotle's famous illustration, if one did not know its normal connections with the human body: the organ, by its very existence, implies the organism it serves.

Just as the anatomist, given the fragment of a human skull, can reconstruct with reasonable certainty many other characteristics of the head and even the rest of the human body, so the religious mind, repeatedly plumbing the depths of human experience, may have a faint twilight perception of the constitution of the universe itself; though no finite mind will ever grasp it fully or exhaust all its possibilities till the end of time: for time, in all its organic and human implications, is part of what must be revealed. Man's deepest needs prompt him to this exploration: the very concept of the stellar universe, as enveloping man's lifetime and persisting beyond it, came from man's deliberate attempt to give a rational account of his own appearance and acts, his birth, his ordeals, his triumphs, his frustrations, and his final dissolution.

Even a false picture of man's cosmic relations—and no picture can be free from many finite human errors—may give a closer image of reality than no picture at all. Granted that man overestimates his powers and over-values his own organs: granted that he often gives too absolute a value to his individual life and its prolongation: granted that he freely projects his own passions and animosities upon the universe itself, as Dante did in his vision of the Inferno—there is still more of the cosmic process in these distorted pictures than in the neat mathematical frame of positive science, which disdains even to place a picture within its boundaries. Partiality and persistent error in a field of genuine interest are more active paths to truth than indifference.

2: THE MYTHOLOGIES OF MAN

Man has told himself many stories about his origin and his destination. Two things are common to these myths: they reflect, with simple childlike unconsciousness, the humble details of his daily life; and they recognize the existence of agents and forces he has never beheld with his eyes or seized with his hand, though in one fashion or another he has had to account for their activities. Admittedly, man cannot discard the suggestions of his immediate environment: the landscape of his daily life envelops his fantasy. If he suffers from heat, like the tribes of the desert, his Hell will be an eternity of fire and brimstone: if he gets lost in exploring the limestone caves of Attica, his Hades will be a cold, pale underground world where half-living souls move about in the leaden light: if a volcano dominates the plains below it, as in Hawaii or in Mexico, the fiercest and most powerful of his gods will spring from that volcano.

This naïveté is not easily put away, even by modern science. If one translated the abstract symbols of present-day materialism into the concrete images that most closely fit them, we would behold a vast automatic assembly line, without a designer at one end or a product at the other, along whose conveyor belt machines assembled themselves by accident and were broken up by intention (fatal law of entropy!) only to re-enter the process once more as belts, shafts, or carburetors, at some point in the assembly line: the gains and losses of this process being accurately tabulated by automatic electronic calculators in a non-existent accounting department.

But these myths have another side to them: neither the quality of man's environment nor the pressure of his daily animal needs fully accounts for their wide scope or their remarkable power of abstraction and detachment. They pose unanswerable questions; or rather, they suggest answers that can be verified in part only by being lived: yet the single life span of the individual man cannot, since the questions concern the cosmos, provide any positive answer. Consider these unanswerable questions, as they come down to modern man from a distant past.

Is man a mote lost in the infinite vistas of time and space, the helpless sport of random forces, the product of indifferent elements, the prey of hostile energies, crippled by savage encounters with Moby Dick—all moving in some cosmic Brownian movement? Is he a smoking candle with a charred wick, giving no light beyond the pale of his own little niche: a poor flame flickering in a wind that will speedily extinguish it? Do his feebleness and his physical insignificance make a mockery of his gigantic exercise of mind; and is this mind of his itself but an accidental infection on the blank face of matter, soon to be absorbed in vaster physical processes? If so, the only way out of man's presumed littleness and helplessness would be to use the feeble light itself, the conscious rational mind, as Bertrand Russell in his youth suggested, to contemplate without hope the greatness that mocks it. The myth is that of materialism; the decision, stoicism.

Or is man the center of all cosmic intentions? Is he, in fact, the prodigal offspring of a loving Deity, who has defied the will of his Eternal Father and gone astray? Has he through his willfulness thrust himself out of his Garden of Eden, where he was at one with all creation, in order to eat the apple of the tree of knowledge, the apple that made him conscious of his short span of individual life and his approaching death; and is he thereby condemned, in his battle against death, to work by the sweat of his brow, laboring ere the night cometh, instead of growing serenely like the lily of the fields?

Does man's nature, then, partake both of the earthly and the divine, but is it steeped in an original sin that springs from his pride and self-love; and is he thus lost and damned forever until divine intervention redeems him? Does man, condemned to daily toil to get his bread, riddled with disease, racked with pain, prone to error and evil, have no true fulfillment on earth? Is it provided that the answers he seeks here and now will be found only if he prepares himself for another world and turns all his hopes and aspirations there? Does he begin his true life only with death: the passage to a life eternal, where he will enact a new role, not subject to earth's burdens—or alas! to its stimulating challenges—so that he will spend eternity solely in the blissful contemplation of God?

That is the myth of Christianity; and with variations, the myth of every other after-worldly religion, which shifts the center of gravity from the earth to heaven, from the kingdom of life to the kingdom of death. For Plato this palpable world was a cave of darkness where man was but a prisoner, forced to spend his days with his back turned to the light: so that all he knew of the verities that lay outside the cave were but the shadow reflections cast upon the wall. The world of his senses was thus a kind of nonsense; and the world unreachable by his senses, but divined with the aid of logic and mathematics, was that in which his deliverance and the final significance of his life lay.

Or is man a being chained to an eternal cycle of recurrence, in which he slowly, with many backslidings, climbs upward in the ladder of being? Does he live in a world where by pious observances of ritual and by progressive spiritual detachment he may ultimately dissociate himself from his animal needs and his exorbitant capacities for pain and misery, concealed even in his briefest pleasures and joys? May he thus escape from the dismal cycle of animal existence: may he, even while he is on earth, by strict efforts and disciplines, cast off his animal role and unite with the source of all energy and life, blessed through spiritual exercises by ineffable illumination (*sattva*), which those of lesser faith and more sluggish energies (*tamas*) will accomplish for themselves only through a long series of reincarnations, till they, too, become part of that Being which is also Non-Being. This is the core of the discipline of many forms of asceticism and withdrawal. United to this conception of many hierarchies of being and godhead, as in Hinduism, or to a depersonalized universe, as in Buddhism, this notion of the cosmic role of man, as a casting off of his animal limitations and a final re-union with Brahma, takes account of every stage of inertia and illumination; yet leaves one with the unaccountable irrationality of the performance itself.

These classic answers about the human predicament themselves raise further questions about the nature of man. Is man merely a paranoid animal, haunted by delusions of grandeur, unwilling to co-operate with the forces that assign to him a more humble position than he fancies he occupies: or is he in fact the offspring of Prometheus, he who stole fire from Olympus, claiming for man that which was once the sole possession of the gods; and are his delusions of persecution not altogether imaginary ones, since the emergence from his animal state brings disabilities that animals themselves have not yet achieved and the gods, so to say, have passed beyond?

Does man live only from day to day, walled in by animal needs he can never escape, and accordingly never more absurdly limited than when he fancies he has stepped out of this modest role: a creature consoling himself for his low estate and his niggardly inheritance by seeking pleasures that will never satisfy him and creating willful illusions that, in his own heart of hearts, he recognizes as little better than the toys and dolls of his childhood: vital lies, puppet creatures of his own fantasy?

Or again, is man, if only a frail reed, still, as Pascal said, a thinking reed: adding to the universe by his very presence something that without his aid, despite countless eons of groaning in travail, it might never have brought forth? Are his sensibilities and his feelings nothing? Are his knowledge and his consciousness nothing? Does their rarity, as one sweeps over the whole range of cosmic forces and events, make them less precious or less significant? If his god is but the enlargement by thousands of diameters of the power, the love, the knowledge he has developed through his own evolution, is that divine quality itself less real because of this?

Perhaps, beyond the scope of these myths and parables, there is some larger purpose and some deeper significance in man's life than any of his historic questions have hinted, or any of his historic answers have proposed. For the more that positive knowledge advances in every realm, from nuclear physics to the inchoate world of the unconscious, the more one begins to detect an underlying pattern, an emerging order of design: a pattern and order through which freedom supervenes upon necessity, purpose upon chance, and the person himself upon the cosmos that envelops him. These questions, at all events, with many parallel ones, are the questions originally set by the classic religions; and though the nature of the cosmos itself keeps any of the answers from being final, the very act of translating these intuitions into acts and observances, into rituals and codes and disciplines for the daily life, yes, into governmental systems and technologies, has itself given a new form and content to human existence. If every institution is the lengthened shadow of a man, as Emerson observed, every man bears a mask upon his face; and that mask is the countenance of his god.

The belief that man's life is not an insignificant local phenomenon, but a meaningful and progressively intelligible part of a cosmic process, is common to all the higher religions: the religions by which the most fully developed and most numerous groups of mankind have lived. Since it represents an experience deeply grounded in human history, this intuition is not lightly to be rejected: indeed, from the standpoint of the present philosophy, it must not be rejected at all: for Man is wiser than men, and the conscious knowledge of any single generation cannot be compared for trustworthiness with the funded experience of mankind. If life is what is at stake, then it should be plain that when men think and feel and act, in relation to an overall cosmic pattern, life flourishes and men grow to fuller stature: as they do not flourish and grow when man's life is held to be no more than the grass that is shoved into the oven and burned.

Man's biological survival, we know now, is actually involved in cosmic processes and prospers best when some sense of a cosmic purpose attends his daily activities. Man's positive knowledge of these processes and purposes is but a film that supports him as the skin on a glass of warm milk supports a fly: he must rest lightly on the surface or perish. When he seeks to drink from the liquid below, he will find further nourishment, no doubt; but it is included in the fact of his own nature that he will never drain the glass dry: measured by his flylike capacities it is in fact fathomless, and at best he may hope that the samples he takes, at various intervals, will reveal something about the constitution of what lies beyond his capacity to take in. That depth of mystery is at once a frustration and a compelling incentive to man's activity: being godlike, he must seek to penetrate it; being finite, he must accept failure.

The other side of the cosmic mystery issues from the nature of man's own limitations. If in some fashion he embodies the creative forces of the universe, he also carries within him, through his continuity with the physical world itself, all those countervailing tendencies summarized in the law of entropy: for life defies this downward tendency, but at last succumbs to it. Eventually, man must come to terms, even as individual men must, with his creatureliness and his finiteness. Nothing that man does endures: none of the values man seeks, none of the purposes he fulfills, none of the knowledge he acquires, is altogether imperishable: the very nature of life itself is to be precarious, insecure, frail, vulnerable, evanescent. When man tries to apply some fixative to keep the color of his precious picture from rubbing off, he falsifies the color in the very act of preservation and thus loses what he seeks to keep: so every attempt to transpose life into eternity, by stone monuments, laws written on tables of brass, or pious repetitions, also arrests life and eventually destroys it.

Only by constant reproduction and renewal can life endure: this is true in the biological realm and equally true in the realm of spirit. In beauty and truth and goodness man finds his highest satisfactions:

the whole experience of the race attests this fact; and to crown these qualities with love is to come as close to the pinnacle of human experience as is possible. But does man fulfill these high possibilities of existence? On the contrary: no small part of man's activities results in the defacement of beauty, the misappropriation of truth, the miscarriage of justice, the perversion of goodness. This potential god, in other words, has a devil in him; his worst suspicions about the universe are confirmed by his own persistent misbehavior. Thus man's life for all its godlike qualities is plagued by perpetual contradictions between his pretensions and his acts: not least between his cosmic intuitions and his more sordid daily occupations: "getting and spending, we lay waste our powers." No small part of man's activities by their very repetition smother those moments of illumination in which man finds himself exalted—and fulfilled.

Plainly, man must come to terms with himself in some fashion, before he can understand the world or transform his own nature, in conformity to ever higher ranges of purpose, ever higher standards of value. No small part of the office of the classic religions has consisted in penetrating man's illusions about himself: in breaking down his rationalizations of his own misconduct, in exposing his pretenses and hypocrisies, in bringing home an appropriate sense of guilt over his failure to fulfill his own potentialities, and in helping him to overcome his animal inertia; since too often he is content to fall back to the survival level of his species, instead of pushing upward to the higher transformations of the person. Religion, even to such a prudent naturalist philosopher as John Dewey, is essentially the "sphere of the possible." The function of the classic religions, as one finds them in history, is to confront the paradoxes and contradictions and the ultimate mysteries of man and the cosmos: to make sense and reason of what lies beneath the irreducible irrationalities of man's life: to pierce the surrounding darkness with pin-points of light, or occasionally to rip away for a startling moment the cosmic shroud.

In brief compass, I shall try now to appraise this contribution, in order to bring out certain common elements which will remain a permanent contribution to every adequate philosophy of human life. In so far as the traditional religions have given expression to these elements and have shaped our response to them, they will, I believe, likewise help express and shape the new personality and the new culture that must emerge from our present chaos of creeds and ideologies.

3: THE EMERGENCE OF THE DIVINE

Because of the narrow time-limits of his own life, it is natural that man should think of the universe itself as having a beginning and an end. Too easily, he conceives of cosmic events as having been set in motion by forces similar to those that intervene in human life. Man himself, as Vico observed, can understand things well only by creating them: so in the effort to understand the universe, he was disposed, in conformity with his own nature, to assume a creator who stands outside his creation and commands it. In an effort to arrive at intelligibility, man placed both the physical agency and the moral responsibility upon the gods, or upon the centralized authority of a single God: omnipotent and omniscient figures who, in their turn, were the reflections of the more mundane control and leadership exercised by the priest-kings of the earlier civilizations in which the high religions first flourished. These were naive presumptions and gratuitous explanations; but natural.

So conceived, as encompassing the universe yet outside it, as moving but unmoved, as immanent in all its creatures yet separate from them by unspeakable distances, towering above them in awful perfections and finalities, God himself has become more of a problem than the problems his existence would solve. In order to come closer to this mystery, man has then conceived God in more human shapes that are themselves equally contradictory and self-negating: as Yin and Yang, as Hora and Osiris, as Eternal Male and Eternal Female, as omnipotent power and all-embracing love: as the phallic principle of fertility and as the divine seed that is buried in the earth in the dying year and resurrected with the awakening of the vegetation in the spring. In one aspect, God is unpicturable fathomless immensity, the nameless one; and in another, he becomes incarnated as Krishna the Archer, as Buddha the Illumined One, as Christ the Saviour. In all these forms, God both accounts for the existence and completes the meaning of human life.

Historically, the sense of the divine is almost inseparable from man's sense of his own destiny; for nothing about his life is more strange to him or more unaccountable in purely mundane terms than the stirrings he finds in himself, usually fitful but sometimes overwhelming, to look beyond his animal existence and not be fully satisfied with its immediate substance. He lacks the complacency of the other animals: he is obsessed by pride and guilt, pride at being something more than a mere animal, guilt at falling perpetually short of the high aims he sets for himself. Behind this strange discontent lies his persistent belief, visible almost from the time that the presence of man can be identified by burial mounds, that the course of life does not fully reveal man's meaning and destiny: that all existence has goals and ends, still almost impenetrable, which in their further unfolding will give fuller meaning to the cosmic solitude and the frustrating brevity of man's life. Even now these ends are difficult to approach by pure speculation; and no wonder: could the earliest one-celled organism anticipate the eventual emergence of a multi-celled, highly organized, self-conscious creature, living in a world re-made in part through his own arts, in colonies and partnerships whose complexity had no parallel in the primal ooze?

This sense of the divine is an historic fact of man's nature: no theory that ignores it or explains it away can do justice to all the dimensions of human existence. What is gratuitous on man's part is the belief that he has any positive knowledge of cosmic intentions or any definite clues to the ultimate goals of this process. What he too confidently characterizes as divine revelation is often premature and presumptuous.

But for man's life to have meaning and purpose, one need not conceive that any part of it existed predetermined, foreordained, from the beginning of time: still less that time itself has a beginning or an ending. Every step in the process of cosmic evolution, no matter how plausible the connections, how closely related the stages when one looks back upon them, may be a magnificent series of improvisations, in which each emergent element, in its very novelty, may suggest a still further step not even dimly defined at the earlier stages of the process. As the action proceeds, it becomes increasingly significant, gathering meaning and value as a snowball gathers bulk and momentum when it rolls downhill.

The universe, like man himself, who is continuous with it, may be in the midst of a process of self-fabrication: chaos shaking down into order: order providing a basis for pattern and purposive transformation: purposes diverging into alternative routes, leading to disengagement and detachment from biological compulsions, and so finally to human freedom. To suppose that this is the work of a detached author, who has written the script and has supervised the performance, is to go far beyond the warranted evidence; while to suppose that it is an aimless accretion of accidents is to claim a far greater miracle for materialism than religion has ever claimed for God.

Plainly, it is man's littleness that has prompted him to affix his own special interests and preoccupations, often of the most limited range, to cosmic and organic processes. We must discount these anthropomorphic projections, even when they appear in the sterile laboratory garb of science. What is at fault is not our sense of mystery and divinity, for this rests on valid translations of human experience: we err merely in our effort to cast this intuition in a too-familiar mold, in order to pass more freely from the known to the unknown. Our mistake has been to regard the process of development as being predetermined at either the beginning or the end: we have looked for an enclosed system with a single cause at the beginning, a single consummation at the end. But the tendency toward organization, development, life, personality does not in fact become wholly intelligible by tracing it back to its origins: the climax of meaning lies, in all probability, in the future.

In other words, a large part of man's nature and destiny must be taken on faith; and the groundwork of that faith is no firmer in science than it is in religion. The equation of life cannot be solved more quickly by sneaking a look at the answer in the back of the arithmetic book. Improvisations and surprises are as deep in the grain of reality as necessity. If the creative power knew the answer beforehand there would be no reason to work it out.

Now the classic religions have not erred in holding that a sense of the divine alters every other perspective in human life. That is a fact of experience, not universal, perhaps, but confirmed in some sense by even the crudest cultures: only an occasional arrested culture, like that of the Eskimo, seems to exhibit a certain cosmic color blindness here. On the present interpretation, however, religion has so far erred in identifying God with totality of existence or being: or, worse, in trying to make God the groundwork of all processes and events: the all-powerful and all-knowing providence. By placing God in a position of active responsibility for the cosmic processes, or for man's special existence, almost every system of theology has saddled itself with false dilemmas, and seeking an answer to the unanswerable, has come up with childish rationalizations.

For mark this: if one puts God at the beginning, as the creator of all things, he becomes a monstrous being, as the God of the Old Testament in fact seemed to the sensitive Manichees, who took note of his irrational angers and his bloody commands long before Voltaire. That

God is a god of matter, bestiality, darkness, and pain: not a god of love and light. If, on the other hand, one attempts to unbind deity from responsibility for having produced a world half lost to the powers of darkness and death, by promising some redemption, at least for man, in an eternal future which will balance up accounts and make love prevail: if one does this one seems to turn a brutal god into a demented one, a creature capable of condemning human beings to an eternity of torture for sins committed in the briefest of lifetimes: a savagely disproportionate system of punishment repulsive to reason and justice. If the God who permitted the slaughter of the innocent in the Lisbon earthquake shocked Voltaire, what would he have said to the God who permitted his creatures to invent the insane horrors of Buchenwald and Auschwitz?

Neither faith nor reason could bring such complete defilements and miscarriages of life within the compass of human acceptance, if a divine purpose actually presided over all the occasions of human life. Plainly, if there is a loving God he must be impotent: but if he is omnipotent, truly responsible for all that happens within his domain, capable of heeding even the sparrow's fall, he can hardly be a loving God. Such contradictions drive honest minds to atheism: the empty whirl and jostle of atoms becomes more kind to human reason than such a deity.

Is the sense of divinity, then, a mere figment of the imagination, a radical misinterpretation of the elements man finds in his own nature? No: it is only as an over-ruling benevolent providence that the divine is a figment. Our logic is at fault in assigning God to the wrong end of the cosmic process. The universe does not issue out of God, in conformity with his fiat: it is rather God who in the long processes of time emerges from the universe, as the far-off event of creation and the ultimate realization of the person toward which creation seems to move. God exists, not at the beginning, but at the end: we shall not find him, except in an incredible degree of tenuity in the earliest stages of the formative process; for he first disclosed himself in a self-revealing and identifiable form, only in the human heart, as a truly personal God. There are, however, many dim foreshadowings of the divine throughout the animal world: without the lower forms of order and purpose in nature, the higher forms he tends toward could not be achieved. Suppose, then, that God is not the active creator, as conceived in the Sacred Books, the Vedas and Korans and Bibles: suppose, rather, that he is the ultimate outcome of creation; so that the Kingdom

of God, latent in nature, is the ideal consummation of the whole process. That assumption, I submit, makes better sense.

If one puts God at the beginning of the whole cosmic transformation,
one adds to the present irrationalities of life, I repeat, the even deeper
mystery and irrationality invoked by the explanation itself. At that
point, the only answer to man's most insistent problems is the peremptory one given to Job: "I am that I am:" which means "Stop asking
unanswerable questions!" But if one finds God at the other end of the
process, not as the foundation which underlies the whole structure of
life, but as the still unfinished pinnacle that may ultimately crown it,
the world's development and human life itself begin to take on a rational form; for man's business becomes not so much the mere contemplation as the active creation of the divine. In the light of the
eventual destination, even earlier steps in development, hitherto meaningless or valueless, even insensate and irrational, become through
this divine foreboding more significant. Begotten in the human soul
itself, but never fully at home there, the divine comes as a further step
in man's detachment from his animal beginnings: a step beyond that
taken through the development of culture itself. This unfinished, still-
evolving deity has never dominated the universe and is not responsible
for its present condition: far from it. But because of his emergence,
nature itself may undergo an otherwise unthinkable transformation.

Something like this was in William James's mind, possibly, when
he conceived God as a limited being, needing our help. If one continued, in the vein of the classic religions, to believe in God's omni-
presence and omnipotence, one would be forced, in order to retain one's
reason and one's reverence for his benign manifestations, to close one's
eyes to the thousand ugly incidents of life that confound any attribu-
tion to this being of either supreme intelligence or unfaltering love.
"Did he who made the lamb make thee?" Distressed by the gritty facts
of human experience, the mystic thrusts the world of sense impatiently
aside in order to reach God directly and bathe in the presence of his
glory and illumination. That is perhaps a happy transitory adjustment; but it hardly reconciles the awakened soul to the frustrations
and evils of life even at its most prosperous moments, to say nothing
of the potential horrors that civilization, by its very advances in science, now holds before us. The "Perennial Philosophy" buys its oblivion too cheaply, by treating as mere illusion that part of man's
existence which it is most difficult to assimilate to reason and love: it

thus turns its back on the love and pity men need in order to maintain its own inner poise.

As soon as religion, in fact, makes its God the creator and all-wise author of the universe, it must either gloze over the evils of existence at the expense of truth, or it must invoke another principle, equally at work in the universe, which brings the creator's work to naught, defacing his creatures and defaming his beneficent intentions. Sheer logic thus drove many of the classic religions to the invention of the Devil or the Destroyer, the mythical equivalent of the second law of thermodynamics, who undermines all the constructive activities of life. As Kali, as Ahriman, as Satan, as Loki, the devil personifies an inescapable fact of human experience: the fact of de-building, disorganization, degradation.

William Morton Wheeler's discussion of Emergent Evolution is exemplary, because he fully reckons with these possibilities of *Abbau*, or de-building; whereas various modern attempts to unify every aspect of man's experience by using a one-directional formula of process and organization, like that of Mr Lancelot Whyte, come partly to grief, because they must either deny the polar alternatives of goodness and badness, of development and deformation, or fail to give an adequate account of these downward tendencies. To the extent that the higher religions have allowed for the fact that integration and disintegration go hand in hand, their mythology is less untrue to the facts of life than the Marxian description, which sees process as working in a single direction.

A sound philosophy, it seems to me, must embrace the facts of human experience hitherto represented in the symbols of a creative god and a destructive devil: the one directed toward greater fulfillment of life, the other tempting it to lose sight of its higher goals and regress to lower planes of evolution. But for the sake of clarity, one should combine these ambivalent cosmic forces into a single figure, applicable to all natural processes; and not confuse two-faced Nature with the emergent aspect of divinity, which derives from the fuller development of the human person.

When one treats God, then, as the symbol for a new emergent, coming at the very last stage of all observable development, one has a foundation for an inescapable fact of human experience, which would otherwise, if God were in fact omnipotent and responsible, be highly disconcerting: namely, that so far from being omnipresent and all-enveloping, divinity is the rarest attribute of human existence. So rare, so intermittent, indeed, is the presence of divinity in human affairs that when it appears in any heavy concentration, it becomes the center of a new way of viewing the world and acting in it, in the person of an Ikhnaton, a Moses, a Zarathustra, a Buddha, a Confucius, a Jesus; and when such a person appears, a whole society takes on a new shape and reveals new possibilities in thought and action and the general conduct of life. In diffused and diluted forms, these potentialities for freedom and creation are always at work, in some degree, in every community. But their intervention is so rare that, when they decisively come forth and work their special transformation, they set human history on a new course.

Unfortunately, that manifestation of an emergent divinity is fragile and precarious: so powerless to preserve itself, that not a single religion has been able to save itself from either corruption or mummification at an early stage. Even while Moses was among the Jews, journeying through the wilderness, his fellow tribesmen turned to the worship of brazen serpents instead of Elohim, the unrepresentable, the unfathomable, the voice in the burning bush. That story stands for a hundred similar degradations in the history of every great religious impulse: witness the transformation of Jesus's essential doctrine and example by the Church that preserved it. The divine may be constantly radioactive; but the human isotopes, which divinity has quickened, have but a short life.

Now possibly a life-conserving inertia is at work here. If God were actually dominant, it would be as if radium were as heavily distributed in the earth's crust as iron: his presence might well consume the universe and blast the life it had come to bless. But the actual situation seems just the reverse of this. Only flashes and glimmers of godhood appear in history, usually mingled, like radium in pitchblende, with vast quantities of baser stuff. Yet those visions of higher forms of existence, of new potentialities for development, if fleeting, are likewise so intense that when they appear they quickly impart their light and heat to a whole society; for when man finds them in his consciousness, he feels nearer to the purpose of his being than at any other moment of his life.

God, in this sense, points to an order beyond the limitations of natural existence, of biological survival, or even of a purely human fulfillment. Yet all the genuine manifestations of God are so uncertain, so unpredictable, that his presence has often been counterfeited for purely mundane purposes: his name has been invoked, too often, to sanctify inertia and to rationalize regression. Though everywhere men have organized institutions and erected buildings to guard their vision of divinity and to re-awaken faith in man's divine possibilities, a faith too often shaken by the trials of life, it is not through buildings and ceremonies, not through the scribes and the Pharisees, nor yet through the Levites, that this service is most fully performed.

Notwithstanding its intentions and its sacred mission, religion, I must emphasize, is open to degradation: perhaps more so than any other human activity. So the apparatus of salvation becomes one of the main obstacles to its own achievement: the doctrines of religion become a device for egoistic assertion, on the part of a tribe or a caste, rather than an agent of universal purposes, dissolving all hostile man-made claims and privileges.

Too readily in history, religion, instead of addressing itself to the general condition of man, has lent itself to buttressing the position and privilege of the ruling classes, preaching humility to those already in humble circumstances, instead of to the proud, and resignation to the victim rather than to his oppressor, as Luther did in his denunciations of the downtrodden peasants who revolted. Even where these perversions have not become flagrant—and what civilization has been immune to them?—there are many inner obstacles to the search for the divine. For divinity, by its nature, cannot be decanted into a bottle and safely corked: it comes like a flash of lightning or like the faint perfume carried on the summer breeze from a distant meadow. Every attempt to capture divinity in some permanent form ends by imprisoning the spirit of man.

Thus God, as I seek here to interpret human experience, is not the foundation of human existence: he is the pillar of cloud by day and the pillar of fire by night that lead men onward in their journey toward the Promised Land. Yet because man finds in himself an occasional spark of divinity, because fitfully a tongue of this flame may illuminate a whole life, man may logically and honestly interpret the entire process of organization and organic development as having, in future, an end other than a mere increase in complexity and heterogeneity. If the universe, as the physicists now suppose, has taken some three billion years to come forth out of chaos and old night, God is the faint glimmer of a design still fully to emerge, a rationality still to be achieved, a justice still to be established, a love still to be fulfilled.

In the best representatives of the human species, God becomes manifest in a profound discontent, an impulse toward perfection, a purpose severed from self-preservation or self-inflation. At the fullest stage of development, man achieves detachment and transcendence: something both playful and purposive delivers him from his hard physical necessities, or the humiliating limitations of his animal drives. Though conditioned to social existence, he may withdraw from society or defy its lower claims in the interests of a higher development, as Francis of Assisi or Thoreau did: though tethered to the will-to-live, a deeper loyalty may cause him to elect death, rather than animal survival, as both heroes and martyrs have often done, valuing life intensely, but valuing the god life has brought forth even more.

Religion develops out of this faith in the meaningfulness of human experience, set against the background of cosmic mystery: faith in the reason that underlies all the irrationalities of existence, faith that a divine purpose, still struggling into existence, will finally prevail.

4: ETERNITY, SEX AND DEATH

Every culture has sought, in terms of its own special situation and experience, for a provisional answer to the unanswerable questions that religion propounds. Some cultures, like that of the ancient Greeks, were mainly oriented toward life; others, like that of the ancient Egyptians, were oriented toward death; still others, like orthodox Hinduism and orthodox Christianity, have attempted to encompass both affirmation and rejection, the secular here and the holy hereafter. But in spite of many points of divergence and contradiction, the historic religions share, in fact, large areas of agreement: so large, so substantial, so significant that the current attempt to reject religion itself, as a meaningless survival, infected with superstition, calling for surgical removal, like a diseased appendix, rests on a more questionable dogma than the dogmas it questions. Freud's attitude toward traditional religions was, perhaps, but the jealousy of a prophet who had, up his sleeve, a religion of his own: a Wagnerian mythology with Eros and Psyche in the roles of Tristan and Isolde, seeking death alone in their lover's cave.

Let us now mark the points where the classic religions come together. All religions, to begin with, lengthen man's time perspective: they bid him pay attention to more than the vanishing moment and the passing years. Sometimes, as with the Jews, religion emphasizes long biological continuities: it promises that the injustices or frustrations of the single individual's lifetime will be redeemed by the further history of his tribe or his species on earth; or, with a sounder naturalism, it notes that the sins of the parents may be visited upon the children, even unto the third and fourth generation. In other civilizations, as with the Egyptian, time passes into eternity and the receding perspective of the dark halls of death occupy the imagination more than the lighted antechamber of life: the finiteness and frailty of the individual life is thus counterpoised by a cult of the after-life: a life whose quality is supposedly determined, at the day of judgment, by the character of one's behavior on earth. In this version, developed further by Christianity and Islam, all the individual's actions are preparatory and incomplete: without immortality, according to this creed, life on earth would lack significance or adequate compensation for its evils and injustices.

Such an indefinite prolongation of life, one may remark in passing, would paradoxically bring to an end the very conditions of life that set it off from brute matter: life eternal is in fact a contradiction in terms. But religion's repeated insistence upon eternity and immortality must have had, in the earlier stages of human development, a salutary practical effect: for this attempt to give the individual life a cosmic perspective offsets the natural foreshortening of time that takes place under biological pressures and passions, when man is tempted to sacrifice his true destiny for minor immediate goods: greedily to prefer his present mess of pottage to his birthright. "Leave now to dogs and apes: man has forever." Those words of Browning's sum up the very essence of the religious view of time; and most of man's durable achievements rest on that foundation.

For man, future potentialities are present realities; indeed Mowrer has experimentally demonstrated that "the essence of integrated behavior is the capacity to bring the future into the psychological present." One cannot doubt, on the evidence of history, that a certain degree of detachment from momentary impulses and short-term gains is essential for human development. For one to do his best in a situation whose outcome he cannot surely predict or wholly by his own efforts determine, or for one to perform the necessary duty of the moment, though that duty is an unrewarding or positively repulsive one, demanding heavy sacrifices, it is necessary for him to widen his time boundaries: to act as if he were in fact immortal. That discipline was more important for man's development than a more realistic interpretation that would have denied the possibility of immortality in any kindred and comforting earthly form. Whether this sense of time was bestowed through the cult of family, as with the Chinese or the Jews, or through the hope of personal survival, as with the Zoroastrians, the Manichees, the Christians, and the Moslems, it bestows on each individual episode a new significance, making it part of an indefinitely prolonged hereafter.

The religious cycle of time is a cosmic cycle: it embraces centuries, millennia, eons. That telescopic view both diminishes the claims of the individual moment and enlarges its ultimate significance. Such a view contrasts with the sacrilegious American jibe: "Why should we do anything for posterity? When has posterity ever done anything for us?" In religion, the time that signifies most is the time that cannot be measured: the place that counts most is that which is never seen. When those convictions are uppermost, man's purposes embrace the greatest range of possibilities and can make the most of them.

Besides this orientation to the timeless, religion brings with it the practice of constant reference, not to man's works and days and habitations alone, but to the cosmic whole. If this is not true of the more primitive religions, with their localized deities and their narrow theater of operations, confined to a river valley or a city, it remains for the most part an essential characteristic of the higher religions. On this interpretation, religion presented in mythic terms, long before biology began to trudge slowly over the same ground, the image of the great web of life: the interdependence and mutual support of all living creatures, with the further dependence of life itself upon the sun and possibly even remoter cosmic energies. Hinduism has perhaps the deepest and richest insight into these universal kinships and co-operations: it was not by accident that a Hindu physicist, Jagadis Bose, not merely measured the sensitivity of plants but discovered the first traces of response in metals.

The facts of mutual aid and of man's total involvement in the universe were first outlined by religion; and this outline has only been confirmed in essentials by the multiplicity of details and the rich palette of colors with which the sciences, during the last three centuries, have filled in the blank spaces. Man is, in fact, the microcosm that religion first conceived him to be: he is involved in a long interplay of processes which reaches from the distant sources of cosmic rays to the innermost recesses of man's soul, from the widest stretches of time and space to the sensorium in which the universe is, in symbolic form, reflected and transformed.

No less important than its orientation to the whole is religion's sense of the sacredness of life. To the act of fertilization, the begetting of a new life, religion in its primitive stages correctly attaches a profound value: an age that makes free with contraceptives loses that sense at its peril. In the magnification of the phallus and the female organ, the magic transmission of strength and potency, the deliberate cultivation, in the corn rituals that underlie so much of the higher religions, of the moment of sexual abandon and surrender, when union is achieved symbolically through eating and drinking the body of one's God—in all these terms religion proclaims the sacredness of sex, as the source of life's own continuity, and as the organic creative act that lies at the base of man's remoter creative acts.

Sometimes religion's magic prescriptions record the fear of this power as well as the impulse to worship it: witness the frequent putting away of the menstruating woman, not merely as unclean but as uncanny, and so inimical. Sometimes it attaches to the sexual act itself a special religious value, as in the dedication of a whole class of women, in many religions, from that of Ishtar to her Hindu equivalents, to temple prostitution. For these early cults, sterility was a curse and a punishment: potency and fertility were themselves attributes of godhead. Horus and Osiris: Isis and Serapis: Cybele, the Great Mother and her lover: Dionysus, god of corn and wine, who rouses his followers to sexual frenzy and abandon: in all these mythical representations the essential sacredness of sex, as a universal power, not to be lightly held, was made manifest. Man's sexuality pervades his whole life; and under various metamorphoses and sublimations it spreads through the higher religions, taking many forms, from that of Mithra and the Bull to the Virgin Mary. The mysteries of generation lie at the gateway to religious explanations of man's lot and destiny; and the rites of marriage and birth, or the countervailing rites of abstention and withdrawal from the duties of procreation, become attached to the religious conception of man's role and even to the possibilities of divinity; for it is out of sex, in the dual roles assumed by the passionate lovers and the compassionate parents, that the gospel of love itself was born. Here ecstasy and union: there detachment and sacrifice.

But the sense of the sacredness of life comes from another source, too: the crisis of death. Man is the only creature in whom the anticipation of death alters his present actions, and in whom the memory of the dead lingers so powerfully as to haunt his dreams and invade his working moments, frequently with images of overpowering concreteness. In some sense, the dead are still alive; yet the living likewise must partake of death even before their life reaches its natural terminus.

Long before Socrates observed that the task of philosophy is to prepare one for death, religion made this its chief concern. Not merely did the early religious cults care for the dead body; but they sought to circumvent the finality of the soul's departure by providing it symbolically with the means of sustenance on its long journey; while out of that journey into the unknown itself they conjured up many homely comforting details, and released, at the final destination, all the desires for bliss that life itself had denied: not least of course the desire of those who have found happiness, that life should have no ending. The historic date for the appearance of these brave fantasies can be fixed in at least one civilization; for in Egypt we can follow the extension of what was at first the special privilege of immortality from the Pharaoh, as the first real person, and a manifestation of his god, to his court favorites, and finally, by a steady process of extension to people of lesser rank. This mode of democratization did not, perhaps, become quite free from restrictions till the advent of Christianity, when the same consummation was offered, for good conduct and timely repentance, to every human soul, slave or free.

Now this affirmation of death often led, as in Egypt, to a serious sacrifice of the claims of the living. The building of tombs depleted wealth and energy that might have improved the life of men in cities. In what sense, then, has that orientation been an affirmation of the sacredness of life?

The answer is not far to seek. If life prospered in all its manifestations, the pleasure principle might well dominate it: out of an overflow of sexual exuberance, the beautiful forms of life, forever caressing and embracing and conceiving, would swarm through existence as they do on the walls of the Ajanta caves. But there are in fact many desolate negative moments in life, observable even in its most fortunate stretches. The de-building principle is at work, along with the creative, at every moment of man's existence: his life is in fact a series of little deaths, and it is out of man's experience of illness, injury, depletion, corruption, that religion dramatizes its final negation, death itself, and affirms as real and significant that which seems to deny the reality of life and destroy its significance.

Man needs no special schooling to embrace life, when it emanates in health, energy, erotic love, joyful dilation and expansion: when the juices flow harmoniously, he "who knows, as the long day goes, that to live is happy has found his heaven." But there is another side to life, no doubt over-stressed in times of trouble, but too blandly overlooked in the optimistic utilitarian and romantic philosophies of the last century: the negative pole of existence, just as real as the positive pole, particularly on the descending curve of life. This part of life must be faced and embraced too: an arduous discipline.

By the time men reach middle age, even the seemingly fortunate have some inkling of this experience; for illness, the impairment of bodily organs, or psychic disintegration come in some degree sooner or later to all men: so too with the loss of one's friends and neighbors or the death of one's beloved—all recurrent events in human existence. Death comes to every household. No Shakespearean apothecary, no unctuous mortician in the Hollywood style, can heal those ills. Often the worst of these evils have nothing whatever to do with one's individual deserts: Job and Oedipus both bear witness to this fact.

Since man cannot evade these negations and irrationalities, religion affirms their final significance. By bringing death consciously back into daily life, the religious mind gives a positive role to the most dismaying conditions in man's existence. Here is the essential explanation, I believe, of religion's apparently perverse concentration, as upon an aching tooth that cannot be removed, on sin and sorrow and pain and death. No liberalism in theology can liberate one from these profound encounters with the forces that limit and curtail life, threatening it with utter defeat: sooner or later some scheme of redemption or transcendence must be proposed.

When vitality runs high, death takes men by surprise. But if they close their eyes to this possibility, what they gain in peace they lose in sensibility and significance; and not least, they then leave themselves unarmed for more serious encounters and more dire defeats. One of the classic missions of religion, accordingly, is to search for values in that part of existence which man, in his purely animal preoccupations, would turn away from, as almost all other animals incuriously turn away from their own dead. Anticipating the fact of death, never losing sight of it, religion restores to the person a sense of his true condition; and when he reaches the downward curve of life, it helps make the spirit ready to accept its fate with resignation, if not with positive hope. Only those who face these negations reach maturity.

Humility, sacrifice, detachment, like faith, hope, and charity, must count among the theological virtues: they belong to the waning phase of life, as pride, generation, and attachment belong to the waxing phase. Man often reaches his best understanding of the ultimate purpose of life when he finds himself in a situation where he must willingly choose his own death or accept that of the one he most dearly loves. Yet for the parent, for example, whose young child has gallantly lost his life trying to rescue a drowning playmate, that deeply painful moment will forever count as one of life's true consolations: too sacred for bitterness.

5: SACRIFICE AND DETACHMENT

If death is the ultimate gauge of religious belief, sacrifice is its chief representative in the sphere of action. To determine how much we value an object, we must ask: How much are we ready to give up for it? If it goes to the root of our being there may come a moment when we are ready to give up everything.

To modern man, for the last few centuries, sacrifice has seemed a primitive and repulsive act, a form of devil worship as Herbert Spencer put it: how infantile to offer one's God seasonal fruits and libations, or present one's precious child to the fiery furnace of Moloch! Those who live, as they fancy, guided by the dry light of science, contemn these irrational practices: yet we have gods of our own that are no less exacting. As an offering to the god of Speed, the American people sacrifice more than thirty thousand victims every year. With such a record, we can hardly afford to look with such cold repugnance on allegedly more primitive practices. But when, after severe examination, we find that a particular sacrifice is justified in our own conscience, we become aware of its religious significance. For there are moments when our self-respect would be undermined if we failed to make the sacrifice. In the very nature of existence we shall find a basis for this ritual and this value.

Human life in all its phases seems to flourish best when some restrictive pressure is exerted against its aimless proliferation, just as a garden must be weeded and thinned to produce a richer growth, a fuller efflorescence. In nature this pressure seems provided by the struggle for existence; but with the increase of mutual aid and the tendency to form harmonious organic partnerships, the highest forms of life must find within themselves some equivalent principles of restriction. Man is a creature whose appetites, if otherwise uncurbed, would grow by what they feed on: with every further satisfaction, his needs become more imperious: so that what was once an occasional luxury too easily, under prosperous circumstances, becomes a daily necessity. If he had no means of releasing himself from this tendency, man would forfeit his freedom and with the resulting sad satiety would lose the capacity for further development. Here religion, with the rise of civilization—that is, an ample food supply and a secure life—pointed the way, through deliberate sacrifice, to further growth and renewal.

In its minor forms, sacrifice consists of fasts, abstentions, renunciation of customary pleasures and indulgences, acts that both mortify the body and discipline the soul, tightening the reins on the lower functions and giving the lead to the higher ones. These religious efforts bear so many resemblances to the exercises used for making a soldier capable of facing hardship and obeying without question commands from those above him in rank, that Tertullian, in his preachments on the Christian way of life, drew constantly upon military precedents for apt figures. Our Western society is now so conscious of the neurotic perversions that may lurk in asceticism that it has overlooked its general prevalence in our own society, particularly in those departments where its advances have been most conspicuous. But, as I pointed out in Technics and Civilization, it was primarily a religious ascetic practice, shaped in the Benedictine monasteries, that brought forth the new conception of the disciplined capitalist man, schooled to regular hours of work, capable of exercising what had been once a slave's devotion to regular and monotonous tasks. Passing from the monastery to the scholar's study and the government office, this discipline eventually became a minimal requirement for business men, administrators, scientists: no matter what their other human failings, the capacity for intense application to the job in hand has given these functionaries no small measure of the dignity and power they enjoy. Savage peoples are notoriously incapable of this sort of life-negating abstention, but it is equally true that no merely Epicurean philosophy, however advanced the civilization, could produce this new ideal type.

In certain religions, unfortunately, the doctrine of sacrifice and detachment from organic needs and vital cravings becomes an end in itself: this leads ultimately to the complete negation of life one finds in early Buddhism. Buddha taught that life, from its beginning at birth, brings suffering. This suffering springs out of the libido itself: all sensations, all feelings, all impulses and appetites, lead men to pain and grief, so that the mass of men, by the very gift of life, are drowned in misery, while even the most fortunate, whose head is temporarily above water, will sooner or later be swallowed by the same flood.

For the relief of this condition Buddhism had a simple prescription: fetter the senses, curb one's animal impulses, reduce all forms of craving! By drying up life at its source, one lessens the daily flow of misery. This is the doctrine of total sacrifice: the whole is forfeited in order to control the part. But actually, if life were as inherently and chronically subject to miscarriage as Buddhism proclaimed, why should one respect the taboo against suicide? The only perfect cure for this disease would be to kill the patient: mere halfway measures savor of superstition and cowardice. Respecting the will-to-live too deeply to challenge this taboo, Buddhism sought to redeem man from life, not for life.

To hold with Schopenhauer, the most consistent Western reinterpreter of Buddha's view, that "the denial of the will to live is the way of redemption" is to turn the world into a penal colony: the self-imposed starvation of every organ would become the only means of release. No doctrine of sacrifice and detachment that so challenges the innate will-to-live can hope to keep its hold on the human spirit: for if it is not, at any particular moment, untrue to the grim facts of life, we know in our hearts that it is untrue to its potentialities.

That is why in history Buddhism preserved itself, happily, through a long series of "corruptions"; against logic, these backslidings once more placed Buddhism on the side of life, binding its followers to their earthly lot by an elaborate ritual and an esthetic effulgence which, so far from denying their mortal appetites, tempted them with ever more sensuous and joyous fare.

In the long-time perspective of religion, it becomes plain that only through the practice of sacrifice and the discipline of detachment can man accept, without overwhelming despair, the facts of his own corruptibility and death. When man has not schooled himself by such practices, when he fosters in himself the illusion that he holds life on his own terms and may expand without limit, he is in no mood to confront the tragic terms of his own existence.

Once achieved, the practice of sacrifice brings a special compensation: the kind of release that comes directly to those who have undergone an ordeal and who know, having survived it, that they are equal to all of life's occasions. Those who accept sacrifice as one of the constant conditions for life's fulfillment and expression, whether in the relations of lovers, of parents, of citizens, are well grounded in the objective conditions under which communities and persons actually flourish. No serious work has ever been done in the world without giving up a large part of what men rightly think valuable in daily living: no higher development was ever achieved without renouncing many of the goods that gave one satisfaction on a lower plane. Unless the great political leader can, at the right moment, give up his political power, as Solon did, unless the loving mother can surrender her child sufficiently to let him follow his own line of growth, the very resources of power and love necessary to nurture the personality will also cripple it.

In the long run, all high human achievement demands sacrifice, since a part of what we do in our present lives will have no fulfillment or completion till such a distant date that it will make little difference to one's own happiness or that of one's immediate descendants. Little efforts may be consummated in the passing hour of the present generation, but great things usually demand a longer period for their fruition; indeed, perhaps the most valuable part of our lives lies in realms that promise least immediate satisfaction. To stand pain, hardship, deprivation for the sake of such distant consummations is part of the lot of the human race. In teaching this lesson, the higher religions taught men to accept reality.

Let me sum up. Though life flourishes only by expressing its immediate needs and fulfilling the biological goals of growth and reproduction, human beings are able, through the discipline of sacrifice, to choose courses that lie outside this natural path, and with this choice a fuller development of the person becomes possible. Sacrifice, in the religious sense, may be ultimately beneficial to the human community; but it is not based on any tangible *quid pro quo:* often what the individual, or even the community, gives up will be infinitely more than what he will get in return. Paradoxically, the more profound the values attached to the sacrifice, the less likely one is in the end to profit by the act. When the matter is important enough to warrant the giving up of life, he who does so gets no earthly reward at all; for who would be so foolish as to count his posthumous medals? But the capacity to make that decision and to act on those terms has its own special justification: it brings one face to face with the divine in human existence. "Indifferent to gain or loss, prepare for battle." Those words of Krishna to Arjuna in the Bhagavad-Gita count among the ultimate words of wisdom; they repeat, with their special accent, the more familiar words of the New Testament: "Whosoever loseth his life, the same shall find it."

When that thought and attitude were first formulated, a new person was conceived, and a new form of society became possible. We shall presently trace some of these consequences.

6: RELIGION'S POSITIVE FUNCTIONS

At this point, it may be well to summarize briefly the paradoxical functions of religion. Religion proclaims the sacredness of life and attempts to further man's insight into his own development. Spreading its net so wide that it hauls in the ugly monsters of superstition and many of the commonplace fish of daily life, religion also includes in its catch the rare flying fish of divinity, the possession of which, even for a moment, somehow exorcises the blind fury of Moby Dick.

In the early cycle of culture, religion overcomes the foolish conceits of barbarous vitality, by confronting man with his tragic destiny; but in the later phases of the cycle, when the attachment to life tends to weaken, then religion performs the function Henri Bergson ascribes to it: it defends man "against the representation by the intelligence of the inevitability of death." Likewise religion protects him against his over-reacting to the sad discovery that there is a constant hiatus between his plans and their day-to-day fulfillment, in a world where man's will and purpose are far from being supreme. Finally, religion gives man a sense of permanence and rationality in a world of flux, accident, seemingly demonic caprice.

On the animal level, the world contains no mysteries, though it may hold many surprises. The animal's understanding is adequate to his environment: the last thing he would be capable of grasping is the fact that his environment is beyond his grasp. Not so with man. Religion teaches men systematically what his dawning intelligence prompts him to suspect, that there are forces beyond his control, time beyond his reckoning, space beyond his reach, mysteries beyond his very ability to formulate the problems that arise from them. In short, the real world is other than what man's naive animal needs have made

out to be. In the light of that interpretation, solid rocks become
transitory and diaphanous and what seemed the passing shimmer of a
dream may last longer than a granite cornerstone.

By centering part of man's attention on insoluble problems, religious thought has schooled man to look below the surface of things:
the deeper he looks, the more effectively, in the end, he acts. Long
before modern physics, high religion detached itself from the illusions of materialism: so, too, its faith in a rational order pervading
the universe gave man the confidence to search for nature's regularities and laws.

These great contributions also define religion's limitations. None of
its concepts offers a causal explanation of any event: it deals with
reasons, purposes, designs—not causes. Many religious intuitions have
proved but childish sketches that anticipated, but could not replace,
the methodical photography of science. Where orderly observation and
systematic measurement are possible in dealing with the nature of
man, the traditional descriptions of religion must be supplemented
with the causal interpretation of science. But the kernel of religious
consciousness is a profound sense of the nature and meaning of life
in all its dimensions: an intuition of the whole. In every religious
myth, from that of Kali the destroyer to that of Jesus, the Good Shepherd, there is a true indication of some portion of man's experience
and aspiration that no causal description, from the outside, can nullify,
or, for that matter, do without.

In the pervasive forms of animism and magic, religious consciousness has doubtless superstitiously served many factitious interests and
local needs: but it has remained a central activity of man because it
relates, ultimately, to that which is central in all existence; and if
every shrine were effaced, every Church destroyed, every dogma ob-
literated, every superstition buried, it would still occupy this place and
perform this special function. The heightened consciousness of what
lies beyond our immediate present state, in space and time, was the
specific contribution of the classic religions. To act in terms of that
consciousness is to acknowledge that no act exists for the actor alone:
not even that which seems most private and inviolate.

Religion, then, is the sphere of the sacred: the ultimate wonder and
mystery of all existence as mirrored in the living consciousness of
man. From this standpoint, a single cycle of life in the tiniest of organisms discloses something about the nature of the entire cosmic
process that a whole eon of stellar evolution, without that stir of life,

would not reveal; while what is relatively even a moment of significant consciousness in the life of man, transforms him from a mere
speck lost in an almost boundless universe, into a progressively boundless mind, capable of devouring that universe. Where sentience, feeling, and thought exist the dumb universe has found a spokesman and
its blind forces a commander.

This view of religion, needless to say, differs in essential features
from all of the existing orthodoxies. While it upholds many of the
divinations and revelations of the classic religions, it does not attribute
factual truth to their mythologies or any finality to their dogmas.

In all humility the present philosophy affirms as persistent that
which every system of revelation tends to coyly modify or arrogantly
deny: the continued existence of mystery itself. Whether we consider
God in the orthodox form as the boundless Being that encompasses
all existence, or as the emergent divinity that realizes the purposes
and potencies that otherwise remain only latent in existence, this view
holds that religion has no special key to the character and nature of
God. In that, we accept the classic Hindu refusal to define God: *Neti,
neti:* that is to say, Not, Not . . . Not Yet.

So, though the presence of "God" and the possibility of communion
with "God" rest on a great mass of human testimony, what it is that
is so felt and communed with is not open to external inspection or
objective assessment: it can only be experienced and that experience
lends itself to diverse interpretations. William James, testing the influence of certain drugs and anesthetics and awakening from a nitrous
oxide dream, felt triumphantly that he held at last the key to the universe. But he found that the precious sentence in which all wisdom
seemed concentrated became, as soon as he awakened, sheer nonsense.
That is one possibility. At the other extreme, it is conceivable that a
person who has the experience of encountering God and being lifted
above all human levels by his presence has found a natural way of
widening the field of his responses; so that forces that have as little
to do with his conscious animal existence as, say, the cosmic ray, find
a path to consciousness that is usually blocked.

On those terms, the resulting sense of illumination and ecstasy
might make more life-limited forms of consciousness seem paltry:
that indeed is what the great mystics have felt and taught. Even such
a resolute agnostic as Dr Horace Kallen has confirmed this intuition
of the divine by personal experiment. To seek such ecstasy directly
would be as worthy of human effort as to seek it in the more tangible

ediums of painting or music, which also have the possibility of seiz-
g and transporting the receptive soul. Are not many of the cere-
onies of religion an attempt to use the conventional vehicles of art
achieve the direct sense of this divine communion? Unfortunately,
attach the word "God" to this experience does not in any sure sense
fine it or give one a more intelligible account of the nature of di-
nity . . . Neti, neti . . .

If this interpretation differs from that of the theologians, it differs
less from the explanations offered by the so-called advanced minds
the recent past: the eighteenth century rationalists, with their con-
ction that religion was a tissue of superstitions, framed by cunning
iests for their selfish ends; or the nineteenth century "scientific"
ew, which rejected even the possibility of a pragmatically useful
perstition and regarded religion as a sort of tumor on the brain of
ason and science. If religion were as accidental and insignificant as
is, it would be an exception to every other institution: indeed, it
ould so extravagantly defy our current systems of explanation that
scientific mind would rest easy till it had gotten to the bottom of
is anomaly.

Here the burden of proof rests rather with the doubter. Even on
nited biological terms, a practice embedded in the history of the
ce must have some value. If man has so long concerned himself
ith the cosmic and the sacred and the mysterious, as a guide to his
nmediate plan of life, the likelihood is that this concern is a re-
arding, life-sustaining quest. There are other parallels to guide judg-
ent here; for the race has often had a dumb persistent feeling that
me field of activity was important long before man has found a prac-
able means for exploiting it. Take the dream of the transmutation
the elements. For ages that dream haunted man irrationally: at the
d of the Middle Ages in Europe the alchemists, becoming more
verish in their quest, even resorted to acts of deliberate charlatan-
m, such as concealing gold pellets in their crucible, in order to have
e false subjective gratification, if not the actual triumph, of achiev-
g it. On the basis of long observation of the stability of the elements,
ere was little hope that this dream could be realized: indeed, the
ore knowledge accumulated, up to a point, the more baseless it
emed. Forty years ago, no one doubted that ninety-two elements,
more or less, existed, though not all of them had yet been brought
light. But let us now admit the facts: the fantastic dream of trans-
utation was closer to the nature of things than the scientific prudence

and common sense that denied it. We have seen the fool's gold of alchemy become the minted sovereign of nuclear physics.

Thus it may turn out with religion: above all, with the special hope of the high religions for enlarging the sphere of the divine, for transmuting humanity into divinity at some far-off moment. The formulas that the Churches have employed for bringing about this change are doubtless as clumsily empirical, as willfully superstitious, as practically futile, as those of the alchemists—though even here one must qualify this dismissal by remembering that the alchemists chose lead as their favorite element for transmutation: a selection from the right compartment of the periodic table. Certainly, no one can examine the role of religion in historic societies without recalling how often the religious impulse itself has miscarried, and how resistant human ways and institutions have been to the radical changes in man's nature which religion has proposed. But these failures must be set beside many genuine gains: for, as the distinguished anthropologist, Dr A. L. Kroeber, has pointed out, the classic religions have done much to transform the infantilism of primitive man; and there is little doubt that human development has gone on most fully and rapidly in those civilizations where a higher religious consciousness has pervaded at least an enlightened minority.

On this view, then, religion is no bedraggled survival from the past, soon to be completely discarded through the advance of positive science. Traditional religion will, rather, be the source of fresh mutations, proceeding from older formulas to more active methods of investigation, experiment, self-observation, utilizing aspects of life and personality that science too long has disdained.

Religion concerns itself with the reaction of man in his wholeness to the whole that embraces him. Instead of abandoning religion as science extends the province of objective description, we must rather increase its scope, so that our subjective contributions will be as adequate and as disciplined as our objective descriptions. The despiritualization of the world—the withdrawal of projections, as Jung calls it—has not brought us closer to reality, but has shut out that aspect of reality which only the fully developed human person with a rich subjective life can cope with. As a result of this process, we have not simply undermined our sense of the divine: we have rather embraced it in an inverted and debased form by giving a fuller scope to the demonic. When the god in him is repressed, the half-gods and devils take possession of man. We have seen that happen in our day, in countries that have too confidently paraded their science and objectivity.

Religion re-establishes man where he belongs in the scale of significance: at the very center of the universe he consciously embraces and interprets. Without excessive pride, we may still nourish the hope that one day man will discover a more viable way than even the saints have yet found to nourish and enlarge the province of the divine. What man still finds within him only at rare moments he may yet project and establish in the world outside: the beginning if not the completion of the Kingdom of Heaven.

CHAPTER IV

THE TRANSFORMATIONS OF MAN

1: THE BIRTH OF THE PERSON

Various classic religions and philosophies anticipated the current discovery that man has two natures: a primitive or original nature, conditioned by his biological inheritance, and a socially acquired nature, shaped by his history and his culture, not least by his aspirations and anticipations. Apart from earliest infancy man's original nature never becomes visible except as it is clothed in its social attributes; for one of man's deepest natural characteristics, as essential to him as the hive-building habits of bees, is his impulse to fabricate and transmit a culture. By this means he not only communicates with his kind and interprets every fresh experience, but modifies his own capacities. He must make himself more than an animal, if he is not to fall below the level of any beast.

As a product of nature, whose past links him with other animal species, whose present condition unites him in complicated ecological partnerships, making him dependent upon even the bacteria and the molds, man's work is plainly laid down for him. Breathe or die! Drink or die! Eat or die! Reproduce or die! Work together or die! These alternatives hold as strictly for him as they do for all the rest of the animal kingdom; and so a large part of his existence must be dedicated to carrying out these functions: the physiological cycles of nutrition, growth, and repair, of ovulation, fertilization, and reproduction account for immense areas of human activity, and leave such a profound impression that they even color remoter spheres of his culture. On the basis of these animal needs, man builds his culture: elaborating in more playful forms the imperious demands of nature.

By the slow accretion of symbols and technical facilities, of customs and ceremonies and rituals, man builds upon the environment he shares with other animals a more artful nature, one he has made more truly his own. If habit becomes "second nature" culture is mainly transmitted habit. The biological differences between the major races of mankind are few, compared to the differences that exist between cultures: for each culture, even if primitive, tied closely to natural conditions and limited in area, tends to become an almost self-contained world, set apart from each other little self-contained world. So dearly won are the achievements of culture, that, once a departure has been made, it tends for long periods to become sacrosanct. "We observe our ancient customs," an Eskimo head-man said to Rasmussen, "so that the universe may be preserved." The comfort that children find in the repetition of a familiar story, or the discomfort they show when a familiar ritual is thoughtlessly omitted, only carries into the present the attitude of primitive man toward the ways of his tribe. So the stereotypes of social habit, though different from those of nature, tend all too soon to become as fixed, rigid, hostile to further change and development. Bergson, in Two Sources of Morality and Religion, has well described the static, immobile, self-preservative culture of tribe and nation.

Once a group has achieved a certain level of culture, its life tends to relapse into a static and repetitive pattern, undergoing changes only in response to outward pressures, coming either from fluctuations in climate and in food supply, or the insurgent activities of other tribes, encroaching on home territory: whence the old proverb, that dates back at least to Heraclitus, that war is the father of change. For the greater part of history, the main source of recent cultural changes, namely mechanical invention, operated only at rare intervals and with great slowness: tens of thousands of years passed before the Old Stone Age, with its hunting economy, gave place to the New Stone Age, marked by the domestication of animals and plants. In the more primitive cultures, man's nature remained almost as limited, as conditioned by the characteristics of his immediate group, as incapable of projecting higher levels for development, as the animal species themselves: for all of life's insurgence and adventure, the whole course of organic development is marked by a series of enclosures and arrests: in human culture no less than in nature.

But at a particular moment of history, a transformation at length takes place. This has proved almost as radically important for man's higher development as his original invention of language. He seeks a new kind of self, organically conditioned by his biological and social roles, and yet to a certain degree released from them: directed toward a path of development that lies beyond mere racial continuity and tribal survival. By an inner reorientation, man detaches himself from the fate of his local group: he becomes part of a more universal society, at first merely an imagined one, and by means of new insights and purposes, he transcends the frustrations of his historic experience and an earthbound community.

One may call this process the birth of the person. Its significance lies in the fact that it makes possible the eventual emergence of united humanity, no longer separated by impassable cultural walls: individuation and unity thus go hand in hand. With this change, man loosens his ties with blood and soil, which bound him to his limited past: all other men become his brothers, the world becomes his home, and the inner transformations of the person take precedence over the shocks and challenges and chance stimuli that come from outer circumstances alone. First he is earth-conditioned: then group-conditioned: still largely the passive product of nature and culture. Finally, he achieves self-direction and propels himself toward a universal community.

Even today this transformation has not yet been widely achieved, though it has been the major effort of the classic religions for the last three thousand years. Let us look at this process more closely; for it has long resisted interpretation: even the best recent descriptions, those of Bergson and Toynbee, have been vitiated by their over-sharp distinction between the tribal and the universal, between the self wholly conditioned by the immediate culture and the transcendent self that is released from its local attachments and is part of a more universal society. Yet the change is in fact a profound one; for it adds to the human character something not given, except in a latent form, in either nature or culture—the glimpse of higher pinnacles of development, in and through and ultimately beyond the person.

So far from being at the end of this development, we may, with the further advance of science, be only at the beginning of a much wider transformation. But to be ready for such departures we must first examine the process that gave rise to the universal religions— beginning perhaps with the abortive effort of Ikhnaton in Egypt to found a world religion under the Sun God, Aton.

2: THE UNIVERSAL MASK

The change I seek to interpret seems to occur at a crucial moment in civilization. Sometimes that change is embodied in myths, and at other moments, it leaves behind its own record, marred by torn or missing pages but still largely decipherable: the Confucian Analects or the New Testament. Up to this point, each member of the community has no part to play except as a subordinate, often specialized, member of the group as a whole: he must obey its laws, and still more strictly, follow its customs on penalty of severe punishment, sometimes even death: its taboos, however irrational, are inviolate, and its gods, however brutal, are unchallengeable. In so far as this community has a mind, it is a common one: the new Chinese character for the generic term, group—man-sheep—applies to all tribal communities even when, as in the great river valleys of the Indus, the Tigris, the Euphrates, or the Nile they reach the complex interdependencies of civilization. Already, perhaps, there is a glimmer of the potentialities of the person, even in the most backward tribes: but if so, it is confined to the local god: the attributes of autonomy, self-transformation, selectivity, freedom do not as yet belong to any being except the god, or his symbolic representative in the community, the Pharaoh or Emperor.

Suddenly—for the first steps in the transformation occur within the span of an individual life—a person detaches himself from the community. He singles himself out from the mass by reason of the fact that he no longer paints his face or tattoos his skin with the typical patterns of the tribe. He is no longer a Babylonian or an Egyptian or an Assyrian: no longer an Eskimo or a Bantu or a Maya: no longer even visibly a Yellow Man or a White Man or a Black Man. He belongs in fact to a new and singular species that has never hitherto had a local habitation: he is a person. In him the natural man experiences rebirth and enters into a fuller inheritance than that of his race or tribe.

The usual questions that one asks about the older forms of man are no longer relevant: What tribe do you belong to and what land do you come from? Who are your parents, your brothers and sisters, your other kinsmen? What is your vocation, your rank and status? What language do you speak: what food do you eat? Yes, this person comes from a tribe, but all the markings have grown fainter; yes: he has sisters and brothers, but he has turned his back on them: he still loves the place where he was nurtured, but the wide world has become his home. He has a vocation, too; is a shepherd, a carpenter, a tent-maker, a lens-grinder; but he purposes to found a new kind of guild, based—to use Fichte's phrase—on the Vocation of Man. This creator of a universally human mode of feeling and thinking and behaving first announces himself by stripping off the symbols of his local culture: in his very nakedness he seems a monster, and in his innocence a cheat. But he leaves on a few open minds an impression so singular they never forget it: they have at last seen a Man. With this avatar of universal Man, this second birth, a new stage of development opens for humanity at large.

What attracts men to this new type of person?—he who urges them to leave their familiar paths in the fertile valleys of life, and climb, with constant effort, with hazard-tempting skill, often facing mortal danger, up to the rocky pinnacles and the ice-clad summits, where finally the climber himself is the only representative of life? Why do men dream, even for a moment, that his way is a better way than their way, and that the lonely climb, with no promise of a safe return, will yield a higher reward than three solid meals, a soft bed, and a warm fire in the ancestral village below?

The reason should be evident, for the greatest of all human rewards is surely not animal satiety: therefore not health, not wealth, not luxury: not a multiplicity of sexual partners or an endless procession of feasts, all followed by drowsy oblivion. The greatest reward is a sense of possibilities above this lowland existence: the inner strength that spurns security: the vision one achieves only from the heights, after the hard effort of the climb. Because the new prophet represents, in excess, the highest but weakest side of man's nature, he exercises a peculiar fascination over his fellows. This weak side, even at the lowest human level, has already helped him to emerge from his grubby animal necessities; but it does not yet dominate them: far from it. Even to believe in its existence, too often requires a special act of faith: "If anyone was unreal," observed Henry Adams, himself the product of a high culture, "it was the poet and not the business man." He spoke thus, not merely for his generation, but for the common sensual man, at all times and everywhere. So fragile is the common faith in all that gives life the sense of some more ultimate goal than the endless cycle of animal necessities.

The new person embodies that faith and confirms it: he speaks from cosmic as well as human perspectives: on behalf of the timeless, the unconditioned, the universal. He gives forth new laws that defy those of the tribe, and outlines new duties that supplant the familiar old ones: his message flows, like a stream of fresh water from the mountain top, to remove the barnacles of superstition that cling to the tribal hulk and hamper even its daily sailings. With the cleansing of

aw and custom, the new self emerges: a self capable of leading a life
ıot included in the tribal pattern, capable of moving outside the circle
ıf the tribe or the city and embracing men molded by other earth-
orces and social pressures: a self capable finally of detaching itself,
n some degree, from even the most urgent biological needs: renounc-
ng life, yet guarding it and fostering it more watchfully than it had
)een fostered and guarded before.

When such a transformation takes place in complete isolation, as
)ne must assume that it often does, the chances will be against the
urvival of either the person or the new way of life. For its successful
:stablishment the human community itself must be prepared for an
ınusual change, for a rebellion against the accepted pattern of life,
)y experiencing some unusual series of misfortunes or frustrations.
Unscathed, untroubled, unawakened, no community would be pre-
)ared for the new person or be willing to take part in the great changes
hat he finally effects. Only out of despair can such hope and such
nvincible effort come forth. This new religious consciousness, as
Toynbee has amply demonstrated, takes form almost without excep-
ion in a Time of Troubles; when the familiar gods have deserted the
:ribe and the familiar ways of life do not bring their accustomed
ewards.

Yet once the situation is ripe, and once the prophet appears, a
whole series of changes will come about with remarkable swiftness;
and though these changes may bring no improvement in material con-
litions, men will turn to their familiar tasks with a new sense of direction and purpose: they will model their whole existence on a non-
tribal, non-animalistic plan. So decisive is this transformation that
presently people will proclaim that the process is a supernatural one:
ı god has been born!

But a god is not in question. The miracle that takes place is without doubt a true miracle; but the marvel of it is even greater because
it does not in fact depend upon a supernatural agency. Changes that
would be inconceivable through the slow secular modifications of tribal
society, changes so great that they would otherwise need a millennium,
take place in fact, at least the grand outlines emerge, under the impact of the new personality, almost overnight: through this form of
social polarization, every element in the community re-aligns itself as
a group of iron filings re-arrange themselves in a definite pattern once
they are brought within the range of a magnet. But do not be misled
by mythological elaborations: the process itself is a natural one. The

new leader need not exercise, or pretend to exercise, omnipotent or even super-normal powers: certainly, in their own lifetimes, neither Solon nor Confucius nor Buddha nor Moses nor Mahomet made any claim to being a God. The magical wonder-working attributes, which are later imputed to the leader, or even to his relics, are probably signs of a declining faith, which can no longer credit the natural properties of the departed leader and feels the need of bridging the increasing psychological distance by a recourse to magical explanations. His followers, inferior to the man, conceal their own littleness by hiding behind the enlarged figure of a God.

But the real miracle is in fact far more astounding than the healing of the sick, the raising of the dead, or the moving of mountains: for the birth of a universal personality is the equivalent, if not more than the equivalent, of the sudden appearance of a new species in nature. Through the creation and incarnation of a universal persona, or mask, a whole civilization may not merely alter its composite face but deeply change many other dynamic constituents of its character. By strenuous discipline and devout imitation, each follower of the new prophet assumes the mask for himself, and in time his own very bones and flesh begin, as it were, to fill in these ideal outlines: by a second birth he achieves a nature no less distinctive than that given by his first birth.

We have still much to learn about this whole change. In some ways, this transformation bears a resemblance to a more common process: that which takes the raw material one finds in any generation of babies and, within a short space of years, with the aid of parental training, social molds, and deliberate educational methods, transforms these creatures into clerks and bookkeepers, into physicians and inventors, into farm laborers and mechanics: creatures adapted to many roles of a most exacting kind, not found in nature or in primitive societies. The creation of such characters, the assumption of such roles, is a common secular process: under sufficient stress, we can even take young men, amiably disposed toward their fellows, used to an easy, over-protected life, and within a half-year turn them into soldiers, ready to endure extreme hardship, to kill ruthlessly, to face grievous injury or death. This last change is, in fact, almost miraculous enough to be called a conversion: but it lacks the spontaneity, the "catching quality," that religious transformation displays.

In sketching this development I but outline a problem. How a person *"becomes* what he at first merely pretends to be,"* as Gordon Allport has pointed out, "is one of the processes dynamic psychology seeks to explain." Unfortunately for science, the most revealing examples of this transformation on a collective scale take place only at rare moments in history; and our chief knowledge must be derived, not from this critical handful of major events, but from various parallel manifestations of the process, visible in every developing life, which take place under far less dramatic and decisive circumstances. As for the later achievements of a persona, which turn people year after year into Hindus, Jews, or Christians, they take place under the slower pressures of custom and habit: the dramatic process of conversion becomes, at this later stage, far more rare. Yet it is only by a repetition of the original experience, by incarnation and conversion, that the original change can keep from lapsing into a social stereotype, given to vain repetitions and empty rituals, incapable of producing the freedom, the autonomy, the creativity of the original person.

One need not wonder, then, that it is from the artist that the best description of the whole creative process has so far come. William Butler Yeats, in his Autobiography, noted that "there is a relation between discipline and the theatrical sense. If we cannot imagine ourselves as different from what we are and assume the second self, we cannot impose a discipline upon ourselves, though we may accept one from others. Active virtue, as distinct from the passive acceptance of a current code, is therefore theatrical, consciously dramatic, the wearing of a mask. It is the condition of an arduous full life." I cannot improve that description.

With the birth of the illumined person, the ritual of a static culture, conditioned by its own past, complacently committed to its ingrown "way of life," vain of its very weaknesses, turns into an active drama, whose plot concerns the conflict between its higher aims and claims, embodied in the person, and its old anxiety to achieve mere security and survival. Every great religious prophet has been the harbinger of a more universal way of life, which unites his fellows into a wider community that ideally encompasses all mankind. In that sense, the new leader is the individual embodiment of a whole society; and from his personality, his new attitude, his fresh aims, his daily practices, not least from little hints he drops by the way without developing them, the complex activities of a higher society will take form. In time a discipline and a common system of education will be perfected in an attempt to carry forward the original miracle of his detachment and transcendence. Yet the pressures of a closed society will limit the full scope of this movement: neither Buddhism nor Christianity nor

Islam, the most extensive attempts at unification, has actually encompassed more than a small portion of mankind. But the original effort, even when it stops short of its ideal goal, profoundly alters every institution; and transfigures every possibility.

This transformation, as I have hinted, has never been satisfactorily described in all its details, though the data for such a description have been accumulated by comparative history and anthropology, and much of it has been conveniently summarized in Toynbee's magnificent work of scholarship, A Study of History. If theologians have tended to overmagnify the more striking moments of this process and to give them an entirely supernatural cast, the ordinary historian or sociologist has been tempted simply to ignore it, because his leading concepts and his method direct his attention to less singular points and less decisive changes. How could conventional modern scholars describe a change that takes place, in the first instance, in a single individual, not in a mass: above all an interior change not verified by substantial contemporary documents, a change whose very existence can only be deduced from its remote consequences? Yet the fact remains that much of this process is of a social nature: the mask would be unimportant if it covered only one face.

3: THE SOCIAL PROCESS OF CONVERSION

In The Condition of Man I sought to summarize the stages of this whole transformation from personality to community under the heads of Formulation, Incarnation, Incorporation, and Embodiment. Here I shall recapitulate this summary, in order to have a firmer base for describing the corresponding process in its counter-development in reverse: Disembodiment, Alienation, Detachment, Illumination.

The first step in the integration of a more universal person, the step of formulation, involves a change of ideas and, more deeply, an alteration of feeling, attitude, and expectancy. This change often takes places on the uppermost level of abstraction: but it eventually brings new perceptions and intuitions to the actual life-situation. Often in the early stages, the new attitude hardly even achieves the status of a full-blown philosophy: it is still too fluid and unformed, too much the product of solitary illumination: the very words to express it are lacking. For a long time the change of attitude produces no definite ideological structure, though it may show itself in such arts as are unbound by practical exigencies, like painting or music: there is something secret and esoteric in these early manifestations. At their deepest levels, they are a wordless sense of fresh potentialities for life.

Consider the coming of Christianity. The ideas of renunciation and otherworldly fulfillment of a supernal kind were already visible in the fifth century mystery cults: baptism, initiation, conversion, all were practiced; and the believer was "saved" by these practices and guaranteed an after-life in heaven. Plato had a more philosophic vision of eternity: but his world of forms complemented the vulgar heaven; and he, too, participated in the general reorientation toward death: the new departure. These life-renouncing ideas characterized the philosophies of Antisthenes and Diogenes, and formed the general medium of expression for the world-weariness that took place in the whole Greco-Judaic world: they had their counterpart in the practices of the Therapeutae and the Essenes. Seeping into Israel the new attitude blended with a growing belief in the end of the world and the coming of the Messiah, so long prophesied in Jewish literature. Beyond this, currents of Buddhism, transmitted through Alexander the Great's conquests, may have re-enforced these native elements.

All these early formulations took place centuries before the ideas were clarified, deepened, and given a dynamic impetus through the act of incarnation: for men become susceptible to ideas, not by discussion and argument, but by seeing them personified and by loving the person who so embodies them. The prophet must live the life so that others may know the doctrine: he hands down the idea in a form deeper than words to his followers and successors; and they, in turn, must dramatically install themselves in his role.

Here, in the history of Christianity, Jesus and Paul of Tarsus played a decisive part. Up to this point, the main ideas of Christianity were still formless and diffuse. They had given rise to more than one partial incarnation, indeed, to a succession of such incarnations from Socrates to John the Baptist; even later manifestations, like that of Mani, were of the same order. But the decisive stage awaited the inner transformation of Jesus. This came after his lonely vigil in the desert: he came forth from that ordeal, not merely prophesying that a serious Time of Troubles was at hand, according to Matthew, but manifesting in his own person a radical change of interest and attitude. Rising above concern for temporal kingship and personal survival, Jesus stressed the new virtues of humility and forbearance and patience: he treated one's duty to one's neighbor as of the same order as self-interest and sought by imaginative insight, through smiling accommodation rather than resistance, to transform aggression. By all these means Jesus created a new basis for human association and a new social agency for living through and transcending the approaching crisis. The person thus gained the upper hand over the forces that threatened it.

Now we come to the third stage. The direct effect of the prophet upon his community is fitful and limited during his lifetime: he reaches only a handful of disciples; and these, as often as not, are the weaklings, the rejected ones, the outcasts, who have nothing to lose. Before he can touch even such people, no small part of his life has been spent in the process of defining his mission, fitting himself for it. This self-transformation, incidentally, is so little understood that a certain biographer of Walt Whitman used the evidence that describes his second birth as a positive proof of the fact that Whitman was a mere charlatan. Even among those who come directly under the prophet's influence, the faithful handful, the process of rebirth and renewal takes place slowly, haltingly: the disciples are at first witnesses rather than active participants: if they are fascinated by this new species of man, they are also full of doubts and resistances and impulses to betrayal: witness Thomas, Peter, Judas. Moreover, those who are most desirous of being re-born are not always thoroughly transformed: even while the master is living they fall away from him, and though their conversion be ardent, they may not in the end succeed in changing their ways as fully as they had, in their first generous espousal, believed possible. Yes: the new mask does not fit easily over the natural face: indeed, in forcing conformity, it will be the mask, not the head, that will be changed. For one who stands on the bank and looks at a swimmer, swimming looks easy; but once the novice takes to the water himself, he can scarcely make half a dozen strokes before he sinks: it takes practice as well as faith to be able to keep one's head above water. So with this greater change.

To give substance to this new personality, one must do more than repeat the master's precepts, capture his gestures, imitate his voice: the whole routine and discipline of life must in time be altered. Once the new person appears, once the new plot and theme are outlined, the stage must be set and special costumes designed for the multitude of new actors. The rites of sex and marriage, the conduct of economic life and the administration of government, in the end every social institution, must be altered so as to support the new person and make possible his social existence and his participation in all the activities from which, in the first instance, he had withdrawn and had apparently left behind him.

In short, if the rebirth begins as an inner private change, it must be confirmed by an outer public one, before the new self can achieve a universal nature, superimposed on the more limited secular culture. Until these processes of incorporation and embodiment have taken place, the new personality will remain unformed, inoperative, insecure, subject to early extinction. In the end, the very environment must be made over: everything, from costume to architecture, will be remodeled and will in some degree record and express further the inner change that has taken place.

By the time the final stage is reached, in which a whole society has been re-shaped by the new doctrine and cult, a further transformation has taken place: this curtails the great leap that the originating personality, departing from existing practices without yet being hampered by the new ones his own doctrine in turn brings into existence, has actually made. For the original intuitions of the new religion, and the image of the new person as partly incarnated in the prophet himself, must pass through many minds before they take hold in society. On the way, they will encounter the inertia and resistance, yes, the downright hostility, of many venerable institutions. For the sake of sheer survival the new religion or philosophy will absorb many contradictory elements derived from the static body of the existing cultures it seeks to re-make: not least it will have to come to terms with old biological claims that it has perhaps too peremptorily discarded.

In the act of adapting itself to the existing order and its favored "way of life" the new religion will, often without any conscious guile, alter the original intentions of the prophet and even contradict his demands: consider the place occupied by image-worship in later Buddhism, or by the saints and the Virgin Mary in the Catholic Church: consider, too, the glaring contradiction between Jesus's injunction about simplicity in prayer with the elaboration of prayer in the Christian liturgy. At many points, then, the need for adaptability, as a condition for survival, may lead to wholesale perversions and betrayals: so the gospel of humility and love will sometimes be carried into action with fire and sword, with arrogance and hate.

The more extensive the claims of the new personality, the greater are the chances for this perversion: Buddhism and Christianity have been more open to self-betrayal than Confucianism or Mosaic Juda-

ism. Every radical transformation takes place within a society that
is, by sheer force of habit if nothing more, deeply alien to the new
impulses and the new forms; for what is any established institution
but a Society for the Prevention of Change? The impetus of life itself, in the great mass of men, is limited by inertia. Left to themselves
many would be content to accept their animal lot: the common tribal
self suffices and one birth in a lifetime is enough for them. So in every
culture, during the period of its reintegration and renewal, there is
a constant tug between the old self and the new self, or as Christianity used to put it, between the unregenerate Adam and the redeemed
Adam. These theological terms refer to observable facts: one could
witness them, during the past generation, operating in Communist
Russia, where very plainly the Old Adam of the Czarist tyranny has
won out. Why, people presently demand, should they seek to achieve
a larger common mold that ignores their racial pattern, their physiological type, their "natural" tribal self? To conform more closely to
the pattern of their tribe is the only re-making of the natural man
that seems to them sensible, and this is so much a matter of merely
deepening ruts that are already deep that it seems part of the way of
nature itself.

Unfortunately, the very qualities of the new personality, which raise
the level of tensions and conflicts, are partly responsible for the betrayals that take place. Though the new prophet wins the faith of his
fellows by reminding them of the claims of their higher functions, his
rejection of nature and habit, of the racial "id" and the tribal "ego,"
is perhaps too peremptory and too unqualified; for however eagerly
man aims at expressing more fully his higher nature, he can never
become a disembodied spirit: such a perfection would remove all further striving. In their very effort to overcome the tendency to slip back
too quickly into tribal norms, the great religious leaders have often
lifted their ideals so high above the vulgar patterns of life that in the
end they have defeated their own purposes. Not content to establish a
central nucleus, around which the new personality can form, they
demand a kind of life from the ordinary man that would, were he
able to follow it faithfully, transform him into a saint. Judging other
people's capacity by his own, the leader makes little of this transformation. Because, for example, he is himself willing to forego all sexual satisfactions, he may hold up an extravagant ideal of perfect
chastity before other men, without in his innocence even realizing
that for most normal people chastity of mind and spirit, so far from

esulting from abstention, is the reward of a loving and harmonious exual life.

From the abyss of a Time of Troubles, these heroic renunciations nay in fact summon up, for a while, a depth and completeness of esponse that a more reasonable expectation of change would not pro-luce: so far they have a pragmatic justification. But the final results re often deplorable and in time they cast undue discredit upon the riginal doctrine: for the more earnest followers of the new faith end to live in a state of constant frustration, inadequacy, and guilt; r to overcome the strain, they escape as soon as possible by degrad-ng the original impulse into a superstitious worship of a remote Di-ine Being with whom mortal flesh can have little in common. This acksliding explains, perhaps, why the historic religions tend to identify he flashes of divine insight the new prophet exhibits with the final ap-earance of God in human form. The mythical figure, growing at the xpense of the human one, becomes more easily assimilated: by widening the breach between the heavenly and the earthly life, sinful nen make it easier for themselves to sink back into the more familiar ound of earthly existence.

So much for the shortcomings of the profound impulses that have ransformed whole societies. But not by such lapses can one account or the new religion's widespread influence and for the amazing per-istence of a new vision of man's potentialities: a vision sometimes ransmitted through tens of millions of people for two or three thou-sand years. What actually survives of the new person is what counts: he image of a human being of the largest spiritual capacities: the nutant of a new social species. Since it is the total personality that ecomes operative in this great conversion, the most effective prophets lisdain to use the written word for transmitting their message: as Walt Whitman put it, "I and mine do not convince by arguments: we con-vince by our presence." So they communicate, even at many removes, hrough a living chain of believers, the true apostolic succession, and by the echoes that still reverberate on the air, the after-image that still lingers on the retina, many centuries after they have gone.

If words alone conveyed the message of the new person, the in-fluence of the great prophets would be hard to understand; for their affirmations and acts differ in no special way from those of many other men of genius. no mere examination of the new doctrine can fully account for their impact. Let us confess it: in Aeschylus, Sophocles, and Plato; in Dante, Shakespeare, Goethe; in Donne, Emerson, and

Melville, there are occasional probings into the very core of human existence that often surpass, in their profundity, any recorded observation of Confucius, Jesus, or Buddha. If scattered intuitions and insights were capable of transforming life, they are indeed present in every great literature in quantities copious enough to produce a change. But the impress of a new personality is of a different order: through him many diffused and scattered ideas unite to produce, not other new ideas, but a man.

All this is part of the natural history of man; and it can be followed, on a humbler scale, with a narrower scope and a shorter time-span, in many lesser incarnations. The influence of Napoleon I presents itself: that model, not merely for the Julien Sorels, but for the masters of finance and industry and politics in the nineteenth century. Even in his own lifetime, Napoleon transformed laws and customs over a wide area; and there was a Napoleon I style in furniture and decoration, as well as in military strategy. With a little more luck and success, he might even have become the titular deity of the new creed of modern man: *Arrivisme:* the religion of the "Bitch-goddess Success."

Does this mean that we must accept the enlargement of the new personality, through the agency of a cult, a priesthood, and a church, into a cosmic myth and a veritable all-embracing God? Not in the least; for an emergent species of divinity, whose potent activating effect upon a whole society we need not deny, has no need for such an imposing background: this trick of enlargement is perhaps but a special case of the general tendency to over-value an object of love. The god that Buddha in time became was expressly denied by the fundamental beliefs of Buddha himself. As for Jesus, there is more ambiguity in his own position and testimony; but though the weight of the evidence would point to his belief in his own supernatural mission, that proof is almost negated by a single passage in which he said: "Why call ye me good? Only God is good." Is that not a simple profession of his purely human dimensions? Those words, left as it were by inadvertence in the New Testament, are so strikingly in contradiction to the usual claims of Jesus's divinity that they have an exceptional ring of authenticity, though they demolish the assumptions upon which most of the New Testament and the Pauline Epistles rest.

Divine or human, heavenly or mundane, the fact is that, at certain intervals of history, the potentialities for a more universal culture, a more co-operative life, and a richly dramatic development of the human theme become visible in the image and example of a single human being. At that moment a universal man appears and under his direction a universal society becomes possible. This but repeats, in a more decisive and transcendent fashion, a natural process that is constantly at work in some degree in every human group and tribe and nation. The imitation of that example provides a new destination for society, and a new set of values and purposes, which start it moving on a new path. Centuries and millennia may pass before that impulse ceases to enrich civilization. But in an age that has rejected the function of personality, in its attempt to achieve statistical certainty through dealing only with mass phenomena, the prevalence of a mechanistic and behaviorist ideology undermines both the sense of reality and the possibility of renewal. Before we can go further, therefore, it is necessary that we should take account of this obstacle and firmly push beyond it.

4: BIAS AGAINST THE PERSONAL

The birth of a dominant personality is the decisive step in the process of making a limited, closed society capable of entering into wider social relations, of a more inclusive and universal pattern. By loving and imitating the parental, life-nurturing image of the new person, by bowing to his wisdom, by following in his footsteps, by accepting his ideal figure as a true and central image of man, toward which all smaller figures should approximate, peoples of the most diverse backgrounds and histories achieve a common bond and pursue a common goal. Through this personal medium they achieve a common understanding and the possibility, despite all diversity, of combining and synergizing their efforts. The process of arriving at this unanimity is no simple one: it demands effort. But the result of that effort is to replace regional, tribal, and national differences, which set men apart, with a sense of their common destiny, arising not out of common animal origins, but out of their unique historic purposes.

There are many factors in our day that make this imitation of the person difficult to understand in theory or to accept in practice. Even when one makes allowances for the historical distortion of this whole process through an over-magnification of the person, there is something about the manner of this transformation that stimulates a resistance in the very groups that should, from their own experience, be in the best position to interpret the workings of personality.

Perhaps the deepest source of this resistance in Western society is the general reaction, since the close of the Middle Ages, against the religious enhancement of personality. Humanism, which made man the center again, lacked the humility to participate in a kind of change that even the uneducated and the illiterate must share. Furthermore, in the pursuit of more accurate knowledge about the behavior of physical bodies, and with the growth of gigantic bureaucratic, industrial, and military organizations, the process of depersonalization spread to every other department. Result: our conscious world is largely a depersonalized world, and our most accurate knowledge is limited to those areas where the person does not operate.

In any account of dynamic social processes, our favored knowledge today comes mainly from those realms where man's behavior is closest to animal behavior: Darwin's pioneering work on animal psychology, which established close relations between human behavior and that of other animals, near or remote, has borne abundant fruit. In so far as we take account of the human personality, we conceive it as being a mere product of its past and its geographic and cultural environment, without any allowance for the fact that at man's level the future, the imagined and projected future, is hardly less effectively operative. We accept the past's drag: we reject the future's pull. If changes take place in man's character and destiny, current thought conceives man himself as being merely a passive creature of forces outside himself: we hold perhaps that little modifications can be made by food and drugs, by habit and exercise, and that further social changes can be effected by mechanical inventions, by laws and codes. By the continued operation of such agents, we even admit the possibility of profound changes taking place eventually in a whole culture. But, in terms of conventional science, we have no need to invoke the direct action of personality to explain any of these changes: even its existence as a psychal "filter" is usually overlooked.

With this bias toward the de-personalized, it is little wonder that we overlook every form of change that works from the top down: that begins with the complex and the unique, the individual human instance, and then radiates through the dense tissue of society. We find it hard, with our pragmatic tendency to equate the subjective with the unreal, to suppose that a change in intention and attitude, an upsurge of new feelings and a crystallization of ideas around the tiny seed of personality, can work any large organic changes within a community or a culture. There is nothing in the observed behavior of other animals to suggest that a transference of love, comparable to that which takes place between a patient and his psychiatrist, can occur on a collective scale and bring about a new orientation in a whole society. If some change like this actually occurs during one of the great religious transformations, our intellectual mentors are hardly equipped to observe it: they will look instead for a fluctuation in the climate or a change in the system of production to account for the observed difference in behavior—if in fact they even notice what has taken place.

To suggest that the person may have a more direct impact on society is, in terms of the positivism that underlies most contemporary thought, to introduce something as impalpable, indeed as inadmissibly spookish, as the concept of the Aristotelian entelechy in biology. But the fact is that this very impersonalism is the source of a radical error quite as deep as that which the classic religions originally made in giving fanciful accounts of the detailed operations of nature: indeed, we have profoundly misread the modes of social change because we seek to interpret them only on those levels that can be understood without reference to the positive growth of the person. Nietzsche, in The Genealogy of Morals, had some genuine insight into the more personal aspect of this process; but unfortunately, in characteristic German fashion, he mistook it to be the work of a superb master-class, imposing its will forcefully upon a servile population.

But if the failure to understand the nature and function of personality is one of the main reasons for our so easily rejecting the larger subjective process that works by conversion and imitation, there are other limitations that spring from internal weaknesses that historic religions themselves have disclosed. No single religion has yet done justice to every aspect of the human personality: hence the new drama, focused on the leading actor, fails to provide parts for many people who are not, by nature, close to the biological type of the dominant person.

In origin, for example, the Christian religion had no civic or domestic role for its adherents, as Renan correctly pointed out: Jesus, centering on his own special mission and the hope of a quick "end of the world," made no provisions for either vital or social continuity. Some twelve hundred-odd years passed before Thomas Aquinas formulated, with any completeness, the Christian response to situations whose very existence Jesus ignored: the just distribution of political power or the erotic responses and duties of man and wife. Hinduism, it would seem, has been more generous to all types of character and disposition: hence a readiness, from the foundation of the nineteenth century Brahmo Samāj onward, to acknowledge the moral insights and the spiritual validity of Christianity and Islam. But unfortunately Hinduism, until our own day, restricted the province of personality, through its doctrine of permanent castes: a denial of the capacity for personal development and transcendence within a single lifetime. Not till the advent of Mahatma Gandhi, deeply permeated through his reading of Thoreau and Tolstoy by the liberating thought of Christianity, was this fatal obstacle to universality challenged.

The other handicap is of a different nature. Once the first strong impulse to honor and love and obey the new parent-image weakens, the instinctual patterns of behavior that have been worked out in a stable closed society, regain their hold: for the new way, by its very liberation, is neither as well defined nor as secure as the old way. These older tribal attitudes often regain their original position by bending to the new universalism and taking it over for their own narrower purposes. The resurgence of Roman officialism, Roman centralization, even Roman materialism and superstition, in the Papacy in the era of Gregory the Great, was an instance of this wily maneuver; and many of the heresies that were rife between the fourth and the sixth centuries A.D. may be looked upon as attempts, on the part of the provinces, to counteract the new imperialism of Rome, masking itself as a universal spiritual doctrine. The same thing has, ironically, happened in our own day with soviet communism; in the very process of inner consolidation, it has come closer to the Muscovite regime of Ivan the Terrible than to the cosmopolitan tendencies of Lenin; and it now imposes its Russianism on Chinese and Poles alike, as an unchallengeable "communist" dogma.

Since modern science has, until recently, led to a mistrust of personality in any form, treating it solely as a source of error and subjective mischief, it is no wonder that people reject the over-magnification of the person, which in so many classic religions turns a prophet of merely human dimensions into a god. That whole process seems to defy both science and common sense, and those who worship these deities cannot see beyond them. But our contemporaries have even better reason for their distrust: they have witnessed a fraudulent godhood, projected before their own eyes, in the systematic deification of Adolf Hitler and Joseph Stalin. The very success that has attended this collective transmogrification only makes it harder to accept a doctrine based on the dynamic impact of the person.

In the case of these false deities the apparatus of inflation and distortion, the propaganda machines, the control of the sources of information, the destruction of all contrary evidence and the murder of all who could bear living witness to the truth, the enforced prostitution of intellectuals who might have exposed the cheat, the constant display of oversized images of Big Brother himself—all this has been as visible to the innocent onlooker as the contrivances by which an inept magician performs his tricks. Even those who most urgently wish to be fooled still know how the trick is done. Though Doubting Thomases are thrust promptly into concentration camps and torture chambers, enough new ones come forth in every generation to make it necessary to keep the engines of suppression working vigorously and vigilantly.

But why should such a show of force be necessary? The answer suggests a profound difference between bastard religions and real ones, though the same social pressures not merely cause the two species to grow side by side, but—as so often happens in a garden—cause undesirable weeds to bear many points of physical resemblance to the flowering plants. The saving fact is this: the false Messiah *may* not be imitated and *can* not be loved; or rather, the more successfully his ruthlessness is taken over by others, the more surely will his regime break up. Since he does not spontaneously evoke love, the very pressure to display adulation and reverence must finally make people burst forth in extreme hate: witness the fate of Mussolini.

Consider, too, the careers of Hitler and Stalin: they reflect on a large scale that perversion of personality which accompanies a disintegrating society and brings about its final collapse. Both Hitler and Stalin, two common men, the first psychopathic and vile, a connoisseur of corruption and cruelty, the second shrewd, relentless, supple, but likewise brutal, have attempted within their own lifetimes to bend millions of men to their will. To effect this they have represented themselves, not as fellow mortals, but as deities worthy of abject worship and slavish obedience. They are the authors of all earthly good: the conquerors of all evil: by their miraculous touch tyranny becomes democracy and conquest liberation. What they have no hopes of achieving by persuasion and spontaneous co-operation, they seek to impose by force, backed by superstitious observances. Fortunately for mankind, unfortunately for the dictators' millennial ambitions, they reverse the process by which personality actually operates in history. Intent on taking advantage of the superstitious over-magnification of personality, which so often takes place even with a cinema star or a radio crooner, they invent an auxiliary apparatus of repression to hasten the process.

Thus these leaders sought to impose a God upon their fellow men, before they had transformed themselves into the image of a veritable person: loving and life-bestowing. Even with mirrors, they could not possibly succeed. What happened when Goebbels magnified and multiplied the debased image of Hitler? Ten years of unqualified success sufficed to seal Germany's fate. The devout imitation of Stalin by his own henchmen can be counted upon to produce their systematic extirpation of each other: this process, begun by Stalin himself, will probably be carried on without restriction upon his death—all past annals support this prediction. Thus the historic "Savior Emperor," that darkly benevolent figure who so often arises in a disintegrating civilization, only hastens that disintegration by his inherent contempt for the normal operations of personality. Precisely because of his love of power, he can make no use of the power of love. So the last stage in the downfall of a civilization is the mutual extermination of the unloved and the unlovable.

5: NEXT DEVELOPMENT OF RELIGION

This discussion should help us now to detect the fallacy in the current hope that traditional religion, particularly Christianity, if it once recaptured the hearts of men, might serve to re-direct the demoralized energies of Western civilization. Even if the present crisis were not on a worldwide scale, no crystallized orthodoxy, Catholic or Protestant, Christian or Oriental, seeking merely to recover ground it had occupied in the past, would be adequate to the catastrophic situation mankind now confronts.

Before any existing body of beliefs can become active again, it must both absorb the fresh elements that Western civilization has brought into the world during the last three centuries, and it must detach itself from the institutional forms that now limit their power and usefulness. If the ascending path of growth leads from the interior outward, from abstract formulation to physical embodiment, the way of renewal proceeds first in the reverse direction: through disembodiment, detachment, disenchantment, finally through the wholesale withdrawal of interest from the existing society. In that state, naked and alone, the spirit may rise to new illuminations and achieve a new center of growth.

To preserve the vital impulses of the traditional religions, then, their followers must escape from their buildings and their rituals, they must withdraw from their prudent attachments to the wealthy and the worldly: they must strip themselves voluntarily of many ancient dogmatic claims that defy reason and so, in the end, unsettle faith. When the process has gone far enough, those who keep to their purpose will reach an inner core. At that point, the possibility of unity and common action will exist. Only from this inner nodule can fresh growth take place; and only by this stripping down of the collective ego, to a point where there is neither white nor black, male nor female, Christian nor Hindu, Theosophist nor Marxian communist, can a fresh start be made.

Those who still believe that Christianity alone can save our civilization, or rather, deliver modern man from the miscarriages of his civilization, are perhaps best represented by Arnold J. Toynbee. This admirable historian has been driven by his convictions into theology, only to become a theologian who, to push his convictions to their conclusion, must turn his back upon history. To arrive at his view, Mr Toynbee assumes two things: one is that the Christian faith is alone the true one, and that Jesus is the only god who ever took human form. The other is that Western civilization, since the breakup of the medieval synthesis, has merely been monotonously duplicating the errors that brought Hellenic civilization low. Into a quite different set of symptoms, he reads the same disease and mechanically prescribes the same original remedy.

As for the first assumption, it is beyond both proof or denial, since it rests solely on an act of faith. But the notion that God manifested himself only once in human form contradicts the postulate of continuity on which the present philosophy rests: so I must challenge it. On its face, this idea is as unreasonable as the notion that a small Semitic tribe that settled in Palestine was the exclusive recipient of divine favor. Though I have no doubt that the advent of Christianity was a singular occurrence which re-polarized the existing historic forces, similar transformations are equally visible in the other civilizations the historian describes. In the sense that Christianity "saved" Western civilization, Buddhism saved that of India, Confucianism China. If the saving, on Toynbee's later interpretation, was through the formation of an otherworldly non-historic society in the form of a Church, then Buddhism, at least, like Islam, shows identic characteristics to Christianity.

The second assumption, however, is open to challenge on grounds common both to Toynbee's philosophy and to one that contradicts it. For the fact is that few of the typical phenomena of a world-weary society, such as that which followed the decay of the Olympian religion and the fall of the Greek city, did in fact come after the disintegration of the medieval idolum: there is simply no parallel. Though the fourteenth century showed a rapid disintegration throughout Western Europe, made catastrophic by the effects of the Black Death, the period between 1400 and 1900 was marked by an equally rapid recovery. During that half-millennium, indeed, an extraordinary outburst of human energy took place: it led to the colonization of the new world, to the mastery of the forces of nature, to the formulation of a new scientific outlook, which built up a method for creating valid knowledge and for controlling natural forces, and, not least, to a swelling wave of sheer animal vitality, marked by a tremendous increase in world population. Productivity and reproductivity went hand in hand.

Hardly anywhere till the beginning of the twentieth century, or rather, till the First World War, were there concrete evidences of those shrinkages and lapses that went on so dishearteningly throughout the Hellenic world from the end of the fifth century B.C., and again in the Roman world, from the second century B.C. onward. Not least, the energies of the West showed themselves in acts of spiritual creativity. The long line of writers and artists, beginning in literature with Shakespeare and Cervantes and Rabelais, in painting with Tintoretto and Breughel, and the equally remarkable line of scientists and philosophers, from Kepler and Vesalius and Galileo, from Spinoza and Leibnitz and Kant to the men of the twentieth century would not indicate a downhill movement in culture, except to someone who was standing on his head. To interpret this whole process as essentially a negative and non-creative one, as Mr Toynbee is tempted to do, is willfully to trim the facts to the theory—if one may speak so harshly of the mistakes of such a genial and humane spirit.

Today the situation, in many quarters, has indeed begun to alter drastically for the worse. Within a half-century, a series of devastating changes, comparable to those that took place in the fatal fourteenth century as recorded by Petrarch, are now visible: this has happened with startling rapidity, as in the spread of cancer cells in a body that hitherto seemed healthy. Today we do in fact—and here Toynbee's insight seems both penetrating and valid—face many end-processes. Schooled in the ideology of progress, our contemporaries have been slow to recognize these dangers, and slower still to correct them. Though they were first pointed out by Jacob Burckhardt, in the heyday of Victorian complacency, and uncovered once again by Henry Adams a generation later, they remained "unbelievable." Our development has not been as harmonious and as triumphant as the philosophers of progress proclaimed: we have now to pay the penalty for our one-sidedness and our externalism, for our devaluation of the personal, for our puerile over-valuation of the machine, for our failure to embrace the tragic sense of life and to make the sacrifices that would, if made in time, have saved our civilization from its corpse-strewn Fifth Act.

This miscarriage of our civilization has come about, however, not through a seepage of its faith or a waning of its energies, but through an over-concentration of its energies, through an excess of zeal, through a fanaticism of scientific rationalism, so proud of its multiplying discoveries and inventions that it continued to run past the danger signals on the road, like a drunken engineer on a streamlined train, unaware that his inordinate speed multiplies all the natural hazards.

The difficulties Mr Toynbee forces himself to read into the earlier centuries of "modern Western civilization" did not exist until a much later period. For the fact is, the crisis of the fourteenth century activated new forces in society that gave life direction and meaning for another five centuries: the adventures of exploration and colonization, the disciplines of capitalist enterprise and systematic mechanical invention, the dionysian reactions of the new painters and poets, symbolized in every aspect by Rabelais's mythical Gargantua, were all life-affirming responses. If there had not been such a wide swing away from the cult of life-negation and otherworldly salvation, the decomposition of the medieval Church would possibly have gone on even more swiftly: and doubtless it would have produced more noxious stenches and by-products: its engines of torture might have been presently adapted to mass-production, instead of giving way, even in Catholic hands, to engines of utilitarian enterprise.

What this decadent Christian civilization would have been, left to itself, one can perhaps detect in those undercurrents of expression from François Villon to Baudelaire and the early T. S. Eliot: symbolic

Fleurs du Mal blooming in what might have been, but for the fresh energies released in the fifteenth century, a universal Waste Land. Modern historians have yet to appraise how decisively the energies of the new industrial civilization, after the eighteenth century, helped to rejuvenate the Roman Catholic Church.

If orthodox Christianity had retained in itself the means of renewing medieval civilization and averting its later miscarriages, it would hardly have lost its grip on Europe. And if the Church was unable to save even itself intact, during a crisis when it was still supremely in spiritual command, what likelihood is there that it will, with only its past insight and its historic forms of conversion, be capable of transforming peoples that are now only nominally Christian and a world that is predominantly non-Christian? The earlier transformation that Christianity actually accomplished was of a simpler nature. For the original Christian answer to the disintegration of classic culture involved merely persuading the proud pagan to let go of something he no longer confidently possessed, or even actively desired. Until yesterday our present civilization showed few signs of such weariness.

What Toynbee's special theory of Palingenesis or Re-Birth does not take into account is the fact that though many of the negative conditions that once made Christianity possible, nay imperative, are again here, the same basis for reintegration does not exist: the formative Christian nucleus, however active through all the centuries, holds now only a tiny portion of its original mass. In origin a fresh form in classic society, Christianity is now only an encapsulated survival in our own: its restoration would betray the very disease of archaicism that Toynbee properly rejects in all other religions.

Survivals, in the nature of things, lack the dynamic force of mutants. Once, Christianity was truly oriented to the future: now it is directed to perpetuating a past that cannot, except in a mummified form, have any continued existence. While the vital truths of Christianity must be included in a new synthesis, this holds equally for other religions and philosophies. To claim unconditional acceptance for Christian dogma as embodied in any of the historic Churches, is to deny the essential idea of an emergent divinity; for, as the Victorian poet sang, "God fulfills himself in many ways, lest one good custom should corrupt the world."

On this matter, I would set Josiah Royce's analysis above Toynbee's; for long ago Royce touched the quick of our present dilemma. In discussing The Problems of Christianity, in 1913, Royce said: "The office of religion is to aim toward the creation on earth of the Beloved Community, the future task of religion is the task of inventing and applying the arts which shall win men over to unity and which shall overcome their original hatefulness by the gracious love, not of mere individuals, but of communities. Now such arts are still to be discovered. Judge every social device, every proposed reform, every national and local enterprise, by the one test: Does this help toward the coming of the Universal Community? If you have a Church, judge your own church by this standard; and if your Church does not fully meet this standard, aid toward reforming your Church accordingly." That puts the case plainly, and it applies to all our institutions. We cannot have unity among the so-called United Nations unless we invoke unity and work for unity at every level of human activity.

By proper extension, one must apply Royce's insight to every other form of religion, including, naturally, the Marxian gospel of dialectical materialism. No present Catholicism is sufficiently Catholic, no universalism sufficiently universal, to join in spirit the divided nations and make possible our imperative goal: One World.

This perhaps explains why the most universal of religious doctrines, that of Baha-'ullah, the founder of the Bahai religion, has not so far prevailed. For the better part of a century the adherents of Bahaism have proclaimed the unity of mankind and the need for world order: their noble intentions, their timely exhortations, their catholic injunctions, represent man's best hopes. But one prophet more, one religion more, no matter how enlightened his aims, is not what the situation requires; nor can rational persuasion alone bring about the essential conversion. When the overall change comes it will spread rapidly from a multitude of centers: it will infuse a religious sense of a common purpose and end, even in departments of life not recognizably religious. To be ready for that opportune moment, each religion, each secular philosophy, each going institution, must widen and deepen its own vein of universalism.

Not by accident, perhaps, one must turn to a Hindu thinker, rather than a Christian one, for an explicit statement of this new universalism. I find it in a passage from Keshab Chandra Sen:

"I believe in the Church Universal, the deposit of all ancient wisdom and the receptacle of modern science, which recognizes in all prophets and saints a harmony, in all scriptures a unity, and through all dispensations a continuity, which abjures all that separates and divides and always magnifies unity and peace, which harmonizes rea-

son and faith, yoga and bhakti, asceticism and social duty . . . and
which shall make all nations and sects one kingdom and one family
in the fullness of time." In that spirit, only in that spirit, will the
classic religions find regeneration: only so can all nations and kin-
dreds and peoples, to use the words of the Apocalypse, come within
speaking distance of each other.

6: THE UNIVERSAL COMMITMENT

Those who are looking for a change to take place, along the classic
lines that Buddhism and Christianity and Mohammedism followed,
are applying, to the unique events of our time, a mode of thought that
over-weights the traditional and the repetitive, and ignores the possibility of a new act of creation. But the change that made it possible
to redeem the Roman world needed a thousand years for its consummation. We know that the living places of our planet may be wiped
out, and our planet itself denuded of life, through the wholesale mis-
applications of scientific power, unless the change that alters the condition of modern man and the direction of his activities takes place in
much shorter order: almost, as one reckons historic time, within the
twinkling of an eye.

No matter how efficacious the example of Buddha or Jesus may have
been, we cannot put our faith in renewal by a similar process; or
rather, though the process itself may be similar, the time in which
it operates must be abbreviated. How can this be done? By looking,
not for a single transforming agent, but for millions upon millions of
them, in every walk of society, in every country: a democratic transformation, dispersed and widespread, to replace those centralized and
authoritarian images which would today, under our current nihilism,
be either ineffectual or tyrannous.

Let us confess it: such a change has never yet taken place in the
past. But the conditions which now make this kind of change imperative have never existed either: the extent of the catastrophe that threatens gives the measure of the transformation that will be necessary in
order to master it. But the fact that there are no favorable historic
precedents is not, for the philosophy advanced in these pages, an un-
climbable barrier: we have learned nothing valuable about man's nature and destiny unless we have learned that man holds, in far larger
degree than the physical universe, the possibility of continuous creation. Thanks to the very form our institutions and machines have taken,

with our multifold channels of communication, millions of minds are now aware of man's dilemma and awakened to the danger that threatens all life: if they are not fully awakened today, they may be roused —even to the point of action—tomorrow.

This fact perhaps makes possible the change of attitude and purpose that will halt the processes of disintegration before they have reached the critical point where they can no longer be controlled. Though no one mind can impart his own dynamic of renewal to a world that is now radically endangered by its paranoia, its incapacity to foster love, a wholesale quickening of many minds might restore the collective balance. If but one person in ten were fully awakened today, fully capable of exercising his higher centers of intelligence and morality, the fatal processes that we have set in motion could be arrested, and a new direction set.

On that possibility, mankind's security and salvation now seem to hang. The task of the individual Messiah of the past now devolves equally on all men: likewise the burden of sacrifice. No Diogenes need run through the streets with his lantern looking for an honest man: no John the Baptist need perform a preliminary cleansing and absolution upon others, while waiting for the true prophet to come. Those are the images and the expectations of another era. Today each one of us must turn the light of the lantern inward upon himself; and while he stays at his post, performing the necessary work of the day, he must direct every habit and act and duty into a new channel: that which will bring about unity and love. Unless each one of us makes this obligation a personal one, the change that must swiftly be brought about cannot be effected.

But all this is beyond historical precedent and probability? Granted. An impossible dream? No. For why should we readily hail marvels like the transmutation of matter and energy, issuing out of the physical world, without our admitting the possibility of equally radical departures issuing out of the subjective world, which is itself the source of our mastery of physical phenomena? All challenges to animal lethargy and inertia begin in a dream; and every dream is "impossible" until the dreamer heeds it, communicates it, develops the rational means of creating its own fulfillment: until the dream, passing into consciousness as an inchoate impulse and stir, at first but a shadowy shape, works itself out into a new reality: the reality of the paintings of the Ajanta caves, of The Divine Comedy, of the Pyramids of the Mayas and Aztecs: the reality of life lived in symbol-laden cities under justice and law. Only one thing is needful: faith in the dream itself; for the very ability to dream is the first condition of the dream's realization. And which is better?—to sink into a nightmare, equally self-fabricated, though we close our eyes to our own constant part in this pathological process—the nightmare of extermination, incineration, and universal death?—or to dream of the alternative processes that will endow individual men and the race at large with a new plan of life? Better the possible self-deception of this dream than the grim fact of that nightmare.

The new age will begin when a sufficient number of men and women in every land and culture take upon themselves the burden men once sought to transfer to an Emperor, a Messiah, a dictator, a single God-like man. That is the ultimate lesson of democracy: the burden cannot be shifted. But if each one of us, in his own full degree, accepts this desperate condition for survival, that which seemed a threat to man's further development will be transformed into a dynamic opportunity.

CHAPTER V.   THE BASIS OF HUMAN
                                        DEVELOPMENT

1: MAN'S WILL TO FORM

The doctrines of Progress and Evolution both supplied modern man
with certain valuable insights absent from most traditional ethical
systems: particularly with the notion that no static system of ethics
could do justice to the still-unfathomed possibilities of human development. What had once seemed to be final revelations of value and
purpose now became limited, provisional, local, relative, the product
of historic events that are open to the correction and amplification of
further experience. Exit Plato's Republic.

But neither doctrine could supply modern man with the materials
needed for a more adequate morality, since one must first formulate
a positive measure of the good before the word progress in an ethical
sense can have meaning. Without a concept of purpose, without an
image of perfection, biological evolution, even when it embraces man's
special nature and needs, can mean nothing more than the procession
of more complicated organic forms in a continuing time-series. The
arrest of such forms at any particular point remains meaningless, or
at least morally neutral, unless some higher goal is definable.

Now man is not merely the unfinished but the self-fabricating animal. What other organisms do by purely organic means, in and through
the structure of their own bodies, man does by extra-organic means,
sometimes within his lifetime, or at least within a few centuries.
Through his culture, man continually remakes himself, recasts his
functions, and gives form to his environment. That will-to-form is itself one of his main distinctions. Man is, as it were, the leopard who
knows how to change his spots; or rather, he is the creature who has
found the secret of becoming at will a fish-man, a bird-man, or a mole-
man—even an angel-man or a demon-man, though angels and demons

are as lacking in nature as warm-blooded animals were in the days when the great reptiles alone reigned.

Instead of taking life as it comes and quietly adapting himself to external conditions, man is constantly evaluating, discriminating, choosing, reforming and transforming at every moment of his existence; and this has been true throughout his history. By conscious selection, man increasingly imposes his own will on nature and not least on that ultimate product of nature, his own self. "Choosing is creating!" And the goal of that choice, in man, is his own fuller and further development. No natural history of man can omit, without grave distortion and error, the place of values in his existence. And any scientific anthropology that attempts to ignore values, as outside the pale of science, or to dismiss values as culture-bound and so self-enclosed, must lack the ability to describe the process of human development, since it has no criterion for distinguishing arrest from progress in the department where it most matters.

Doubtless simple modes of estimation and appraisal begin far below the level of man. Every creature must distinguish food from poison, security from danger, friend from foe: even the lowly amoeba, as H. S. Jennings describes its behavior, seems to know what it wants. Judgments of value long antedate judgments of fact; and no judgment of fact is uncolored by values, since even the desire for neutrality or unemotionality is itself an expression of human value. The very mode of science that proclaims the non-existence of values in nature is itself the product of man's over-valuation of mechanical order, and his special regard for those elementary truths that can be established best on an impersonal basis.

Man can apparently make intellectual errors of a flagrant kind without suffering too seriously in consequence: indeed, not till man seeks to form a coherent world picture does it matter to him that his own uncorrected fantasies have distorted or utterly effaced many patent objective facts. Knowledge of good and evil, on the other hand, lies at the very root of human existence. However poor man's positive knowledge may be, he must constantly affix positive or negative values to every event, in order to guide his own life in the direction of development. To know the difference between right and wrong, between good and evil, is the basis of survival, even before it becomes the condition of renewal. In this department, any serious misappraisal will have formidable consequences.

Most of man's evaluations and choices, naturally, were made long ago by the society and culture in which the person finds himself. Significantly, in their origin, the words ethics and morals are equivalent to habits and customs; and firm social habits, since they are the very basis of orderly and calculable behavior, are fundamental to all higher forms of development. While we may rise above our habits into freedom, we must never sink below them into random caprice. Life would be one long blundering frustrating confusion if each generation had to discover entirely by itself what was good for it. That is why a purely experimental ethics, worked out from day to day in the light of the situations encountered in a single lifetime, will ordinarily lead to disaster. (If there may once have been doubts about this observation, the experience of the last two generations has harshly confirmed its truth.) But even when human conduct is based on sound tradition and guided further by reason, sound choices are not automatic or infallible; nor is there any assurance that good intentions will produce good results. Even when values are well established and widely assimilated, they must still in each particular case be recognized as appropriate to the occasion and carried out. The habitual, the traditional, the conservatively moral, are necessary starting points for the proper conduct of life; but they do not in themselves guarantee man's development.

The reasons for this limitation should be plain. As human life rises above its primitive concern with bodily security, the nature of good and evil becomes less obvious. In all the higher expressions of life there is need for greater intelligence and sensibility and understanding to aid in discrimination, and for greater wakefulness, to recognize occasions for intervention or departures from the prescribed norm. The higher the development, the wider the margin of freedom—but also the more serious the consequences of perverse desires and bad choices. There is hardly a phase of human life, from diet to dress, from sexual practices to religious ceremonial, that does not show regressions from sound choices, lapses sometimes made far down in the evolutionary scale. The passage from tribal society, where goods have been stabilized and routinized, toward an open society, where goods are subject to re-appraisal and new choices become possible, is a critical one in human development; for often a sound instinctual pattern may be destroyed by half-baked intelligence long before anything worthy of taking its place has been achieved. The self-confident iconoclasts in Bernard Shaw's The Philanderers or Getting Married knew far less about the nature of sex, love, and the family than the fecund Victorian couples against whose prim household gods they were in revolt.

Man's constant re-shaping of himself, his community, his environment, does not lead to any final state of equilibrium. Even the notion of self-perfection implies the further projection of a self beyond that which may be momentarily achieved: only death can end the dynamics of growth, crisis, and transcendence. And tempting though it may be to do so, one must not confuse the good with what is socially acceptable, or that which promotes the adjustment of the self to the group or the community. Pragmatists and totalitarians have both made this radical error; by their insistence upon conformity to an external pattern, whether imposed by authority or by a mechanistic apparatus, they have proved hostile to creative processes that have a subjective and internal origin.

There are moments when the continued growth in the person demands the endurance of maladjustment: moments that may be accompanied by complete alienation from the community, and require a readiness to encounter the active hostility of its members. These moments are known to saints and martyrs at the very point when they are exerting their unique influence: indeed, every innovator and inventor, even on a more pedestrian level, must often bear the penalties of his nonconformity in rejection and poverty. Without such oppositions and tensions, without such lonely defiance, the pressures of the group might stifle all growth. In some degree, nonconformity is a necessary condition for human development; and that is why the age that produced an abundance of nonconformists in Western Europe was one of the most creative and fruitful the world has known.

The attempt to shift the ethical center from the person to the group overlooks their actual relationship. The group molds the person and gives him a function in his community, provides him with a role to play, bringing out the possibilities of social man: but the person, when he has absorbed and made over what the community provides, in turn, by his very detachment, gives the group itself the possibility of acting with some of the freedom of the person. Eventually the person must take the group with him on the path of development or perish for lack of support. Nationalism unfortunately misreads this interplay between person and group: from Fichte onward, the philosophers of nationalism have held that the nation encloses all possible goods: it falsely identifies the good with the tribal, the customary, the traditional life of kin and kith, while it identifies the not-good or evil with the outsider, the foreigner, the barbarian. "Blut und Boden," "Sacro Egoismo," the "American way of life," thus become mythic deities, whose worship inflates nationalists with a spurious sense of their own virtue, spurious since every other community has a similar set of tribal gods and a self-sufficient ideology just as fatal to human unity and co-operation.

Even in the somewhat more innocent form of a wholly social theory of ethics, the identification of the person with the group overlooks the very condition that is essential for their reciprocal development: the maintenance of tension between the actual and the potential, between achieved goods and possible ones. To make the good consist in conformity to the group pattern does away with this tension in the name of a pre-established harmony and conformity. So far from restoring human values that have been lost during the last three centuries, nationalism, in both its naive and its sophisticated forms, whether democratic or totalitarian, would attempt to restore an obsolete tribal pattern of identity and unanimity. The engines for creating such a limited human type are more powerful today than ever before: for the psychological laboratory and the propaganda machine and the school are now re-enforced by the terrors of the corrective labor camp and the torture chamber. The final outcome of that process has been foreshadowed by more than one imaginative writer, from Čapek to Zamiatin: nowhere more horribly, perhaps, than in George Orwell's realistic nightmare: 1984. It comes to nothing less than the annihilation of man.

2: NEEDS AND VALUES

Life is the source of all human goods, even those that transcend it. To foster life, to select higher forms of life, and to project further goals for life's development—this is the grand human imperative. All our special obligations and duties, as citizens and workers, relate to this higher one. To serve life well, over a long span of time, man's immediate purposes must, in the long run, fit into such larger organic and cosmic purposes as he can discern and interpret. As a species, man has a moral obligation to be intelligent, as well as an intellectual obligation to further his own moral and esthetic development.

Man's own needs and functions are many and various: what sets them apart from their purely animal counterparts is that they lend themselves to a far greater degree of elaboration, for they draw on emotions, feelings, and fantasies whose expressions overlie and sometimes almost conceal the organic purpose they serve. What begins as a bare physical need becomes elaborated into ritual and, under pressure of a formative idea and purpose, may rise into a dramatic action. Take the simplest case, the need for food: common to all animals. If that need halted in man at the instinctual level, it would remain like even more pressing needs, those for air and water—too peremptory to be a source of value. But the expression of the need for food is not confined to the digestive tract: it awakens activities and interests that involve the whole organism; to get food and make it fit for his eating, man uses a hundred ingenious devices for hunting and cultivating, for preparing and preserving, that no other animal has ever, in their immense variety, approached. Expanded by this total engagement of the organism, the original need, once capable of being satisfied on the crudest terms, becomes transformed into a series of social and personal acts. Eventually esthetic delight and gustatory excitement, hospitality and friendly intercourse, even religious ritual, enter into both the getting and eating of food. This tempering of greedy desire, this embroidery of need, this "working over of the raw fact," in short, this involvement in man's whole nature characterizes a large part of his values.

Though the value of food for man originates in his physiological structure it does not remain there. Even the imperious and unbearable stimulus of extreme hunger may be curbed by a cultural taboo, like that of the Moslems against pork. So, too, the infant who is offered food without friendly intercourse and love, as in an old-fashioned orphanage, may reject it or fail to be nourished by an otherwise adequate diet: the very processes of digestion prosper only if re-enforced by attitudes and feelings that have no direct bearing on the function in hand. Just as thought itself may be partly interpreted as an arrested impulse to action, which allows a wider canvass of the whole situation and a more adequate response, so value may be described as a need that has found expression by a circuitous route that draws into it other functions of the organism and brings about a wider sharing of the occasion with other members of society. The organic need subserves symbolic expression: in the act of satisfying his wants man makes them more interesting.

What we properly call a value in life is precisely this organic mixture of need, interest, feeling, purpose, and goal: the physical or physiological impact of a need is only a small part of its expression. It follows, then, that a scheme of life founded on raw human needs alone, without any further efflorescence in values, must remain at a sub-human level; for a life that is stripped, in theory or in fact, to the ingestion of so many calories of food, the performance of a specified number of man-hours of work, the achievement of a certain number of orgasms, is incapable of embracing the social and personal satisfactions to be found in eating, working, and mating. Even the most primitive cultures at the lowest margin of subsistence do more for their members than this.

Perhaps the best recent discussion of values was that of Dr Edward L. Thorndyke, in Human Nature and Society. This perceptive treatise is all the more remarkable because it came from a psychologist who had attempted for the better part of his life to establish purely quantitative methods, without reference to values, in psychology. But even he showed a tendency to define values as goods in themselves. Thus Thorndyke said, by way of illustration, that "sunshine is in general better than inky darkness," curiously ignoring the conditions essential for sleep; or that laughing is better than wailing, overlooking the fact that grief makes laughter acutely painful, and that when one is confronted by an occasion for grief, the ability to express it in tears and sounds of anguish is preferable, even on the lowest grounds of health, to bottling it up. (Note that the suppression of tears and the abandonment of the traditional rituals of grief in modern civilization, mainly through our withdrawal of interest from death, in itself points to an erosion of values.)

There are no intrinsic goods apart from the purposes and needs of men: only in relation to him do some goods become absolute. The only unconditional good, as Immanuel Kant truly observed, is the will-to-goodness. Values arise out of the natural occasions for living; and they serve to magnify beyond their immediate deserts the processes of satisfaction and fulfillment. Conceivably all our needs could be satisfied directly in a push-button world, contrived exclusively to our convenience; but such a life would be more empty than even that of an embryo, since it would lack the specific conditions for human growth —namely, that in the course of fulfilling our needs we should also enter, by this useful back door, into the domain of beauty and significance.

Now, in all going cultures, man is born into a world of established values: here every instinctual need is broadened, yet partly concealed, by a social form, as the naked body is soon covered by decorations or clothes. The production and conservation of values is one of the main concerns of human existence: all that a man does and is depends upon his taking part in this process. Thorndyke is right, therefore, in remarking that if one graded value from the intensely good to the intensely bad, only a small part of the things that one does and acts and handles are of a neutral nature: they are either life-furthering or life-impeding. "Values to man and men," says Thorndyke, "may be infinitesimal, and approximate a neutral zone or zero between good and bad, for many or all persons under most or even all conditions. It consequently does little harm to think of the value, say, of having one grain of dirt washing to the sea or dredged out of the sea as zero. But the number of events which are really neither good nor bad in the slightest degree is much smaller than common thinking would estimate." . . . These facts of natural history are important to bear in mind: ethics rests on them.

Life is a selective process: that is one of the conditions for all growth. Though the organism is sometimes pictured as a sort of filter or membrane, these figures hardly do more justice to its activities than the neutral blank sheet of paper on which Locke erroneously supposed the environment left its definite mark. For the fact is that all organisms are striving and forward-moving creatures: even their most passive responses are still determined by general goals derived from their organic plan of life: they actively reach out for one kind of good and reject another. Some of the selections that the organism makes have become so deeply ingrained in its behavior that it cannot, even under pressure, even under threat of defeat, alter its disposition: it must stick to the goods of its own species, the goods that honor its own style of life and that allow it to fill out, in time, its proper shape.

Many of these commitments are so old and have involved so many co-adaptations with other species that it is impossible for the organism, so to say, to change its mind. Though faced with starvation through lack of herbage, sheep do not become ravening creatures, living off rabbits and mice: their very tooth structure is a guarantee against their so defying their own sheepish nature. By contrast, man lives in an infinitely various environment and his choices, through his wide range of inventions and adaptations, are multifold. Relatively, man is an uncommitted animal. As compared with other animals, man is so unset in his ways, so dynamic, so full of unfathomed potentialities, so capable of coming up with more than one answer to the same question, that the tasks of selection become major ones for him.

Indeed, the higher man rises in his own development, the less fixed are his responses and the wider his range of choices: likewise the greater opportunity he encounters for perversions, maladaptations, that more limited animals escape. The institution of war is such a large-scale perversion: in origin, it may have sprung out of a struggle for a limited food supply in a narrow area; and this act may have been prolonged beyond its natural limits because it lent itself to ritualistic elaboration, which lessened its deadliness and turned it for primitives into an exciting game. With the very advance of civilization war became a collective drama: not justified by animal needs or tangible economic gains, but expressive of ideas and purposes of a peculiarly human sort: irrational but imperious. So in modern times this monstrous negation of values has captured and drained off energies that should have gone to the culture of cities and the development of man.

In making evaluations to further his own growth, civilized man merely carries forward habits that took form at a much lower level of organic development. What is abnormal, what is fatal, is to have no standards of value and no methods of evaluation. When David Hume reduced value to whatever served impulse, he took the first intellectual step toward the nihilism that threatens to engulf our age. Today, unfortunately, a large number of people, not merely Soviet Commissars but appointed leaders of democracy, show evaluation blocks, similar to the "reading blocks" which teachers sometimes encounter in young children. Such children often have normal organs and normal intelligence: but they have never performed the mental leap which gives to groups of letters a name, a sound, and ultimately a meaning that, when treated as separate visual elements, they lack. People with evaluation blocks can go through all the operations of intelligence, and they can reason correctly from premise to conclusion: but they fail to attach positive and negative values to their actions, and therefore, from their own vantage point, they can do no evil. They reserve the term bad solely for the behavior of people or conditions that oppose their impulses and obstruct their private plans.

Such moral idiocy, sometimes naked, sometimes disguised, is the typical response of disintegrating civilization to its own aimlessness: with Diogenes, it reduces human life in general to the level of a dog's life, or, with the amiable Dr Kinsey, it reduces human sexual needs to their valueless common denominator with even unrelated species of animals. The most flagrant example of this devaluation was the adoption by the democracies, during the Second World War, of the fascist practice of random extermination, by bomb and fire and atomic fission, from the air. This moral debasement was followed up in the United States by a wholesale concentration, after 1945, upon instruments of genocide, from the atom bomb to biological weapons of an even more wanton and uncontrollable order, as a cheap substitute for war: a gross military error and a moral sin for which many innocent Americans may yet lose their lives. . . . But where was the moral reaction that should have taken place, after 1945, if not during the Second World War, against such anti-human purposes? There is but a short step from such moral perversion to rabid madness. Only a civilization that had everywhere extirpated its living sense of good and evil could make such a fatal mistake.

3: THE CASE FOR PURPOSE

"What is the good of life?" This question, certainly, does not ordinarily occur to a person in health and prosperity, when the appetites of the body provide their own answers: then every minor good seems to bear witness to the general good of merely being; and to prolong that being brings its own reward. But we know that this question, rising as a wail of despair, occurs on a grand scale when a civilization is losing its grip; when its daily activities are not self-sustaining and self-rewarding; when every effort meets an obstacle, when every plan miscarries and every new turning seems to take one farther from one's goal. To answer that question satisfactorily at these moments—and we are now in the midst of such a dismaying Time of Troubles—requires both historic and cosmic perspective.

"The great use of life is to spend it for something that outlasts it." No doctrine of ethical conduct that overlooks this wider destiny for person and community has anything but a stopgap value. Though habits of discrimination exist below the human level, the sense of conscious participation in a durable, all-enclosing purpose is an entirely human one: perhaps it came to man first in the Chaldean faith that his life was in some way bound by iron necessity to the course of the planets. Scores of centuries elapsed before man found evidence for purpose, not in astrological conjunctions, but in the structure and function of living organisms, in relation to their environment and their projected existence through time.

Now this sense of a presiding purpose in its most common form has been attached to a theory of divine revelation. In the general reaction against theology during the last three centuries the concept of purpose itself was accordingly lost: instead of finding a purposeful world, scientific materialism professed to discover only a blind accidental one. As a result, many people still tend to overlook the immense body of evidence in favor of purpose that has piled up since Darwin's day. One of the strictest and most meticulous of bio-chemists, Lawrence J. Henderson, even demonstrated by an analysis of the properties of the physical world that the very disposition of chemical elements, with their specific properties, on this planet would indicate purpose, in terms of eventual life. While accident occurs throughout nature, and statistical order largely governs the physical world, all manifestations of life bear evidence of a sustaining and widening purpose: a purpose that begins to achieve consciousness in man.

Spinoza, in his Ethics, dismissed the notion of cosmic purpose, or finalism, by saying that "nature has no fixed end in view, and . . . all final causes are merely fabrications of men." During the last three centuries that attitude became ingrained among men of science; but Spinoza's dismissal, for all that, was more than a little specious, because there is a great difference between having no fixed aim and having no aim at all. To say that one has laid out at the beginning no rigidly pre-ordained route is not the same as to say that one has no provisional destination.

At the time Spinoza uttered this judgment there was, indeed, good ground for his taking that position; for the scholastic belief in final causes (purposeful processes and ultimate goals) had led to an attempt to deduce all the forms of existence from the presumed nature of God. Fortified by such dogmatic convictions, scholars avoided detailed inquiry into cause and effect and neglected concrete observation: they presumed, for example, that the course of the planets was a circular one, because the circle was supposedly more perfect than any other figure; or they imputed to providence the detailed evolution of nature, without being curious as to the methods and means, taking for granted that the world had been designed, from the beginning, with a single view to man's use. In this crude form the doctrine of final causes was an encumbrance to thought; and before it could be more adequately re-stated it no doubt needed to be completely rejected.

Two generations ago, a fresh attempt at a more adequate formulation of the theory of purposes and ends in nature was made by a French philosopher, Paul Janet: a treatise too premature, perhaps, to have the influence it deserved. This effort must now be carried further, in order to make intelligible the very facts that causal inquiries in many sciences, particularly biology, have revealed. Perhaps the simplest way of re-stating the doctrine of finalism is to say that in organic change the present may be as much determined by the future as by the past: that causal mechanisms operate in organisms precisely by being attached to goals. At the human level, hope, aspiration, plan and design modify the impact of past events and serve in some measure to order their further transformation. This is not to say that ends are wholly predetermined or fixed, even in brute nature: still less to say that the acknowledgment of purpose in nature frees one from the operation of mechanical processes or releases the observer from detailed investigation of causes and consequences. So far from making mechanistic interpretation unnecessary, finalism does just the opposite: it makes it more significant.

Speaking mythically, one may say that Nature works according to plan; but, as with organic works of architecture, the plan may be revised in the very middle of construction. Hence to read nature's intentions too specifically or too comprehensively is as deceptive as to suggest that she lacks them entirely. When one conceives final causes, one does not, as Janet points out, have to think of a hidden force or Aristotelian entelechy, acting without physical agents: that is the straw man erected by scientists who seek to get along without acknowledging teleology, because this dummy is so easy to demolish. "He who says end," Janet goes on to say, "at the same time says means—that is, a cause fit to produce such an effect. To discover this cause is in no way to destroy the idea of end."

Janet's whole discussion of this problem seems to me so pertinent that since his book is now inaccessible I shall quote a whole passage:

"We give the name of *end* to the last phenomenon of the series, in reference to which all the others are co-ordinated; and this co-ordination of phenomena and actions is explained for us in the simplest manner by the supposition of an anterior idea of the end. I know very well, for instance, that if I had not beforehand the idea of a house I could not co-ordinate all the phenomena whose conjunction is necessary to construct a house. I know very well that it has never happened to me to succeed in making a phrase by taking words at random from a dictionary; I know that I have never succeeded in composing an air by touching at random the keys of a piano. . . . I know that I cannot co-ordinate the elements of matter in a whole without having previously formed the idea of that whole. In a word, I know that with me every induction, and every art, supposes a certain end, a certain finality, or as we have expressed ourselves, a certain determination of the present by the future."

This issue was evaded by the leading thinkers of the nineteenth century: theories of laissez faire, which mystically assigned to blind chance the role of a rational providence, and to cumulative accidents the effect of functional design, were transferred from the world of business to that of nature. Properly rejecting Archdeacon Paley's conception of an Eternal Clockmaker, who designed and wound up the universe, fashionable thought also denied that clocks showed, by their structure, an intention to tell time: it did not occur to them that the clockmaker and the timekeeper might both be concealed in the clock and indistinguishable from it. Unfortunately for this curious form of mysticism, which flattered itself on being hard-headed, the facts of teleology are conspicuous throughout the organic world. Such facts cannot be explained away by the glib device of referring to mechanisms of adaptation. That is a semantic contradiction. For what is a mechanism but a specialized contrivance for producing a predetermined result? In short, a conspicuous example of teleology.

The alternative to this slippery logic was to make Chance itself become a sort of operative entelechy: this is the role that Darwin actually assigned it, in his non-Lamarckian moments, in the guise of Natural Selection. Chance was not merely responsible for variations in the organism, which might lead in time to the complete transformation of species: it was also responsible for co-adaptations, like that between the yucca plant and the yucca moth, equally positive, equally remarkable, in the "environment." Likewise, presumably, chance was responsible for cumulative changes in a single direction, since in many instances small changes would not have the effect of enhancing the prospects for survival until the entire change was accomplished: that is, until the designated co-operation had been achieved.

In short, an age that rejected miracles assigned to chance a series of purposeful transformations quite as extraordinary, on the doctrine of statistical probability itself, as any amount of special supernatural intervention. And unfortunately, our ethical life during the past century has been undermined by the vulgar assumption that this miraculous but purposeless system of nature corresponds to the actual world. That conclusion is without foundation.

Must one not hold that the argument in favor of final causes has not been closed? Just the contrary, it is only now since we are in possession of sufficient data, drawn from the detailed investigation of countless biological and social phenomena, that the whole argument for final causes, that is, for a teleology pervading all life, can be confidently opened again. Once we get over this hurdle in dealing with nature, we shall have no difficulty in applying the concepts of purpose and "plan of life" to man.

4: THE NATURE OF DESIGN

To say that life is by nature goal-seeking and directional, and that human life in ever greater measure is consciously and deliberately purposeful is not to describe except in the vaguest outline the nature of this purpose, or to forecast, with the slightest sense of sureness, life's ultimate goals. At this point, he who pretends to have an explanation, or even a system of explanation, not merely lacks modesty: he shows plainly he has not taken in the dimensions of the problem itself. By analogy, we may infer that a grand design has encompassed all the little designs whose pattern we can trace; but that pervading unity must be taken on faith.

True: certain nearer goals are not completely hidden from keen analysis or deep intuition. History provides us with suggestive parallels. Six centuries before the invention of airplanes and motor cars, the monk, Roger Bacon, predicted these mechanical contrivances: from his knowledge of processes at work in himself, he was able to anticipate "the next development of man." Glanvill, in the seventeenth century, predicted the possibility of communicating at a distance without visible material means. Where design is present, a fragment may give a sufficient clue to the whole.

But since life is not a circular process, doomed to endless cycles of recurrence, each emergence to a higher level brings with it unexpected and unpredictable elements. Even apart from this, many purposes are not in fact consummated; and many consummations remain cryptic and hidden until they actually come about. The game of "cheat the prophet" as Chesterton called it in The Napoleon of Notting Hill is doubtless as old as prophecy. Even nature seems to change her mind: having invented a painless method of childbirth in the marsupials, she capriciously threw that valuable invention on the scrap-heap and elaborated the clumsy, painful system still used by the placentals: highly difficult and dangerous to a creature with man's capacious brain case at birth.

Obviously, nature has left no blueprints around, to disclose her purposes and her final intentions. And the process by which purpose and design have appeared in the universe seems just the opposite of that sudden miracle by which, in the Book of Genesis, God telescoped the work of eons into six days, and created man as his crowning labor in this swift operation. If man himself were the end nature originally had in view, it might seem absurd—at very least downright incompetent—to arrive at that end by such a protracted and devious route. The answer to this dilemma, as I have pointed out, is provided by the doctrine of emergence: processes are not merely modified by their ends, but, when they reach a certain point of development, they reveal unexpected characteristics which surpass the limitations of their earlier conditions. As in the creation of a work of art, there is a reciprocal interaction between the artist's intention and the means he uses: so that the final result, no matter how firmly conceived at the beginning, usually brings with it a considerable element of surprise. But design is needed, before one can have events sufficiently out of the pattern to be "unexpected": in a world governed wholly by chance, only order would astonish.

Every purpose is transformed by the medium and the mechanism through which it is expressed: wherefore every distant end undergoes a change during the time taken to reach the last stage. On the analogy with art, as sentience and feeling and intelligence developed in the evolution of species, the idea of man, so to say, became clearer. By the time man emerged from earlier animal species, however, certain irrevocable decisions had been made, some of them highly embarrassing to the new creature who was to appear. Thus nature's abortive but stubbornly persisted-in experiment, of making the nose the dominant sense organ, had finally been abandoned in favor of the eye and ear: a great aid to man's dawning intelligence. Some experiments still remained in the neutral zone: plainly it made no difference to man that his liver and kidneys were built essentially on the same pattern that had been used in humbler creatures at a far earlier stage in evolution. But on the other hand the close association of the organs of reproduction and excretion became a handicap to man's increasing playfulness in sexuality; and this was offset only in part by the heightened erotic responsiveness of woman's breasts. As for the upright position, with the free arm, the mobile dexterous hand, the unobstructed binocular vision—that did more to release man from his flat, four-footed animality than anything else, perhaps, this side of spoken language: but all this is so belated it seems almost a postscript.

Man, with his short span of years, is impatient: "no sooner said than done" is his motto. But time-saving, like economy, is a human invention for which there is no counterpart in nature: the mills of the Gods, proverbially, grind slowly, and except in man's reckoning, a million years are as a day. For purposes that work so slowly, pushing over so many obstacles, disclosing intentions at such a remote end, patiently "muddling through" without anything that can be called a consistent plan of action, however purposeful each event and however remarkably co-ordinated the general result, man lacks the necessary parallels in his own life to aid his understanding. This weakness holds particularly in our own time, whose pride it is to hasten all natural processes. But the builders who designed the cathedrals at Köln and Ulm, neither of which was finished till the nineteenth century, might have felt a little closer to the ways of nature had they bothered to look into them.

Let us make, then, a necessary correction in the older doctrines of finalism. When we accept purpose and plan and goal as essential in the barest definition of life, we do not deny the existence of causes and events that lie outside this living system and are often, as we say, at cross-purposes with it. Nor do we deny, within it, the necessity for many experimental trials and rectifications. So far from saying, with Walter Lippmann, that a plan that can be changed is not a plan, I would say just the contrary: a plan too rigid or too brittle to be changed does not belong either to the organic or the human world, for life cannot function effectively within such hardened molds. All organic change partakes of creation; and our clue to creation comes, not through the investigation of mechanical sequences viewed by an external spectator or operator, but through the observation of purposive action in man's own creative acts. Without reference to these higher processes in man, one cannot perhaps make an adequate interpretation of what goes on in earlier stages of organic development.

Since these concepts are still unfamiliar, I must make use of a homely illustration. Take the creative act of writing. I do not know, at the moment I write this sentence, exactly what my next sentence is going to be, though an anticipatory feeling of what will carry the thought further has already formed. But I know, even as I now type it, that it is the result, not merely of what I have said in the previous sentence—and in turn in the book as so far written—but also of what

I have in mind further to express in order to complete the general thesis of the book. This sentence might have taken many alternative forms without departing from the plan; and one of those forms has now actually appeared; but whatever form I might choose—and at the moment I said it the words came as a somewhat unexpected revelation—its character as well as its meaning is determined by its place in the structure of the book and the extent to which it participates in and furthers the overall purpose of the book.

Before the book is finished that sentence may be deleted; yet it will, by having once served as a link in the chain of argument, have performed a genuine purpose, even though it disappears: it would still, in other words, have been molded at its point of origin by a future goal and in turn contribute to the fulfillment of that goal. The meaning of the single sentence, in other words, derives from the larger design; yet even the author could not describe in advance all the details of that larger design, for the design itself will not be coherently organized or effectively expressed, until the last page is ready for the printer. In other words, it is characteristic of purposive organization that, though the future determines the present, the future itself is subject, both in detail and even in the overall pattern, to many further modifications. Yet even if I abandoned the book in the middle, the words, as so far written, would have been determined by the goal I originally set before myself. That degree of purpose would exist.

The acceptance of a pervasive teleology or finalism, uniting the cosmic and the human, now becomes our operational postulate and living faith. All life is purposive and goal-seeking; and human life consciously participates in a more universal purpose and seeks goals that lie beyond the mere survival, in a state of animal torpidity, of the species. Though many of the details of this teleological system are substantiated by observation, the purpose of the whole, the grand design, cannot be established either by experiment or by observation—and neither, for that matter, can it be refuted or discredited by such means as long as living organisms survive.

All one need say is that if purpose exists in the basic structure of things, it calls for a far less incredible succession of miracles than a world subject wholly to random processes, which has nevertheless achieved such abundant manifestations of purpose and design. In the larger terms of existence, both purpose and chance lie beyond effective demonstration; but it is more sensible to admit the existence of purpose, modified by fortuities and necessities, than to suppose that chance is uppermost and then be compelled to avert one's eyes from every evidence of purposive transformation.

At all events, we begin perhaps to see why the sense of a pervasive purpose that encompasses all creation enters into every reasonable definition of the good. This purpose existed in nature, before man identified nature with the larger order of his own being. A purposeless life is in fact a contradiction; for as soon as life becomes purposeless the very possibility of its continued existence comes to an end: in man, that irrationality and futility bring about self-destruction. Cancer is, from the standpoint of the organism, prolific but purposeless growth, and all purposeless growth must produce death.

By the same token, a purpose that reaches beyond any immediate satisfaction and gives direction to the whole course of life, or that even spans the lives of successive generations, is a powerful agent of social and personal integration. To prefer the durable to the ephemeral, the consistent to the inconsistent, is the essence of "character." That was what the Jewish prophets, from Moses onward, meant when they sought to interpret God's intentions to man, and to make man's daily arrangements fit into the larger scheme of probation and salvation that was, according to their view, being worked out in history. Though they often crudely over-simplified this vision and doctrine, by making reward and punishment more swift and sure than they actually are, they at least emphasized the fact that the good is no wholly self-contained entity and no purely human illusion: every good is the vehicle, not merely of immediate personal fulfillment—sometimes indeed that is withheld—but of continued growth and development and renewal.

The understanding contemplation of the ultimate goal enables it to be to some extent manifested and realized in the present moment: if in one sense life involves perpetual struggle and self-transcendence, there is at the same time a quiet pool of being in which the most distant goal is mirrored; so that even if frustrated or cut short in his efforts, the person's ultimate fulfillment is nevertheless partly realizable in the acts that lead to that goal. No small part of the function of art is to bring those moments into the busy marketplace of life. What one calls the timelessness of art is its capacity to represent the transformation of endless becoming into being. Without allowing for this realization of purpose in the active present—what Emerson probably meant when he said that life was a matter of having good days— a doctrine based on purpose alone might, like totalitarian communism, subordinate all immediate personal goods to the ultimate distant goal.

By over-emphasis of a purely compensatory after-life Christianity for long made the same error.

The binding force of an ethical system based on purpose has been dramatically confirmed in the history of the Jews: its practical consummation in our own time perhaps merits our special note. Scattered to the four corners of the earth, the Jews, during the long period of the Dispersion, still retained their faith in a divine promise: in the restoration of Jerusalem, in the advent of a Messiah, and finally, in the prophecy of Isaiah, of the coincident coming of a day when the nations will no longer war against one another, but join together in ways of peace.

All these purposes may well, at many grievous times during the last two millenniums, have seemed delusional projections: the reactions of desperate souls to unfortunate political and social conditions: reactions bearing every mark of a collective neurosis. By holding to these purposes, the Jews kept together as a people under conditions that would have ground any less hopeful nation out of existence: that itself would constitute a pragmatic justification of purpose. But these goal-seeking people have done more than hold together, while their conquerors and oppressors, given to ephemeral satisfactions and immediate aims, vanished. Today the Jews have performed the incredible feat of returning as a unified political group to their native home in Palestine. Thus a collective purpose, working over an almost cosmic stretch of time, has brought its own fulfillment. By that fact, every contributory ceremony and ritual and prayer, every hardship and sacrifice, has been retrospectively justified. The mere existence of Israel today is a testimonial to the dynamics of purposive development. If the Greeks had had such a vision of life, they might have left an even deeper impression upon modern man.

So far, then, we have established three large criteria for an ethics of human development: Reverence for life in all its manifestations. The development of evaluation and selection, of a constant discrimination between good and bad, as an inherent need of human life. Finally, the acknowledgment of the purposive nature of all living processes, and the conscious formulation of ideals, goals, and plans as being an essential carrying over of natural teleology into the development of man. By entering into purposes that transcend the limits of any single life, sometimes of any historic period, man endows his own limited needs and values with a meaning that outlives their temporary satisfaction or their equally temporary defeat.

5: THE ORGANIC HIERARCHY

Man's goods spring directly out of his vital and social needs, even before he elaborates the cultural forms and the personal values that widen their province in life and ensure their continuity. At their point of origin, these needs are on the same level: some may be more imperious than others, but they all work equally for the maintenance of the organism and keep it in the state of dynamic equilibrium necessary for growth and self-fulfillment.

Within the body itself there is a hierarchy of functions, however, and this hierarchic order leaves its imprint on many remoter areas of life. There are, for instance, supernumeraries, like the appendix and tonsils, trusty domestic servants, like the stomach and bowels, willing manual workers and clerks, like hands and legs; and their status and office are well defined. One may get along famously without one's tonsils; and reasonably well without an arm or a leg; but if one is deprived of even a square inch of the frontal cortex, the entire organism may be thrown completely out of adjustment. There is no question as to what is the dominant function in the body, or in what direction the organic hierarchy leads. The highest functions are those of the nervous system; and they culminate in the over-developed and still only partly used organ that is responsible for the effective working of the whole. Common American speech recognizes this fact, when responses are tardy or reflexes fumble, in the sharp admonition: "Use your head!"

Ethical conduct affirms this organic hierarchy of functions in the body and develops it further, in application to the person and the community, by discriminating between higher and lower ends. Unfortunately, at this point one historic doctrine after another has been tempted into a too easy solution based on the simple dualism between body and soul. This overlooks the fact that it is within the body itself that the qualitative difference between higher and lower is first established. Nietzsche sought to make high the equivalent of "high caste": whatever people of birth and breeding and aristocratic purpose proclaimed as fit for their own kind; while for him the low consisted in the values to which the poor, the humble, the conquered clung.

Both distinctions are false, for the natural hierarchic order cuts under such factitious historic divisions. The human organism functions well only when the subordinate organs are in harmony with the higher processes, not in a state of mute resentful rebellion. Between the lower and higher centers a continuous traffic goes on: the first supplies energy and vitality, feeling and emotion, to all that the mind undertakes, thus enlisting the active aid of the whole organism; the second makes use of its special capacity for abstraction, symbolization, co-ordination, and vigilant anticipation to bring the organism into fuller relation with other men, with the environment, and ultimately with more universal processes.

Now, the dominance of the lower functions by the higher ones is always fitful and uncertain: the conscious, rational mind, established later than the lower functions, is like a wise ruler, resisted by his unruly subjects, who would prefer to be left alone in their gross customs, without having their attention directed to great projects for the improvement of the whole community, to which they will have to contribute their taxes and their work. A drink of gin or a depressing sight may impair the finest kind of mental creativity: fatigue, pressure, repetition, may reverse the natural order and put the subordinate organs or the reflexes in a position of control. This explains the humiliating fact about illness: that it upsets the natural dominance of the higher functions. The diseased organ, the lung or heart or liver, often takes possession of the whole personality and overpowers it, putting the mind itself at the service of the ailment. Thomas Mann exquisitely revealed this transmogrification in The Magic Mountain.

Judged from the standpoint of survival, the most indispensable life-need, and therefore in one sense the surest good, is air: if deprived of air for as little as three minutes, most men will die. Suppose, however, one were granted five hundred years of continuous life on the sole condition that all one's natural functions were paralyzed and one were kept "alive" in an iron lung, committed to the single function of breathing—who would not reject life on those terms? Air is indeed vital to man; but not for the sake of more air. When the brains of the aged begin to break down, they sometimes maintain a vegetative existence, without memory or hope; and with what lingering spark of mind remains they will often resent this state as life's final indignity: they eat, they breathe, they move, often in perfect health: but in a meaningless world. That is neither life nor happiness.

"Happiness," as that wise old observer of life, John Butler Yeats, once put it in a letter (1909), "happiness is neither virtue nor pleasure nor this thing nor that, but simply growth. We are happy when we are growing." To that observation an ethics of development would add one further note: the means for continuous growth are provided, not in the physical organism as a whole, but in the higher functions. Up to the point that bodily deterioration undermines the higher functions, their expansion and renewal are the main conditions for a good life: a life of increasing sensitiveness, deeper love, richer meaning.

The essence of wisdom, then, is to pay sufficient attention to the lower functions to ensure their fullest contribution to the whole process of growth; but not to allow them to usurp the place of the higher functions or to disrupt the whole. Any special attention one may pay to the lower functions—as in fortifying the body by hard exercise— must be for the sake of giving more scope to the higher functions. But with reason, the ancient Athenians disparaged the professional athlete, whose personality became an appendage to his muscular skill; hence indeed their distrust for all forms of specialization, which give to a single function the over-riding place that reason alone, in their scheme, should occupy.

Does one solve the ethical problem, then, simply by arranging the goods of life in a vertical order, as Plato did in The Laws, observing that "the right way is to place the goods of the soul first and highest in the scale, always assuring temperance to be the condition of them; and to assign the second place to the goods of the body and the third place to money and property"? This seems a convenient practical division; but it is in fact an imperfect one; for it fails to do justice to the need for organic harmony or to suggest any principle for achieving it: even more serious, its order is a static one and does not provide for those occasions when the lower functions must be in ascendancy to restore balance. Christian doctrine, for example, followed Plato closely in differentiating between higher and lower qualities: so far well. But in the Christian's extravagant pursuit of disembodied virtue he often upset the unity of the personality, causing inner division and neurosis: so much so that Ignatius Loyola, that subtle and wary psychologist, was always quick to caution novices against excessive zeal in mortification, as no less hostile to spiritual perfection than over-indulgence.

The servile functions exist for the sake of the self-governing ones: the automatic and habitual for the selective or spontaneous: the reflexes for the sake of the released functions, which lend themselves to art and thought: so much is clear. But the higher can no more do without the lower than the lower can do without the higher, or rather somewhat less: for the physical body often survives in old age when all the higher processes of thought and emotion have disappeared. If the lower self must not dominate the higher, neither must the higher seek to extirpate the lower: for at that moment it removes the energies needed for its own propulsion. The increasing dominance of the higher functions, which is the condition for all truly human development, is not for the sake of suppressing the lower functions, but of using them more fully for ends that they themselves cannot encompass; for choices that, left to themselves, they could not make.

In short, the meaning of hierarchic organization in both the person and in society is to secure conditions favorable to freedom: to release the person from automatism and give him an increasing degree of self-direction. Freedom for man in large part is an effort to escape the age-old stereotypes of his lower functions and to exercise constant choice and discrimination: what applies in the personality applies also in the community. In no sense does freedom mean the casting off of restraints, the destruction of inhibitions, or the denial of duties and responsibilities. Man loses his freedom through poverty, ignorance, and disease; and again, he may lose his freedom through the over-development of a single organ or function, or through over-commitment to mechanical or social processes not under the control of the personality. That is why money and property, up to a certain point, are as much a condition for the development of the human personality as direct access to the non-material elements in a culture, and to pretend that their absence does not matter is hypocrisy or dishonesty.

In view of man's hierarchic internal organization of needs and functions, the place of freedom in the moral life becomes plain. Man is not born free: at the moment of birth he is the helpless prey of his reflexes, and the passive recipient of the conditions imposed on him by his family and his culture. He can exercise no initiative: make no decisions. His education, up to the point where it meets arrest, is a slow induction into the possibilities of freedom: a transfer of restraint from the outer world to the inner man, and a progressive increase of choice, as intelligence and experience and imagination widen the range of his vision and increase the number of alternatives before him. Increasing selectivity and increasing self-direction are the rewards of man's capacity for freedom: and all his organic processes are so arranged, as Coghill and Angyal have shown, as to assure the ultimate dominance of the higher over the lower functions and to make the life he thereby develops an infinitely more rewarding one than that which other creatures, or men themselves at a lower stage in their development, have been able to live.

Even a purely physiological analysis of man's behavior, then, establishes the fact that there are higher and lower goods; and that the higher goods are those leading toward freedom and multiple choices, toward esthetic sensitivity and symbolic interpretation, toward the domination of the parts by the whole and the subordination of organic functions to a guiding purpose: in fine, toward the creation of a meaningful and valuable world. The slightest impairment of activity in the forebrain, either through drugs or overt injury, first destroys the symbolic functions and the ability to co-ordinate, as Goldstein and von Monakov have demonstrated: the world becomes less meaningful and less valuable: along with this goes a breakdown of inhibition, that capacity upon which all positive choices are based.

One of the reasons, perhaps, why there has been a widespread ethical disintegration in our whole civilization is that we have created an interlocking machinery of schools, factories, newspapers, and armies that have artificially destroyed the higher centers, have impaired the power of choice, have reduced the symbolic functions to an almost reflex level, and have removed the capacity to co-ordinate from the person to the machine process: the whole system powerfully re-enforced by narcotics and other drugs, from alcohol and tobacco to marijuana, cocaine, phenobarbital and aspirin. The utopia of the conditioned reflex.

The final degradation in this dethronement of the higher functions consists in the systematic confusion of names, which both Nazism and Stalinist communism have cunningly employed. By the same token, the first step toward freedom will be a new respect for the symbol, a purification and clarification of language itself, an abstention from unclean slogans and conditioned verbal reflexes. The death of the advertising agency and the propaganda bureau will be one of the surest signs of the birth of a new society.

6: THE CONTROL OF QUANTITY

The constant discrimination between good and bad, and the unremitting pursuit of goodness are vital requirements for human development. He who would deny the importance of these efforts would abolish man's very humanity. To substitute power for goodness is simply to turn a single aspect of life into an absolute: an error which denies the essential fact about life, that all its functions and goods are inter-related and organically conditioned by each other. The obligation to recognize the good and to pursue good is absolute. But goods themselves are relative: each has its time, its place, its function, in the economy of the whole. If goods must be chosen and pursued with respect to their ultimate capacity to raise the level of human development, they must also be chosen in the right order and the right quantity.

While qualitative discrimination is essential it is not enough: there must be quantitative discrimination at the same time. In addition to affixing a plus or minus sign to all experience, one must add a numerical indicator for "how much?" Now the present age with its scientific background and its pervasive money accountancy takes pride in the fact that it is quantity-minded: yet both piety and cynicism have, from quite different motives, overlooked the radical way in which goodness is conditioned by quantity. Both the absolute pacifist, unwilling to take any life, and the complete nihilist, contemptuous of all life, unite, for example, in their refusal to admit any difference between the restrained and directed violence of war and the unlimited violence and random extermination of genocide, as practiced in so-called obliteration bombing, whether by incendiary bombs or atom bombs. But just as the practice of enslaving prisoners was morally superior to killing the victim outright, so war itself, even in its insanely destructive modern forms, is still morally preferable to random extermination and random destruction. War at least limits the area of violence and murder to designated, identifiable groups. Genocide knows no limits of any kind: it accordingly flouts the dictum Kant uttered in his Essay on Universal Peace, that one should never employ a method in war that would make it impossible to make peace with one's enemy. Here the absence of quantitative judgment has led to further debasement; for to kill a million men is not the same as to kill a thousand men: it is precisely a thousand times worse.

The pursuit of the good involves one in constant estimations of quantity; and the disciplined control of quantity is therefore one of the marks of the maturing person. The vulgar hold that one cannot have too much of a good thing; but their own experience, if only they reflected upon it, would show that this is untrue. Whether a thing is good or bad often depends in no small measure upon how much of it one takes or consumes or does. Over-indulgence in the appetite for food or drink or sexual intercourse is normally, in due time, self-correcting: indigestion, headaches, lethargy, impotence curb the overdriven impulse and restore the organic balance. There are, however, as Herbert Spencer observed long ago, people who indulge themselves unduly in scientific pursuits; people who, like Darwin, on his own pathetic confession, let their emotional responses dry up, in their very concentration upon one of their higher functions alone. So even the higher goods, if quantitatively overdone, can turn into their opposite: a fact Plato recognized when he said that "temperance must be a condition of them." The virtuous must occasionally recall The Preacher's sanative injection: "Be not virtuous overmuch: why shouldst thou destroy thyself?"

Now both Confucius and Aristotle were aware of the need for quantitative discrimination as one of the chief components of an active mode of ethics: both the Greeks and the Chinese observed the doctrine of the Golden Mean: they were wary of extremes, even in matters that were excellent and estimable in themselves. But to be golden the mean must be no mere mathematical mid-point: the useful mean takes into account the time, the place, the circumstance, the organic capacity. By causing men to follow its general counsel of moderation, this doctrine helps to rectify in some degree even qualitative misjudgments; for evil, if not manifested in inordinate amounts, can be assimilated and overcome.

The doctrine of the mean, however, is subject to one correction: it must in practice be limited by its own canon. There is a golden mean even in applying the golden mean; for to reduce every action and every impulse to a nicely regulated not-too-little-not-too-much is to overlook those occasions when, in the interest of an eventual equilibrium, one must abandon this too-even form of control. As a rule, eight hours of work is more than enough for a day, and in some professions, like writing, possibly twice too much. But in an emergency one must work around the clock, and if one held back in the interests of moderation one would forfeit the very life one seeks to conserve. There are often brief periods in life—military combat or creative work in art or science—when to live a balanced and harmonious existence is impossible: at those moments, moderation itself becomes the dangerous extreme. In so far as ethics provides a sound guide to living, it must have life's own attributes: its pliability, its adaptiveness, its sensitiveness to the occasion. "Wisdom," old Theognis said, "is supple: folly keeps a groove."

Now modern civilization, during the last three centuries, has given itself over to quantitative production, and has thrown off the natural limits that once existed on the food supply, the birth-rate, the amount of power a single individual could exercise or detonate. As a result, the control of quantity has become one of the dominant moral problems of our age: a problem all the more difficult to solve because we have treated our permissive ability to remove quantitative limits as a command. At every stage of production we enlarge, we expand, we multiply, we accelerate: but we lack both the will and the means to direct the instruments we have created in the interests of life; and when they threaten life, to contract them and to bring them to a halt.

Precisely because we are now capable of inundating the planet with more human bodies than we can nourish, with more printed matter than we can assimilate, with more knowledge than we can apply intelligently, our whole culture is in the position of the Sorcerer's Apprentice: we do not know how to decrease or to turn off the power we once fatally invoked, and can now only increase. Until we master that lesson, all life is in danger.

In short: qualitative discrimination and selection and quantitative control are both essential elements in an ethics of development. Where their practice is not deeply ingrained in custom and habit and conscious self-direction, a disordered life will result. Who in our time has not witnessed and participated in this disorder?—often with a false feeling of emancipation and pride, coming directly from the fact that we had overthrown old rules and norms on the supposition that they had no place in a universe interpreted by the sciences. And one does not have to seek far to detect such sinners: one need only honestly examine one's own life. Once the constant need for discrimination and self-direction is admitted, as an unfailing condition for a truly human life, every day becomes a day of reckoning.

CHAPTER VI.   BEYOND MORAL AMBIGUITIES

1: "MODERN MAN CAN DO NO WRONG"

"Is it not evident," wrote the painter, Eugène Delacroix, a century ago, "that progress, toward good or toward evil, has brought society to the edge of an abyss into which it may very well fall, to make way for a state of complete barbarism?"

Actually, our age now hovers on the verge of that abyss: part of our society has already plunged into it; and the condition of man therefore calls for radical improvement. Unless that improvement touches every part of our culture, reversing the movement of many dominant forces, transforming our institutions, above all, producing an inner change in men and women that will radiate in every direction, a more complete disintegration may come about. Now that certain life-preservative taboos have generally broken down our present leaders would be capable, in a conflict between the nations, of turning the whole planet into a cindery radioactive waste, or into one vast plague-infested lazaretto, under the wholly insane conviction that a "victory" bought at this price would be worth the victor's having. Scores of bombed cities and millions of displaced persons, starved, bitter, hopeless, are prophetic witnesses to the possiblity of our creating a universal wasteland.

But the invisible breakdown in our civilization is more insidious, and possibly even more destructive: the erosion of values, the dissipation of humane purposes, the denials of any distinction between good or bad, right or wrong, the reversion to sub-human levels of conduct under the pretext that man's progressive emergence from his instinctual state has no significance. In a society whose values are still operative, the bad man knows that he defies society and his own better nature when he robs or kills or rapes: sometimes he even courts punishment after the act, because part of his self still accepts the standard his conduct has defied. In a nihilistic order there is a complete unonsciousness of guilt: who can indeed admit responsibility for evil cts, if he does not admit the existence of evil?

The social breakdown of our time has shown itself in at least three vays: philosophically, ethically, and politically. Philosophically, this reakdown has disclosed itself in the cult of general nihilism, a cult vhich rejects the reality of those fundamental discriminations between ood and bad, between higher and lower, that are the very bases of uman conduct. At first defacing only values, nihilism must, to remain theoretically consistent, also deny meanings, since meaning merges from human existence by the same process that creates and onfirms values: by providing consistent clues to life-furthering procsses and actions and states. The cult of Da-da, which took form in the wenties in esoteric intellectual circles, was the perfect symbol of this hilosophy: it treated all attempts at significant expression as pompous nd irrelevant. The final achievement of this nihilism, if it did not alt itself on its way to extinction by attributing to power the sole neaning of life, would be a stuttering helpless imbecility. Instead of oing that far, it debases every concept it touches: witness Nazi anhropology, Aryan physics, Stalinist science. The ultimate effect of elieving that values have no meaning is to proclaim that meanings ave no value. At that point the truth and the will-to-believe become ndistinguishable: even the capacity to lie effectively is lost.

Politically, our moral breakdown has taken precisely the turn predicted by Henry Adams fifty years ago, and by Oswald Spengler, with even more brutal realism, after the First World War. This state has rought with it the general debasement of justice, the disregard of aw, the attempt to concentrate power in a ruthless minority which, inder whatever convenient ideological mask, sometimes fascism, ometimes communism, sometimes capitalism or nationalism, seeks only to perpetuate the lethal conditions of its own existence. The notion hat justice is but a convenient disguise for naked power was formulated by Thrasymachus in Plato's Republic, echoing a popular thesis t the beginning of another period of violent social disintegration; and that same notion has now spread from active exponents, like Lenin and Hitler, to many lesser practitioners in our society.

Now, if those who govern are not bound by law, if they are not under continuous moral judgment, based on historic precedents and common human standards that transcend any particular social order or caste, then physical force will entirely displace moral authority, instead of merely supplementing it when the latter is too weak to prevail. As a consequence terrorism, torture, arbitrary compulsion, have already been elevated in many states into normal methods of political government, and every state tends to become a police state: witness the ominous growth and ubiquitous pressure of the Federal Bureau of Investigation in the United States: an agency whose operations are immune to public scrutiny and may presently, like those of its totalitarian counterparts, be beyond control.

The cult of nihilism thus tends to issue, by swift steps rather than slow, into a cult of violence and methodical terror, expressing a total contempt for life. And we should be deceived if we clung to the belief that these results have appeared only in totalitarian countries. In an active or latent state, nihilism is at work throughout our civilization.

This brings us to another set of symptoms that indicate the general breakdown in Western civilization. In many areas, we are now faced with the dissolution of long-established habits of communication, communion, and co-operation: the narrowing of intercourse to people of the same isolated nation, race, religion, or class: even the progressive disappearance of genuinely international congresses and meetings, at the very moment we create a vehicle, in the UNESCO, to produce the maximum amount of common effort among educational and scientific groups. Not merely has there been a wiping out of previously established collaborations: positive barriers have now been raised, of an even more impenetrable character: barriers which operate against the free interchange of opinions, the free rivalry of opposing beliefs, the free flow of ideas, to say nothing of more commonplace traffic that also acts as a solvent of prejudice and provinciality.

During the century before 1914 our planet had become, to a degree never achieved before, a single unit: indeed a worldwide community, beyond the limit of all previous empires and civilizations. An invisible network of equitable law and widely accepted custom covered the planet: the scholar, the financier, the actor, the harvest hand, the hotel waiter, the tourist, traveled in peace and security throughout the planet, without any other credential than the fact that they were human beings. Violence had become so petty, so sporadic, so unthinkable, that the hero of H. G. Wells's novel, The New Machiavelli, writing in exile, boasts that no despotic ruler could keep him from freely expressing his ideas. That illusion did not survive the First World War.

Now, in all organisms, upbuilding processes and breaking-down processes are constantly taking place. What is true of life in general, is likewise true of man's communal and individual life. There has never been a period, probably, when certain symptoms of moral weakness could not be detected: for even a stable, fully integrated society may, by its very stability, fail to meet the problems and pressures brought about by the need for further development, the most constant of all human needs. Out of its very rigidity such a society may contribute to moral relapses. Healthy organisms, moreover, may often show local impairments and deteriorations; yet, as in a body attacked by a fatal disease, the larger number of organs may, till the end, function vigorously and partly overcome the failure of the weak organ. Even today, possibly three-quarters of our society is still organically healthy.

Unfortunately the presence of this large amount of healthy social tissue is perhaps unduly reassuring: while the buildings show unbroken windows, while the trains run punctually, while the markets are still heaped with food, it is hard to realize that the forces of disintegration may already be getting the upper hand. But the fact is that the most disturbing symptom of disintegration is an inner one. What keeps men from recognizing the danger of their present state is not merely the old stereotypes of progress, but a more sinister belief, implicit if not avowed: *Modern man can do no wrong.* Unable to discriminate between good and evil, incapable of taking moral responsibility, unwilling to accept blame, confusing goodness with power and evil with impotence, turning a lurking sense of guilt over his sins into the only sin he will acknowledge—doing all this, modern man has undermined all his solid foundations. While the physical superstructure may still look sound, the underpinnings of value and meaning have been eaten away.

The healthy organs of modern society are happily still of service and may eventually help save us: fortunately there are still many sound institutions and virtuous people even in countries like Russia and Germany and Japan whose physical existence has been most severely impaired. But if we are to re-establish the foundations of our humanity, we must first re-acquire those essential capacities of feeling and discrimination that will direct men toward the right and the good and the spiritually profitable: in short, toward life. The conviction that "modern man can do no wrong" is the ethical source of his brutalities, his destructions, his self-contempt, his ultimate suicide.

2: CONDITIONS FOR MORAL RENEWAL

The conditions for re-establishing ethical values in our civilization are those under which conscious moral direction originally came into existence. As respects qualities, the first essential change in attitude is an increase in sensitiveness and fellow-feeling: the precise opposite of Nietzsche's inverted morality of the superman. Not *Be hard!* but *Be tender and sensitive.* In the most concrete and literal sense, the moral life needs mothering. To be in a condition to do well with one's fellows or to pursue one's own self-development, one must be touched to the depths by the impression our conduct makes on others: to feel sorrow when they are in grief, disappointment when they are frustrated, joy when they are uplifted: even to sympathize with their hostility and aggression, to the extent of being able to recognize how far one's own conduct shows similar traits and is in fact partly responsible for producing it. These are the first lessons of parenthood: without such love, the next step, toward self-discipline and responsibility, the acceptance of the super-ego, will not be made.

By contrast, the most deadly sin is that of cutting oneself off from other men. Brutality, unfeelingness, insensitiveness, isolationism, the paranoid rejection of fellowship, are the enemies of the moral life: hardness of heart, as every moralist has proclaimed, is another name for moral deadness. Common experience confirms this judgment: the worst crimes are those committed by people who, through ideological or chemical means, have blunted their natural responses. The very name assassin reminds one of those professional murderers who prepared for their crime by eating hashish, just as their modern counterparts in gangsterdom go to their violent rendezvous after taking cocaine or heroin. These extreme examples prove the conditions under which vice and crime normally flourish. Even hardened criminals may still do violence to their nature when they kill in cold blood. Only those who have spent time in a totalitarian extermination camp, or its equivalent—see Dostoyevsky's account of his Siberian imprisonment—know how low human conduct can sink through sheer hardness of heart.

But we must be equally on guard against insensitiveness that is promoted, not by drugs or by the animal effort to survive, but by ideological means. The fanatic Marxist who characterizes members of the bourgeoisie as vermin, like the Nazi who so characterized the Jews and the Poles, finds it easy to take the next step: to exterminate his victims like vermin. Even without warped ideological support, this hardness may be promoted by the psychological distance between cultures—the curse of imperialism—or even by the physical distance which permits aviators to drop bombs on innocent men and women, with no sense of any result except the pattern of the explosion: this is also to exterminate one's victims like vermin. The willingness to participate in cruelty and murder, when presented in mystery novels and radio programs and "comics" is not, it goes without saying, the only source of contemporary crime: but who can doubt that the mental habituation to violence so provided makes it easier to engage in both individual and collective crimes, or to turn our faces away, indifferently, when they are committed.

In the phase of disintegration, each civilization seems to find a special way of keeping to its downward course by reversing the values of life: unable to identify and promote the good, it embraces a variety of evils and calls them good. What the Roman gladiatorial spectacles did for the Romans, our age has achieved through motor races and plane exhibitions, designed to produce maimings and deaths, by wrestling matches and boxing bouts in which brutality is far more visible than sportsman-like skill, in concentration on more lethal weapons of war, instead of on measures that would produce co-operation and peace. But the first step toward moral renewal should be plain: we must overcome the present cult of callousness; and we must abandon the morality of the "dead pan," which characterizes our whole style of life, cutting off every warmer manifestation of human feeling and turning unemotionality and impassiveness into the only accepted values. Our fear of emotions, our habit of treating normal emotions as deplorably sentimental and strong emotions as simply hysterical or funny, betrays fundamentally our fear of life.

What our civilization needs today, as a condition for increasing human maturity and for inner renewal, is the cultivation of an exquisite sensitivity and an incomparable tenderness. . . . Unnameable horrors have paraded before us and worse evils threaten because we have been unable to wipe the blank stare of indifference from our stony tearless faces. We are too numb even to hate what is hateful. Lacking the capacity to feel, when feeling is an imperative condition for living on a human plane, we also lack the capacity for action. Those who most prided themselves on their absence of righteous anger and anxiety, when the Nazis threatened to subdue the world to their systematic barbarism, were precisely those who lacked even an animal sense of danger: their coolness and impassiveness betrayed their failure to recognize life's demands.

No nation perhaps is collectively hardened down to the level of its criminal or psychopathic elements. Even the German people, though steeped in a brutal authoritarian tradition, sought to hide from themselves the hideous practices of the extermination camps. But a tendency toward the psychopathic, if one may judge by the growing occurrence of vicious crimes in otherwise normal children and adolescents, is far more serious today than people ordinarily estimate. My own experience as a teacher in getting student reactions to situations that involved the acceptance or the moral reprobation of senseless criminal violence, makes me believe that perhaps as much as a third of our student population of college grade may, for all practical purposes, be considered moral imbeciles, or at least moral illiterates. So poorly have the moral values that still remain partly operative been transmitted to these students that they are potential, if not active, delinquents. Though they have been screened by intelligence tests and personality tests before entering college, they have not yet acquired the moral values and purposes that would enable them to function as fullgrown human beings. Masked by more adult habits that they share with the rest of the community, their values remain infantile, if not brutally criminal.

The qualities of vigilance and wakefulness were rightly emphasized by the Christian Fathers as essential to moral life: everything that induces anesthesia or lulls one to sleep is an obstacle to moral development. But to fortify sensitiveness still another quality is needed: sobriety. Not to be unduly elated at success, not to be unduly depressed by defeat, to preserve equanimity in the face of danger, and moderation and reserve in embracing wealth and good fortune: these are the characteristics of sobriety. They are symbolized for us by the figure of Socrates, he who could arise from the longest drinking bout with a steady head: he whose conduct at Potidaea, as described in The Symposium, was as untroubled as his behavior on the last day before his death. A sufficient increase in sensitiveness to re-establish moral values, without a proportionate strengthening of sobriety, might result in pain and anxiety that would nullify the capacity for effective response.

With sobriety go two other qualities needed for moral renewal. One of them is the cultivation of far-sightedness: the common-sense requirement for an effective attachment to ultimate ends and goals. Now ethical conduct often has its rewards and fulfillments in the present: it is an academic superstition to hold that it is always better to defer immediate satisfactions in favor of remote ones—as if the remote did not at some point become immediate. But far-sightedness is necessary in order to do justice to immediate goods in their proper order and to anticipate their probable consequences: the moral bankruptcy of Neville Chamberlain and the moral capacity of Winston Churchill, with respect to the immediate issues of war and peace in 1939, derived largely from the short-sightedness of the first and the far-sightedness of the second. The other necessary quality is timeliness. The good consists not only in the right quality in the right quantity in the right order: it must also be brought into action at the right time and place. Misplaced or inopportune virtues are often as much an obstacle to human development as positive evil would be.

But the overwhelming need to renew moral values in our civilization, and to establish, by nurture and education, the habits that grow out of them, should not lead us into the error of moralism. Conduct may be, as Matthew Arnold used to say, three-fourths of life; but the aim of ethics is not simply to promote good conduct: its essential aim is to further life; and this means something more than the capacity for ethical evaluations and acts. Here lies the mistake of all pharisee-ism and to some extent one of the recurrent errors of religion itself. The vigilant application of ethical norms is essential in every living function; but one misconceives this duty if one holds that goodness displaces every other kind of value: that for the sake of "being good" one may and should renounce love and marriage, art and science, sport and play. Such desert island virtue is as meaningless as it is easy.

The whole process of moral evaluation and choice and directed development is justified in the long run only by the sort of life it facilitates and the sort of personality it produces: but in that process something more than mere goodness is achieved. To live only to be good is to become goody-good. People whose life is confined to obeying the prescribed rules for conduct tend to belittle the very purposes for which ethics exists: that is, a life both more abundant and more significant. Such people, smug, placid, untormented by strong impulses, over-impressed by their own righteousness, too often lack any capacity to grow: thus, in their blameless existence, they may negate the very conditions that give meaning to moral evaluations and choices.

For this reason, an adequate ethics must not only enable one to embrace in due measure the concrete goods that life offers, instead of drawing back from them as wanton distractions: it must also find a place for the dynamic role of evil: since the goods of life, by a curious process of transmutation, often come forth from conditions that would seem to oppose them.

Such an ethic will accept denial and sacrifice in order to make possible the fullness of giving: that is why it usually comes into existence first, not among the prosperous and the satisfied, not in an "economy of abundance," but under conditions when men face death willingly together. This simple fact was well put by an American soldier in combat during the Second World War: "It's hard," he wrote, "for men who live only because they co-operate, to explain things to people who live only as semi-isolated individuals. A front-line soldier will almost always *give* you half of his last dollar or one of his last two cigarettes. An American civilian finds it hard to lend you half of his surplus." These men, facing death daily, knew that "you can't take it with you." Only the understanding acceptance of man's tragic destiny will make possible that wider giving and taking of love which will lead to man's further development. The knowledge of this fact was the essential strength of traditional Christianity: it is part of the ultimate wisdom of an ethics of development and fulfillment.

3: THE CHALLENGE OF EVIL

In most historic definitions of the good there is a tendency to affirm as a conclusion the very question one has asked. The old Stoic dictum, "Nothing but goodness is good," is only a caricature of every other definition: not excluding, of course, that which I have attempted to give. For the good, as Thomas Aquinas observed and as Aristotle taught before him, is in one sense the very property of life itself: "The good is being as an object of appetite." Life itself is its own blessing and when man appeared matter at last laughed. Taking life as the very core of goodness, the Greeks before Socrates naturally rated health as the supreme good of life, and after health, beauty. But this youthful over-emphasis on bodily delight unfortunately is too innocent to provide for all of life's occasions. Are no goods left when youth has disappeared and energy dwindled?

When one follows the full trajectory of life one must face the fact that human beings, even before life reaches the downward curve, often face painful crises and suffer penalties: we may encounter crippling accidents and fatal diseases, as well as consummations, gains, and fulfillments. An optimistic ethics, which makes health and prosperity the central, or even the supreme goods, becomes childishly bewildered and helpless when overtaken by bodily disaster. By contrast, a pessimistic ethics, deliberately embracing the bad in order to fend off something worse, partly fortifies the spirit, as Mithridates did his body, by taking a daily dose of poison. But by its own logic such an ethic is forced to assert that love is a snare, that joys are worthless because they vanish, and that prosperity is only a more subtle kind of misfortune.

Now, no matter how bad life may prove, we need an ethics that will do justice to its benign moments; and no matter how good it may become, we must still reckon with life's final undoing. With wise teaching and provident laws and improved technics we may abolish poverty, crime, and disease, or reduce them to minimal amounts, as Robert Owen once preached: that hope is a wholly legitimate one. But in some form, deviously if not directly, the forces of evil will still beset life, if only because there is a widening discrepancy, as man advances upward in the scale of being, between his own purposes and the lower order of nature.

These extraneous forces will threaten man's plans sometimes with the appearance of concentrated malice, such as enraged the soul of Captain Ahab, sometimes with the drooling inconsequence of an idiot giant whose fumbling hands may strangle a baby as easily as a mouse. An earthquake, a bolt of lightning, a raging fire, a falling meteor, a plague, a plane wreck, though they be events in an orderly and purposeful world, nevertheless cut across the path of some living creature's growth and development. From the standpoint of life, such happenings are senseless and evil: yet this not-goodness that overpowers goodness is closely bound up, at every stage, with man's existence. One can recognize all these facts without, like the fashionable existentialists, making a religion of that recognition. Evil, by its constant threat, introduces an element of tragic struggle into a world that would otherwise be in a state of effortless enjoyment, like some smiling Polynesian island; but by the very fact that it rouses life to fuller effort, it may be essential to human growth and renewal.

Are evil and good polar opposites, then, so intimately related that one could not exist without the other? Or are they, as Augustine thought, substance and shadow, so that evil is only the absence and dearth of the good; or are they each positive but not necessarily inter-dependent aspects of life? Or finally, is there something ambiguous in their character, which neither the doctrine of absolutism nor the doctrine of relativism sufficiently acknowledges? I put off this question for later discussion in order to deal with still another doctrine widely held today, that evil is merely a projection of fears and anxieties, and that, by proper psychological therapy, it may be removed from the mind and will therefore have no objective existence. This view was put forward, with no little acumen, by Mary Baker Eddy, who with psychosomatic insight even applied her philosophy to such bodily evils as disease. Since then it has been taken over, on a materialistic rather than a transcendental basis, by many psychiatrists, who would be somewhat embarrassed by this underlying association with Christian Science.

There is no doubt whatever that evils may have a subjective or psychal origin: but this fact in no wise lessens their reality; nor does it in the least prove that extirpation of a sense of guilt solves the problem of evil in any case except a neurosis. Evils that are of human origin require constant rectification; and the doctrine that "modern man can do no wrong," which so easily absolves him of all sense of self-condemnation, has the effect of increasing the social burden of evil by lifting responsibility from the shoulders of the evildoer. By that fact, it removes the impulse to repentance and self-correction, both essential for moral development.

Recently, an intelligent and earnest group of people in Texas resolved to come to grips with the cause of the domestic and international tensions that are visible today: they formed a co-operative group and enlisted aid from the outside, in their search for a method which would banish the fear and anxiety which, following current psychological fashion, they took to be the only source of positive evil.

The general premises of the Behavior Research Project can be summed up, in their own words, as follows: "If we are to reduce human fears in order to eliminate evil, we can no longer use the devices of blame and reprisal in our social action in community life. Blaming the other fellow (or ourselves) is further punishing the already insecure personality. This creates greater fear and generates more 'evil' counteractions. . . . If the problem of evil is the problem of fear, we must find the causes of fears, ease them, and thus triumph over evil." These premises are highly characteristic of the general attitude toward evil in our civilization: one which reduces life to a sequence of external causes and effects, and has no place for human reason and purpose; for, on these popular terms, reasons are merely rationalizations that cover brute impulses, and in a non-purposeful world, the means generate their own ends: "the going is the goal." The issues raised by this group were so general, that I will illustrate my point further by giving with slight amplifications my own comments on their inability to overcome their own inertia.

"The dilemma in which you find yourselves reveals, from my standpoint, what was wrong in your original approach and what, I fear, will vitiate your further work, unless you can bring yourselves to re-examine your original assumptions.

"The unexamined premise is, as you must know, the chief source of radical errors. Your unexamined premise is the belief, which seems to you axiomatic and unquestionable, that evil has only one source, fear, and therefore the simple, indeed the only way, to eliminate evil is to reduce fear. This for you, following many latter-day psychiatrists, means banishing any sense of guilt; and to do this effectively you must nullify the tendency to blame other people or even to blame oneself.

"I question this whole set of assumptions, including your notion that any evil that does not derive from fear is 'mystical,' that is, unreal or without objective foundation. You have closed your eyes to a large body of evidence when you define fear and evil in such narrow terms: you forget that both Greek and Christian culture, with a far longer experience of life than modern psychiatry, have attributed the chief source of sin, not to fear but to pride and self-love, which are only exaggerations of the constructive virtues of dignity and self-respect.

"Now even fear has a proper function in the organism, if it is fear of a real danger, not of an imaginary one; and similarly, blame has an effective part in the human economy, if he who is blamed has in fact committed a wrong action that greater conscientiousness or wakefulness might have avoided. In the extreme case you will of course acknowledge this: you will admit that no amount of love and fellow-feeling and psychological understanding should lead one to withhold reproach from, say, a locomotive engineer who has fallen asleep on the job and caused a wreck. Because all of us wish social approval in some degree, blame becomes a means of re-enforcing the super-ego, when it might flag in its supervision; or when, to protect himself from undue pain, a person might seek to anesthetize his conscience.

"An honest ethics, it seems to me, cannot attempt to lift the burden of guilt from one who has sinned or committed a crime. What it will seek to do, rather, is to appraise the evil that has been done, sensitively and understandingly; it will discourage excessive neurotic reactions to the normal errors, and be lenient or merciful to the extent that others have been implicated or must bear some of the burden of the guilt. Thus if the engineer fell asleep because he had been overworked by his superiors, the latter would share a large portion of the responsibility. But avoid fixing blame altogether? No. The truth is that people in our culture have a morbid tendency to avoid blame, because they do not wish to take the trouble to change their conduct in any way: blame-avoidance and blame-transference are therefore endemic amongst us. These are substitutes for repentance and renewal.

"In fine, the way to neutralize evil tendencies is not to deny the objective existence of evil or to avoid hating what is hateful and blaming what is blameworthy, but to accept the fact that we have in our own conduct the very tendencies we dislike and see so plainly in those who oppose us; and without abating our legitimate responsibilities to correct acts in others that need correction, to call upon our fellows in turn to help correct them in us. An ethics which seeks to promote good without recognizing any evil but that derived from fear, and which offers rewards without daring to inflict penalties, will prove a much more formidable obstacle to human co-operation than the systems it seeks to replace.

"Let us grant that some forms of evil must be treated as a remediable disease, as Samuel Butler first satirically suggested in Erewhon. But if all evils were of a purely neurotic origin, the psychotic's gifts for murder or torture would be indistinguishable from acts of love since they leave him with no sense of guilt or remorse. That is the *reductio ad absurdum* of your attempt to reduce evil to fear and to banish all blame and guilt: 'goodness,' on those terms, would merely be a name covering large areas of unacknowledged evil."

4: THE SALT OF LIFE

In practice, evil offers a dramatic contrast to good and heightens its quality, as vinegar or salt bring out the taste of food: the fact that life turns out to be a dramatic struggle, rather than a pageant, is due precisely to this constant clash of impulses and forces, within and without. But let us not repeat the common mistake of an exclusively dialectical analysis of this struggle: the value of the good is not positively increased by its negation. Food would be nourishing even if starvation never threatened one, and friendship would be rewarding even if enemies did not exist. Theoretically, then, one may easily conceive a world in which there would be only a choice of lesser or greater goods.

The dream of such a world of innocence and plenty, health and joy, has haunted man from the beginnings of his consciousness of pain and evil; and one finds it expressed in all the great literatures: in Hesiod's picture of the Golden Age, in Chuang-Chou's description of a similar state, and of course in the Biblical account of the Garden of Eden. Even now, this is the world that our more naive contemporaries believe we are on the point of establishing through the advances of medical science, mass production, and an "economy of abundance." A world in which every disease will be cured by magic drugs, every pain effaced by anesthetics, a world where no inordinate desire will exist that the industrial mechanism cannot gratify, since by sedulous training human beings will be conditioned to express no desires that cannot so be met.

So man might mature as the trees grow: self-contained, filling out his shape, never experiencing disharmonies, never encountering crises, wholly at one with himself and with his environment. William Morris, in News from Nowhere, conceived such a two-dimensional wallpaper world, without strong highlights and without depths; but he was honest enough to admit that the possibility of murder would remain. Indeed, in a letter written in 1874, his insight into the nature of evil in the human economy went even farther: "Years ago," he wrote, "men's minds were full of art and the dignified shows of life, and they had but little time for justice and peace; and the vengeance on them was not increase of the violence they did not heed, but destruction of the art they heeded. So perhaps the gods are preparing troubles and terrors for the world (or our small corner of it) again, that it may once again become beautiful and dramatic withal."

Even were the equable self-fulfillment of a Golden Age actually achieved, it would in its very perfection bring about a new kind of evil: it would arrest life and stultify it; for it would no longer produce the kind of disruption and conflict out of which higher forms of life become possible. The fact is that temporary chaos, if it does not harden into a pattern of disorder, may be more helpful to man's development than a regularity too easily accepted, a happiness and equilibrium too effortlessly achieved: it is not in the hothouse, under "ideal" conditions, that one grows life's most perfect fruit. If life is to escape the cycle of repetition and mere survival on a dull animal level, some measure of disintegration, as Lloyd Morgan pointed out, is essential to its higher emergence. The seed must be buried, the husk of the seed must rot, the body must die to its old habits and constraints, if a higher order of growth is to come forth.

In some sense pain and organic disharmony and psychological conflict, so far from being wholly deplorable accidents, are among the requisites for development: for growth is a state of unbalance on the way to a higher equilibrium. In this sense, crises are normal events in growth. Childbirth, teething, the first coitus, not merely painfully punctuate the successive phases of bodily maturity but have their parallels in the spirit. Graham Wallas collected a long list of biographies of exceptionally gifted people, whose opportunity for a more intense and fruitful development was furthered by illnesses or disabling accidents. Many of the experiences of life which one would avoid as evil, or at very least as damnably unpleasant, if one had the possibility of rejecting them, often turn out to be conditions for adequate growth. That is why those who have been able to assimilate their experiences in war usually have a far higher degree of maturity than those who never faced extreme hardship and terrifying danger. If one had life completely on one's own terms and lived it solely according to the pleasure principle, as people so often dream, it would probably turn out to be as vapid and empty as the historic lives of the ruling classes: lives so flavorless that the aristocracy, in their boredom, must provide themselves danger and difficulty in the form of polo or mountain climbing or duels of honor in order not to lose their appetites entirely.

This does not mean, however, that good and evil are everywhere quantitatively equal; or that they are the right and the wrong sides of the same coin, inseparable by nature. And it does not necessarily lead to the conclusion, to which Dr Reinhold Niebuhr comes in his Interpretation of Christian Ethics, that the possibilities of evil inevitably grow with the possibilities of good, so that "human history is therefore not so much a chronicle of the progressive victory of good over evil, of cosmos over chaos, as the story of an ever-increasing cosmos, creating ever-increasing possibilities of chaos." These are, no doubt, theoretic possibilities, and sometimes they have had historic existence: indeed, they would fit very closely in a "diagnosis of our own time." But there is no ground for thinking that such possibilities are constant necessities. On the contrary, viewing life as a whole, one may say that within its realm order has been on the increase and the realm of the good has widened. The complex symphonic order that life seeks is of a more unstable kind than the order of the physical universe; and precisely because it is so complex and so delicately balanced and timed, it carries with it the constant possibility of retrogression and complete disruption. So far Niebuhr is right.

But many communities that have freed themselves from leprosy and typhus have not merely decreased the quantity of evil from that particular source: they have at the same time lowered the general death rate. If the processes of improvement were as self-negating as Niebuhr makes them out to be, even such a temporary gain could hardly be expected. The whole case for ethical guidance, indeed, rests on the fact that both relatively and absolutely the quantity of good can be increased and the quantity of evil reduced. As I have said elsewhere, evil, like arsenic, is a tonic in grains and a poison in ounces: hence its decrease is a major goal of human effort. But all goods are perishable, and evils, like weeds, continue to spring up: so that every generation must continue its discriminations and persist in its efforts.

If there were not this difference in favor of the good, if, speaking mythically, the devil were fully the equal of God, and not an inferior power who schemes to overthrow his lord but never quite succeeds, there would be hardly any sense in preferring good to evil, since any gain in the first would only make the second more formidable. On those terms, life would be doomed to inescapable frustration. But that is like saying that the better a city is planned and built, the more slums it will show, or the more law-abiding citizens there are in a country the more criminals they will have to fight: propositions contrary to both reason and observed fact. (Thanks to good laws and vigilant moral discipline, it was once possible for Daniel Webster in all honesty to boast, so low was the rate of crime in mid-nineteenth century Massachusetts, that no householder had to lock his door at night.) Every assumption that the proportion of good and evil is unalterable must lead, as it has constantly led in Christian thought, to a doctrine of quietism: a false creed which, incidentally, is fatal to the pursuit of justice and the exercise of civic virtue.

Our second problem is whether moral principles are absolute or relative. That is an ancient theme in ethics; but the modern displacement of positive standards began in the eighteenth century with that representative philosopher, Denis Diderot: in some ways the first and the most admirable of the "moderns." In his annotated edition of

Shaftesbury he noted that "there is no moral principle, no rule of virtue whatever," that could not be contradicted by customs and conditions in some other race or climate of the world. The observation was true; but the implied conclusion was unsound.

This devaluation was founded on a romantic exaggeration of the importance of the surviving primitives; and it failed to distinguish between forms of life that are repetitive, stultifying, infantile, and the forms produced by the higher civilizations which, for all their sins and lapses, have tended toward development, maturation, emergence. Civilized man has indeed much to learn from primitive peoples; but those tribes and communities that differ most widely in moral values from the universal standards of civilization have contributed few important values to the rest of mankind. Against many minor departures from the common norm, which back up Diderot's dictum, one must place the much more significant fact that the majority of civilized people for the last three thousand years—billions as compared to a few poor millions—have lived by progressively universal principles, whose similarities are far more significant than their differences.

Within the great circle of the historic civilizations the main directions of morality have been well set: to follow customs and frame laws that regulate social relations, in order to make conduct predictable, instead of wholly erratic and self-willed; to respect symbols and conserve values; to refrain from murder, violence, and theft; to respect organized and sanctioned forms of sexual relationship; to nurture the young and stand by them as long as they are helpless; to tell the truth and to refrain from falsehood—though as to lies, violence, and thefts the Greeks of the Homeric poems were still a little shaky. This basic morality is in fact common to all human society: what distinguishes civilization is a heightened consciousness of the occasions for moral choice and a positive effort to extend the benefits of the moral code outside the community where it originated.

These, and many similar precepts and regulations, are deeply ingrained in the human tradition: they remain operative as long as that tradition is deliberately passed on from parent to child, from teacher to student, from master to disciple or apprentice. Customs and choices may, in minor respects, differ; but to have no customs and to make no choices—on the ground that obvious historic and natural differences make them all meaningless—is to be demoralized. So, too, to make any "original" departures from the common norm, such as

Nietzsche made when he extolled torture, is to open the way for such psychopathic conduct as Hitler and his followers practiced.

Plainly, some norms of conduct are better established than others: some are still reserved for in-groups and denied to the out-groups. But except in times of social disintegration (when they are widely rejected) these norms help to establish an essential part of man's humanness.

Now, none of mankind's present "absolutes" in morals existed from the beginning: man was not born, in his primitive state, with a special moral sense that enabled him to distinguish at once these universal principles. Each is the result of long-continued efforts, experiments, appraisals: trials that must still go on. By now, however, certain questions, like cannibalism or incest, are no longer open ones. The fate of the human race today depends largely upon our moral decision to place torture, war, and genocide under the same inviolable rule. Relativism, by its indifference to the universal, by its insistence that all goods are equally valuable expressions of local taste or ephemeral impulse, actually places itself on the side of the tribal, the static, the unprogressive: processes and states that obstruct human growth. Even the most hidebound ethical system is still more favorable to life than a relativism that denies the possibility of universal principles and stable standards, or whose one form of obligation is conformity to external change.

Good and evil nonetheless remain in an ambiguous relationship; and in interpreting their operation further we shall, incidentally, do justice to the element of truth in the relativist's position.

5: CHRONOMETRICALS AND HOROLOGICALS

Perhaps the classic statement of this two-faced role of good and evil is to be found in the novel, Pierre, by Herman Melville: a novel whose sub-title, The Ambiguities, underlines the discoveries that Melville himself made in the very course of writing it, and embodied in the paper attributed to the Transcendental philosopher, Plotinus Plinlimmon, a curious spiritual caricature of Hawthorne and Emerson.

The title of the paper, Chronometricals and Horologicals, points to the relationship between the absolute and the relative. Here Melville shows that in the modern world absolute time, as reckoned by the planetary movements, is set by the observatory at Greenwich; and every vessel setting out from London checks its ship's chronometer by Greenwich time. But by the time the ship reached, say, China, its captain would discover a startling discrepancy between his own accurate chronometer and the local clocks or sundials. If the captain tried to conduct the day's business by a schedule that kept to his own Greenwich time, he would be sleeping by daylight and making sociable calls when his Chinese neighbors were in bed.

So with the highest principles of conduct. Each generation, Melville observes, produces a few rare souls who try to guide their lives by heavenly time, and seek to make that absolute and universal: they are ready to sell all that they have and give to the poor, or to turn their right cheek when their left is slapped. But men in the mass live their lives by local time; they desire to reach heaven before giving all they have to the poor; although, as Melville ironically remarks, they will find it easier to practice this virtue in heaven, since there are no poor in that place. From the smug standpoint of the local time-observers, it is heavenly time that is wrong.

All this brings out a fact that Niebuhr has skillfully, indeed brilliantly, developed: that our ideals, however imperative and absolute, must nevertheless reckon with the fact that we live in the realm of the historically conditioned, subject to pressures and environmental limitations that cannot be entirely put aside. In other words, the moral ideal is a compass point, not a destination: while a fixed orientation to north and south is essential in order to find one's way to port, one may have to tack one's ship, now to the east, now to the west, in order to move in the general direction one has chosen; while if one sets one's course unconditionally to north or south, one will find oneself at last only in a polar waste. One steers by the fixed North Star, not in order to reach an ideal north, but in order to find a fair haven.

Pierre makes some of these discoveries for himself; but unfortunately neither he nor Herman Melville drew the correct conclusions. In his endeavor to confound the morality of prudence, exemplified by Pierre's worldly mother and her spiritual counselor, the Reverend Mr Folsgrave, Pierre brings disorder and disaster into the lives of all those around him: his "noble" unconditioned conduct, released from all traditional guidance, penetrates the patched garments of convention like an X-ray, only to attack the living flesh beneath. His mother, his new-found half-sister, his wife, and finally himself pay the penalty for his proud intransigence. In pursuing the absolute, with his eyes fixed only on the distant horizon, Pierre stumbles into deeper sloughs than he would have encountered if he had never raised his eyes from the ground and attempted merely to leap over the mud-holes that blocked his path, or pursued a circumspect course around them.

Wherein lay Pierre's radical error? Mainly in the fact that he forgot it is only at Greenwich—at an ideal point—that absolute and local time coincide. Worse, he forgot that once the Astronomer Royal leaves his observatory, he must keep time by an ordinary watch, an imperfect instrument which gains or loses time or flatly stops and must be wound up: such time will no longer coincide with astronomical observation, if he moves east or west of the meridian line.

Melville may be right in saying that the saints are those who live closest to this zero meridian; but that does not make them infallible in their daily living, nor does it condemn as untrue to Greenwich time the timekeepers that are followed in other lands, provided they have made their own corrections with reference to astronomical time. In other words, there is no abstract formula for virtue that yields an unconditioned result. What do Pierre's unconditional idealism or his sexual purity profit if they lead to frigidity and impotence, to hate and anguish, to misery and suicide? Melville was as wrong-headed as Pierre in his conclusions; and the black disaster that finally envelops his hero and those whom he loves was the natural climax to his error: repeated once more, in effect, in his personal life.

There is no virtue that may not, at any moment, turn into its opposite. Humility, pursued too steadfastly, may give rise to pride over its very achievement: Pierre's absolute integrity produces disintegration. "The good in goodness often find an enemy to dread," as an ancient Hindu scripture observes. By the same token, there is no vice so desperate, no impulse so depraved, that man may not out of his depths, by reaction, create an otherwise unattainable good. This explains Jesus's preference for the sinner to the Pharisee: it was not only that the sinner needed more urgently to be saved, but that, once saved, he would perhaps be a better man than his more studiously virtuous rival.

As essences, good and evil are poles apart: fixed poles. But in existence, they are the algebraic signs that indicate positive or negative quantities; and they change values as the symbols of life shift from one side of the equation to the other. Was not this the meaning of Emerson's Uriel: "Evil will bless and ice will burn"? These paradoxes and ambiguities in the moral life are well illustrated by two contrasting historic occasions: at Athens in the time of Demosthenes and in England in the days of Churchill. The Athenians, unable to depart from their beloved way of life, doomed themselves to defeat; whereas the moral readiness to face danger and death brought life to the British and reversed a long series of disasters, occasioned by their earlier unwillingness to encounter positive evil.

That change, as we know, brought compensations that other countries, which shrank collectively from making the same choice, did not share. The high morale of Britain after the war, with its equable system of rationing, "fair shares for all"; the resolute effort to cope with economic difficulties through the exacting discipline of the austerity program; the statesman-like surrender of its rule in India—all these positive moral gains were made possible by the original decision to accept death and destruction. As long as Britain sought safety and peace, its very life was in danger: as soon as Britain dared to face insecurity and even extinction, it was saved. That algebraic shift is a constant factor in the moral life: hence the need for unremitting watchfulness.

If fullness of life fits the positive definition of the good, this plenitude does not belong to life in its primeval innocence, overflowing with fresh animal spirits and radiant health: it comes only with knowledge of good *and* evil, with action on behalf of one and against the other. Ambiguously, though evil itself must be combated, diminished, forced into retreat, it enters the human situation as one of the conditions for life's highest fulfillment. Evil and good are both phases in the process of growth and self-realization: who shall say which is the better teacher? In other words, the very forces which, if triumphant, would destroy life are needful to ripen experience and deepen understanding.

Those who aim at a particular good, are often carried to their destination by the very path they consciously seek to avoid. In achieving a life abundant, accordingly, success lies not in altogether escaping evil, but in being able to turn the negative forces to the account of the personality itself. For those unprepared to cope with evil, life's injurious moments count only as a dead loss. But once evil is accepted, as an element as much in the run of vital processes as waste and fatigue, the law of compensation may operate; and in energizing the spirit evil may—as Helen Keller's life reminds us—sometimes give back more than it has taken.

The good, then, is that which furthers growth, integration, transcendence, and renewal. Evil, by contrast, is that which brings about disintegration and de-building, arrests growth, creates a permanent unbalance, dissipates energy, degrades life, baffles and frustrates the spirit, and prevents the emergence of the divine. Not sin but indifference, not erroneous knowledge, but skepticism, are the chief aids of the destroyer.

The concepts of growth, emergence, and transcendence take us far in the interpretation of human life: but they provide no terminus for human effort; and in that sense, even if life went well at every stage, they would leave each of us with a tantalizing sense of incompleteness and non-fulfillment, an endless stirring and striving, without any goal except a provisional one: a continued ascent of pinnacles that revealed only further peaks to climb. But actually, at least in human life, a provisional stopping place is provided, in the sense that one may have momentary glimpses of the end of the journey and of all that one could accomplish if one had endless days to command. The need for some such finality undoubtedly has led to the conjuring up of eternal heavens: mirages of unqualified beatitude, enjoyed forever; but there is a more functional interpretation of this idea of heaven which places it, not in a period after death, but in the midst of life itself.

Mary Boole remarked that "anything which seems to you worth doing you will never be allowed to do long: 'pour vous empêcher de routiner.' " This is true of all man's most intense or highest experiences: from the delight of a common orgasm with one's beloved to the joys of intellectual illumination. But it is in such moments that life seems irradiated in every direction: moments detached from all preparatory activity or further result, moments so intensely good in themselves, so complete, so all-satisfying that neither further emergence nor transcendence seem needed, since they are present in the experience itself. These are the moments when art seems poignantly to encompass all of life's possibilities, or, by the same token, when life reveals the significances of art.

Without such consummations, without such precious moments, man would be but the traditional donkey, flayed by a stick behind, lured by a deceptive carrot in front of him. To be alert to seize such moments of high insight, unconditioned action, and perfect fulfillment is one of the main lessons of life: endless activity, without this detachment and contemplation and ultimate delight, cannot bring life's fullest satisfaction. What man creates in art and thought justifies itself, not only by contributing to life's development and the emergence of new values, but by the production of significant moments. Those who have encountered these moments, who have held them close, can never be altogether cheated or frustrated, even by life's worst misfortunes or by its untimely curtailment. An education or a general mode of life that does not lead—though by indirection—to such moments and heighten their savor, falls short of man's needs.

6: REPENTANCE AND RE-AFFIRMATION

We are now prepared to understand the significance of the Jewish-Christian insight into the nature of evil: in particular, its perception of the fact that the assumptions that man is naturally good or that he may, by trusting entirely to scientific thought and technical invention, avoid any contamination of evil, are both illusions. Evil is as much a part of human existence as entropy, or the running down of energy: in one sense, it is the human counterpart of entropy and chance, breaking down organization, direction, and purpose. In this respect, Greek philosophers, who took pride in their own goodness even when they denied the certainty of truth or the usefulness of positive science, and humanistic philosophers of the eighteenth century type, who believed that man was born good and was corrupted only by external institutions and wily authorities, both failed to take in the facts of existence.

Unfortunately, the illusion that man is naturally good and can at will avoid evil is almost as much an obstacle to human development as the philosophy that man is naturally bad and cannot, by any efforts of his own, attain to the good: both of them leave human nature in a static condition, incapable of achieving wisdom through trial and error or reflective insight into its own actual nature. In a time of social disintegration, both these interpretations of the dynamic interaction of good and evil not merely share the field: they impede the necessary transformation of personal conduct and social plans. For the fact that evil is a constant element in life does not mean that one must submit to it; but it means that, if one is to get the better of it, one must acknowledge it, and above all, one must repent of it—repent in the literal sense of changing one's attitude and turning away.

As a protection against altering their ways, modern people tend to recoil from the very word sin: they will not admit, first of all, that they are capable of sinning, and they regard a sense of guilt as an unfortunate mental disturbance that should be removed, as promptly as possible, by a psychoanalyst. These blameless people, in their massive serenity and self-complacence, are probably a greater block to the renewal of life today than the most brutal dictators, whose nefarious designs often awaken the very opposition and struggle that produce change. It was the blameless statesmen, too rational to entertain a conviction of sin—the Blums, the Benešes, the Chamberlains—who led their contemporaries into appeasement and surrender: it was a good and upright man, an exemplary citizen, Henry L. Stimson, sure that his own decisions were untainted by evil, who not merely sanctioned the use of extermination bombing but even after there was time for reflection continued to justify that infamous policy.

These blameless ones do not repent: in a mood of fervid self-justification they continue their follies and magnify them. That rigid sense of self-righteousness, with its inability to confess the evils it commits and bring them to an end, is perhaps the chief mark of a dying civilization. If it could admit the possibility that it was on the wrong course, and that every extra effort only hastened the moment of destruction, it would be able to change its direction. Not wishing to be other than they are, the blameless ones, in their self-love, cannot conceive the real alternative: another self, cleansed of guilt and freed from folly, capable of renewal.

This general sense of blamelessness has been abetted, in our time, by the fact that our most extravagant sins, perhaps, are less sins of violence than sins of inertia. There have perhaps never before been such a large number of people in the world who live blameless lives: people who work regularly at their jobs, support their families decently, show a reasonable degree of kindness to those about them, endure colorless days, and go to the grave at last without having done active wrong to a single living creature, except the god within themselves. The very colorlessness of the existence of such people—like the colorlessness of sea water in small quantities—conceals the collective blackness of their conduct. For this kind of sin consists in the withdrawal from more exacting opportunities, in a denial of one's higher capacities: in a slothfulness, an indifference, a complacence, a passivity more fatal to life than more outrageous sins and crimes. The passionate murderer may repent: the disloyal friend may regret his faithlessness and fulfill his obligations of friendship: but the mean sensual man, who has obeyed the rules and meticulously filled out all the legal papers, may glory in what he is—and that is a deeper misfortune; for it is in his name, and by his connivance, precisely because he sees no need for changing his mind or rectifying his ways, that our society slips from misfortune to crisis and from crisis to catastrophe. No wonder that Dante consigned these blameless ones to the Inferno—

those who were neither for nor against the good. The hell of our times is in no small part of their making.

On this matter, Christian theology has perhaps shown a more profound insight than any other religion or philosophy; and though the essential doctrines relating to evil, sin, repentance, and renewal are too often set aside in the Churches today on the ground that they affront modern man, proud of his neutral, scientific, sinless world, these insights constitute the living core of Christianity, which every fuller synthesis must make use of. The fact is we must admit the constant possibility of sin, at every stage of life, indeed at every moment: partiality, narrowness of vision, self-seekingness, rigidity, miscalculation, stiff-necked pride, involuntary involvement with evils that carry one along in their surge, as an innocent man may be caught in the midst of a homicidal mob—all these have us in their grip. In our civilization, the very impersonal forces that preside over so much of our destiny implicate each of us, almost automatically, in sinful acts. Whether we are conscious of it or not, prisoners are mistreated, insane people are neglected, poor people are allowed to starve, beastly weapons of genocide are manufactured, and a thousand other evil acts are committed, not without our connivance. We are involved in these sins and can correct them only if we confess our involvement and take upon ourselves personally the burden of correcting them.

If the men who misguided France during the fatal decade that ended with the surrender of France to Hitler could have had the courage publicly to confess and repent, they might have brought back the general capacity to think and act in a more heroic mold. If the men who misguided America since 1945, giving away the fatal secret of the atomic bomb by exploding it, full of misplaced confidence in atomic and bacterial weapons of genocide, failing to place our full force and authority behind the United Nations, following the wholly negative policy of "containment" toward Soviet Russia, could have confessed their sins, at any moment we might have made a new start, on a basis that might have brought the world into measures of co-operation still unthinkable. Instead, they magnified the enormity of their military errors and their moral guilt—their lack of even a self-preservative life-sense —by commissioning the manufacture of the hydrogen bomb.

If resistance to such an inner transformation continues, our whole civilization will harden further in the very mold that will paralyze what benign forces remain and prevent us from escaping a worldwide catastrophe. Only people strong enough to admit their constant tendency to err and sin will be capable of finding new paths: only those who confess their sins will be re-activated sufficiently to attempt the transformation that must now take place in every institution, in every group, in every person.

But the negative side of this change is not enough; for no one can really turn aside from evil unless he has some positive vision of the good. Alongside repentance goes a process too often overlooked: the re-affirmation of virtues and goods. No more than evil can goodness be taken for granted. One cannot hold fast to any good and hope that it will remain intact, like a buried treasure: the best tradition, the happiest state, will dry up and disappear unless one constantly reviews it, replenishes it, and re-affirms it. Nothing that we do by routine and habit is safe from corruption. In order to keep old truths alive, we must re-think them, every year and every generation, testing them in the light of further experience, altering the very terms and words with which we express them in order to be sure that our thought is still active and dealing with realities. In order to keep good institutions in operation, we must re-dedicate ourselves to them, correct the errors time constantly discloses in their workings, even deliberately break up regulations and conventions that are about to crystallize to a point where they resist human intervention.

Without a poignant consciousness of the goods of life, in all their freshness and intensity, without some daily glimpse of beauty, some expression of tenderness, some stir of passion, some release in gaiety and laughter, some quickening of rhythm and music, our very humanity is not safe. To summon up the courage to go through our daily tasks, above all in a Time of Troubles, where no goals can be reached without sacrifice, we must remind ourselves, by conscious daily dedication, of the goods we desire and value. This dedication is perhaps the psychological core of prayer; and every concrete expression of the good, in a song or a symphony, a poem or a loving embrace, has some of the quality of prayer. There is no creation, in the end, except in the mood of love; and if we are impotent to love, the mere recounting of our sins will leave ashes in our mouths and cinders in our eyes.

Indeed, in the process of making over our lives, so that a new pattern, more favorable to growth and renewal, may be designed, we shall not merely re-appraise but re-savor all life's multifarious goods: making the most of them, no longer snatching and filching them with a sore conscience or a sense of personal inadequacy and positive shirking. For the final effect of repentance and affirmation is a fresh appetite for life, all the keener for the fastings, abstentions, renunciations that must necessarily precede it. The pain of rebirth will turn, on delivery, into a shout of joy. The fellowship of those who have experienced renewal will be written on their faces: in a good-humored patience, and tenderness, in an outer resolution tempered by an inner mirth.

CHAPTER VII.　　　THE FULFILLMENT OF MAN

1: THE FALLACY OF SYSTEMS

Most ethical philosophies have sought to isolate and standardize the goods of life, and to make one or another set of purposes supreme. They have looked upon pleasure or social efficiency or duty, upon imperturbability or rationality or self-annihilation as the chief crown of a disciplined and cultivated spirit. This effort to whittle down valuable conduct to a single set of consistent principles and ideal ends does not do justice to the nature of life, with its paradoxes, its complicated processes, its internal conflicts, its sometimes unresolvable dilemmas.

In order to reduce life to a single clear intellectually consistent pattern, a system tends to neglect the varied factors that belong to life by reason of its complex organic needs and its ever-developing purposes: indeed, each historic ethical system, whether rational or utilitarian or transcendental, blandly overlooks the aspects of life that are covered by rival systems: and in practice each will accuse the other of inconsistency precisely at those imperative moments when common sense happily intervenes to save the system from defeat. This accounts for a general failure in every rigorously formulated system to meet all of life's diverse and contradictory occasions. Hedonism is of no use in a shipwreck. There is a time to laugh and a time to weep, as The Preacher reminds us; but the pessimists forget the first clause and the optimists the second.

The fallacy of systems is a very general one; and we can follow its ethical consequences best, perhaps, in education. The moral becomes equally plain, whether we consider a fictional or an autobiographic account. One thinks, for example, of Sir Austin Feverel's system in Meredith's The Ordeal of Richard Feverel. Full of reasoned contempt for the ordinary educational procedures of his culture, Sir Austin contrives a watchful private system, designed to avoid current errors and to produce a spirited, intellectually sound, thoroughly awakened, finely disciplined young man. But the system-maker had not reckoned upon the fact that a young man, so trained, might, as the very proof of the education, fall in love with a young girl not duly accounted for in the system and elope with her in marriage; and that when the system intervenes in this marriage in order to carry out its own purposes, it would bring on a far more harrowing tragedy than any purely conventional mode of education, less confident of its high intentions, less set on its special ends, would have produced.

Or take an even better case, none the worse for being real: the childhood of Mary Everest, that extraordinary woman who eventually became the wife and helpmate of the great logician, George Boole. Mary's father was the devoted disciple of Hahnemann, the philosopher of homeopathic medicine; and he applied Hahnemann's principles, not merely to illness but to the whole regimen of life. Following strictly the master's belief in cold baths and long walks before breakfast, the system-bound father practiced upon his children a form of daily torture that drove Mary Everest into a state of blank unfeelingness and irresponsiveness. She hated every item in the strict routine; and her whole affectional and sentimental life as a young girl, in relation to her parents, was warped by it. The resentment she felt against this inflexibility and this arbitrary disregard of natural disposition is indeed still evident in the account she wrote at the end of a long life.

Believing blindly in the system, Mary Everest's father never observed what was happening to his beloved children in actual life: for the sake of carrying through the doctrine, he blindly disregarded the testimony of life and took no note of scores of indications in his children's conduct and health that should have warned him that he was working ruin. Every intellectually awakened parent who applied one or another of the rival systems in psychology and education that became fashionable during the last thirty years can testify out of his own experience, if he reflects upon it—or at least his children could testify—to the fallacy of over-simplification that is involved in the very conception and application of a system. Life cannot be reduced to a system: the best wisdom, when so reduced to a single set of insistent notes, becomes a cacophony: indeed, the more stubbornly one adheres to a system, the more violence one does to life.

Actual historic institutions, fortunately, have been modified by anomalies, discrepancies, contradictions, compromises: the older they are, the richer this organic compost. All these varied nutrients that remain in the social soil are viewed with high scorn by the believer in systems: like the advocates of old-fashioned chemical fertilizers, he has no notion that what makes the soil usable and nourishing is precisely the organic debris that remains. In most historic institutions, it is their weakness that is their saving strength. Czarism, for example, as practiced in Russia during the nineteenth century, was a hideous form of government: tyrannical, capricious, inwardly unified, severely repressive of anything but its own orthodoxy. But, as Alexander Herzen showed in his Memoirs, the system was made less intolerable by two things that had no lawful or logical part in it: bribery and corruption on one hand, which made it possible to get around regulations and to soften punishments; and skepticism from within, on the other, which made many of its officers incapable of carrying out with conviction and therefore with rigor the tasks imposed. In contrast, one may note in passing, the relative "purity" of the present Soviet Russian regime serves to buttress its inhumanity.

This tendency toward laxity, corruption, disorder, is the only thing that enables a system to escape self-asphyxiation: for a system is in effect an attempt to make men breathe carbon dioxide or oxygen alone, without the other components of air, with effects that are either temporarily exhilarating or soporific, but in the end must be lethal; since though each of these gases is necessary for life, the air that keeps men alive is a mixture of various gases in due proportion. So it is not the purity of the orthodox Christian doctrine that has kept the Eastern and Western Churches alive and enabled them to flourish even in a scientific age, but just the opposite: the non-systematic elements, seeping in from other cultures and from contradictory experiences of life: covert heresies that have given the Christian creed a vital buoyancy that seemingly tighter bodies of doctrine have lacked.

The fallacy of exclusive systems has become particularly plain during the last two centuries: never have their errors, in fact, proved more vicious than in our own time.

Since the seventeenth century we have been living in an age of system-makers, and what is even worse, system-appliers. The world has been divided first of all into two general parties, the conservatives and the radicals, or as Comte called them, the party of order and the party of progress—as if both order and change, stability and variation, continuity and novelty, were not equally fundamental attributes of life. People sought, conscientiously, to make their lives conform to a system: a set of limited, partial, exclusive principles. They sought to live by the romantic system or the utilitarian system, to be wholly idealist or wholly practical. If they were rigorously capitalist, in America, they glibly forgot that the free public education they supported was in fact a communist institution; or if they believed in communism, like the founders of the Oneida Community, they stubbornly sought to apply their communism to sexual relations as well as industry.

In short, the system-mongers sought to align a whole community according to some limiting principle, and to organize its entire life in conformity to the system, as if such wholesale limitations could do justice to the condition of man. Actually, by the middle of the nineteenth century, it had become plain that the most self-confident of the systems, capitalism, which had originally come in as a healthy challenge to static privilege and feudal lethargy, would, if unmodified by other social considerations, strangle life: maiming the young and innocent who toiled fourteen hours a day in the new factories, and starving adults wholesale, in obedience to the blind law of market competition, working in a manic-depressive business cycle. As a pure system, capitalism was humanly intolerable; what has happily saved it from violent overthrow has been the absorption of the heresies of socialism—public enterprises and social security—that have given it increasing balance and stability.

Now a system, being a conceptual tool, has a certain pragmatic usefulness: for the formulation of a system leads to intellectual clarification and therefore to a certain clean vigor of decision and action. The pre-scientific age of abstraction, as Comte originally characterized it, was a general period of un-knotting and disentanglement: the numerous threads that formed the warp and woof of the whole social fabric were then isolated and disengaged. When the red threads were united in one skein, the green in another, the blue and purple in still others, their true individual texture and color stood out more clearly than when they were woven together in their original complex historic pattern. In analytic thinking one follows the thread and disregards the total pattern; and the effect of system-making in life was to destroy an appreciation of its complexities and any sense of its overall pattern.

Such a sorting out of systems, with its corresponding division into parties, made it somewhat easier, no doubt, to introduce new threads of still different tones or colors on the social loom: it also encouraged the illusion that a satisfactory social fabric could be woven together of a single color and fiber. Unfortunately, the effort to organize a whole community, or indeed any set of living relations, on the basis of making every sector of life wholly red, wholly blue, or wholly green commits in fact a radical error. A community where everyone lived according to the romantic philosophy, for example, would have no stability, no continuity, no way of economically doing a thousand things that must be repeated every day of its life: left to spontaneous impulse, many important functions would not be performed at all. By whose spontaneous desires would garbage be collected or dishes washed? Necessity, social compulsion, solidarity play a part in real life that romanticism and anarchism take no account of.

Similarly, a community that lived on the radical principle, divorcing itself from its past and being wholly concerned with the future would leave out as much of the richness of historic existence as John Stuart Mill's father left out of his education: by cutting off memory, it would even undermine hope. So, too, a thoroughly Marxian community, where no one had any life except that provided by the State on terms laid down by the State would do away with the possibility of creating autonomous and balanced human beings: thus it would forfeit—as Soviet Russia has in fact forfeited—the generous core of all of Marx's own most noble dreams.

In short, to take a single guiding idea, like individualism or collectivism, stoicism or hedonism, aristocracy or democracy, and attempt to follow this thread through all of life's occasions, is to miss the significance of the thread itself, whose function is to add to the complexity and interest of life's total pattern. Today the fallacy of "either-or" dogs us everywhere: whereas it is in the nature of life to embrace and surmount all its contradictions, not by shearing them away, but by weaving them into a more inclusive unity. No organism, no society, no personality, can be reduced to a system or be effectually governed by a system. Inner direction or outer direction, detachment or conformity, should never become so exclusive that in practice they make a shift from one to the other impossible.

None of the existing categories of philosophy, none of the present procedures of science or religion, none of the popular doctrines of social action, covers the method and outlook presented here. Not personalism, not humanism, not materialism, not idealism, not existentialism, not naturalism, not Marxian communism, not Emersonian individualism can comprehend the total view that, in the name of life, I have been setting forward in these pages. For the essence of the present philosophy is that many elements necessarily rejected by any single system are essential to develop life's highest creative potential; and that by turns one system or another must be invoked, temporarily, to do justice to life's endlessly varied needs and occasions.

Those who understand the nature of life itself will not, like Engels or Dewey or Whyte, see reality in terms of change alone and dismiss the fixed and the static as otiose; neither will they, like many Greek and Hindu philosophers, regard flux and movement and time as unreal or illusory and seek truth only in the unchangeable. Coming to the practical affairs of life, this philosophy of the whole does not over-value any single system of property or production: just as Aristotle and the framers of the American constitution wisely favored a mixed system of government, so they will favor a mixed economy, not afraid to invoke socialist measures when free enterprise leads to injustice or economic depression, or to favor competition and personal initiative when private monopolies or governmental organizations bog down in torpid security and inflexible bureaucratic routine. This is the philosophy of the open synthesis; and to make sure that it remains open I shall resist the temptation to give it a name. Those who think and act in its spirit may be identified, perhaps, by the absence of labels.

The skepticism of systems is a basic thesis of this book; but it has another name: the affirmation of organic life. If no single principle will produce a harmonious and well-balanced existence, for either the person or the community, then harmony and balance perhaps demand a degree of inclusiveness and completeness sufficient to nourish every kind of nature, to create the fullest variety in unity, to do justice to every occasion. That harmony must include and resolve discords: it must have a place for heresy as well as conformity: for rebellion as well as adjustment—and vice-versa. And that balance must maintain itself against sudden thrusts and impulsions: like the living organism, it must have reserves at its command, capable of being swiftly mobilized, wherever needed to maintain a dynamic equilibrium.

2: THE REASON FOR BALANCE

Modern man, committed to the ideology of the machine, has succeeded in creating a lopsided world, which favors certain aspects of the personality that were long suppressed, but which equally suppresses whatever does not fit into its predominantly mechanical mold. Every effort to overcome the strains and distortions that have been set up in society by the general process of moral devaluation that has taken place during the last century, must have as its goal the restoration of the complete human personality.

All life rests essentially on the reconciliation of two opposite states, stability and change, security and adventure, necessity and freedom; for without regularity and continuity there would not be enough constancy in any process to enable one to recognize change itself, still less to identify it as good or bad, as life-promoting or life-destroying. The fixed structure of determined events—as Melville beautifully put it in the mat-weaving chapter in Moby-Dick—is the warp on which the shuttle of free will weaves the threads of different colors and thicknesses which form the texture and pattern of life. Internal stability even of temperature, independent of a wide range of changes in the outside world, is a mark of the higher vertebrates; and since man, at the head of this vertebrate mammalian stock, has the widest range of responses of any organism, he likewise needs extra mechanisms, which he develops in mind and culture, for creating within himself the equilibrium that is essential for both survival and growth. To achieve balance without retarding growth, and to promote growth without permanently upsetting balance, are the two great aims of organic education.

Without balance there is defect of life; and if any proof were needed of that miscarriage, the increase of neuroses in our civilization, even apart from the number of people so ill that they are admitted to hospitals and asylums for the mentally unbalanced, would almost be sufficient. We have created an industrial order geared to automatism, where feeble-mindedness, native or acquired, is necessary for docile productivity in the factory; and where a pervasive neurosis is the final gift of the meaningless life that issues forth at the other end. More and more, our life has been governed by specialists, who know too little of what lies outside their province to be able to know enough about what takes place within it: unbalanced men who have made a madness out of their method. Our life, like medicine itself, has suffered from the dethronement of the general practitioner, capable of vigilant selection, evaluation, and action with reference to the health of the organism or the community as a whole. Is it not high time that we asked ourselves what constitutes a full human being, and through what modifications in our plan of life we can create him?

Now, the notion of balance has something of the simplicity and naturalness of the conception of the human body as most admirable and beautiful in its nakedness, which the ancient Greeks arrived at and made visible in their sculpture. Seemingly, that naked beauty was present from the beginning. But when we observe other cultures we see that the naked body in all its simplicity, developed in every part, undeformed and undisguised, is in fact a positive achievement. No small human effort, before and after the Greeks, has been spent on concealing the human body, on decorating it with garments, on mutilating it or scarifying it, on painting it or fantastically tattooing it, on altering the natural shape of the head, like the Peruvians, binding women's feet, like the Chinese, on carving the face or on creating fantastic ducklike lips, like the Ubangi, on covering the head with a wig like the Egyptians or the eighteenth century Europeans, on exaggerating the nose or the ears or the buttocks.

In fine, the Greek notion of letting the body arrive at its full growth, without distortion and without concealment, finding beauty in its visible harmony and inner rightness, was a revolutionary conception. To delight in the human body without shame, to enjoy it without adulteration, is no simple human prerogative: it comes only at the summit of a high culture.

So with the notion of organic balance: both in the community and in the person. In the long history of civilizations the balanced personality, even as an ideal, stands forth as a similar rarity. Perhaps the reason for this rarity springs out of the peculiar nature of civilization: the fact that in origin it was based on the division of labor and on compulsory work: two measures that increased efficiency in production and multiplied the power of the ruling classes, at a general sacrifice of life: so that almost every people looked back to an earlier period of balance on a more primitive level as their veritable Golden Age. The conception of the balanced person, the Whole Man, first was put forth, perhaps, by the Chinese: in the person and teachings of Confucius, they beheld such an image and were profoundly affected by it.

But it was the Greeks of the fifth century who arrived at the fullest expression of the balanced person: first in life and then in reflection. Witness the living example of such a man as Sophocles, handsome in body and great of soul, capable of leading an army and writing a tragic drama, ready to move through every dimension of human experience, keeping every part of his life in interaction—here was the balanced person in its fullest development; and the culture of Athens, which produced such a man, also brought forth within two centuries a greater number of such men than history has shown anywhere else.

That balance and that fullness of life were not long maintained. As Plato recognized in The Republic, even Athens at her best had never found a place for half the human race, its women, in its plan of life: the inner conflict between romantic homosexual love and domestic heterosexual love produced a fissure that weakened this whole society. All the attempts to renew this society from Plato and Epicurus to Paul, from the early mystery religions to Christianity, sought to give woman a role the fifth century Athenians had denied her; but by the time this was achieved, the conditions that had been so favorable to the balanced personality in the fifth century had been undermined: a Time of Trouble is, almost by definition, a time of imbalance and distortion.

But there was likewise a good reason for rejecting the classic doctrine of balance in its original form; and this is that the early formulation of it was a static one. From our insight into process throughout the universe, above all from our knowledge of the living body, we know that the stability we seek is not that of a closed system, which has achieved a fixed and final shape, like the stability of a crystal, and might remain the same for ten thousand years. All living creatures are open systems, constantly seizing energy, converting it into "work" and dissipating it and then replenishing it over again: so that the only form of balance that is truly conceivable or desirable in the human organism is a dynamic balance: that of the fountain, endlessly changing, though within the pattern of change retaining its form. Even the figure of the fountain is inadequate to describe organic forms, for dynamic balance itself undergoes shifts and changes through the cumulative effects of memory and through the further effects of time and fresh events and new purposes on maturation and growth.

As with walking, one achieves balance in life only by a series of lunges, which are in turn compensated by other lunges: to arrest that movement, in the interest of equilibrium, would be to paralyze the possibility of growth: the very condition that the equilibrium itself, in living organisms, exists to further. The events that most upset the balance of the personality in actual life, illness, misfortune, error, sin, grief—events that would deface any system of static perfection, as a blow with a hammer would deface a marble statue—have the effect of furthering spiritual growth and transcendence far more positively than any condition of effortless ease and freedom from sin would produce. The hot house fruits of life, the product of the "best possible conditions," have perhaps a waxen beauty and freedom from surface imperfection that fruits grown in the open, susceptible to wind and weather, to worm and blight, do not possess: but the latter have the finer flavor, and, at least in the personality, the most interesting and significant marks of growth.

The classic notion of balance allowed no place for the negative moments of life: it dreamed of a timeless perfection that made no use of time itself, nor of the process of maturation, nor of trial and error, nor of sin and repentance: that is to say, it denied the processes of growth, which upset the possibility of static perfection in the act of enlarging the domains of beauty and significance. In this respect, the Christian understanding of the radical imperfection of life provided a better interpretation of man's essential biological as well as his personal nature than the classic one. Balance is valuable as an aid to growth: it is not the goal of growth.

But the ideal of balance is too central ever to disappear completely. In partial form it reappeared in the Benedictine monastery, with its life devoted to work, study, and prayer: a life whose concern for the manual arts rectified the bias of earlier leisure-class schemes. In the Renascence, partly under the influence of Platonic ideas, the ideal came forth again in the dual conceptions of the gentleman and the artist. In both these personalities there was an effort to do justice to the whole man: the warrior, the priest, the philosopher, the athlete, the manual worker, were united, in non-specialized forms, in a single human organism: the gentleman. Alberti, Leonardo da Vinci, Michelangelo, were equally developed on the side of thought, feeling, emotion, and action: the painting of the Sistine Chapel was not merely a work of imagination, but a gymnastic feat that demanded hardihood and daring. Among the aristocracy, during the Renascence, women played a fuller part than they had done in Greece: and therefore the social balance was more effective. But neither slavery as practiced in Greece, nor the combination of feudalism and early capitalism that prevailed in Western Europe during the fifteenth century made it possible to extend the ideal of balance to every member of the community: so at the very moment that balance and unity became visible in the great personalities of this period, a paralyzing specialization and subdivision of labor made its way into the community at large: robbing the manual worker of such autonomy and balance as even the peasant once had at a low level in his daily life. Still, the ideal of the gentleman, fully cultivated in every aptitude of mind and body, lingered on into the nineteenth century: there was some of the Renascence facility and roundedness in men like Goethe and Jefferson; and this was incarnated, in more democratic form, in a Thoreau, a Melville and a Whitman, with their capacity as gardener, surveyor, woodsman, farmer, printer, carpenter, sailor, as well as writer.

The growth of a mechanistic culture, during the last three centuries, has confirmed the older habits of caste division and specialization, by narrowing the province of the individual worker, by multiplying and refining the particular forms of specialization, by lessening the personal significance of his task. Those who still sought for some sort of wholeness, balance, and autonomy were driven to the outskirts of Western society: the pioneer alone preserved the qualities of the all-round man, though he was forced to sacrifice many of the goods of a rich historic tradition to achieve this. In general, the notion of the segmentation of labor was carried from the factory to every other human province.

In accepting this partition of functions and this over-emphasis of a single narrow skill, men were content, not merely to become fragments of men, but to become fragments of fragments: the physician ceased to deal with the body as a whole and looked after a single organ, indeed, even in Dr Oliver Wendell Holmes's time, he remarked on specialists in diseases of the right leg, who would not treat those of the left. In similar fashion, each man tended to nourish in himself, not what made him a full man, but what made him distinguishable from other men: mental tattooing and moral scarification were supposed to have both high decorative value and immense practical efficiency. Such people cheerfully bartered the fullest possibilities of life in order to magnify their power to think, to invent, to command.

As a result, the apparently simple notion of the balanced person, like the notion of the naked body, symmetrically grown and harmoniously developed, without the over-emphasis or distortion of any organ, a person, not rigid and hard-shelled, but supple and capable of making the fullest response to novel situations, unexpected demands, emergent opportunities, almost dropped out of existence: repressed in life, rejected in thought. Even groups and classes that had once espoused the aristocratic ideal of living a full and rounded life, shamefacedly dropped their traditional aspirations and made themselves over into specialists, those people Nietzsche pregnantly called *inverted cripples*, handicapped not because they have lost a single organ, but because they have over-magnified it. Upon the ancient Babel of tongues was erected a new Babel of functions; and the human community tended to turn into a secret society, in which no person was sufficiently developed as a man to be able to guess what the other person, equally undeveloped as a man, was thinking and feeling and premeditating. Naturally this is an exaggeration: yet it hardly does justice to the loss of the facilities for communication and communion that has taken place. Only men who are themselves whole can understand the needs and desires and ideals of other men.

Historically speaking, the periods of highest vitality, fifth century Athens, thirteenth century Florence, sixteenth century London, early nineteenth century Concord, are those in which most men have been whole, and in which society has found the means of supporting and furthering their wholeness. In such cultures, organs and capacities and potentialities have been so generally developed that each person could, as it were, change places with any other person and still carry on his life and work: a general life-efficiency more than compensated for the special facilities derived from narrow concentration. I see no reason to think that Bacon wrote the plays of Shakespeare; but human potentialities were so evenly developed during this period that the hypothesis is not altogether absurd: not more absurd than to suppose that Shakespeare might have written The New Atlantis or The Advancement of Learning. In those periods of balance and completeness —and completeness is an essential attribute of the balanced person— Hegel's definition of an educated man still magnificently held: "He who is capable of doing anything any other man can do."

This view of human development contradicts the central dogma of modern civilization: that specialism is here to "stay." Rather, to the very extent that the perversions of specialism are accepted as inevitable, the civilization that clings to them is doomed. Our deepening insight into the needs of organisms, societies, and personalities supports just the opposite conclusion: specialism is hostile to life, for it is the non-specialized organisms that are in the line of growth; and only by overcoming the tendency to specialization can the community or the person combat the rigidity which leads to inefficiency and a general failure to meet life's fresh demands. Let our over-specialized sluggards consider the ant: in sixty million years formic society has undergone no change and the experience of the ants has led to no further development, precisely because of the miracle of adaptive specialization that brought perfection and stability at the ant's level and closed every route to change and betterment.

The central effort in the renewal of life today must be to bring back the possibility of wholeness and balance, not indeed as goods in themselves, but as the conditions for renewal and growth and self-transcendence. We must break down the segregation of functions and activities, both within the personality and within the community as a whole: hence moral evaluations and decisions must not be intermittent acts, but constant ones, whose main purpose is to maintain the balance that is partly achieved and assist in those further developments, which, by upsetting balance, lead to growth and increasing fullness of life.

To this end, our sterile mechanistic culture must be exposed to an even more thorough drenching of the emotions than the earlier romanticists dared to dream of. Without re-establishing the capacity for strong expression, for erotic passion and love, for emotional exuberance and delight, we shall also be unable to establish the inhibitions and controls needed to escape automatism and to further autonomous activity; for inhibitions, imposed on life that is already tamped down and denied, are almost a sentence of death. Only those who have said Yes to life will have the courage to say No when the occasion demands it. Those who are starved will say Yes even to garbage—the current offal of the popular press, radio, television—because they have not yet tasted food.

Now the notion of balance in the personality is itself a many-sided one. Theoretically it derives primarily from a close study of organisms—internally, by physiologists, externally and socially by ecologists. Claude Bernard was the first to establish scientifically that a dynamic equilibrium in the internal environment was essential for the exercise of man's higher functions: he also proved that very small quantitative chemical changes could upset this balance and impair the higher functions. But the more thoroughly one studies both organisms and groups of organisms, the wider becomes the application of these leading ideas: in the diet, for example, even faint traces of copper or iodine may be essential to the proper functioning of the whole. Balance in other words is both quantitative and qualitative; and this general condition for effective life applies to every human activity. Balance in time, which is equally important, is established not by repetition but by rhythmic alternation, as of day and night, exertion and rest, expression and inhibition: small variations in rhythm may here prove to be as important for the full functioning of the organism as the presence of tracer elements in the diet; and a routine of work which ignores the need for rhythms and change may lead to frustration, impairment of function, and productive inefficiency.

I purpose presently to carry further the idea of balance: between the external and the internal, between the individual and the group, between autonomous functions and collective ones, between the transitory and the enduring: finally, between the local and tribal on one hand, and the cosmopolitan and universal on the other. By our systematic scientific insight into balance today, we can carry the whole process much farther than was possible through the earlier Greek or Renascence intuitions. But here I would emphasize one special aspect of balance that has a profound bearing upon the good life, all the more because it is an aspect that has, in our generation, been generally ignored: the balance that must be maintained between the expressive, life-asserting moments and the negative, inhibitive, nay-saying moments.

In reaction against the forbidding rigidity of feudalism, modern man sought to remove all boundaries and throw off all restraints. Blake's dictum, *Damn braces, bless relaxes,* might have served as practical guide. Such freedom was mainly escapist: freedom from arbitrary coercion, from stagnant duties, from outworn obligations. But "freedom from," even when amply justified, must be attached to a positive ideal of "freedom for": and this by its nature involves a new restraint—fixation on a self-imposed goal. The freedom of the spoiled child, who has everything he might wish for and lacks only the power to wish or the patience to see his wish through, is the worst of slaveries. Freedom in love, for example, demands an inner readiness to *be* in love, freedom for commitment and continuity, not just for new erotic adventures. The Casanova who flits from lover to lover loses by that inconstancy one of the qualities of mature love: the totality of its attachment, the need, despite fluctuations of passion, for a long-continued union. There is no freedom in wandering unless one is equally free to stay home. So in other phases of life, inhibitions are as essential to freedom as to balance. Relaxes *and* braces, expressions *and* inhibitions, in a rhythmic interplay. That is a prime secret of balance.

Here I cannot improve on the observations of that wise woman, Mary Everest Boole, when she said: "The ordinary man thinks of physical temperance as a process of sacrificing the lower pleasures to the higher; he does not understand that the rhythm of temperance should be kept especially in what he calls the highest. The true prophet, on the contrary, knows that *nothing* is good except in rhythmic alternation. He is no more a glutton intellectually than physically; he no more desires the constant enjoyment of what is called realizing the Presence of God than he craves for unlimited brandy; he no more aspires to a heaven of constant rapture in the intercourse of Jesus and the Saints than to a Valhalla of everlasting mead-drinking in the company of ever lovely Valkyries. He desires, for every fibre of his body, and every convolution of his brain, and for all the faculties he may hereafter acquire that each may be the medium of an occasional revelation. . . . He no more desires for his children incessant health or prosperity than he desires for his vines a uniform temperature."

Actually, the imbalance between the organism and the environment, or more specifically, between the personality and the community, becomes increasingly fatal as we do one of two things: multiply the stimuli and pressures that come from without, or decrease the number of impulses and controls that originate from within. To achieve balance requires quantitative control on both sides; and the greater the means at our command, the greater becomes the need for continence, for discipline, for continued selectivity. Very definitely, therefore, the notion of quantitative restriction enters into the conception of even physiological balance, as it does with no less insistence into any scheme of positive morality: constancy and continence: the reduction of the maximum possible to the optimum assimilable. As we enlarge the sphere of interest and the field of operations, we automatically increase the number of shocks and stimuli that may throw the personality out of balance; and therefore we must counteract this tendency by building up protective inhibitory reactions, by lengthening the circuits of emotional response, and by slowing down the whole tempo of life.

But note: the ideal of balance must be applied in society before it can be fully effective in the life of the person. No amount of watchful self-discipline can create the necessary conditions for achieving equilibrium and growth within the life of the single individual or the isolated group: that is the fallacy of all fugitive and cloistered virtue. Even the Stoic boast, "Nothing can hurt me," was a piece of self-deception. Every system of moral or religious discipline that puts the whole weight of change upon the isolated individual does so by minimizing the actual influences and pressures that are at work in his life, and by voiding a large part of their significance. Profound transformations may and do take place first in the individual person: but they must come speedily to an end unless the condition for a more stable equilibrium is maintained by widening the social base.

The static balance of a life focused completely within itself and lived to itself, the balance of the self-absorbed and self-enclosed mystic or yogin is, in a sense, too easy to achieve; it is like walking firmly on a board laid on the ground: whereas the dynamic balance needed for spiritual growth is like that called into play by crossing a chasm on a single plank. The risk and the achievement of it are due to the constant operation of forces, within and without: the walker's giddy imaginative projection into space, his latent tendencies to suicide, weaknesses in the plank, the pull of gravity, the presence of another person treading on his heels, all give meaning to a process that would otherwise lack both tension and exhilaration. If a hermit's life is not more empty than it is, it is because he has internalized so many of the pressures of society: in fantasy he is still a social creature, tempted by lusts that do not have to have outward existence to be effective.

While the person, then, is an emergent from society, it is within society that he lives and functions; and it is for the purpose of sharing values and meanings with other persons that the moral life becomes something more than a lonely tight-rope walk in a private theater. Not merely are we, in the strict Pauline sense, members one of another; but balance and purpose require for their sustenance a community whose activities and institutions work to the same end. . . . Without that constant support, without that interplay between the person and the group, only a meager and half-awakened life is possible. It is partly in other men's eyes that one sees one's true image; it is partly through other men's example and support that one fathoms one's own potentialities; and it is toward a purpose that we share increasingly, not merely with our immediate fellows, but with all mankind and with generations still unborn, that we rise as men to our utmost height.

Many thinkers of the nineteenth century, even before specialization had been carried to its present pitch, were quick to recognize these facts, as I pointed out in The Condition of Man: this indeed is the one common element that brings together thinkers as diverse as Spencer and Marx and Kropotkin, artists as varied as Nietzsche and Ruskin and Walt Whitman and William Morris. Though the ideal of the balanced man has been less often stated during the last half-century, one can find it, once more, in the work of later thinkers, as individualized in their philosophies as Patrick Geddes and Havelock Ellis and A. N. Whitehead and Karl Mannheim, to mention only the dead. In the

United States, the ideal of the balanced personality has been put forth by Professor F. S. C. Northrop, in his attempt to unify the ideas of the East and the West; and no less significantly, it has been restated, as an essential condition for overcoming the corrosions and devastations of our age, by such a rigorous psychologist as Edward Tolman, in his essay on Drives Toward War.

After discussing the governing personality-images of Western culture in the past—the Spiritual Man of the Middle Ages, the Intellectual Man of the Enlightenment, the Economic Man of the Victorian period, Tolman goes on to say: "The underlying thesis of the present essay will be that still a fifth myth (or, if you will, a fifth ideology) is now nearly ready to appear, and that it must be made to appear. I shall call it the myth of the Psychologically-adjusted Man. It will be the myth, the concept, that only when man's total psychology is understood and all his absolutely necessary psychological needs are allowed balanced satisfaction, will a society permitting relatively universal happiness and welfare be achieved and war be abolished. It is the myth (or rather, I dare hope, the ultimately true concept) that man is, societally speaking, not a spiritual, intellectual, economic, or heroic being, but rather an integrated complex, the entirety of whose psychological nature must be understood if general happiness and welfare are to result."

The chief changes my own analysis would lead me to make in Tolman's statement would be to add that it is not merely necessary to understand man's complex wholeness, but as a further act of understanding, to create the positive channels through which it can be expressed. One of the road-blocks that halt this achievement is that we cannot achieve wholeness, either intellectual or personal, merely by uniting in their present specialized forms the existing body of men and institutions. Such an encyclopedic massing of specialisms—which H. G. Wells tirelessly advocated—will not produce synthesis in thought, any more than an assemblage of specialized functionaries within a community will produce a whole and balanced society. Such mechanical cohesion, whether promoted arbitrarily by the state or through more private initiative, can only produce a state of arrest: not to be confused with the state of dynamic integration. Hard though it may be for our age to accept the fact, we cannot become fully alive again without being prepared to sacrifice the over-development of any particular valued function, and being ready to subordinate it to the dynamic good of the whole. This will mean, in almost every activity, a decrease in productiveness: happily that decrease will be offset, in the end, by an increasing fullness of life. Faced with the life of the ordinary machine-worker, for example, we must be ready, if necessary, to dismantle the assembly line in order to re-assemble the human personality. In the interest of creating better citizens, better lovers and fathers, better men, we may have to lower the number of motor cars or refrigerators produced by the factory: balancing that loss by the higher output of men.

This same rule will apply to almost every specialized facility. Thus the scholar who values wholeness, who cultivates the ability to look around his subject, to include every aspect, to throw forth tentacles into related fields, will not be able to rival in quantitative productivity the work of his predecessors, who confined themselves to a narrow segment. In each case, something must be sacrificed: if not the man himself, then mechanical skill, refinement of detail, speed, output per man hour or per lifetime. Though productivity may decrease, the durability of the product will go up. With our new standard in mind, it is apparent that a large part of the past two centuries' production, in both cities and institutions and books, will have to be done over—and done right.

3: TYPES AND TEMPERAMENTS

One of the most pressing problems of our age, that of creating the human basis for our universal culture, would be easy to solve if all human beings were fundamentally alike in their constitution and their functions: the assumption that one could pay attention to human likenesses and disregard their differences was, indeed, one of the beliefs that buoyed up Christian missionary enterprise and made somewhat too lightly sanguine the rational-minded philosophers of the eighteenth century.

By now, however, we are almost inclined, by reason of the vast amount of scientific data that has accumulated in both physiology and anthropology, to over-emphasize men's differences: apart from the obvious differences in color that men have always recognized between the major races of man, we find differences in blood-types and various other physical components: we even assume, with a fairly high degree of probability, that no two sets of fingerprints are identical. No longer do we expect to find universal man in nature: he is not a natural organism but an ideal type, a product—to the extent that he exists at all—

of effort and culture; a type that overlays biological, regional, occupational, cultural differences.

In the matter of balance, we encounter the same original difficulties that we do in the case of universality. From the time of the Greeks, if not before, students of human nature have recognized definite physiological and temperamental types. The classic division between the choleric and the sanguine, the phlegmatic and the melancholy, has in our time been re-discovered and re-appraised through our increased knowledge of the functioning of the endocrines and their effect upon bodily structure, functional response, and character. In personal expression, another kind of division discloses itself: that named by Jung in his description of the extravert and the introvert: the first outward-turning, active, dominating, externalized, the second inward-turning, passive, withdrawing, internalized. Nothing is more rare, perhaps, than an even distribution of character-traits or a fine, delicately maintained balance between introversion and extraversion.

If a division corresponding to the four temperaments were a clear-cut one, as some of the cruder accounts of physique and character have assumed, there would be little hope of creating balanced personalities: at best, one would have to outfit each particular temperament with a philosophy and a code of ethics suitable for it, without even William James's hope of finding some pragmatic middle way between the tough-minded and the tender-minded. Fortunately, Dr William H. Sheldon has made a radical reorientation in this whole field, by finding a more fundamental kind of constitutional division than earlier investigators had discovered: a division related to that which goes on in the developing embryo when the three layers of the blastula—the ectoderm, the mesoderm, and the endoderm—differentiate into their special organs: the nervous system, the skeletal and muscular structure, and the internal organs. Obviously every human being contains all three elements: Sheldon's special contribution is to attach a numerical scale to each component. This device enables him to describe personality, not merely by the dominant traits—sometimes misleading, always incomplete—but by the proportions of the mixture.

Dr Sheldon calls his personality types the cerebral, the visceral, and the muscular types. The first tends to think its way through life: the second to feel its way: the third to fight its way. Withdrawal and inner concentration go with the cerebral type: for the sake of the mind, he minimizes bodily enjoyment and shrinks from activity. Sociability and hearty bodily appetites go with the visceral type; while muscular exercise and organized activity go with the muscular ones. The way of the first is a difficult, lonely climb, with sparse rations and a slippery foothold, mainly for the sake of enjoying the view when he reaches the top. The second performs a Bacchic dance through life, up hill and down dale, with quick senses and "storm-swift" feet: ever ready to pause for wine and food, for sexual intercourse and blissful sleep, not least, for dreams. The third type marches through life, often in squads and companies, muscles tense, eyes aggressively set on the enemy, never stopping to meditate or to feel: becoming easily demoralized, like Samson in Delilah's arms, if once he relaxes into the life of feeling.

In sociological terms, first outlined by Auguste Comte, the cerebrals become, ideally, the intellectuals: the theologians, the philosophers, the scientists, the symbolizers and system-makers: the viscerals are the "women," or as Geddes and Branford termed them, the emotionals and expressionals: artists and poets and lovers, articulate in their senses, rich in images and sounds, their minds nourished and fertilized by their erotic life: while the muscular types are the chiefs, the leaders and organizers, the men of action, distrustful of all thought or feeling that would weaken their capacity for struggle or divert them from their practical goals. By various combinations of these fundamental attitudes, one arrives at the almost inexhaustible richness and variety of human society, in which pure types are an impossibility, relatively pure types a rarity, and a balance between the three in any one personality perhaps even more singular.

There is nothing esoteric or academic about the general theory of bodily types in relation to character and human potentiality: it is rather massively confirmed by common observation. The differences in outlook and capacity between Prince Hal and Falstaff, between Don Quixote and Sancho Panza, are properly associated in our minds with their respective physical appearances. Similarly the Greeks, in their idealizations of womanhood, differentiated between the lithe muscular huntress, Artemis, the cerebral Athene who had even been born from the brow of Jove, and the visceral Aphrodite, who would have been spoiled for the offices of love and their further consequences in childbirth, if her muscles had been hardened and tightened in the chase, or if intellectual specialization had anesthetized her capacities for erotic response—that curse of the intellectual woman, unwilling to yield to her body or abate the compensatory exercise of her cerebral functions. Mind and spirit operate in and through the body: even when they transcend it, they are modified by its existence. If man's life were only a passing thought in the mind of God, that thought would have to include man's bodily characteristics in order to evoke anything that could be identified as man. That is why incidentally there is more reason in the primitive Christian notion of the resurrection of the physical body on the Day of Judgment, than in the gnostic fancy that spirit has no need of matter. To be delivered from the prison of the body, one must assimilate the social ways and spiritual creations of other bodily types and characters.

If man had lived according to his own nature exclusively, he would still exist in a state of animal-like obedience to his instinctual impulses and his endocrines: the history of human society, therefore, is the story of the increasing influence of nurture over nature, of ego and super-ego over id. To some extent, every individual must respect his biological endowment and live in accordance with it: at the moment of crisis, in Shaw's Androcles and the Lion, the giant Ferrovius discovers that he is no meek Christian, but a man of angry passion and aggressive muscular strength: had he failed to heed that call, he would have died of frustration or humiliation. But one of the reasons for understanding one's nature more thoroughly is to cease to be an automatic victim of its pressures and claims: just because one is human, with all three components present in one's body, one may by education and deliberate culture alter one's original balance and offset the bias of constitution and temperament.

Every theory of types, whether physiological or social, that seeks to re-enforce the type at the expense of one's common humanity must prove in the end antagonistic to growth. This, in fact, is the curse of every caste system, and equally the curse of every static division between functions and processes, which assumes that the only partly used human being should conform to that division. If there were no other reason to seek balance and universality, the need to remove blockages to human growth and development would be sufficient to justify it.

One of the reasons for the failure of the universal religions, perhaps, to achieve the wide and inclusive mission they set for themselves, is that the ideal person who gave the religion its stamp still bore too plainly the mark of a single biological type: the cerebral one. Now that mankind, to guarantee its survival and go further with its development, must create a universal society, capable of embracing all men as brothers, it must have as its dominant persona a mask that will fit every face, and a goal that promises to bring together, at a common point, every particular mode of life. With the ideal balance dominant, we shall offset weaknesses, correct partialities, and lay a basis for mutual aid and reciprocal understanding. As the division of labor between the sexes is justified by their union to bring forth a new human being, so the division of labor between the three personality-types will be justified by their common parturition of a new kind of man, capable of living in a unified world, adaptive to every kind of regional environment, embracing every manner of person and culture.

4: THE WHOLE MAN AS IDEAL TYPE

In reacting against tribalism, the classic religions have often underrated the qualities that are in fact conserved and furthered by the life of the primary group and must, in some form, enter into its most ideal expressions. The great historic exceptions to this generalization are, it would seem, Confucianism and Olympian Hellenism; though in as far as Jesus accepted the law of the Old Testament as basic for the New, which transcended it, he, too, did justice to man's original nature and tribal culture. Each of these did in fact take in so much of the in-instinctual human nature as to seem, to the followers of other religions, essentially worldly; or at all events insufficiently concerned with the universal and the divine.

In analyzing the fundamental religious attitudes, one finds that they correspond broadly with three general ways of approaching the world: to attack, to hold fast, to retreat. Early in the present century, these attitudes were characterized by the British scholar, Dr D. S. MacColl, as the way of the Titan, the way of the Olympian, and the way of the Pilgrim: respectively struggle, domination, withdrawal. Recently these three attitudes have been further differentiated and described by Charles Morris in a book called The Paths of Life. Here, following Sheldon, Professor Morris distinguishes between the promethean, the dionysian, and the buddhist components in all religions.

From the familiar example of Christianity, the Buddhist element seems to most people the specifically religious one: the attitude of detachment from earthly life, leading to withdrawal, rejection, inhibition. This element contrasts with the life-affirming dionysian element: the exuberant display of animal vitality and the heightening of all the moments of sensual erethism and efflorescence, in which the visceral emphasis even turns the figure of the god, as in the various

Greek representations of Bacchus, into a feminoid form, with prominent breasts, smooth musculature, rounded buttocks and a soft face. The third component is that of Prometheus, engaged in a manful struggle with the conditions of life: he who in our age exercises all those faculties that go into mechanical invention and political organization, but who was originally symbolized by the mythical hero who stole fire from the gods for the sake of improving the lot of men on earth.

If Dr Sheldon's analysis of constitutional sets proves valid, then Morris's endeavor to describe ideological interests and total life-response in terms of the physiological type of the believer is equally sound: though only on the same terms of inter-mixture that Sheldon has established for body and personality. The domination of one or another attitude in the original formulation and incarnation of a religion tends to explain in no little degree what happens at a later stage, when it draws in an increasingly nondescript and non-selective body of believers. At that moment, every universal creed must find a way of providing for the participation of people whose organic dispositions provide a different constellation of natural needs and interests than those that entered into the early intuitions and dogmas.

All these compensatory phenomena, which to the practitioner of religion seem backslidings and betrayals, can be interpreted in a more understanding psychological way. What are they but attempts to re-establish an organic balance which a too one-sided insistence on a single need and response has upset? At some time in every religion, the ideal type that has been chosen must confront that part of the personality it has left out of account: it must face the facts of nature and include them within the purview of its ultimate ideal.

The ideal types that Charles Morris has ably interpreted are capable of one further correlation: that in time. This increases their value from the standpoint of the philosophy of balance. Going back to Mac-Coll's division, the three phases of personality may likewise be correlated in his scheme with the three main phases of life. The olympian or dionysian element, springing out of vitality and health, tending toward playful expression and enjoyment, with its dilation of the senses and its exuberance of erotic activity—what is this but the phase of youth? Here are the potentialities of the normal human being, before illness, family responsibilities, vocational disappointments, or physical injuries have subdued its vitality. The olympians know neither satiety, exhaustion, nor the prospect of death: in the gleam of each new morning, they recover their youth.

As for the promethean type, which MacColl calls the Titanic, with its high degree of purposive activity, its inventiveness and its systematic effort, its concentration on work, its acceptance of hard tasks and responsibilities, its constant struggles and agonies, its narrowing down of the sensuous life, with its tendency to over-value its vocational skills even to the point of accepting bodily malformations, like the blacksmith's callus, the professor's stoop, this is surely the idealization of man in middle age, wracked and buffeted about, like cunning Odysseus, in the long Odyssey of middle life. Promethean man, who has put his youth completely behind him, despises the dionysian elements for the same reason that the utilitarian Gradgrinds of the nineteenth century, who built Birminghams and Manchesters where even children were given no chance to play, despised the frivolous idlers of the British aristocracy, the surviving olympians of another order.

Dedication and commitment: blood, sweat, and tears: that is the way of Prometheus; and the work of the world is carried forward by those who are prepared to sacrifice their digestions and even their warm domestic relationships to see that it gets properly done. Without the toughness and discipline of the muscular types, who impose their mesomorphic pattern of life more or less upon all those of middle age, the tasks of the organizer and the soldier, the colonizer and the administrator, the engineer and the business enterpriser, would be only half done. Countries like China and India, where the cerebral types have dominated, and literary scholarship is the main requirement for administrative office, now find themselves handicapped in their attempt to create a more balanced civilization by an absence of prometheans, people capable of standing up under the burden and the heat of the day, who actually enjoy the struggle with refractory materials or hostile men, which is so distasteful to the buddhist or dionysian temperament.

Finally, there comes a dark moment when the original life-impetus begins to falter; when the animal vitality of youth and middle age wane: when one's best efforts have ended in at least partial failure; when accident, disease, vocational crippling, have all taken their toll; when the pleasures of the table or the bed no longer are irresistible, or in fact seem a little childish, perhaps because the senses are becoming dull, perhaps because one has repeated these acts once too often: when, with lowered capacity and strength, the personality is pushed down almost to the invalid's level; and in order to have something like an adequate response, one must reduce the number of possible occasions, guarding time, hoarding vitality, in order to make life go a little further.

Enter the Pilgrim: no longer bent on achievement but rather ready for disengagement and detachment, passing on the burdens of office to others and even taking, like a Hindu holy man, to the open road. At this point, life can be lived more completely in the mind, if only for the reason that the other avenues of expression are slowly closing down. At its best, this is the period celebrated by Po Chü-i in his poem On Being Sixty. Between thirty and forty, he observes, one is distracted by the Five Lusts; while between seventy and eighty one is a prey to all manner of diseases; but from fifty to sixty, one is done with profit and fame and has put behind one love and greed: "calm and still—the heart enjoys rest."

At this downward cycle of life, every man becomes, if he is conscious of his destiny, a "Buddhist." For now death makes his appearance, not as a passing stranger to whom one waves at a distance and never expects to meet in one's home, but as a constant companion whom one cannot shake off. By this time, in the normal course of age, the death of friends, relatives, companions, magnifies the steady shrinkage of life that is going on in a man's own body: the dimming of the eyes, the falling out of the hair, the wrinkling and sagging of the skin, the increasing sense of fatigue in tasks one once took in one's stride. With this shrinkage goes a further withdrawal of interest from the external world: the inner deafness and blindness of the aged, which so often precedes any actual impairment of their organs. To make the most of what remains, one must turn one's back on life's fullness: it is a time for reducing the intake of food, for curbing too exhausting exercises, for falling back on memory, reflection, revery—and in happier souls, a time for a more intense inner life, like Titian and Renoir, still painting gloriously in their eighties.

From the outgoingness of youth to the withdrawn-ness and ingoingness of age: from the visceral life of infancy through the muscular life of maturity on to the cerebral life of senescence: that is the trajectory of life. Yet as all three components of the body are present, in some proportion, at every stage, so all three components of time are likewise present in every moment. Life as a whole exercises a determining influence upon each phase that it enters; and too great a segregation in time is as conducive to unbalance as too complete a segregation of functions and activities. Each part of life is good in its own right; yet part of its meaning lies in what it contributes to other phases. Education, in the past, tried to turn children prematurely into adults; but today there is a tendency to isolate childhood and to limit its activities to those that give pleasure or make sense within its own limited role. The principle of balance applies likewise to time: *each phase should bear within it, either as experience or symbol, some portion of the absent whole.* Shallow is the youth that is not by anticipatory dream committed to maturity: unillumined is the maturity that has not achieved the self-criticism that comes with detachment: empty and dry is the old age that has not a touch of youth's irresponsibility and levity.

Is it any wonder, then, that all the phases of life have been embodied in the great religions; or rather, that each of them has claimed for itself one sector or another of the great arc so described, and has even tended to give that phase of life exclusive right to represent the whole? But no historic religion has yet sought to sustain life in its fullness and wholeness.

There is one other point that remains to be noted in this correlation of the phases of religion with the constitution of persons and the cycle of life. Because all these processes, all these types, belong to life in its full development, there is a sense in which they are interchangeable, too. The young who went to war and faced deprivation and death every day, came back, even if they were not physically mutilated, far older than their outward appearance indicated: old men, blessed with a premature patience and resignation that had nothing to do with their years, often cursed by the memory of horrors they were too tender to look at, still less to endure. Similarly, a severe illness, a crippling accident in early life—see that fine human document, The Little Locksmith, by Katharine Butler Hathaway—will bring about an attitude of senescence even in earliest childhood.

But in a culture like that of contemporary America, just the opposite change may happen. Because we are committed far too heavily to the promethean way of life, a bastard dionysian element may be introduced as compensation: infantile oral sexuality in the form of smoking, or equally infantile sensual enjoyment through overdoses of candy, ice-cream sundaes, and similar sweets. Such rituals at once promote further business and offset at a low level the effects of mechanical concentration. Similarly, this suppressed dionysian element will draw even the aged into sexual exploits that no longer comport with either their years or supposed experience of life. Note how the matrons of this culture will undergo endless efforts of gymnastic and cosmetic to heavily counterfeit the vitalities that are naturally at the disposal of their daughters.

What holds for the individual again holds in civilization as a whole; for though the personality is an emergent from community, the relationship is interdependent and interacting. Faced with the terrible devitalizations produced by the Black Death in the fourteenth century, the first response to death was that of withdrawal. Even so worldly a writer as Boccaccio disclaimed his popular erotic tales and turned to writing the soberest religious tracts, precisely as Tolstoy, facing old age and death, deserted his magnificent novels. But presently the emphasis shifted again in the sixteenth century from senescence to youth: with rising vitality came a promethean concentration on the machine and a dionysian interest in sexual expression; and these two movements led to the recovery and expansion of Western civilization, after it had reached a lower state of physical depletion than Rome had reached at the end of the fourth century.

In every phase of life, then, we can single out moments of affirmative absorption and moments of negation and detachment: moments of elation and engagement, and moments of desolation and disengagement: while between them there stand out moments of activistic struggle, to which both plus and minus signs may be prefixed. In other words, the Dionysian, the Buddhist, and the Promethean are always with us: indeed, if they have their roots in the constitution of the body itself, as we have reason to think, this could hardly be otherwise. But it is only as concepts that these forms can be found in a pure state: life makes mock of purely logical divisions. Buddhism itself, for example, would seem free from any ideal propensity to transform the environment by the application of technics: yet a promethean element crept into the inner core of this religion, in prayer itself, through the invention of the prayer wheel: a means of ensuring salvation by the mass-production of prayers.

So, too, in Western culture, with its devout worship of its own Holy Trinity, Militarism, Mechanism, and Money, a strong life-denying element persists. Even today—and of course still more under the capitalism of the nineteenth century—the exhausting routine of the factory and the office, the harsh drill and discipline of the army, reduce the urges and enjoyments of organic existence to a minimum. Read the biographies of the early inventors and entrepreneurs: above all the story of the workers who were sacrificed to their hard, inhuman ambitions: you read a story of mortifications and self-flagellations that

match anything in medieval hagiology. Robert Gair, the paper manu-
facturer, abandoned a honeymoon in order to consummate a profitable
business deal. That tale can be repeated with a hundred variations.

The sense of worldly guilt and damnation, which Protestantism
found in its soul, was no doubt eased by this new form of self-punish-
ment, though it worked out ambivalently, since great were the financial
rewards of those who thriftily renounced immediate enjoyment. Even
more definitely, a cerebral element of life-rejection enters into the
dominant attitude of the scientist: it is the essence of the post-Galilean
methodology. For the world, as conceived by Galileo, Newton, and
Descartes was a world stripped of all its dionysian qualities: a world
in which color, form, pattern, sound were meaningless, except as
mathematical quantities, and in which feeling and desire and imagination were disreputable.

This translation of Christian life-negation into a far more pervasive
and inescapable system of rejection and mental ascesis was one of the
feats of cultural sleight-of-hand that accompanied the transition from
the medieval to modern order. Perhaps some of the spiritual authority
that now adheres to science derives from the fact that the scientists
have been the authentic saints of the modern age. From Copernicus to
Pascal, from Faraday and Henry to Einstein, they have set an example
of high spiritual devotion, untainted by the pomps and lusts of a
wicked world. This has given their mode of thought the authentic religious stamp that moves the masses of men.

As for the promethean religious ideology, it is associated with the
effort of the activist, energetic, muscular types to turn their own bodily
prowess first of all toward the direct domination and enslavement of
other men. The Persians, the Spartans, the Norsemen, the Moslem
Arabs, and the Turks conceived existence as a struggle, with hardships
and penalties as a natural accompaniment to all activities. Meeting
obstacles in the purposes of other men, these groups intensify their
own naturally aggressive and sadistic reactions: with whip and rod,
with fire and sword, with plague and famine, they and their Gods seek
to dominate their fellow-men. The world, during the last three centuries, was colonized by Prometheans, who treated nature as ruthlessly
as they treated the underlying populations: today the very existence
of life on this planet is threatened by their pathologically one-sided
descendants, whose commitment to the destructive processes has now
been amplified beyond all sanity by the conquest of atomic energy in

the West, and the building up of great nationalist military machines in Russia and China.

Promethean forms of religion, and notably that of Russian communism, in our own day, are an expression of the over-valuation of struggle as a formative element in life: it was not for nothing that Marx and Engels hailed Darwin's "struggle for existence" as an essential ingredient of dialectical materialism. This prometheanism has little use for the slow processes of maturation and growth: rather, it must deny slow organic procedures in order to confirm its own conviction that physical power, if wielded ruthlessly, can avoid the need for more complex and co-operative methods of change: mutual aid. Though the aim of the Prometheans is power, they punish themselves almost as violently as they punish their conquered peoples: witness the cruel disciplinary practices in the British public schools in the heyday of the Empire, or the whole training and discipline of the Prussian officer caste, including the saber cuts that the members of the student corps proudly courted and counted on their own faces.

The chief refractory element in a society dominated by promethean values is woman; for she cannot, without renouncing her own biological role, turn away completely from sensual delight and organic fulfillment in child-bearing: against the relatively katabolic and destructive male, her own body preaches the lessons of consumption and growth, of yielding to life and enjoying its fruits. Promethean man, not able to take woman's role seriously without partly denying the validity of his own narrow concerns, reduces her to a plaything: typically, the delectable houri in whose arms the Moslem warrior, dying in battle for Islam, will transact an eternity of sensual bliss. Even here promethean man is often the victim of his paranoid ambitions and his compulsive routines: he loses the sympathetic delights of sexual union in a tyrannous routine of record-making.

Each of the classic religions, we see, reveals and in some degree depresses the ideal dimensions of the human personality. Under the pressure of the immediate historic situation, in which these religions took form, they have failed to embrace the full life of man, in its organic diversity and variety. No matter how catholic or universal the professions of the classic religions, they have left out of account much that it was important to include both in doctrine and in practice: wherefore the wisdom of the race is contained, not alone in the sacred books, but in the immense secular literature that has grown up beside these books. In the effort to achieve a balanced personality and a universal culture, we must offset these tendencies to over-prize a single type of personality-structure and a single way of life.

On this point, Patrick Geddes's words confirm the intuitions and practices of Sri Ramakrishna, he who sought to understand other forms of religion than his own by putting their doctrine and precepts experimentally into practice. These insights are a salutory challenge to the tendency of every religion to regard its own truth as the highest and completest form of revelation: so high that it can overlook other truths, so complete that it can exclude them. "All the gospels," Geddes affirmed, "are various views of life, and *all true*—as far as they go. All the myths are true, too. It is pitiful nonsense that one has heard, ever since Darwin frightened the curates: 'Do you mean to say you believe in the Bible?' spoken in a fearful voice by would-be scientific folk. Of course I believe in the Bible . . . and in the Koran, and in all the bibles of all peoples, whether savages or Buddhists, Celts or Christians. To those storehouses of past wisdom one makes one's own contribution. I make mine by seeing that life is bigger and more wonderful than has been thought; and that all the gospels put together cannot encompass it."

Just as in the coming Constitution of a World Government no tribe or region must be overlooked or neglected, or permitted to remain cut off from conversation and co-operation with the rest of mankind whenever it manifests a desire for them, so no part of the human constitution may be neglected in our effort to achieve the universal: we must even provide harmless outlets for irrationality and aggression, in order that we may not be maimed by their repression and unseemly eruption. Every personality bears the stamp of its individual uniqueness, irreplaceable in every dimension, identifiable in the very whorls of its fingerprints. Each personality, too, bears the imprint of its type, its biological type, its social type, its class-conditioning and its total cultural conditioning, so that its uniqueness still falls into many definable types and categories. Finally, every personality bears the imprint of the universal: that which is viable in all situations, translatable into all tongues, not merely because it issues out of the common human lot, but because it indicates a resolution to create and participate in a common destiny. When man ignores this universal aspect, his whole life breaks down, and in compensation he will seek to make some minor form of unity, that of the tribe or the self-enclosed ego, take the place of the whole. Every mode of unity by suppression mars the purpose it professes to serve: only unity by inclusion in an expanding and

ereign states, an effective World Federation. The method was as admirable as the objective: for Mr Humber understood that no universalism was possible that did not have its origin and its sanction in the local community. By reasoned argument and quiet persistent effort this one man started a movement of great potentiality—though it has since been thwarted by servile fears and reactionary suspicions. But had there been as many as a dozen men, similarly possessed by this idea, similarly ready for action, similarly capable of self-sacrificing personal effort, neither the Republican nor the Democratic parties would have lapsed so quickly into an improvident belligerence or a pusillanimous isolationism—both based on a superstitious faith in the magic properties of the atomic bomb.

These are but a few examples, accidentally known to me, among thousands, scattered through every country: equally heroic and decisive. By such a willingness to break with the comfortable automatisms of the past and to participate in acts of world unity and integration, a new attitude will be passed from these leaders to other members of our society: each personal choice, each individual commitment, will confirm the new ideology and put it to the test of effective action. On the other hand, without the support of an ideal purpose, framed in a conscious philosophy, even the most impersonal and self-sacrificing acts, like those of the soldiers who fought under the United Nations flag in Korea, will fail of their full effect.

From many possible witnesses, in our own age, I shall turn to one whose long career affords a classic example of renewal and integration. I choose Albert Schweitzer because his life is in outline already familiar to many readers; and because his books, the conscious expression of his philosophy, are accessible in many languages. But it is on his life rather than on his writings that I shall concentrate; for his actions have transcended the limitations of his thought. Schweitzer's conscious philosophy, from my standpoint, is sometimes contradictory and inadequate: in the world of ideas, to speak with candor, he is not one of the greatest luminaries. But his intuitions are better integrated than his reasons; and the transformation effected in the life and work of Schweitzer is more profound and more widely significant than the best ideas he has yet formulated. From his actions, one may deduce a fuller philosophy than that which has consciously guided him. And through his masterly example, the task of formulation becomes an easier one.

Consider the course of Albert Schweitzer's life. He began as a student of philosophy who turned to Christian theology; and in his early twenties he did so brilliantly at his chosen career that honors and fame would have come to him rapidly, had he been content with the role of pastor and theologian. Within the theological world, he was plainly one of the olympians: he might have lived and died in that role, like so many other churchmen, preaching the doctrines of a religion he had never tested or practiced by any major act: the willing observer of outward forms and ceremonies, the happy recipient of worldly courtesies and worldly honors.

Fortunately, one of Schweitzer's early studies was an intimate examination of the life of Jesus, whom he rescued from the fashionable impugners and devaluators by a more rigorous use of the very historic method they had used for deflating him. This brought him to the conviction that a true believer in Jesus must, in the twentieth century, take up the cross himself and perform some redemptive work of sacrifice. Such a work would not bring fame and honor, but, more probably, neglect, ill-health, possibly death, if not also contumely and oblivion. Plainly many evils need to be abated: many sins Western society has committed cry for atonement. With a vigilant eye, Schweitzer picked a classic example: the degradation of primitive peoples through imperialist exploitation, often coming on top of a primitive life that in itself, by reason of its own ignorance, superstition, and brutality did violence to the human spirit.

Hence Schweitzer decided, like many another fervent Christian, to become a missionary. But since nothing could be more ironic than to carry the word of redemption to people too sunken in disease to be made whole, Schweitzer again followed Jesus's example: he would heal the sick while bringing the Gospel to them, and that healing should be no small part of his gospel. With that decision, the neophyte threw aside the honors of the theologian and settled down to the hard discipline of the medical student: the "Buddhist" gave place to the Promethean.

Those four years of medical preparation were doubtless difficult enough in themselves even to an able student of the humanities, trained in the rigorous scholarly discipline of a European university like Strasbourg; but they required a further intensity of concentration for the reason that Schweitzer, instead of closing up all the other channels of life, kept his emotions and feelings quick, by his cultivation of music as an organist. Through his special knowledge of Johann Sebastian

Bach, Schweitzer brought into circulation again many precious scores that had been completely overlooked. As organist, as musicologist, above all as lover of music, Schweitzer served Dionysus as well as Christ: that constant concern with music, throughout his toilsome life, made his wholeness and balance an exemplary one.

In philosophy or theology, in medicine or in music, Schweitzer's talents were sufficient to guarantee him a career of distinction: as one of the eminent specialists of his time, in any of these departments, his success would have been prompt and profitable, just to the extent that he allowed himself to be absorbed in a single activity. But in order to remain a whole man, Schweitzer committed the typical act of sacrifice for the coming age: *he deliberately reduced the intensive cultivation of any one field, in order to expand the contents and the significance of his life as a whole.* Doubtless the humility that made it possible for him to entertain such a sacrifice derived directly from his Christian convictions: yet the result of that sacrifice was not the negation of his life but its fullest realization; for even in the humid jungles of Africa, where he finally made his home, he kept alive his highly cultivated interest in music: not merely having his organ by his side, but finding time, despite a lack of the usual scholarly apparatus, to write a life of Bach.

Both in his work as a medical missionary and in his public appearance as an organist, Schweitzer, who was a German by birth, performed another act of symbolic importance: an act perhaps easier, more natural, in the international world before 1914 than in our own day. For Schweitzer's field of action was less in his own original fatherland, among the people who spoke his preferred language, than in the country of its rival, and presently its active enemy, France: in that sense, he was another Jean-Christophe. So it was to an unattractive colony in French West Africa, in the steaming equatorial jungle, that he turned for a field of endeavor. There, with occasional intervals abroad for lecturing and organ playing—including the interval he spent as a prisoner of war in France, in the very hospital at Saint Remy where Van Gogh, another imitator of Jesus, had been confined—he has lived his life: serving a God who recognizes neither white nor black, neither French nor German.

Without that devaluation and renunciation of nationalism no life worthy of the name can now be built up. He who is one hundred per cent an American or a Russian, a German or a Frenchman, a European or an African or an Asiatic, is only half a man: the universal part of his personality, equally essential to his becoming human, is still unborn. Every act that softens the egoistic claims of nations and accentuates the unity of mankind, adds another foundation stone to the new world that we must now build.

All the great spirits of our time participate with Schweitzer in this devaluation of nationalism and this lowering of barriers. Vivekananda, breaking the Brahmin's rule against overseas travel to come to the Congress of Religions in America and to carry his mission to Europe: Patrick Geddes, spending ten of the best years of his life in India, exploring its living resources and planning its cities in consonance with its own mode of life: Gandhi, breaking down caste lines that are even more inviolate and obsessive than national barriers: Nansen, the explorer, engaged on a universal rescue expedition, so that even the form of an international passport under the League of Nations, the first prophecy of world citizenship, bore his name—all these people, breaking down the walls of hateful egoism and aggressive pride, which keep men apart, are at the same time bearers of cultural pollen: producers of those cultural hybrids which, Flinders Petrie long ago remarked, are no less superior in civilization than in farming.

By the same token, the intense isolationism and xenophobia of the Russian communists has undermined the original universality of their doctrine, even as that of the Daughters of the American Revolution, a somewhat less influential body, has undermined the universal principles of an earlier American revolution. Nothing could in fact prove more surely that Russified communism is not the creed of the opening age, but rather its desperate antagonist, its would-be destroyer, than the fact that it now denounces "cosmopolitanism," and not merely fails to propagate, but even refuses theoretically to sanction, any ideas and forces of a universal character. There is something colossally comic in the essential identity in attitude toward the universal expressed by the Soviet rulers, the reactionary and repressive sons of one revolution, and their spiritual counterparts in America, the equally reactionary and would-be repressive daughters of another. Against such perversions and pandemonium the universalism of Schweitzer's mission stands out.

Schweitzer's arduous career as a medical missionary condemned him to a long period of relative obscurity. But at the same time it gave him a perspective on Western life that determined the further direction of his thinking: it was such an act of detachment as leads to a more inclusive view of man and his destiny than any closer involvement in immediate issues can give. As a result, Schweitzer's two-volume diagnosis of our Time of Troubles counts among the earliest contributions to an adequate self-analysis of our civilization: differing from the earlier forecasts of Burckhardt and Henry Adams because Schweitzer, like a good physician, regards his prognosis, not as a death sentence, but as an incentive to rational action.

Published a few years after Spengler's Decline of the West, Schweitzer's studies, grouped under the general title of The Philosophy of Civilization, were plainly conceived independently of Spengler's work and were unaffected by it, though they pictured, as unsparingly as Spengler had done, the disintegrating forces that were already visibly at work. The lack of human values and ethical principles, in our positivistic, mechanical civilization, was on Spengler's diagnosis the most serious cause of our ills. Instead of urging, as Spengler did, a willing submission to the processes of barbarism, as the implacable destiny of Western man in our time, Schweitzer urged a return to the generous cosmopolitan humanism of the eighteenth century.

Here is an indication of Schweitzer's intuitive grasp. Though he himself followed the way of Jesus, he recognized the original limitations of Jesus's thought: it was the product of a parochial, self-centered culture, obsessed by the myth of national deliverance through the agency of a Messiah, while Jesus himself, as Schweitzer had demonstrated, erroneously regarded the approaching end of the world as a determining factor in human conduct. Schweitzer saw that the ethical foundations for a world society had been laid, not by Jesus nor even yet by the Christian Church, but by the great Chinese sages, Confucius, Mencius, and Mo-Ti: the translation of their thought, even indirectly, which accompanied the introduction of porcelain and silk and wallpaper into Europe, had a formative effect on some of the best minds of the eighteenth century and gave to its ethics, no less than to its gardens or its tea-tables, a Chinese cast: Chinese in origin but as wide in its province as humanity itself.

Coming from a Christian, a Christian by active consecration as well as formal espousal, Schweitzer's doctrine revealed the depth of his insight; for against the formalism of theology, he saw that the eighteenth century had been, in fact, a time when Christian doctrine, often abandoned in formula, was perhaps as active in actual life as it had been in the Middle Ages, encouraging men to mildness of conduct, even in the midst of war, to a common understanding and a tolerance of underlying differences, to universal enterprises that tended to make

the world one. This century produced international philanthropis
like John Howard and international patriots like Thomas Paine.

Men like Howard and Paine undoubtedly under-rated the forces
a closed society, as did the new eighteenth century Order of Fr
Masonry; by failing to do justice to the domestic self-containment
the primary group, they perhaps even contributed in some measur
to the nationalist reaction, which began ideologically with Roussea
and Herder, and practically, with the French revolution. But the belie
in the possibility of universal standards and universal goals, applyin
to the actions of men because they shared a common humanity, wa
a healthy one; and Schweitzer recognized that fact. Note that th
title of Part Two is not Religion and Civilization but Ethics an
Civilization.

Among American theologians it has become the fashion to speak o
ethics without religion as a mere cut flower, with no roots in the soi
of life: beautiful, perhaps, but doomed to wither. But careful histori
analysis shows that just the opposite is the truth; for ethics lies in th
common earth of life, with roots that go deep into our animal ances
tors; while religion, though it takes us to the mountain top and dis
closes vistas that stretch far beyond our common daily horizon, pro
duces wider ethical imperatives only because it rests securely on a
older ethical order. On the basis of animal loyalty and love the highe
values, the divine sanctions, become possible.

Schweitzer's affirmation of eighteenth century cosmopolitanism, lib
eralism, and optimism, contrasts with Reinhold Niebuhr's unfavorable
interpretation of the same period. Though Niebuhr's insight into the
shallowness and vanity of the eighteenth century *philosophe* is a salu
tary corrective to latter-day smugness, Schweitzer's appreciation of
valuable insights that have been lost or actively discarded seems to me
equally relevant. How difficult it is in our time to achieve this univer
salism, Schweitzer's own work abundantly demonstrates; for though
he wrote an extensive critique of Hindu philosophy and religion, even
he has been tempted at times to over-stress the differences between the
Christian and the Buddhist doctrine of love, treating the first as if it
were more life-furthering than it often was in practice, and treating
the latter as if it were wholly negative and life-denying, in its substitu
tion of pity for love and abstention from violence for active succor.

Aware of the static nature of Hindu civilization, Schweitzer even
overlooks the affirmative aspect of the popular doctrine of reincarna
tion, failing to interpret its truly progressive character and failing to

see that it provides a more logical system of rewards and punishments than the Christian conception of atonement; since it proportions heaven to one's deserts. For all his scholarship, such partiality to Christian revelation weakens Schweitzer's insight as an interpreter of the Hindu religions: he lacks in some degree the catholicism and the charity of Archbishop Söderblom's interpretation of The Living God. Despite this, Schweitzer characteristically owes a great debt to Hindu religion no less than to Chinese philosophy: for it is from Hinduism, rather than from Christianity, that Schweitzer consciously or unconsciously derived his central ethical doctrine: the reverence for life.

The transvaluation of established values, which Schweitzer has so magnificently carried out in his own person, has been only partly fulfilled in his philosophy: his ideas lack the organic wholeness of his life. This arises from the fact that he abandons the attempt to achieve a world picture capable of embracing both nature and man: though he valiantly bases his interpretation of the non-human world on the systematic effort to achieve truth, he founds his system of ethics on something apart from this: the will-to-live.

Fundamentally, Schweitzer's ethical doctrine merely turns that of Schopenhauer upside down: instead of preaching that the will-to-live is a curse, he embraces it as a blessing. But by divorcing ethics from the larger evolutionary process, Schweitzer's reverence for life must in the end confront this final paradox: if all forms of life prospered equally their very success would bring about life's own end; and before that happened the higher forms would die out. No choice can be sanely made in terms either of the will-to-live or the derivative doctrine of unqualified reverence for life.

Fortunately, this criticism of Schweitzer's philosophy does not subtract any value from his example as a teacher; for there he occupies a special pinnacle, by reason of his declared intention, so largely fulfilled in his actual writings, to follow truth to its ultimate goal and to abide by his findings. Note that intention and consider its applications: it contrasts favorably with the attitude of many scientists, who mean by truth only their system of truth; and who refuse even to look dispassionately into evidence that might compel a radical revision in their own assumptions.

No integration is worthy of our time or adequate to its challenge that seeks to unify men through a private system of truth: pace Gurdjiev and Steiner. However feeble science and collective research have been in establishing a valid life-wisdom, it is partly by further efforts in science and philosophy, equally respectful of "hard, irreducible facts" in departments so far ignored, that we shall correct these failings. In the highest type of person we can create today, fine thinking is as much a mark of excellence as human-heartedness, and an unconditional dedication to verifiable truth is the manifestation of its righteousness. Only through the guidance of man's highest function, his mind, can the claims of the rest of his life be fully expressed.

If Schweitzer's conscious philosophy is not adequate to express all that is implied in his living example, his life fortunately bodies forth much for which even categories or symbols are lacking in most philosophies: in the drama of his life, the philosophic implications of his position become crystal-clear. As theologian, physician, and musician, as thinker, man of action, and saint, Schweitzer has accepted all the hard claims of our time and performed, in admirable fashion, the corresponding duties. None knows better than he, through experience, that balance cannot be achieved without sacrifice: yet that balance itself counterweighs and nullifies the sacrifice by intensifying and expanding the possibilities of life. Schweitzer's moral greatness derives from the fact that he has shown that it is feasible, without renouncing the methods and insights of modern science, to achieve that which no science, no philosophy, no religion as yet adequately teaches: the possibility of becoming a whole man and of living, even under hostile circumstances, a whole life.

In every conscious act, Schweitzer has gone about the process of renewal with exemplary swiftness, simplicity, and directness: a further testimony to the soundness of his life-plan. One of the nurses in Schweitzer's hospital has borne witness to this genius for simplification. "I have never before," she writes, "seen an institution as personal as this one; nor have I seen one in which there is such a painstaking, hand-made element. There is originality and simplicity in the way everything is arranged. Emphasis is always laid on whatever is most practical." One might have deduced as much; but that testimony remains precious. Embrangled in its complexities, our civilization has an especial need for such direct action, and such straight moving, such rational simplification.

Albert Schweitzer's life, therefore, is a sign and a pledge. His life says, better than any book he has written, that however deeply our own lives suffer from the passive breakdown or the active destruction of our civilization, it is still possible to create a plan of life based on more solid foundations and directed toward higher ends: a life more organic in structure, more personal in expression, no longer the victim of specialism, nihilism, and automatism.

That this change cannot be effected easily goes without saying: nothing short of an heroic effort, widely participated in, will suffice. Perhaps few of us, no matter how resolute our understanding, will be able to achieve the even development of our parts or the all-embracing harmony that Schweitzer in his own person has achieved. Nor need we exaggerate Schweitzer's own success in order to make the goal seem more desirable: we must rather assume, since Schweitzer is but human, that there are weaknesses, contradictions, failures in this life: that in some degree he, too, remains incomplete, unbalanced, unfulfilled. All of us must live and act before we have perfected ourselves for our new parts, since only through the action can we become more perfect. So in the nature of things our best efforts will fall short.

But these reservations in no wise lessen the love and reverence Schweitzer's example commands: they are indeed assurances that the ideal he sets before us is not an unapproachable ideal: rather, it is just sufficiently beyond our normal habits and powers to introduce a salutary tension into all our activities. In this true person, the springs of life have started to flow again: presently, from a hundred similar sources along the mountain side, other springs will pour their waters, and a mighty stream will begin to carve a new channel through the valley below. This new type of man, so different in his balance from the Athenian or the Renascence gentleman, demonstrates the possibility of re-directing the forces of our civilization, and creating a new working unity between our powers and our purposes, which will utilize every suppressed or mutilated human potentiality.

External events beyond our human powers of control may for a time make this growth abortive: that has happened before and it may happen again. But if Western civilization escapes the evil fate that its over-commitment to mechanism and automatism, its wholesale denial of humane values and purposes, now threatens it with, if it overcomes its delusions of atomic grandeur and its psychotic compulsions to suicide or genocide, then the form that life will take, and the type of personality that will nurture it, is the form and the type that Albert Schweitzer has embodied. On such a basis, the renewal of life is possible.

CHAPTER VIII.   THE DRAMA OF RENEWAL

1: THE OPTIMISM OF PATHOLOGY   •

Every formative movement in culture, if profound enough to begin a new cycle of development, seems to start as a reaction against an inner disruption of society—what Gilbert Murray called a "loss of nerve." Almost overnight the familiar life that people have lived becomes meaningless: though they go through the routines of the day, inhabit the accustomed buildings, and worship their usual gods, their whole life suddenly becomes hollow. In a going culture, even the trivial details of existence become significant through their relation to the whole. In a disintegrating one, even great ambitions and plans seem insignificant, because a living sense of the whole has disappeared. At that moment, speech becomes da-da: once dynamic leaders become dangling puppets: life itself suddenly gets deflated, with an obscene snort, like a toy balloon ripping on a nail.

Thenceforward a culture may for many centuries go on repeating the old pattern of activities and ceremonies: it may even revert to archaic modes in order to overcome the dismaying discovery that the pattern is becoming dimmer as life itself proves emptier. But this crisis may cause a decisive reaction. If the forces of life rally, a new movement begins: the old ideas, de-polarized and freed from the pattern that can no longer use them, become re-united around a new organizing idea: the farther the disintegration has gone, the wider is the area on which the new idea can draw for sustenance. While the process of syncretism and synthesis can be traced with classic clearness in the history of Christianity, it is more or less present in every great transformation. When a civilization begins to develop around such an idea, it is potentially saved: that is, the lost members of this society—lost because they have been excluded from it or have found no common goal—become re-united: supported by the new ideology, they devise a new plot, wear a new costume, build new scenery, engage in a new drama. More often than not the excluded ones, the Gentiles, or the barbarians, the proletariat, the despised minority, take the lead in this transformation.

In this whole process there is a certain "optimism of pathology," as physicians used to call it: that is, where conditions seem worst, as in the delirious fever that precedes a crisis, they often have a higher chance of becoming better. Only after a certain agony of disintegration has been experienced is the soul ready, it would seem, to take on the otherwise insupportable burden of creating a new form of life. If the social crisis does not bring about death, it may foster fresh growth, in the way that a plant whose leaves have been stripped by beetles may, even late in the season, put forth fresh leaves. Often the creative period in a culture is the moment of rebound from a hard, almost fatal challenge: witness Athens after the Persian war, the Jews after the escape from Egypt.

More than one encyclopedic philosopher of history in our time has exerted much effort to understand how and why a cycle of culture or civilization develops, flourishes, and comes to an end. Spengler, using the simplest but most deceptive of analogies, suggested that all cultures went through the cycle of the seasons: forgetting that, if he took his figure seriously, he would have to account for the possibility of cultures situated in regions without any marked quarterly contrasts between cold and heat, growth and dormancy. Toynbee, building on Spengler, has gone exhaustively into various aspects of growth, arrest, and disintegration, with far more concrete detail and a more generous allowance for contradictions and discrepancies than Spengler. Unfortunately, at the end, Toynbee comes forward, if I understand him, with the suggestion that the mission of a culture in its final stages is to produce such a state of collapse and torment and irremediable disintegration as to make people give up all hope of earthly fulfillment. This leads to the development of a new type of Heaven-centered society—inconceivable, it would seem, to the whole and healthy—directed toward Eternity and functioning "out of time." On Sorokin's interpretation cultures fluctuate between ideational and sensate types, the first mystic, inward, otherworldly, the second pragmatic, externalized, positivist: a view which, despite the wealth of scholarship that supports it, seems to combine the weakest features of Spengler and Toynbee, though it tries to avoid the arrogant dogmatism of the first and the anti-historical otherworldliness of the second.

Now there are crushed and splintered fragments of truth in all three interpretations; and I would willingly utilize them: often the splinters penetrate deep. My own interpretation, however, is based on the assumption that man has repeatedly altered his archetypal biological plan of life by creating, through his culture, a social ritual and a drama, formed by his own special needs and conforming to his own emerging purposes. This new drama was, perhaps, a natural result of the increasing division of labor; for with such division went a multiplication of roles: choices thus opened before the members of such a society, not given altogether in their ancestral patterns. Within a developing society, fresh tensions arise and struggles ensue, between the old static tribal selves and the new cast of characters. This dramatic conflict heightens the interest of life: in search of it, men leave the custom-bound village and go to the city, for the city, out of its variety of human resources, provides a new mode of unity other than repetition and ritual: unity of dramatic theme. This theme is defined and modified by recurrent collective choices.

Drama, taking form in the theater, constantly appears as a symbol of a culture, at the moment the culture itself transforms stereotyped routines into unexpected dramatic actions, rich with new possibilities for life. For over the drama of the higher cultures presides a general guiding theme, a plot that encompasses every part of society and that involves each actor in a role other than his natural biological one, or the fixed prescriptions of social ritual. Thus emerging and developing social purposes get the better of habit and custom, tempting man into efforts that call forth otherwise unused stores of vital energies. In this drama of a culture man takes a further step in the process of interpretation that began with his utilization of the dream in art and his invention of language. By dramatic enactment, which encompasses his place, work, and folk, the scene, the action, the lines, and the plot, man interprets a larger range of phenomena than he could by any system of limited observation: he takes it in not merely as spectator but as participant: as playwright, manager, and scene-builder, too. This multi-functional role, enclosing every aspect of life, yields a fuller knowledge of the possibilities of existence, of man's nature and destiny, than could be achieved by any narrower means; for it invokes the widest kind of collaboration, and brings about the utilization of every possible aptitude and function.

The conception of the plot and the building up of the main themes of culture is one of the principal offices of religion. That which moves men to dramatic action in roles other than their natural ones is in fact their religion, no matter by what name they may call it. Thus the active religion of the Romans was not the pious performances attached to moth-eaten cults of local deities, but the construction of the Roman imperium: that of the American pioneer was not Protestantism, but the conquest of nature and the winning of the frontier. It was for these ideas that men struggled and sacrificed and willingly died. The detailed working out of these dramas in successive scenes and actions lies at the very heart of human history. What stands outside the collective drama belongs to the lumber room of history or to the heating and plumbing system of the theater: necessary incidents to producing the drama, but with no specific reference to what takes place on the stage. Who would go to the theater if all that happened was a series of scenic changes and fresh lighting effects, staged for their own sake? Man is easily bored by all the preparatory activities Nature forces on him: his drama is precisely what makes life interesting to him.

The rise of civilizations, from this point of view, is associated with the formulation of a dominant unifying theme and the creation of a central role for the hero, with subordinate roles for the supporting cast. But in the further development of the drama, more than this is required: the building of a special stage, the design of fresh scenery and properties, which will provide a symbolic background for the action, the further elaboration of roles, so that every member of the community will have a significant part to play. Meanwhile, the action tends to shift from the original central characters to the whole society that supports them.

Naturally, the lines of this drama are unwritten: the play itself is full of unplanned-for surprises, misplaced climaxes, prolix interludes, disconcerting breaks in action, awkward passages from comedy to tragedy: at best, it is a sort of *commedia dell' arte*, in which the actors improvise the lines as the plot progressively unfolds itself and, through their own fresh interpretations, gathers point and significance. Every culture produces a drama and *is* a drama: it interprets life and *is* life. Threatened by regressions to man's animal past, or by arrest in tribal rituals, man escapes from these limitations through the invention of drama, in which he renounces the perfection that animal societies know, and the stability that tribal societies achieve, by enacting the plot of the possible: choosing his costumes, his scenery, his lines, in order to give new meanings and purposes to human life. In the drama of a culture, man both holds the mirror up to nature and discovers potential selves that would otherwise lie dormant and unformed.

This dramatic interpretation of human culture does not seek to replace other interpretations, the economic, the religious, the psychological, the geographic: its merit is that it includes them and exposes the partiality of the effort to single out any aspect of the performance as the sole significant one. And if this is in fact a clue to the development of cultures, it is likewise perhaps a key to their decline. When a culture begins to disintegrate it does so, not because the seasons have changed, not because it is old and decrepit, not even because it has met an external injury or shock, but because its guiding theme, which bound all the parts of it together, political activities and economic affairs—and art and philosophy, too—has become exhausted: the acts of progressive self-revelation and self-understanding have been played out to their appointed end. The operative cause, which touches every institution simultaneously, is the collapse of meaning: the disintegration, not simply of this or that part, but of the overall pattern. As soon as this happens, the old scenery becomes irrelevant; the stage becomes cluttered with useless properties, which are themselves obstructive to fresh action: no longer impelled by its plot, the culture lacks choices, and even when presented with them, its leaders are incapable of making fresh decisions.

So, what begins in the growth of civilizations with the quickening of traditional ritual into a dramatic struggle, with challenges made and accepted, with purposes carried out or frustrated, falls back into a smooth, sordid-morbid routine. Yes: the old words have been spoken once too often: the old gestures have become a compulsive tic: life becomes full of vain repetitions, and the tensions and the ambitions that roused men to play their parts cease to be satisfactory even as ritual. The essence of drama is action and struggle in an important role, working up to an undisclosed climax through choices freely made. When the tension relaxes, the end itself disappears and the whole meaning of the performance evaporates. If the actors do not have the sense to leave the stage when that moment comes, then a tedious epilogue will be recited, just interesting enough, perhaps, to keep the audience from dispersing: witness Egypt after 1200 B.C. or China after the Sung Dynasty. At this point the actors, who had once thrown themselves into their work, leaving their everyday selves to take on their higher roles, refuse to take their parts seriously, particularly if the acting demands some strain and effort. They are tempted either to clown it or to fall back on their natural off-stage selves. This phase of vulgar naturalism is the end of all the arts: not least the art of life.

Now historically this relapse into the "natural self" is usually accompanied by an outbreak of rampant vitality: not the meaningful vitality of culture, but the blank raw vitality of barbarism, the regressive "barbarism of civilization," as Vico called it. With this the forces of the id, which had been held in restraint by the very requirements of the drama, manifest themselves in an upsurge of untrammeled lust and aggression, greed and senseless violence. Since men do nothing without some form of ideological disguise, if not support, this dethronement of the super-ego, this debasement of the ego, this magnification of the id, is accompanied by a deliberate cult of the primitive and the infantile. At this moment, all the more mature and more significant forms of life are dismissed, with contempt, as a mere hypocritical mask, an empty show. Effortlessness and purposelessness, the positive denial of significance and order, become qualifications for public success and approval: the chief reason for existence becomes a denial of any reason for existence. Nausea, followed by vomiting, not merely becomes almost a dominant symptom of the spiritual life, but the vomit itself is prized as life's essential product: *the* ultimate reality in all its sour denial.

Short of this final rejection of life, in anything but a physiological sense, each organ seeks its own separate satisfaction, as each member of this disintegrating society seeks his own temporary safety and prosperity, or as much of it as he can "get away with." If they still go through the motions of work it is only to make possible their dissipations and distractions and debaucheries. Neither direction nor self-control is left in such a society: its only form of inhibition or repression is that exercised *against* the higher functions. The plot of such a society is an inverted drama: it begins with the murder of the hero and successively mutilates, tortures, or exterminates every subordinate character. Boasting his decapitation, modern man parades, like a figure by Dali, in a blasted landscape, kicking his own head before him. The raw id, like unscreened energy, is fatal to what is specifically human: the new barbarian, with not even an animal's life-plan to guide him, must debase even his animal functions. So Hitler and his accomplices invented new mutilations of the human body in order to defile the spirit more effectively. The very idea of hell, an eternity of torture, was the subjective by-product of such a disintegrating society.

Emerson's estimate, that one-half of man is expression, becomes even truer if one realizes that this is mainly dramatic expression: indeed that his whole history is essentially a psychodrama, or rather a series of such collective dramas. Man is never so fully himself as when he is acting a part: when he is transforming the raw materials of life into art. Similarly, men are never such sorry creatures as when they have reached the end of one drama and find themselves without any part: each the undistinguished member of an aimless crowd of unemployed people. In such a state, only one thing can save the lost individual or his society: a new drama. When they are unwilling to throw themselves into this task they will seek a substitute in one-dimensional salvation: salvation by correct diet or by right posture or by dream-analysis or by orgasms.

Western civilization has now plainly come to a point where all the processes of disintegration and barbarism I have been abstractly describing are fully in view: the faceless and heartless man, the gangster, the connoisseur of violence who has devaluated everything about life except the instruments for defacing it, the inventors of the extermination camp, the agents and potential practitioners of random violence who devise H-bombs and biological instruments of genocide: all these are not merely in our midst but they include supposedly honorable and intelligent members of our society: the final proof of our extreme debasement. The processes of negation they have set in motion threaten to bring ruin to what is left of our civilization: carrying destruction over wider areas, and hastening its pace more effectively than ever before, precisely because we have placed all the highest capacities of scientific abstraction at the disposal of moral imbeciles and psychotics. In this manner the drama of the machine will come to an end: if it goes a scene further, there will not even be corpses left on the stage.

But what has happened in history before, may happen again: after disintegration, renewal. If that were not so it would be foolish to waste one's time considering alternatives to the catastrophe that is already so close to us. "Each age is a dream that is dying and one that is coming to birth"; and if the stench of a universal extermination camp now hangs prospectively over the planet, the possibility of a new life-drama has also appeared. We may not be spared the last act of disintegration: handcuffed together, the Automaton and the Id may march to their common doom. But already the script for a new play—or at least the synopsis—has been written and the new scenery and props are already in the wings. We have now, as a means of survival and a prelude to our further development, to throw ourselves into a new drama, in which elements of the human personality that have been repressed or mutilated by older institutions will form the core of a new synthesis.

Against the domination of the machine, we shall restore fresh energy to the word and the dream: we will bring forth ideal projects, plans, dramas, related to the whole personality, and to the community that sustains it and enhances it. Whereas the mark of the machine age was the dehumanization of man, the new age will give primacy to the person, so that ethics and the humane arts will dominate politics and technics. Many of these changes and transformations have long been in process. Our present task is to identify the emergent elements and to find a method, open to each of us, for bringing them together. In this process, much that is merely new we must be ready to reject; and much that is old will still prove of service.

2: DOCTRINE OF THE WHOLE

If the present diagnosis is correct, modern civilization cannot be sufficiently improved to escape disintegration by forms of science and politics and religion that now actively prevail: in all these domains a new orientation must be conceived, and more positive modes of action provided. Out of the division of peoples and races, we must create unity: out of the separation of classes and cultures, we must create common goals that will unite them, without permitting any permanent state of dominance and inferiority: out of intellectual specialization, we must create synthesis; finally, by overcoming the long-maintained hiatus between the subjective and the objective world, we must create a new person, who is at one with nature, and a new concept of nature, which does full justice to the person.

With the insights and the methods that are now in use, such a deep organic transformation in every department of life is inconceivable, except by slow piecemeal changes. Unfortunately, such changes, even if they ultimately converged on the same goal, are too partial and too slow to resolve the present world crisis. Western civilization needs something more than a drastic rectification of private capitalism and rapacious profiteering, as the socialists believe; something more than the widespread creation of responsible representative governments, cooperating in a world government, as World Federalists believe; something more than the systematic application of science to social affairs, as many psychologists and sociologists believe; something more than a re-building of faith and morals, as religious people of every creed have long believed. Each of these changes might be helpful in itself; but what is even more urgent, is that all changes should take place in an organic inter-relationship. The field for transformation is not this or that particular institution, but our whole society: that is why only a doctrine of the whole, which rests on the dynamic intervention of the human person in every stage of the process, will be capable of directing it.

On piecemeal terms, such a change is impossible: indeed inconceivable: so those who know no other method of approach are, if they be honest, corroded with cynicism and despair. But those who come to our present disorders with such limited expectations of surmounting them are like the pathetic armchair admirals in the United States Navy in the early stages of our conflict with Japan: these individuals predicted that the conquest of Japan would take at least ten years, since they could conceive no other way of effecting it than by capturing each island base, one by one, from the Caroline Islands upward. As long, indeed, as we cling to the present piecemeal method of attack, our problems will remain largely insoluble, unless we allow such a span of time for their working out that the crisis we now face would be unaffected.

But one of the reasons our society has become so incapable of controlling the automatic processes it has set in motion, is that its most potent and reliable method of thought has been basically at fault. Primitive man mistakenly treats things as if they were persons: but modern man treats persons as if they were things; and that is perhaps an even more dangerous superstition. The primitive's habit of mind at least did justice to the potentialities for life which matter, even in its less organized forms, actually possesses. But the modern bias reduces higher functions to lower ones, misinterprets as external events alone the processes of integration and development, and offers no clue to the nature of an organic transformation, which pervades the whole at the very moment that it brings about critical changes in the part.

Up to now, the closest that Western thinkers have come to a philosophy of the whole, capable of doing justice to the nature of organisms, societies, and human personalities, has been in the Marxian doctrine of dialectical materialism: especially as that doctrine was expounded by Friedrich Engels. What was important in this conception was certainly not Marx's vulgar materialism: what was important was the original Hegelian conception of the organic unity of natural and social processes, in their continuous evolution and transformation. This unity underlies even conflicts between the dominant forces of society, since each resolution of thesis and antithesis in turn produces a synthesis which reconciles their claims in a new emergent pattern. What success Marxism has actually had in the world has been partly due to the confidence and resolution that the very idea of such a possibility of unity gives to the believer: in that respect it rivals Islam as a religious doctrine.

Unfortunately, in suppressing the Hegelian part of its heritage, with its emphasis on subjective forces and ideas, Marxism gave rise to as great a distortion as the non-organic, piecemeal view of the life-process given by post-Newtonian science. In addition, the very conception of the dialectic process itself is too limited to account for all types of change: Marxism does not do justice to non-dialectical changes, like maturation: it takes no account of the processes of de-building and disintegration, which often fail to produce any reactive change in the opposite direction: above all, it has no place for freedom, that essential attribute of personality: for Marx limited freedom, in so many words, to "the conscious recognition of necessity." Hence Marxism has no theory to account for its own corruption, though the stench of that corruption in Soviet Russia is the most signal manifestation of Marxism today.

Even if one added Hegelian idealism to Marxian materialism to form a theoretic whole, Marxism would be an inadequate doctrine; for the reason that it makes the processes of history external to human choice and plan, and buries the person in society. Instead of understanding that the person is a higher emergent from the community, Marxism personifies the community and endows its leaders alone with the true attributes of persons: this is in fact a regression to the theology of the Egyptian pharaohs, for whose personal enhancement a whole society worked and slaved. The tributes offered to Stalin on his seventieth birthday did in fact endow him with every attribute of Godhead. Meanwhile dialectical materialism has been transformed in the USSR into a system of totalitarian compulsion, in which the ruling classes protect themselves from the challenge and struggle inherent in the dialectic process itself by holding that they have arrived at perfect and final truth. This "truth" may of course change from year to year as a matter of expediency; but the Stalinist Marxian denies the validity of any rival form; despotic fiat takes the place here of cooperative verification and correction.

Far from creating dynamic unity and synthesis, this dialectical system, despite Engels's original effort to make it organic, creates a static monolithic body of dogma: insulated from criticism and from the challenge of rival ideas. Even worse, it creates a dualistic theology, with a special God, "communism," and a new devil, capitalism. This theology becomes all the more quaint because communism has been transformed, in the course of a generation, into a full-fledged fascist system, marked by the absolute control of a single party, by compulsion and terror as normal adjuncts of government, by the abject worship of the Leader, and by a paranoid isolationism; whereas in almost every country capitalism has been steadily modified by an influx of socialist measures which equalize wealth, distribute power to the workers, guarantee economic security, and promote human welfare: in short provide many of the tangible benefits promised by communism without abolishing political and intellectual freedom.

The time has come, therefore, for a more profound transformation than the purely materialistic conceptions of revolution could envisage. The present crisis calls for an axial change in our whole system of thinking and in the social order based on it. Deliberately, I use the word "axial" in a double sense, meaning first of all that there must be a change in values, and further a change so central that all the other activities that rotate around this axis will be affected by it. Such a change must be based on a fuller understanding of human life, in all its dimensions, than the naive philosophies of romanticism and socialism or any other form of eutopianism were able to entertain. The new philosophy will treat every part of human experience, from the enduring structure of the physical world to the briefest incarnation of divinity, as an aspect of an inter-related and progressively integrating whole. It will restore the normal hierarchy of the organic functions, placing the part at the service of the whole, and the lower function at the command of the higher: thus it will establish once more the primacy of the person, and the function of man himself as the interpreter and director—not the passive mirror and ultimate victim—of the forces that have brought him into existence.

3: ON REACHING A SINGULAR POINT

So far the best insight into the creative factors in history comes from an almost forgotten memoir by the great physicist, James Clerk Maxwell. In this letter, following up a mathematical clue first traced by

Babbage and Boole, he sets forth his doctrine of Singular Points. Clerk Maxwell observed that science is organized to study continuities and stabilities; and selects by preference those fields where these attributes are significantly dominant. But even in the physical world, he adds, there are unpredictable moments when a small force may produce, not a commensurate small result, but one of far greater magnitude . . . "the little spark which kindles the great forest, the little word which sets the whole world a-fighting, the little scruple which prevents a man from doing his will."

"Every existence above a certain rank," Maxwell continues, "has singular points: the higher the rank, the more of them. At these points, influences whose physical magnitude is too small to be taken account of by a finite being may produce results of the greatest importance. All great results produced by human endeavour depend on taking advantage of these singular states when they occur." And Maxwell goes on to quote Shakespeare's famous passage from Julius Caesar about a tide in the affairs of men which, taken at its flood, leads on to fortune. At such moments that which is impossible on any common-sense calculation, may not merely become thinkable but enactable; whereas predictions based on regularities, continuities, stabilities, also observable in the same society and usually sufficient for its description, would prove misleading as a guide to decisive action or as a clue to future tendencies. What informed Roman observer, as late as the second century A.D., could have believed that his great empire would be taken over, from top to bottom, by the followers of an obscure Galilean prophet, hardly known by name to the educated?

What follows from this doctrine? As regards all that touches the thousand routine functions of society, with its mass movements and its mass organizations, Maxwell's observation remains inoperative for the greater part of their history: to keep even the meanest community going from day to day calls for an enormous mass of repetitive effort, putting brakes on dangerous tendencies, speeding remedial actions, bringing about detailed reforms and improvements. The doctrine of Singular Points countenances no suspension of these daily needs and fulfillments: no putting off of the numerous concrete tasks needed to support the life of the community: no passive waiting around for the great moment that will bring about some different constellation of forces. Indeed, Maxwell's doctrine presumes the existence of these regularities and continuities.

But Maxwell adds something both to the scientific description o
social change and the life of any society that may be so described
For he points out that at intervals, at critical moments in crises, a sup
plementary method of inciting change may be a decisive one, particu
larly if its importance is recognized and the nature of the moment it
self correctly interpreted. At such a pass, the human personality may
produce an effect out of all proportion to its physical powers, just as
tiny seed-crystal, dropped into a saturate solution, may cause the whole
mass to assume a similar crystalline form. Such timely intervention o
a "physical magnitude too small to be taken account of by a finite be
ing" may produce an effect equivalent to a cumulative and widespread
change accomplished by a much greater expenditure of effort through
the normal channels of social change.

This doctrine accounts for the major operations of personality in his
tory: it likewise accounts for the rareness of these occasions. Even wher
such a change is brought about, however, it must be confirmed and car
ried through by the same forces that operate through institutional
mechanisms from day to day. (In terms of our sociological schema the
personal processes of formulation and incarnation must be followed
through by the social processes of incorporation and embodiment.)
In both cases, we are dealing with natural events, operating on the
plane of history: one proceeds by an accumulation of small changes:
the other by a singular change that irradiates through and transforms
the whole society.

Maxwell's doctrine, now confirmed by physical research, casts a
further light on the means by which a new type of personality, Confucian, Buddhist, Christian, Mohammedan, Marxian, gathers to itself
sufficient power to overcome the normal resistances to wholesale change
that every society exhibits. At moments of crisis, where the roads to
disintegration or to development separate, as on a watershed, a single
decisive personality, or a small group of informed and purposeful
men, may by a slight push determine the direction and movement of an
otherwise uncontrollable mass of conflicting social forces. At such moments not a single institution or group, but a whole society, will be involved in a change far beyond its ordinary capacities for adaptation:
yet the dynamic agent in this transformation, the "spark which kindles
the great forest," will be the individual human person; for it is he
who precipitates the change in the social order by first initiating a
profound re-grouping of forces and ideal goals within himself. At such
a moment the human integer represents the whole and in turn has an

effect on the whole. Only within the compass of the person can a total change be effected within the span of a single generation, sufficient to produce the necessary effect on civilization at large: like the seed-crystal, he passes on to the whole the new order of the part.

The point to observe is that what science calls "nature" or the "external world" is partly a projection of the human personality, modified by its capacities and its needs and its cultural forms. Instead of beginning with nature and eliminating, as far as possible, the operations of the personality, we must begin with the human personality, as the most inclusive and complete of all observable phenomena, since every other kind of force and event can be mirrored in it and interpreted by it; and we must pay particular attention to those kinds of events that are not patent in the more stable and repetitious cycles of nature.

In taking this position I would recall certain illuminating perceptions of William James, which unfortunately he never sufficiently developed in his own philosophy. "The spirit and principles of science," he observed, "are mere affairs of method; there is nothing in them that need hinder science from dealing successfully with a world in which personal forces are the starting-points of new effects. The only form of thing that we directly encounter, the only experience that we concretely have, is our personal life. The only complete category of our thinking, our professors of philosophy tell us, is the category of personality, every other category being one of the abstract elements of that. And this systematic denial on science's part of personality as a condition of events, this rigorous belief that in its own essential and innermost nature our world is a strictly impersonal world, may, conceivably, as the whirligig of time goes round prove to be the very defect that our descendants will be most surprised at in our own boasted science, the omission that to their eyes will most tend to make *it* look perspectiveless and short." (The Will to Believe.)

The whirligig of time has now gone round. On the ideological basis of the person we must now make a fresh start.

Instead of the self-abdicating view of the post-medieval world, which put external nature in a position of dominance, we now give primacy to the historic person, with his values, purposes, ideals, ends. As soon as we accept this interpretation as the only one that is capable of doing justice to every aspect of human experience, uniting the inner and the outer, the private and the public, as well as the subjective and the objective, we have a firm hold upon the whole gamut of human experience; for, among other things, we can then give due weight to non-repeatable events and to singular moments.

Much has happened even in science during the last half-century to make this change possible. Not the least important observation of Freud's was the discovery that single events—traumas or injuries—that took place in earliest childhood, might leave traces on the human personality that would outweigh in their effect a lifetime of habit. Though Freud may originally have over-stressed the pervading influences of isolated injuries that occurred in childhood, there is little doubt that such events, both in childhood and much later, may profoundly re-shape the personality. Not only a trauma but a benign occurrence may have such a disproportionate effect—a sentence casually dropped by a teacher in the midst of a lesson, a single act of heroism or generosity or sacrifice, may even without visibly standing out in memory operate under the surface and determine a score of later events.

Shall we neglect these occasions because science in the past had no place for them in its limited method of interpretation? Shall we deny their importance because they are quantitatively insignificant, or because they occur in a non-repeatable and unpredictable fashion? No: for what holds true for the individual holds likewise for groups and communities: in some measure the person operates at every level. Just as we know that infinitesimal traces of chemicals, like copper or boron, may be vital to organic growth, so mere traces of personality may alter the pattern of historic events.

For the last four centuries man has disciplined himself to achieve a view of the external world in which his own wishes and hopes and fantasies should play as small a part as possible in coloring the results. In consequence of this displacement of the person, he has achieved law and order, regularity and predictability, over large tracts of external existence: a superb achievement, which redounds to the benefit of the human person itself. But now, in order to give full weight to every aspect of life and to restore parts of experience that were suppressed in this effort to achieve order, man must complement this gain in objectivity by creating a new form of subjectivity, one which will not infringe in arbitrary fashion on scientific order, but will do justice to forces and potentialities that still lie beyond it.

Not merely does it take a person to understand a person: but one must use the categories of personality to understand a lower order of life that has begun to partake of the personal. The release of these subjective factors may now even be a necessity of survival; for only by a recovery of esthetic and moral sensitivity can we escape from the maiming brutalities which a cult of the impersonal has imposed as a matter of course.

In any generation, only a few people reach the stature which makes them capable of dealing with the emergent forces and singular moments of history either as interpreters or actors: Burckhardt, Henry Adams, Kropotkin, Patrick Geddes, showed such powers in recent times on the theoretic side as Gandhi, Wilson, Lenin, and Churchill did in action. If the process of de-personalization went on indefinitely modern man would give up all possibility of directing and controlling the lethal automatisms that have gone along with it. Even now, the pervasive present sense of helplessness before a man-created catastrophe has caused many Western men to fall back to the superstitious level of a primitive tribe in the face of a volcanic eruption: too awed even to flee from the spot. Were Mr Roderick Seidenberg's analysis of this situation correct, there would be no way out.

So far from accepting that analysis, which projects our present life-denying tendencies into an indefinite future, I look forward to a contrary reaction: one which will reclaim for the human personality much of the ground that, during the last four centuries, it voluntarily surrendered. Not neutrality and one-sided objectivity, not impersonality and hardness, will be the marks of the new personality. Those traits, once sedulously cultivated as "scientific," are already in fact old-fashioned: they perhaps reached their final limit of life-negation and life-debasement in the Nazi extermination chambers where once reputable physicians, with high standing in science, subjected their victims to endless ingenuities of pseudo-scientific torture. The new personality will round out the discipline of the impersonal with the fullest expression of sympathy and empathy, with the most exquisite responsiveness to all modes of being; with a readiness to embrace life in its unity and wholeness, its uniqueness and its freedom and its endless creativity.

Far from certainly, yet very possibly, Western civilization may be on the verge of such a crucial transformation today. A singular moment, which may hold incalculable practical consequences, may actually be at hand: perhaps, in some far corner of the world, it has already taken place, without being reported: for possibly not until long after that moment has passed will we have the means of verifying its existence—unless indeed the singular point should have a negative issue, and lead us to final disaster.

But if we understand the nature of the personality, and the way that it is operative in history—steadily in small increments, intermittently in potent quantities—we shall be ready to take advantage of a singular point when it occurs. There is even a special touch of encouragement in Maxwell's dictum that the higher the rank of existence the more frequent the occurrence of singular points.

There can be little doubt that mankind reached such a singular point at the end of the Second World War. At that moment an awakened personality in the presidency of the United States, with enough courage and vision to have committed the country unconditionally to the principle of responsible World Government, backed by even much wider acts of succor and co-operation than UNRRA and the Marshall Plan envisaged, might have led all mankind toward positive peace. That effort would by its own inner dynamic have challenged and overthrown the fascism and the frightened isolationism of the Kremlin. Such a point may presently occur again: sooner than any calculation of probabilities would expect. If we fail to take advantage of that second moment, the rest of our voyage may in truth be "bound in shallows and in miseries."

4: AN ORGANIC SYNCRETISM

The ideas and the ideals that will transform our civilization, restoring initiative to persons and delivering us from the more lethal operations of automatism, are already in existence: let me emphasize this fact. Indeed the very persons who will make critical decisions, when a singular moment presents itself, are already, it seems probable, alive: it is even possible that a decisive change is already in operation, though as thoroughly hidden to us as the future of Christianity was to Pontius Pilate. If it were otherwise, the outlook would be black; for no change as thoroughgoing as that which will start our civilization on a new dramatic cycle can be effected overnight.

Just as the upbuilding and de-building forces are continually at work in society, so many of the ideas and institutions necessary to offset the now obsolete ambitions of "Faustian Man" have long been in existence. For at least two centuries a series of new values and goals have been projected in this society. Even though they have failed to change markedly the course of events, they have served to correct some of the distortions caused by a one-sided commitment to Moloch and Mammon, the twin deities who would sacrifice life to power, prestige, and profit.

Some of these compensating influences have come from surviving traditions and customs, the debris of civilizations that were kinder to the whole man: others represent new social mutations, hardly capable of surviving in the existing order, but quite capable of becoming the organizing nuclei in a new civilization. The coming together of these ideas and ideals, their re-polarization around the concepts of the balanced man, the self-governing group, and the universal community is the first step in syncretism: the forerunner in the mind of a new general pattern of life.

Let us make a brief canvass of the elements that were repressed by the dominant culture of the past century: for they will probably dominate the coming one, while the forces that have hitherto been uppermost, mechanization and quantification, will be incorporated in the new society as either recessives or survivals, not entirely lost or neglected, we shall hope, but subordinated to more vital purposes.

From the eighteenth century on the chief challenge to the machine came from romanticism, for by this time the medieval culture was in a state of advanced decay, and the regenerative movement of Protestantism had in its turn capitulated to capitalism. In protesting against this erosion of traditional values, the romantics, led by Jean-Jacques Rousseau, sought to undermine the whole mechanical conception of human improvement: significantly Rousseau proclaimed in his first dissertation that the arts and sciences themselves tended to corrupt morals, as Augustine had held long before. Romanticism, seeking to make a fresh start, returned with Vico and Rousseau to a mythical primitivism.

In order to reinstate the suppressed vitalities of man, the romantics turned their backs on culture and sought nature, unsullied, untouched: Rousseau's nature, not Newton's. But what they called nature was in fact the art and politics and morals of more simple societies: Corsica served as well as Polynesia. They found their new ideals in the art of the folk ballad, in the politics of the village community, in the morals and the life-nurturing activities of the peasant household and village, elegiacally recorded by Gray and Goldsmith, dynamically espoused by Rousseau, Herder, Scott and their nineteenth century followers.

Romanticism, thus conceived, was a return to the continuities of history, which had been disrupted by the new power ideology of despots and centralized organizations; and it was conceived as a protest against the utilitarian man, the new ideal type: it reinstated the elements in life that the mechanical ideology left out, spontaneity, impulse, freedom, love: practices that defied repetition and disrupted routine.

All in all, romanticism made many contributions to a more organic conception of human life. Everywhere it introduced an element of playfulness and spontaneity into a civilization where the mechanical discipline of capitalism was adding to the older constraints of institutional formalism: it furthered a rustic simplicity in dress, a peasant homeliness in cooking, an unaffected directness in manners, and above all, a respect for the childlikeness of the child in education, and for the lovingness of lovers in marriage. Even in the arts and crafts, the romantic emphasis upon the person brought about a restoration of sound handwork, at a time when the old methods and processes were in danger of being cast completely aside. The Kindergarten and the Garden Suburb were the supreme embodiments of romantic doctrine.

Unfortunately the romantics lacked a general principle of integration; for the romantic was so eager for freedom that he was at home only in a despotic society of one. But the prophets of romanticism, from Rousseau to Ruskin, from Herder to Hugo, from Scott and Froebel to Walt Whitman and William Morris, brought back into Western culture many important elements that had been jettisoned in the swift change-over to the machine. Romanticism was an emotional oasis in the desert of industrialism: by popularizing the picnic and the summer vacation it altered the very rhythm of machine civilization. Its more positive, non-reactionary ideals, the appreciation of spontaneity it shares with Taoism, its emphasis on feeling and emotion and sensibility, its respect for the organic, its affirmation of the imaginative arts are all precious and permanent gifts to a balanced culture.

One of the great contributions of the romantics was the attempt to strip life to its essentials: this tendency only carried further an affiliated movement in the historic religions. Though one of the effects of science was to close men's minds to religion, another was to give religion a compensatory role; and this led, like the romantic movement itself, into an attempt to establish continuities with an older and deeper past.

This movement had first taken shape, in Christianity, in reaction against thirteenth century capitalism; the first efforts of the Waldensians and the Lollards aimed at a de-materialization of the physical symbols and rituals of the Church. This came to a climax in the comprehensive negations, the life-affirming denials, of the Society of Friends. Calvinism, at the same time, gave back to the congregation, a group of persons, the initiative that had been lost through the one-sided Caesarean organization of the universal Church; and the general political concepts of democracy owe far more to the self-governing Churches, which flourished from the sixteenth century on in the English-speaking countries, than to the once-democratic self-enclosed guilds, which became centers of oligarchic corruption and decay. To the Quakers we owe such democratic simplicity as we have achieved in clothes, such directness of manners, such absence of empty ceremonial, and such mildness and amity as we show in collective deliberation. This survival has still almost the vigor of a mutation: an essential contribution to the new personality.

In other historic religions, similar movements have taken place: notably in the purification of Hinduism undertaken by Mahatma Gandhi. Gandhi's translation of religious faith into a working political creed, based on the Tolstoyan principles of non-violence and the duty of manual labor, were declarations of the primacy of the person at the very point where modern man was tempted to minimize the impact of personality, and to over-value that of organization. This, too, will be one of the formative contributions to the new integration; for without the capacity for direct action that Gandhi, above all other leaders, showed, we shall be pinned to the ground like Gulliver in Lilliput.

5: EUTOPIANISM AND UNIVERSALISM

Along with the romantic and the religious sources of renewal comes a third movement that must not be under-rated, for it now constitutes an active recessive, if not a dominant, in most parts of Western civilization. This one may call eutopianism: the belief in the possibility of renovating society, through the application of reason and social invention to political and economic institutions.

The central themes of eutopianism were first expressed by Thomas More in his Utopia (1516); and they cover every aspect of eutopianism, from the constitutional reform of governments in order to equalize power and further the democratic process, to the just sharing of the annual productivity and the accumulated wealth of the community by every willing and working member of it. In its faith in invention, in its concentration on mass production—which means ultimately the widest distribution of the product—even modern capitalism shows a beneficent eutopian side: so that it was possible for a utilitarian mind like Edward Bellamy's in Looking Backward to look forward to the attainment of Eutopia by a general election, which would alter the control of industry without altering essentially either the process or the product.

Now ours is a planet where the greater part of the population still lacks the bare essentials of life: where even in the richest country almost a third of the population, some fifty million, live below the margin of physical decency, with ramshackle and overcrowded housing, a poor diet, insufficient medical care, and grossly inadequate opportunities for education and spiritual development. Hence it should be plain that the eutopian movement, which emphasized the importance of many functions neglected not only by private capitalism but by romanticism and religion, has still a vital part to perform in the renewal of life. Those who dodge this fact, by confining renewal to an inner change, as if the higher functions could flourish while the lower ones were starved and mutilated, overlook the unusual nature of their own security and comfort: we who have a more organic philosophy cannot share such irresponsible, egoistic perfectionism.

So far from recoiling at communism, because of the current totalitarian perversion of its original life-furthering purposes, we must clearly understand that every country, whether nominally agrarian or capitalist or socialist, is bound, in support of a life more abundant, to seek a progressive equalization of opportunities and goods for all its members. De Tocqueville, a staunch conservative, correctly observed a century ago that this movement toward equalization was the guiding principle of the last seven hundred years in Western civilization: it is in fact the essential democracy that underlies other possible forms of democracy. Christianity recognized the fundamental equality of men in Heaven: eutopianism extends that recognition to the earth. The program of socialism has still a considerable distance to go, even in such advanced countries as Great Britain, Norway, or Sweden, before each citizen will have by right his basic share in all the goods of life, as preliminary to whatever else his special talents or exertions may bring him. Admittedly, this movement is not free from dangers: the dangers of totalitarianism, automatism, purposeless materialism, psychological "over-protection." By its unqualified success it might create a universal squirrel cage, occupied by well-fed squirrels, too fat and bored even to work the wheel that will ensure their continued existence. But those dangers, though already pressing in our over-organized technical society, will be diminished under an ideology and mode of life that restores the primacy of the person.

Now the greatest of the repressed components in present civilization I have left to the last: this is universalism. During the nineteenth century universalism was expressed in forms that awakened antagonism and resistance in those parts of the world that most heavily felt its presence. Religiously, universalism took hold in an increased spread of Christian missionary enterprise, continuing a development begun first by the Apostles and renewed once more by Francis of Assisi in the thirteenth century. Politically, universalism expressed itself in the even more one-sided and arrogant form of imperialism: the exploitation of distant lands and peoples for the benefit of investors at home and a new class of colonial rulers abroad. Technically, universalism meant standardization and uniformity, first in the instruments of production and finally in all the means of life: eventually in the end-products as well.

Each of these forms of universalism had serious human defects: above all a blindness to the values it suppressed and replaced and an unwillingness to admit variety and autonomy. If the religious missionary patronizingly gave without taking, the trader and colonizer rapaciously took without giving: in the very act of spreading the real goods of Western civilization, these representatives contrived to make even its virtues odious. The age of exploration and colonization, of the steamship and the ocean cable, laid solid foundations for a world community: but it was content to erect on these foundations a flimsy sheet-iron warehouse, a temporary structure to store raw materials before shipment home. Technical universalism provided the basic conditions of peace, order, and co-operation, but for lack of insight into the higher principles involved it presently became lost in the Heart of Darkness—to recall Joseph Conrad's deeply illuminating fable.

Despite these failures, universalism lies at the very center of a new integration of life: the stone defaced by the nineteenth century builders must now be recut with fresh and true surfaces. Perhaps the most significant part of the development of science and technics during the last three centuries has been its many universal by-products: a universal standard of weights and measures, a universal method, that of scientific observation and experiment, and a universal principle of association, based on freedom of thought and communication, and voluntary affiliation under the forms of democracy. The development of international congresses of science and scholarship and religion during the nineteenth century were the first steps toward a world parliament: at the great Paris Exposition of 1900, one hundred and twenty International Congresses were held.

Meanwhile, the invention of improved mechanical methods of travel and transportation and communication created, for the first time in history, an all-embracing community. With the further development in the twentieth century of the telephone and the radio—and ultimately television—all the inhabitants of the planet could theoretically be linked together for instantaneous communication as closely as the inhabitants of a village. Indeed, it is conceivable—though not at all probable—that the Sermon on the Mount could now be preached to the greater part of mankind at the moment it was uttered, provided such a notorious agitator as Jesus of Nazareth could be admitted to studios controlled mainly in the interests of commercial advertisers or totalitarian governments, and allowed to speak without submitting a prepared script.

So powerful were these universal agents up to 1914, so thoroughly in accord were the peoples in the West as to their beneficence, that the regressions that subsequently took place through war, nationalism, and isolationism were for them almost unimaginable. But those who believed in universalism were too little conscious of the arrogance and one-sidedness that characterized its premature conquest of the planet: the provinciality of its law and order, the failure of humility that marked even those who professionally preached the gospel of humility. What is worse, the technical and economic forms of universalism were pushed much faster than the social habits that would have supported a worldwide community: apart from spontaneous local efforts like pidgin English, there was little serious effort to create a truly universal language for the practical tasks of world intercourse: a language logical, fixed, and brief, like Basic English, but without the unconscious provinciality of Messrs Ogden and Richards's invention, with their retention of English words and English sounds, even English spelling. Esperanto was only a shade better: it preserved the vices of a natural language without achieving the grammatical simplicity of Chinese or the facile euphony of Hawaiian. The lack of such a universal language, in an age that has the technical means of broadcasting by short wave from any one spot to any other part of the earth, reduces the efficiency of our powerful machines to a mere fraction of their possible maximum. This deep inner contradiction runs through all our universal mechanical instruments: and the only thing more strange than the fact that it exists is the further fact that so few people seem aware of its absurdity.

What is true in technics holds equally for politics. Though at the end of the nineteenth century a first feeble start at creating a body of world law and a government capable of framing it and executing it was made in the Hague Conference, imperialism and nationalism moved in the opposite direction: toward war and conquest: toward segregation, non-co-operation, isolation. This general political regression reached its climax in the economic autarchy actively practiced by Nazi Germany and the New Deal in the United States in the nineteen-thirties, and in the segregation and isolation now hideously visible in both Soviet Russia and the South Africa of today. By contrast, the old-fashioned imperialism of the nineteenth century was enlightened and humane in a high degree: for it is more human to exploit one's brother than to deny that he has any claim on one's attention. The failure to create a world government, capable of establishing order and law, to take the place of force and fear in the relations of peoples, brought to an end the spontaneous universalism of the nineteenth century. The War that began in 1914 is therefore, in consequence, not yet ended.

The naive form of universalism, as expressed by science and technics, no less than by missionary enterprise and imperialism, was itself a partial movement. Technical universalism needed the correction of eutopianism: a positive concept of justice and mutual aid, to take the place of the "white man's burden," and an open-minded receptivity to the products of other forms of culture, as they seeped into other parts of the world, through the efforts of traders and scholars, explorers and scientists. Even within the domain of technics, universalism too easily forgot its debt to other forms of life than its own: the fact, for example, that perhaps half of the world's food crops today derive from primitive cultures that had no contact with the West during their great period of plant domestication. Without these crops the world would be closer to starvation; without the Amazon aborigine's gift of rubber, half our wheels would cease to move.

The abortive universalism of the nineteenth century was nevertheless a happy beginning: the task of the coming age will be to provide it with the human elements it lacked the insight to discover or the courage to invent: a universal morality, as a basis of friendly political intercourse: a universal language, taught as the second language to all children in all schools, to make world communication possible: a world government, with a world capital in every continent, transmuting national struggles and conflicts, which will continue in some form to exist, into habits of law and order, of restraint and positive co-operation: a world citizenship for every human being on the planet, with increasing energy and time devoted to travel and intercourse on a world scale, and interchange of workers and students between regions now ingrown, suspicious, and hostile through their isolationism. To supplement a universalism based on mere mechanical uniformity and on a breaking down of physical barriers in time and space, we must create a universalism based on the spiritual wealth and variety of men: their unity in diversity achieved by working together for common ends. Out of that may come, in the fullness of time, a truly universal religion.

Through this worldwide unity, the human personality, now suppressed and deformed by the very agents and organizations it has created, will begin to unfold and expand in all its dimensions: mankind will enter upon a higher stage of development. This is the new heaven and the new earth that beckon us beyond the disorders of our apocalyptic age. But only whole men, liberated from the automatism of both instinctual and rational organizations, integrated in all their functions, will have the vital energy to take part in this drama. By building the foundations for such a structure, our generation will invest the work of the next era with purpose and significance.

6: THE NEW MUTATION

The re-polarization of the existing creeds and ideologies and methodologies, which now function at cross-purposes, could take place only under one condition: through the appearance of a new concept of space and time, of cosmic evolution and human development.

Such a mutation of ideas has in fact been taking place during the last century: particularly during the last generation. One associates this dominating concept with the new insights into the nature of the organism and of the ecological processes in biology: with the exploration of the pre-rational and unconscious and self-determined elements in human behavior, which makes it possible to include art and religion in our total understanding of the nature and destiny of man. Finally, one associates the new concept with the emergence of a sociology and a philosophy capable of doing justice to every aspect of human life, the inner and the outer, the individuated and the associated, the symbolic and the practical; that understands both repetitive processes and singular moments, causal sequences and purposeful goals.

Now the new polarizing element is the concept of the person: the last term in the development of the organic world and the human community. Instead of taking as fundamental such a derivative concept as the physical universe, our thought now begins with the agent through whose history and development such a concept becomes possible. In other words, we begin with man himself, at the fullest point of his own development, his emergence into a person: with man as the interpreter of natural events, man as the conservator of meanings and values and patterns of life, with man as the transformer of nature, and with man, finally, as the projector and planner of new purposes, new destinies, not given in nature, man transcending his own creatureliness in his forecasts of further creativity. Even in the physical cosmos, considered by itself, the new astronomers and physicists tell us, creation may be a continuous process, perhaps the primordial one, while what we once regarded as the "real" world, with its stabilities and regularities, may be only a relatively inert residue—the detritus of this creative process.

At all events, only when we begin with the person can we fill out the blank spaces in our understanding left by the purely causal interpretations of science. Causal explanation endeavors to understand the complex by means of the simple; breaks up the whole to deal with the part; treats all events as determined sequences, as they in fact are —once they have taken place. Teleological explanation seeks to understand processes in terms of goals, the thread in terms of the pattern, the part by its dynamic relation to the whole. So, too, it interprets the past with reference to the future, the necessary in relation to the possible, the actual as revealed in the potential. From this new standpoint, we realize that facts are no more primary than values, that mechanical order is no more fundamental than pattern and purpose, and that we have not fully understood the cosmos until we have explored all the dimensions—visible and hidden, actual and potential—of the person.

Man's world, as we now conceive it, is a multi-dimensional one, both in time and space. To take full account of it, we must include both its subjective and objective aspects: not casting aside qualities or patterns or purposes because they are irrelevant when we wish to measure the speed of a falling stone or the motion of a planet. Into the person, the mechanical, the organic, the social all enter: from the person, creativity and divinity emerge. To interpret the whole, we must approach experience at various levels of abstraction and concretion; only by so doing can we even partly grasp its dense, inter-woven, many-layered complexity. Even in the physical sciences, from which so many essential attributes of organic life are eliminated, there is a molar aspect and a molecular one, an astronomic field and an atomic field: and between these extremes there are many levels of experience and consistent interpretation. When we begin with the person, which includes even the most elementary physical phenomena, we penetrate life at every level, and reject nothing that is given in human experience, even if it appears but once.

With this new orientation man now resumes the place that he voluntarily abdicated three centuries ago, when Western man overlooked his own creative properties and gave precedence to matter, motion, quantitative change. The order and continuity man finds in nature, he takes to himself, in order to further his own development. Likewise the variety and adventure, the creativeness and expressiveness he finds in himself, he reads back into nature, with new insights into events that remained meaningless when taken in isolation, cut off from their final destination. Through the new sense of the organic and the personal come the auxiliary notions of dynamic equilibrium and creative emergence. There is no phase of knowledge or practical activity that will not be affected by this re-establishment of the primacy of the person.

Such a polarizing idea, when it takes hold in a society, plays the part of the "organizer" in cell growth: it provides the spatial pattern and the temporal order through which every activity becomes interrelated in a new design. The idea of a physical world from which many of the higher operations of personality were excluded, which was the very basis of the scientific and industrial civilization of the past, was such a polarizer: the progressive dehumanization and annihilation of man in his conquest of the planet and his exploitation of power, was partly the result of this limited concept. In so far as the idea of the person does fuller justice to the order of nature and the condition of man, it may in the days to come offset the errors of the past and lay the basis for a worldwide integration of both thought and life. Our machines have become gigantic, powerful, self-operating, inimical to truly human standards and purposes: our men, devitalized by this very process, are now dwarfed, paralyzed, impotent. Only by restoring primacy to the person—and to the experiences and disciplines that go into the making of persons—can that fatal imbalance be overcome.

The new formulations of organism, community, and personality are now increasingly operative in many departments of life: in medicine and psychological guidance and education, in community development and regional planning, not least in technics, where an understanding of organisms has enabled the inventor to pass from the limited world of pure mechanics to that of organically conditioned mechanisms, such as the electronic calculating apparatus. In human beings a dynamic balance is the condition of health, poise, sanity; and faith in the creative processes, in the dynamics of emergence, in the values and purposes that transcend past achievements and past forms, is the pre-condition of all further growth.

CHAPTER IX.   THE WAY AND THE LIF

1: PREPARATION FOR DEVELOPMENT

"Know thyself," the motto written over the Temple at Delphi, i
one of the most tantalizing admonitions that has ever been addresse
to man. For there is no part of the world that seems as accessible a
one's self; yet that very intimacy has long prevented knowledge of an
kind from being achieved without the most strenuous and exacting di
cipline. For at the very gateway of such knowledge one discovers a
obstacle equally intimate: self-love, a protective pride that not merel
maintains one's proper self-respect but covers smoothly all one's weak
nesses. To correct that blind spot one must first realize how large
patch of the world it hides. To shape a new self one must first kno
the properties of the raw material one must make over.

In the past there has been a succession of masters of self-knowledg
whose efforts to come to terms with themselves are still precious t
those who would follow their trail. One of the first of the great seeker
was Socrates, the Socrates Plato has set before us. His first concer
was to divest the self of an unjustified sense of security in the knowl
edge it possessed, beginning with the verbal terms it used to expres
that knowledge. If, as Socrates taught, men act on their knowledge
and act badly either through ignorance or through false knowledge
the way of right living seems plain: for no small part of our defect
of character, our lapses into sin and crime, could then be traced t
the meretricious unexamined premises upon which our actions ar
based.

From Socrates' standpoint, the evil we commit is fundamentally th
result of our defective thinking, or at least our failure to use fully th
processes of logic and dialectic in examining the course of our ac
tions: we fail to identify or define rigorously the terms we use, lik
justice, love, power, and knowledge itself; and all our choices ar
therefore befouled and obscured. There is a fragment of truth in thi

criticism: the truth that discloses itself particularly to a society that is passing beyond the stage of custom, and needs some more intelligent and intelligible guide to action than the assurance that "it has always been done."

Yet with all of Socrates' patient examination and self-exposure, I cannot recall any point in the Dialogues in which he examines his own conduct in relation to his wife, Xantippe, in order to find out why she had, in fact, turned out to be such a shrewish bad-tempered woman. The answer might have told as much about Socrates as about Xantippe. Had Socrates inspected his own behavior, he might have discovered that love of knowledge in itself does not automatically produce virtue: that there is a tendency in all people, including Socrates, to reject as irrelevant, indeed, as non-existent, those forms of self-knowledge that would lame their pride. None of the classic schools of philosophy, in fact, made this discovery: they dreamed that reason could make men lead perfect lives, and often had the illusion that this or the other philosopher was in fact leading such a life. That insidious pride had first to be broken down, before even the wisest soul could come close to himself.

The reason for Socrates' failure was discovered by another great explorer of the soul, Paul of Tarsus. More rigorous in his inquisition, Paul discovered that the self, however much it might seem guided by intelligence, did not act on purely rational premises nor seek undeviatingly what knowledge established as good: Paul observed that the good he supposedly sought he denied by his actions, and that the evil he consciously rejected, he did. In short, human conduct is laden with ambiguities because the order and purpose and knowledge man developed in his post-animal career must contend not merely with animal impulses that are now far more unsure and disruptive than they ever were at the animal level, but also with perversities that knowledge itself brings: insolence, a failure to reckon with one's creatureliness, over-confidence in the intellect itself. Knowledge is not enough: to achieve self-knowledge one must become as a little child again: breaking down the fences of class and caste and role, including the fence that encloses a philosopher, and discarding the garments of pride that conceal spiritual sores or deformities. The notion that a more rational education will cure all the ills of society, if we start early enough, fails to reckon with this fact: hence the weakness of every program, from that of Robert Owen to that of John Dewey, which over-weights the operations of intelligence alone.

Actually, the rationalist analysis of the self fails in both directions if it refrains from plumbing the lower depths, the processes largely insulated against reason and positive knowledge, it also falls short of assessing the heights that are possible, by reason of propulsive energies also drawn largely from the unconscious, in the very teeth of cold-blooded reason: energies that give rise to a self that transcends its ordinary limitations, in acts of sacrifice or creative insight. Out of the same obscure recesses of the self, where the demonic, degrading elements lurk, angels and ministers of grace come forth, making possible liberating flights far above the pedestrian levels of conscious knowledge, although the trudging intelligence will eventually perhaps reach the same heights by slower means. In short, the self holds both a hell and a heaven that rationalism, too confident of the powers of reason alone, never penetrates.

In the great period of detachment from the folkways of the Middle Ages, when the conventional corporate self, fostered by the Church and the guild, no longer was competent to meet life on its new terms, two great masters of self-knowledge appeared: Shakespeare and Ignatius Loyola: incomparable psychologists both. Loyola knew better than most saints the perversions of the self brought about through a too wholesale commitment to virtue: he realized better than St Paul that contempt for the law of the body might bring about ailments of the soul quite as serious as those produced by letting the body have the upper hand.

Long before Loyola, Plato had realized, indeed, that no amount of self-analysis can sustain one in virtuous conduct unless one brings about constitutional changes in the social order, and provides the kind of education and political institutions that are, in themselves, conducive to human development. Brought up in the medicine of the Hippocratic school Plato realized, too, that the spirit was transformed by food and gymnastic and medicine: in other words that the self could not be detached, even in the pursuit of its highest ends, from the elementary organic conditions that govern human existence: it was part of a greater whole.

Loyola accepted this conception of the self and went further: he knew that time and place and circumstance likewise alter the self: hence one can know the self in its full dimensions only by participating in its drama and applying to it, at every moment, a vigilant discipline. Loyola was perhaps the first psychologist to do full justice to all the dimensions of the self: to combine in a single discipline the

Socratic, the Hippocratic, and the Pauline observations on the nature of man. The failure of secular education to understand the nature and value of his Spiritual Exercises, and to adapt them to the science and culture of our own day, is a witness of the superficiality of both psychology and education during the last three centuries.* The recasting of these exercises will, perhaps, be one of the signs of our capacity to transcend the automatisms of both archaic tradition and current civilization.

Fortunately, more powerful aids to the study of the self have come into existence: they make possible new disciplines and new directions. Consider briefly two such forms of analysis, one directed inward, the other outward: Dr Sigmund Freud's analysis of the dream and Matthias Alexander's analysis of posture. I put these two contrasting methods of examination and diagnosis side by side, not because Alexander's work is comparable with Freud's in significance, but because they thus emphasize an important point about the organic knowledge of the self: namely, that one can approach self-knowledge from either the outside or the inside, by way of the body or by way of the mind, and provided that one pushes far enough one will find the unrepresented portions reappearing in the full description.

Alexander's approach to the self begins with the human body as the outward manifestation of every inward tendency. He himself was cut short in his chosen career as an elocutionist by his developing a persistent harshness of voice. By careful mirror-analysis of his method of speaking, he discovered that his habits of holding his head, depressing his diaphragm, and constricting his larynx were responsible for the final symptoms in his vocal cords. By consciously altering the relation of the head to the spinal column he corrected his ailment; and his success with himself led to similar efforts at diagnosis and correction in others. Since we have abundant evidence to show that in many cases psychological interpretation has removed physical symptoms there is no reason to doubt that the reverse method of approach, correcting the psyche by means of studied bodily readjustments, may be equally effective.

To become conscious of how one stands, how one walks or stoops or sits, may disclose inner tensions and contractions: the first move toward their conscious release. Such revelations may be just as hard

* In 1944, in a class on the Nature of Personality at Stanford University, I made an experimental approach to this problem; but my withdrawal from university duties brought this prematurely to an end.

to accept as the grimmest pictures of distorted impulses the psycho-analyst exposes; for eventually one must face, not just the outer symptom but the inner source.

Freud approached the self by a more devious inner route. By means of his analysis of dreams Freud and his followers reached areas of the self that had been neglected in more rational methods of analysis: the most primitive impulses, the most infantile memories and practices, the most deeply covered-over scars, disclosed themselves under the symbolism of the dream and threw light on large active areas of the personality that displayed themselves in daily life. The existence of this primeval layer of the self, the id, the unmodified, unsocialized "it," partly accounted for both the irrational and the pre-rational characteristics of the person: it was, as it were, a dungeon in which the discarded selves of the race lived on, claiming much of the food and drink that might have nourished the inhabitants of the castle above.

Those accustomed to the hygienic practices of the nineteenth century, sure that men were moved by pleasure and pain, or by enlightened self-interest, found it hard to accept the existence of these age-old prisoners of the unconscious, who sometimes made sudden raids into the upper floors, to rape or slay the inhabitants, only to scramble back again, cowed and cringing before the authority of the ego, to rattle their chains or to fill the night air with obscene curses.

Whitman, picturing himself as stuccoed over with beasts and reptiles, had anticipated this discovery in his Song of Myself: but Freud spelled it out in dream after dream. Fantasy and dream, hitherto discarded by the more rational approaches to self-understanding, threw a new light, not merely on the waking moments of the individual, but on the whole collective development of the race. One had to reckon with the forces of the id if one were to do justice to the aspirations of the super-ego: the dark prisoners themselves needed, not the chains and straitjacket, but sympathetic understanding and guidance: large areas of the primitive, to change the figure, could be redeemed, once one took possession of this unknown country, as the jungle itself has been turned into plowland: "Where id was," as Freud himself put it, "there shall ego be"; and one may add, to correct Freud's hostility to the super-ego, where ego is there super-ego shall be.

The organic picture of the self that is now available, when one puts together the data of physiology and psychology and sociology, has the dimensions of both depth and extension that were hitherto lacking. If the id unites man with his animal ancestors, the super-ego unites him with his historic social heritage, that is, with the super-organic and ideal worlds he possesses in partnership with other men. Despite Freud's rejection of organized religion, he re-discovered the doctrine of original sin in his theory of the Oedipus complex; and he re-instated, in modern terms, the therapeutic practices of the Christian confessional.

Unfortunately Freud made the mistake of letting absolution follow unconditionally from the confession itself and refused to take on the priestly role of guidance. This meant that he and his followers projected their own unexamined set of values and devaluations upon their patients, under the guise of scientific neutrality. But the practical gifts of analytical psychology, which derive unmistakably from Freud's genius, outweigh its ideological defects.

On the basis of the essential knowledge first revealed by Freud, various short-cuts to the examination of the self have now been effected. One of the most notable of these is the extremely sensitive form of psychodiagnostics, devised by Rorschach and perfected by his followers: a method that reveals, as even the elaborate Freudian analysis does not, the bodily as well as the intellectual and emotional components of the self. This method of analysis is almost comparable to the invention of scale maps for the description and further exploration of the terrestrial globe: it not merely enables the observer to chart familiar territory more accurately, but it brings into view undiscovered land in related areas.

The success of the Rorschach ink-blot interpretation is due to the fact that at every moment in his life the person is projecting himself and transforming every part of the world he sees and touches, leaving some trace of his personality on all that he does, recording his frustrations if not his controls and expressions. There will doubtless be further refinements on the Rorschach method: the Murray-Morgan Thematic Apperception Tests bring out other areas of the personality, often indicating more fully immediate stresses and strains. In addition, the projectives techniques may be applied further, not in a static record, but in a dynamic interaction, as J. L. Moreno has demonstrated in the psychodrama, in an effort to combine insight with guidance and positive therapy, in a series of dramatic scenes, enacted by the subject.

Each of these methods is a kind of mirror; and the best method, I have no doubt, will be a combination of many mirrors, which will reveal the self from every side: both the partly visible self, as photographed and diagnosed by constitutional psychologists like Sheldon, and the partly invisible self, as revealed in the Rorschach blot or the psychodrama. One may even look forward to a time when it will be as commonplace to possess such an objective psychological picture of oneself with all its wealth of inner detail as to have a snapshot. That will be an important instrument of self-direction and self-education; though it will require guides and interpreters of a higher order than have yet appeared.

We may begin with the process of self-knowledge at any level: with the discriminating assessment of sin (Loyola), with an analysis of speech habits and meanings (Korzybski), with an interpretation of dreams (Freud) or ink blots (Rorschach) or pictures (Murray-Morgan): with an examination of posture (Alexander) or a participation in a psychodrama (Moreno): with a comparative study of civilizations (Toynbee, Kroeber, and Sorokin) or a comparative study of primitive cultures (Malinowski and Mead).

Any one of these methods, if treated organically and carried far enough, must in time foreshadow and embrace the findings in every other department; since even the masks of the self are part of the individual and the collective act that it puts on: episodes in the larger drama of a culture. Only those who have achieved self-knowledge and are constantly seeking both to enlarge it and apply it in their daily living, are capable of overcoming their automatic reactions and reaching their own ideal limits. Hence the achievement of this wider knowledge is an essential basis for ethical development: indeed the basis of any sound education. In future, the school that neglects to provide teaching and guidance in these departments will be recognized as even more deeply defective than one that neglects to teach reading and writing.

But note: there are certain aspects of the human personality that no present system of diagnostic completely embraces, and no future one in all probability will be able to encompass. For the self is no fixed entity: an essential part of it is revealed only in action through time; and except in those parts of the personality that have been definitely crippled, it is impossible to expose every human limitation or potentiality before time has ripened it. In physical illnesses, patients not seldom recover from diseases eminent doctors have pronounced incurable or fatal; and similar mistakes will doubtless be disclosed in reading human character, even after psychologists have made a sufficient sample of "normal" personalities to discover how many such people have case histories almost identical with those who have succumbed to grave mental disorders. Those who wish to qualify as guides, must do so under the constant discipline of humility—on guard against the cockiness that scientific knowledge, by reason of its very triumphs, promotes.

The effect of self-inquisition should enable one to understand oneself and to do justice to oneself: that is, to correct one's blind drives, to overcome one's partialities and unconscious distortions, to establish a dynamic equilibrium, to release the latent potentialities which either outside pressures or failures of insight have kept in check. Self-knowledge is essential to the cultivation of that kind of humility out of which effective co-operation and mutual aid are born: it is the antidote to self-righteousness, to excessive self-esteem, to arrogant self-assertion.

All this is true for both the individual and the collective self. So the American who understands the historic errors made by our forebears in displacing the Indian and enslaving the Negro cannot, without also a chastening self-correction, condemn the masters of Russia for liquidating the bourgeoisie and enslaving the opponents of its regime so ruthlessly: but by the same token, a Russian who understood that his government deliberately committed against economic classes and rival systems of thought crimes of the same order that other nations have committed against races, would realize how lacking in essential humanity and justice his method of installing a new social system has been.

Without an adequate self-knowledge, without searching exposure, without a consequent positive effort toward self-transformation in person and group, the forces that now threaten to barbarize or exterminate mankind can hardly be overcome. Such knowledge alone can save us from the paralysis of complacent routine, and provide sufficient stimulus to unearth the hidden or unrealized potentials of life—for each of us is but an embryo of the self that may one day be brought to birth. Thus the Socratic injunction, Know yourself, the Aristotelian injunction, Realize yourself, the Christian injunction, Repent and renew yourself, the Buddhist injunction, Renounce yourself, and the Humanist injunction, Perfect yourself are each and all partial but essential recognitions of the fact that the final goal of human effort is man's self-transformation. All our ceaseless daily efforts to carry forward civilization will fail, unless we re-instate this human goal: for it is toward the making of persons that all these preliminary activities tend.

2: THE INNER EYE AND VOICE

Each one of us is like Saul of Tarsus on the road to Damascus: at any moment we may be struck by a blinding light and hear a voice, a voice that will tell us what we already know: that much of our present life is actually hateful to us, that many of the impulses we have suppressed and reviled, in order to conform to the fossilized or decaying institutions of our time, are precisely those impulses that should be respectfully heeded and obeyed. We know that the destination of this society, unless it changes its mind, is death: the death of purposeless materialism and sophisticated barbarism, or the more insidious death of "post-historic man," the simulated life of automatons, operating in a collective process that has passed out of human control. And just as for the early Christians the gods of classic civilization became the demons of the emerging one, so for us, the dominant pseudo-progressive elements in our present society constitute our danger, while the suppressed impulses, weak and shadowy though they now seem, the dreams of love and brotherhood, the will to create a universal society of friends, alone hold promise of salvation.

When that light strikes us we may still, in all humility, falter: it is easier to acknowledge a new truth than to find a method for fulfilling it. So the question for each of us is how he will take hold of himself: not merely what he will think, but how he will act and what he will do, in order to bring about in himself, at least partly, the changes that will finally transform society and make possible new forms of life. Before a new structure can be built, we must first clear the ground for it: this means that we must throw off much of the burdensome apparatus of our present life: we must break the prevailing images, abandon the glib routines and empty ceremonies: challenge the existing ideological archetypes, and return, as near as possible, to the naked person: alone with his cosmic over-self.

In this field, each of us is a learner and a novice: so let me drop for a moment into an I-and-Thou relation with the reader, to emphasize the fact that every suggestion I put before him is meant as much for myself as for him.

The first step, then, is withdrawal and rejection, a course that may bring poverty, hardship, sacrifice; certainly it demands a readiness to accept insecurity—though security naturally has become the obsession of our disintegrating culture. Those who seek to take part in this transformation, even if their rejection does not take the heroic form shown by a Thoreau or a Péguy, a Van Gogh or a Schweitzer or a Gandhi, will still have to devise disciplines and exercises that will confirm their detachment from the prevalent customs and restore initiative, once more, to the human soul. From my own experience I can testify that this is hard counsel: the world is too much with us and too easily we lay waste our powers.

Do not be unduly alarmed: withdrawal makes no public demands. In large part, it will consist of little undramatic acts, hardly visible even to your closest associates, concealed perhaps from your wife or your husband or your bosom friend: indeed, it will be hard at first to convince yourself that anything so quiet, so modest in dimensions, so unpublicizable, could help bring about a profound change. Yet this very chastity and insignificance is perhaps what indicates it to be a major break, entirely out of the style of our existing society. Epicurus's injunction, Hide yourself, is the first move toward having an inner life: something that will ultimately be worth showing.

The first impulse of many people, when they perceive the need for a social change, is to sign a pledge, to fill out a blank, to enter a subscription, to join a party: thus they become visibly a member of a group that will perform what the individual seeks to avoid doing by himself, or even doing at all. The hundreds of organizations and associations that function in a big metropolis bear witness to this impulse: in large numbers they are merely mechanisms of vicarious atonement, for actions unperformed. What I suggest here, as a first step toward integration, is just the opposite of this: withdrawal from extraneous activities, as the first step toward conscious, directed, passionate commitment and participation. The loneliness of this original move is part of its discipline.

The prime purpose of withdrawal is to find yourself, to establish a fresh starting point. You must answer the questions: What am I and where am I? Why am I doing what I do, and why, despite my many deliberate convictions, do I omit to do so much that I should do? Without that act of detachment one must remain only an appendage of a household, an office, a school, a factory, a party, a guild, a nation.

Once you begin to use your detachment for self-examination, which is the next step, you will be surprised to find out how much of your life has been covered over by conventional routine, and how little arises out of felt needs, clear convictions, intelligible and communicable purposes: you have lost the surety of the wild animal's reflexes only to succumb to a series of social reflexes, quite as blind and as fatal to self-development. But if you are entirely candid with yourself, as unsparing as Melville's Pierre tried to be, you will find something worse and better than you had taken for granted. Better because even if you are past your nonage you will still find traces of many possible nodes of growth that remain unbudded: potentialities that the best men and women recently found for themselves, for example, even in late middle life, only under the strange new exactions of total war: the ability to take responsibility, to break through the barriers of class and custom: to face danger, torture, death.

But there will be dismaying discoveries, too, even in the happiest of lives: there perhaps worst of all. You will find that success in your vocation, a comfortable income and a smooth-running household, all the felicities that seemed to offer great reward when they were beyond reach, have become dust and ashes, or at least obstacles to further growth, once they are attained. If you dig deeper, you may find worse: in yourself are the aggressions that you find so disruptive in other men, in your own heart are the lusts and infidelities that would be so disturbing if they came to light in your married partner: there is scarcely a crime that you have not committed in your mind, or become an accessory to in your imagination. "Every man bears within himself the germs of every human quality," Tolstoy remarked; and if you are honest you will think better of evil men, because you are their very brother, and worse of your own goodness, which is stained with so much patent or repressed evil. That inner inspection ends all complacency, all self-righteousness.

Most men, Thoreau observed at a far more favorable moment in Western culture than this, live lives of quiet desperation. Before they are thirty they have a sense of being caught; and they lack both the energies and the tools to extricate themselves from the debris they have allowed to block their return to life. Deficiency of life, and because of that deficiency an almost unendurable boredom, hangs over our civilization: the mechanism busily purrs and ticks; but the days of the favored groups and classes are empty as a handless clock. The dumb mass of men, preoccupied with the struggle for existence, do not lack an immediate purpose; but their existence is cursed by the same ultimate sense of futility.

While our individual acts often make sense, the whole plan of life in which we are involved has become senseless and unrewarding: men dream of rocket flights to the moon, stereotyping and extending their typical present activities, because they mistakenly attribute significance to mere motion or change of position, or because, after all, they wish to escape. But in fact, the more they move the more they stand still—indeed slip backward into the non-human. Radio and gambling, cocktails and promiscuous fornication, soporifics and aphrodisiacs, television and motor trips and sports, preferably sports that threaten loss of limb, are all the fillers-in of deficient forms of life: witnesses to the disruption of the family, the renunciation of parenthood, the retreat from citizenship, the failure of education to make whole persons. To the extent that we have accepted our mechanical apparatus as a substitute for man's more vital and human activities, we have accepted this depletion, staleness, emptiness: so that even in our amusements, we make a ritual of mechanical repetition—the very condition that menaces freedom, spontaneity, growth.

As our inner selves diminish, our very self-confidence naturally disappears. We ask a thousand minute questions about the mechanisms and the institutions that surround us: the one question we do not dare to ask is: What is our true nature? What are our own desires? What demands would a more human plan of life make? No small part of our energy goes into patchwork repairs and piecemeal reforms, because we have taken all the dominant tendencies in our civilization as fixed. For lack of any positive vision of life and health, the best that we can dream of is security—absence of want, absence of disease, absence of fear, absence of war, as if by adding these negations together we could create a valid substitute for life.

This is why the first step toward a better life involves a recovery of inner autonomy. To this end we must recognize the pragmatic importance of dream and ideal: they must be tended and minded with the care we now give only to motor cars or airplanes. This notion has all but disappeared in the United States and is passing out of fashion everywhere, the more people submit to the forces of externalization: objectifying their emptiness. . . . Once I had the good fortune to hold a seminar for a group of educators: men and women thoroughly trained in the use of their tools, most of them doctors of philosophy, people who had already achieved eminence in their profession or were on the way to it. I asked them how many spent as much as half an hour a day in complete solitude, with no outside interruption. Most of them confessed that they had never even considered the need for such a period: if by rare accident they fell upon such an empty hour, they felt obliged to "do something" with it; as busy people they were on the go from whenever they rose to when they went to bed again. Self-directed thought? No. Reverie? No. Dreams and fantasies? A thousand times no! Then I asked them what part of the day they spent in the more subjective arts: reading poetry, making music, painting or actively looking at pictures, or in prayer. Only one participant—by general agreement the most brilliant mind in the group—confessed to anything but the most cursory and passive activity here; bashfully, he admitted that he prayed.

Here was a group, professionally devoted to directing the most vital activity in others' lives, their education, without the faintest insight into their own radical deformity: their studious over-concentration on the external and the impersonal, a bare half of the real world. The autonomous, the inwardly directed, the self-prompted, the spontaneous, the images and dreams and ideals that modify the whole course of life—these existed, if at all, only in shriveled forms and covert manifestations, without the vigilant guidance and discipline that the inner life needs. As a result, these well-intentioned men and women were always reacting and responding to something outside themselves: adjusting and conforming, without any ability to take the initiative and to make a genuine departure of their own. David Riesman has admirably documented these deficiencies.

No wonder these educators had fallen prey to an educational philosophy based on docile conformity to existing institutions and a one-sided adjustment to the dominant social groups. No non-conformists, no innovators, no creators could come out of the schools they would organize except by a deplorable accident. And mark this: for lack of a disciplined interest in the inner life, their control of the outer life likewise became feeble: in education, as in politics and international affairs, "things take their own course," as if things alone were endowed with the properties of life. When life follows its autonomous pattern, things do not have their own way and mechanization issues no commands.

Now such busy people, such externalized people as these educators are, from the standpoint of a philosophy of the person, only partly alive. They present a sad contrast to such an arduous administrator as Goethe, who counted the day lost when he had not at least contemplated a beautiful print, or to Gandhi, most powerful of practical men, who reserved not an hour a day, but a whole day every week to a silent withdrawal, immune to outward invasion or even self-prompted action. How poorly equipped are such educators even to advance the sciences they admire, if they are unaware that a great scientist like Faraday had, on his own confession, an imagination as susceptible to believing the marvels of the Arabian Nights as of a chemical reaction.

Long before I came upon Gratry's Logic—a book full of wisdom and illumination—I reached through experience the same conclusion he did: that the setting aside of half an hour a day, in solitude, free from the possibility of interruption, void of any conscious reflection or directed thought, is essential for the recovery of spontaneity and autonomy, for the opening up of depths of one's mind that are otherwise closed by any sort of activity—even of a mental order. In those moments, as Gratry put it, God may speak to one: or, to put it naturalistically, hidden potentialities may become visible. Even if nothing happens—and only rarely can one hope to awaken the divine—one becomes strengthened, through the very act of detachment, for the performance of one's habitual duties. Too many of us wait for an illness, when our psychal powers are at lowest ebb, to entertain such moments; and though a long quiet convalescence may sometimes bring an illumination that will radically change the course of a life, we should not depend on such accidents to make a timely reorientation possible. A half hour of solitude, detached and "empty"—that is essential for a new beginning.

3: TIME FOR LIVING

During the last century, the tempo of life has been vastly speeded up by our new mechanical instruments; and the overcrowding of our days gives to all who profess to participate fully in our civilization the sense of breathless activity: unfortunately the time-clock and the engagement pad not merely pace the hours, but limit their contents. To travel ever faster, to do more things in a shorter time, never to alter one's speed except to accelerate it—these are the implicit imperatives of our age, derived mainly from the feats of the machine or the ambitions of those who think, with Poor Richard, that time is money and that money is the key to a valuable life.

Because of this unceasing pressure, one of the first measures for restoring an inner equilibrium is to escape from this time cage: deliberately to thin out one's activities and slow down one's responses, letting events sink in, mulling them over, lingering over their significance, before advancing to the next task. Children perhaps have a natural tendency to behave in this fashion; and the mechanical pace and discipline imposed by the school often is an active source of their maladjustment and unhappiness: for no one can give himself fully to a task if his ear is half-cocked for the signal that will compel him to abandon it.

In a purely negative, defensive way, the industrial worker, during the past half-century, has learned collectively to practice the slow-down in work: sometimes taking his revenge on those concerned with efficiency and profit by not even pretending to exert his full capacities. Primitive peoples and most of the cultures of the Orient, above all the Hindu, have never fallen under the spell of this modern time-obsession; and we have something to learn from their ways. If they possibly need a greater willingness to accept external order and regularity, we in the West need a more ready submission to the demands of life.

At critical moments of pressure a single pause of short duration may become an act of large dimensions. Skilled administrators have learned to walk out of their offices and be by themselves for five minutes before making an important decision; but something far more pervasive and ramifying than this is necessary before we shall do justice to the time we command. We must not merely introduce more breaks into our compulsive routines: we must slow down the whole tempo of activity and spread attention more evenly over every part of our day, altering the mechanical beat of our lives, transposing events to other parts of the day than their usual appointed place. The threat of dullness in married life, for example, may be partly due to the fact that too often sexual intercourse occurs only during the jaded hours that end the day; while the undue charm of extra-marital erotic adventure may be due to the fact that it often breaks with this routine: late afternoon was traditionally the favored hour, in Paris, for illicit lovers' assignations. The change of time and place by themselves may have the quickening effect that people often seek only through a change of partners.

The first public acknowledgment of the creative pause was, of course, the Jewish institution of the Sabbath: a social invention of the first magnitude. But in our Western culture the day of rest has now become another day of busy work, filled with amusements and restless diversions not essentially different from the routine of the work week—particularly in America: from the Sunday morning scramble through the metropolitan newspaper to the distracting tedium of the motor car excursion, we continually activate leisure time, instead of letting all work and routine duties come serenely to a halt. Even in Wordsworth's day the pressure to be up and doing must have been heavy: why, otherwise, his lines: "Think you, mid all this mighty sum of things for ever speaking, that nothing of itself will come, but we must still be seeking?" That wise passiveness in which the soul lies open to whatever forces from any direction may touch it is a highly necessary counterpoise to over-narrowed and over-directed forms of activity, particularly to drilled submission to the machine.

But note: the deliberate break in routine must be more than an occasional exercise: it has a constant place in every well-organized activity. Even factory managers have come to realize that a period of rest and recreation within the work day is necessary in order to keep up the pace of machine production: though few industrial plants are yet planned with sufficient areas for spontaneous recreation close at hand. In his account of the Second World War, Mr Winston Churchill has told us how necessary a nap in the afternoon was for him to re-gain the power to work, when pressed, far into the night. Similarly the Mohammedan, with his repeated prayers, disengages himself from immediate demands and importunities, and comes back to them, one would guess, with a better perspective and a serener grasp. Reflection, daydreaming, quiescence, sleep—all these alterations in the tempo, driven out by the pragmatic demand for visible action and visible achievement, are essential for keeping conduct truly responsive to reason. Many foolish habits and routines would not survive if we dared to pause long enough to look at them.

We shall not make the effort to control time, unless we realize how much of our work routine is not merely compulsive but obsessive: a neurotic attempt to create a refuge in external regularity from internal disorder, to retreat, with an energetic appearance of victory, from the unsolved problems of life. Compulsive work and the general speed-up indeed kept people "out of mischief" by diverting their libidinous fancies, and the daily absorption in work lightened sorrow and di-minished the tragic sense of life: if one "filled one's time" with work, all one's personal and domestic frustrations would seem less exacer-bating, and the gnawing sense of a more ultimate emptiness would be effaced. Western man, then, temporarily found in work a relief from the unanswerable problems, the mysteries, that give life its wider di-mensions.

But there is no purpose in incessant systematic work, or in the leisure that the machine has already introduced, unless we make a different use of the time so put at our disposal. To practice an external speed-up without an internal slow-down that brings with it a more copious supply of personally usable and enjoyable time, is an extravagant misdirection of our time and energy. From a human standpoint, the chief purpose of time-saving is to decrease the time spent in unrewarding instrumental and preparatory tasks, and to increase the time spent in consummations and fulfillments. Where the process itself is a creative and enjoyable one—like the work of the artist, the scientist, the skilled craftsman, the teacher—reduction of time is actually a curtailment of life.

Even in the most rewarding vocations, some time-saving may be needful, in order that we may each assimilate in fuller measure a world whose boundaries in time and space now spread far beyond the narrow circle of the limited individual ego. We must save time in the present, in other words, in order to spend time more actively in the past and the future; for it is by his critical assimilation of history and biography—the individual's and the world's—and by his selective forecasts and projections into the future, that modern man differs most decisively from the representatives of other cultures.

Now specialized thinking, which proceeds along a single track and avoids all side excursions, was mainly a time-saving device. In our need to create balanced persons, we must resort to polyphonic or contrapuntal thinking, thinking that carries a series of related themes together so that in the process they simultaneously work upon each other and modify each other. By its very nature, contrapuntal thinking is a time-consuming device, inimical to any form of speed-up: it is quicker to rehearse a solo part than to bring an orchestra to perfection.

Take the case of a heart specialist who examines a patient with a functional disturbance of the heart. When that organ is considered as an isolated fact, the main points to be determined are those revealed only by physical examination. But a true physician, guided by a philosophy of the organism, must make a much more subtle and complex approach to the problem. He thinks not of the abstract anatomical heart, but of a particular heart—in relation to his patient's history, which is a biological and social fact; in relation to habits of nutrition, which is a physiological and social fact; in relation to occupation, which is an economic fact; in relation to home environment, which is a geographic and personal fact; and in relation to psychological and sexual problems—all of which contribute to the whole picture.

Permanently to effect a change in the faulty function, the physician may have to prescribe a different vocation or a psychoanalytic treatment.

Such diagnosis and therapy will often lack the swiftness and patness of the old-fashioned specialist's method: to arrive at a competent diagnosis and bring about a permanent cure will often take far more time. Even if one allows for intuitive shortcuts, they can hardly be safely practiced without a circumspect check-up of many facts not visible in the doctor's office. Without a slowing down of the tempo, we cannot in fact do justice to all the levels and aspects of contemporary knowledge. Contrapuntal thinking itself, if widely practiced, will help to slow down the tempo of life: it will even reduce that overproductivity which threatens to choke up the very sources of knowledge. Once we begin to think organically, that is, simultaneously at every level, the results should be far more sound and durable, when they are achieved: but they will be scantier in quantity. In future, people will perhaps be happy to accomplish in a whole lifetime, as part of a fully integrated effort, what they now do in the course of a decade, with a few of their functions over-stimulated and over-tasked, and the rest of their capacities in a state of inanition or collapse. On this basis, both knowledge and life will gain.

One of the great problems of the transitional era, then, is to reconcile the external, mechanical, public time-schedule that now governs so much of our activities with organic, personal, self-controlled time, associated with metabolism, memory, and cumulative human experience, dependent upon the rate of growth, the intensity and extent of activity, the capacity for assimilation. The first contributes a great potential margin of free time, and along with it the free energy needed for enjoying it, leisure and energy on a scale no other civilization has ever offered to so many of its members, except under a constant threat of dearth and starvation. But the second, which has so far found no adequate forms in our society, must now be consciously developed, in order to take full advantage of this opportunity. Subjective time—Bergson's *durée*—keeps a different rhythm from the planets and the clock.

Though our first reaction to the external pressure of time necessarily takes the form of the slow-down, the eventual effect of liberation will be to find the right measure and tempo for every human activity, and to introduce, at will, appropriate variations: in short, to keep time in life as we do in music, not by obeying the mechanical beat of the metronome—a device only for beginners—but by finding the appropriate tempo from passage to passage, modulating the pace according to human need and purpose. We shall not be fully in control of our civilization, or able to express the higher qualities of life, until it is possible to reduce the tempo or accelerate it in response, not to the machine's requirements for production, but to man's requirements for a full and harmonious life. When we reach that stage, even our *accelerandos* will become more meaningful. Instead of hastening all our activities, under the vain conviction that "we are getting somewhere," we shall take our time—knowing that even the spacing of the silent intervals is part of the music.

4: THE GREAT GOOD PLACE

In time, if the practice of withdrawal becomes general, we will have to create a special social structure for it: let us call the new form of cloister The Great Good Place in honor of the fable in which Henry James not merely diagnosed the formidable pressures of our time, but also indicated in an imaginative way the kind of environment and routine needed to overcome them. No house in the future will be generously planned that does not have its closet or its cell, to supplement the only equivalent for it today, the bathroom; no city will be well designed that does not set apart places of withdrawal: solitary walks, secluded woodland hideouts, unfrequented towers hard to climb, devious paths, like the old Ramble in Central Park, no fewer of these than of public places where people can go in groups for social communion or common recreation. The whole tendency of our minds, during the last century of mechanized urban expansion, was so opposed to this need for withdrawal that the ideal of almost all town planners, up to now, has been to make all places equally accessible, equally open, equally public.

Now so far the cloister has performed only an involuntary part in the re-building of the person and the community. Though monastic withdrawal was dismissed as a medieval superstition by the rationalists of the nineteenth century, the fact is that it continued to operate: for the cloister had its part in transforming the vision and personality of the great revolutionary leaders, in repeated periods of forced retirement to exile in foreign countries, above all in the abstemious regular discipline of the prison. From Karl Marx to Lenin and Stalin, from Herzen and Kropotkin to Dostoyevsky and Hitler, from Mazzini and

Garibaldi to Gandhi and Nehru, a great succession of leaders submitted, however unwillingly, to the inner concentration that prison life brought with it. For many a young man, during this period, long voyages at sea played a similar part: it was at sea that Henry George got his first intuition of his intellectual mission; and Herman Melville quite rightly called the whaling ship he sailed on his Harvard College, indeed one may well trace to his long meditations on the maintop much of the originality of vision he brought into the world.

Plainly a habit of life so precious must not be left to chance: nor need it be confined to the archaic forms that have been preserved in the Catholic Churches—though the silence and inner concentration of the monastery will long serve as an archetypal pattern of The Great Good Place. We need not court political repression or social disaster before we make use of the salutary function of the cloister: in our search for wholeness and balance we shall rather seek to democratize this institution and make it more generally available. This involves likewise a rearrangement of our time schedules. One of the marks of the new school and the new university will be the provision of hours of withdrawal, not spent in classroom study or in sport, in the midst of its regular work day: a period of concentration and reflection, in which the work of active selection and spiritual assimilation can go on.

The physical adjunct to this concentration is the absence of visible distractions: an architecture, as Henry James put it, "all beautified with omissions." This ensures the positive presence of esthetic order and clarity. At best, the alternating rhythm of wide landscape or seascape and walled room or closed garden is what brings the inner life to highest pitch: provided that there are no intruders from the outer world during one's period of concentration. Mr. Arnold Toynbee has well emphasized the process of "withdrawal and return" in creating leaders with new schemes and bold plans. Perhaps Adolf Hitler was never so dangerous to the world, in his corrupt intuitions, than when he withdrew frequently to his eyrie in Berchtesgaden; similarly, he was never so stupid, crass, and uninventive as when he immersed himself in the details of war, and lost the detachment and the wide perspectives he gained in his more or less solitary retreats. Roosevelt found a similar detachment in a ship at sea.

Those who omit this act of recuperation and re-creation, by oversubmission to the pressure of practical affairs, lose their hold over these affairs: they mechanically plod along the course on which, by external accident rather than positive choice, their feet have been set.

Detachment: silence: innerness—these are the undervalued parts of our life, and only by their deliberate restoration, both in our personal habits and in our collective routines, can we establish a balanced regimen.

At first, the discipline of withdrawal will be painful, since the tread-mill of our daily life leads us to go through so many smooth involuntary motions. Mere abstention involves a mighty effort. The very feelings we restore to consciousness will be painful and the actions that may follow difficult: for we must first say No to the dominant claims of our time, before we shall be able to say Yes to those we shall create to replace them. Perhaps the chief curse of our condition, at first, will be the realization of how far we shall have to go before we become self-acting, self-directed, self-confident persons once more: how far the events that have victimized the last two generations, the series of wars, revolutions, economic catastrophes, and more wars, culminating in the prospect of even more meaningless forms of random slaughter, are the result of our own continued self-abdication. The goods of this society we have taken to ourselves; but the evils we have not resisted, since we did not dare to find them in ourselves, but attributed them to wholly external machinations or circumstances.

Even in little ways these truths are open to demonstration. In my class on the Nature of Personality at Stanford University, I once asked my students, as part of a weekly exercise, to make a plan for the way in which they intended to spend a whole day; and then, when the day was over, to set down what they actually did hour by hour and compare it with their original program. That proved a useful exercise: for each student was surprised to find how easily his firmest intentions had been diverted by a little succession of outside pressures and stimuli over which he had exercised no control. This was not the miscarriage of Napoleon's set plans of battle, a matter through which Tolstoy sardonically illustrated the opposition between reason and calculation and the unexpectedness of life itself, since battles too easily get out of hand through forces too complex for human control. No: in the case of the students it was a demonstration, quite typical of our whole culture, of how the infirmity of our inner convictions and intentions, indeed our profound lack of self-respect, makes us the easy prey of chance stimuli, which exercise undue authority merely because they come from the outside.

Today external arresting sensations take the place of rational meanings as in advertising: external stimuli replace inner purposes; and so we drift, from moment to moment, from hour to hour, indeed from one end of a lifetime to another, without ever regaining the initiative or making an active bid for freedom. Since we do not discipline and direct our dreams we submit to nightmares: lacking an inner life, we lack an outer life that is worth having, too; for it is only by their coeval development and their constant interpenetration that life itself can flourish.

The moral should be plain: if, as Gregory the Great said, he who would hold the fortress of contemplation must first train in the camp of action, the reverse, for our times, is even more essential: he who would sally forth with a new plan of action must first withdraw to the innermost recesses of contemplation, on whose walls, when he becomes accustomed to the solitude and the darkness, a new vision of life will appear: not the objective after-image of the world he has left, but the subjective fore-image of the world he will return to and re-make.

5: THE NEED FOR TWO LIVES

There is one further reason for the practice of withdrawal and spiritual concentration: perhaps the most important reason of all. To live wisely, each of us must lead a twofold life. We must live once in the actual world, and once more in our minds; and though we cannot give the same amount of time to the second as to the first, we can use the economy of symbols and images, as we do in nocturnal dreams, to encompass as much life in a few minutes, if we secure the free time in the first place, as we could by actual hours of living.

John Dewey has emphasized, quite rightly, the fact that thought which does not ultimately guide action is incomplete. But the reverse of Dewey's dictum is likewise true. Action that does not, in turn, lead to reflection, is perhaps even more gravely incomplete. For one person who is lost so completely in reverie or abstract thought that he forfeits the capacity to act, there are now a hundred so closely committed to action or routine that they have lost the capacity for rational insight and contemplative reconstruction: therefore they have lost the very possibility of re-formation and self-direction. But it is only by constant reflection and evaluation that our life, in fact, becomes fully meaningful and purposeful. In addition, when we prolong the good moments, by holding the flavor of them on the tongue, we achieve a sense of completion and fulfillment that comes by no other method. This is one of the reasons perhaps for the deep inner joy and perpetually self-renewing life of the great painters. In the humblest life that has achieved the capacity for reflection—and in rural cultures the gift is still not unknown among simple people—the second living sweetens and deepens the first.

Now life is the only art that we are required to practice without preparation, and without being allowed the preliminary trials, the failures and botches, that are essential for the training of a mere beginner. In life, we must begin to give a public performance before we have acquired even a novice's skill; and often our moments of seeming mastery are upset by new demands, for which we have acquired no preparatory facility. Life is a score that we play at sight, not merely before we have divined the intentions of the composer, but even before we have mastered our instruments: even worse, a large part of the score has been only roughly indicated, and we must improvise the music for our particular instrument, over long passages. On these terms, the whole operation seems one of endless difficulty and frustration; and indeed, were it not for the fact that some of the passages have been played so often by our predecessors that, when we come to them, we seem to recall some of the score and can anticipate the natural sequence of the notes, we might often give up in sheer despair. The wonder is not that so much cacophony appears in our actual individual lives, but that there is any appearance of harmony and progression.

In some respects, education gives us a foretaste of life and a little anticipatory practice: it serves us best perhaps in naive forms, as in little girls' play at keeping house and tending dolls or the games and tests young boys devise for themselves. But there is no more time to anticipate life in detail than there is to re-enact it in detail. In the nature of things, each one of us, no matter how conscientious his intentions, commits many errors in living: but fortunately, it is not by the avoidance or the denial of these negative moments but by their assimilation and their eventual transformation that the human person grows.

Before we have acquired any large degree of skill in living, we have already made momentous decisions or have had them made for us; and we have committed ourselves to courses that may turn out to be fatal to our best impulses. What is more, in the act of sailing before the wind, we may be deflected, through absorption in the activity itself and the feeling of effortless movement that attends it, from the course we have deliberately chosen. All these choices, decisions, commitments, if allowed to accumulate, become progressively more irremediable. In our very desire to get more swiftly to our goal, we may neglect to look at charts or to take soundings, till suddenly we feel our ship scraping bottom—if we do not in fact crash more disastrously on the rocks. If most of us realized early enough the fact that we have only one life to lead, and that every moment of it that escapes reflection is irretrievable, we should live it differently. Too often, halfway through the journey of life, we suddenly awaken to the fact that we will have no second chance on earth to rectify our errors: a decisive, often a tragic moment.

This day of reckoning is fatal to the extent that it has not been anticipated. Consider the woman who, absorbed in her professional career, has too long postponed having children: one day she finds her period of childbearing is nearing an end; and if she labors under any physiological handicaps she may, despite all efforts at retrieval, have missed this part of her destiny: too late! Or take the man who has failed to give himself to the life of his family: preoccupied with his advancement in his business or profession, or even with a dutiful attempt to "provide well" for his household in an economic sense, he may have deprived his wife or his growing children of companionship or the more inward manifestations of love. Too late, he may awaken to find that his best opportunities have slipped from him: his sons and daughters have grown up and even if they have not been made resentful by his neglect, are out of his reach: he will be lucky if he finds the satisfactions of vicarious fatherhood as grandfather. So with a hundred other commitments. One cannot at the end of one's life redeem one's earlier mistakes: for it is not atonement that one needs but a chance to re-direct one's efforts.

How, then, may we curb these fatal commitments and correct our errors before we are undone by them? There is, I believe, but one answer: we must extend the dismaying shortness of life by living it twice, as we encounter it day by day: that is, each of us must slow down his pace sufficiently to follow up his daily performances with the constant practice of meditation and reflection: a daily re-living, in which we examine our target, appraise our marksmanship, re-adjust our sights. On the positive side, we shall thereby prolong and enhance by further reflection whatever has given us sustenance or delight: a great boon in a time of violence and trouble, of interrupted lives and premature deaths, like the present era. A large part of life, particularly the succession of functions and actions that punctuate the stages of growth, is non-repeatable except in the mind: one must correct the mistakes of youth by appropriate actions in youth, not by compensatory efforts in maturity; and so with each other phase. Perhaps the best part of psychoanalytic therapy is this second-living; but it needs to be supplemented by the Calvinist habit of the daily self-examination.

All this is but to repeat, in another form, the advice of Father Zossima, in The Brothers Karamazov: "Every day and every hour, every minute, walk around yourself and watch yourself, and see that your image is a seemly one." Only by an act of planned detachment is the living of this second life possible: that is why withdrawal requires a form: a time and a place and even if possible a structure that is dedicated to one's second life—not as an escape from one's active existence, but as the means whereby it is completed, and in turn gives fresh impulses and fresh values to the future. Lacking this second life, we neither carry over consciously what is valuable from the past, nor successfully dominate the future; we fail to bring to it the energy and insight we have potentially acquired in the act of living: rather, we let ourselves be carried along by the tide, bobbing helplessly up and down like a corked bottle, with a message inside that may never come to shore.

6: STRIPPING FOR ACTION

The Swiss historian Jacob Burckhardt predicted that the corruptions and weaknesses already observable in Western civilization by the middle of the nineteenth century would result in the coming of the Terrible Simplifiers: people who, with ruthless decision and unstinted force, would overthrow even the good institutions that were, in fact, stifling the growth of the human spirit. "People," he wrote, "may not yet like to imagine a world whose rulers completely ignore law, prosperity, profitable labor, and industry, credit, etc.," a world governed by military corporations and single parties: but such a world becomes possible when the majority no longer, through orderly means, exercises the initiative in continuously re-forming and re-directing institutions to serve human purposes. What the virtuous will not do in a reasonable constructive way, the criminal and barbarian take upon themselves to do, negatively and irrationally, for the sheer pleasure of destruction. When individuals shun responsibility as persons, their place is taken politically by a tyrant, who recovers freedom of initiative through crime.

Even before Burckhardt, Dostoyevsky had predicted, with remarkable prescience, what would occur. In that enigmatic narrative, Letters from the Underworld, in which Dostoyevsky put so many challenging truths into the mouth of his sniveling, repulsive chief character, the veritable prototype of Hitler, he described the utilitarian heaven of the nineteenth century: the heaven, still, of popular current science, in which all the questions that had heretofore troubled men would be precisely answered and all human acts would be mathematically computed according to nature's laws, so that the world will cease to know any wrongdoing. Then he observes: "I should not be surprised if, amid all this order and regularity of the future, there should suddenly arise, from some quarter or another, some gentleman of lowborn—or rather, of retrograde and cynical—demeanor, who, setting his arms akimbo, should say to you all: 'How now, gentlemen? Would it not be a good thing if, with one accord, we were to kick all this solemn wisdom to the winds and send these logarithms to the devil, and to begin to live our lives again according to our own stupid whimsy?' "

This is the nihilistic answer to the serious condition that every civilization at length finds itself in: the result of over-organization, the multiplication of superfluous wants, an excess of regularity and routine in the conduct of daily life, a fossilization of even happy rituals: all resulting in a failure of human initiative and a dull submission to what seems an overbearing impersonal determinism. In such an existence people eat for the sake of supporting meat packers' organizations and dairymen's associations, they guard their health carefully for the sake of creating dividends for their life insurance corporations, they earn their daily living for the sake of paying dues, taxes, mortgages, installments on their car or their television sets, or fulfilling their quota in a Five-Year Plan: in short, they satisfy the essential needs of life for extraneous reasons. Just as in the business organizations, run on such terms, the overhead tends to eat up the profit, so with life in general, the preparatory acts deplete the appropriate consummations.

Such a society as ours eventually ties itself up into knots by its inability to put first things first. When a community reaches a point where no one can make a decision of the simplest sort without bringing into play an elaborate technique of research or accountancy, without enlisting the aid of innumerable specialists who take responsibility for only their minute fragments of the process, all the normal acts of living must be slowed down to such an extent that the economies originally achieved by division of labor and large-scale organization are nullified. Thus the technique of diagnosis becomes as burdensome to the patient as his disease: indeed it becomes an auxiliary disease. At that point, the life of a community will be stalled and frustrated: it will not be capable of anticipating or circumventing the simplest crisis.

But no community can permit itself to be stalled for long; for if we do not find a benign method of simplification, then the Terrible Simplifiers will come on the scene, recapturing freedom through savagery and charlatanism, if not through the polite forms sanctioned by an over-developed civilization. When our apparatus of fact-finding and truth-proving becomes too complicated, the Terrible Simplifiers will resort to brazen lies and childish superstitions. If our factual historians ostracize the Burckhardts and the Henry Adamses for daring to look into the future on the basis of their knowledge and wisdom, people who seek guidance will take to astrological horoscopes as a substitute.

To escape the Terrible Simplifiers one must recognize the actual danger of the condition through which they obtain their ascendance over the frustrated majority: for the condition these charlatans profess to correct is in fact a serious one. Instead of closing our eyes to its existence, we must use art and reason to effect a benign simplification, which will give back authority to the human person. Life belongs to the free-living and mobile creatures, not to the encrusted ones; and to restore the initiative to life and participate in its renewal, we must counterbalance every fresh complexity, every mechanical refinement, every increase in quantitative goods or quantitative knowledge, every advance in manipulative technique, every threat of superabundance or surfeit, with stricter habits of evaluation, rejection, choice. To achieve that capacity we must consciously resist every kind of automatism: buy nothing merely because it is advertised, use no invention merely because it has been put on the market, follow no practice merely because it is fashionable. We must approach every part of our lives with the spirit in which Thoreau undertook his housekeeping at Walden Pond: be ready, like him, even to throw out a simple stone, if it proves too much trouble to dust. Otherwise, the sheer quantitative increase in the data of scientific knowledge will produce ignorance: and the constant increase in goods will produce a poverty of life.

There is no domain today where methods of simplification must not be introduced. Because of the uninhibited production of books and scholarly reviews, there is, for example, hardly a single province of thought where the human mind can make an adequate survey of the literature on any subject, except of the minutest province, come to intelligent conclusions, or move confidently from reflection to practice. Our ingenious mechanical methods of solving this problem, like the invention of the microfilm, increase the size of the total burden: the only true salvation, in this and every other sphere, is *voluntarily to restrict production at its source and to increase our selectivity:* both true simplifications, though only the enlightened and the courageous can apply them. This holds for the whole routine of life: never to use mechanical power when human muscles can conveniently do the work, never to use a motor car where one might easily walk, never to acquire information or knowledge except for the satisfaction of some immediate or prospective want—such modes of simplification, though individually insignificant, add up to a considerable degree of emancipation. A popular mentor, himself no enemy of the profit motive, once suggested that one should never waste time opening second class mail; and if that advice were generally taken, at least in America, a vast amount of time and energy would be saved: indeed whole forests would be preserved. Many other institutions will, in time, follow the example of a progressive school in New York: a school that once gave all its students intelligence tests and heaped up a vast mass of unused and unnecessary data. Now it has destroyed these files and it gives special tests only to those who gravely need such additional checks.

In Western countries one of the prime marks of an organic change in our culture—the hallmark of a new brotherhood and sisterhood—would probably be the drastic reduction of the now compulsive habits of smoking and drinking: along with this would go a return, on the part of women, to a mode of wearing their hair which would forego the elaborate mechanical or chemical procedure for producing fashionable uniformity of curl after original Hollywood models. Hundreds of thousands of acres of land would be freed for food-growing by curtailment of tobacco alone, along with some slight direct improvement of health, and a release, if the movement were spontaneous, from neurotic obsessions. The fact that even in a time of worldwide starvation, after the Second World War, no one dared to suggest even a partial conversion of tobacco land to food-growing, shows how rigid, rigid almost to the point of *rigor mortis,* our civilization has become: with no sufficient power of adaptation to reality. Nor is this demonstration lessened by the fact that there is record of starving men asking for tobacco ahead of food: that merely shows the depth of our perversion of life-needs.

Many effective kinds of simplification will perhaps be resisted at first on the ground that this means a "lowering of standards." But this overlooks the fact that many of our standards are themselves extraneous and purposeless. What is lowered from the standpoint of mechanical complexity or social prestige may be raised from the standpoint of the vital function served, as when the offices of friendship themselves replace, as Emerson advocated in his essay on household economy, elaborate preparations of food and service, of napery and silver.

Consider the kind of frugal peasant living that Rousseau first advocated, when he chose to live in a simple cottage, instead of in the mansion of his patron, surrounded by "comforts": all this wipes away time-consuming rituals and costly temptations to indigestion. Or consider the gain in physical freedom modern woman made, when the corset and petticoats, the breast-deformers, pelvis-constrictors, backbone-curvers of the Victorian period gave way to the garb of the early 1920's, without girdle, brassière, or even stocking supporters: a high point of freedom in clothes from which women sheepishly recoiled under the deft browbeating of manufacturers with something to sell.

Naturally the sort of simplification needed must itself conform to life-standards. Thoreau's over-simplification of his diet, for instance, probably undermined his constitution and gave encouragement to the tuberculosis from which he finally died. By now we know that a diet consisting of a single kind of food is not part of nature's economy: the amino acids appear to nourish the body only when various ones are present in different kinds of food: so that the lesson of life is not to confuse simplicity with monotony. So, too, a tap of running water, fed by gravity from a distant spring, is in the long run a far more simple device, judged by the total man-hours used in production and service, than the daily fetching of water in a bucket: as the bucket, in turn, is more simple than making even more frequent journeys to the spring to slake one's thirst directly. Simplicity does not avoid mechanical aids: it seeks only not to be victimized by them. That image should save us from the imbecile simplifiers, who reckon simplicity, not in terms of its total result on living, but in terms of immediate first costs or in a pious lack of visible apparatus.

Sporadically, during the last three centuries, many benign simplifications have in fact come to pass throughout Western civilization;

though, as in the case of women's dress just noted, they have sometimes been followed by reactions that have left us as badly off as ever.
Rousseau, coming after the Quakers, carried their simplification of
manners through to diet, to child nurture, and to education; while
Hahnemann began a similar change in medicine, a change followed
through by Dr William Osler, under whom hundreds of spurious drugs
and complicated prescriptions were discarded, in favor of the Hippocratic attention to diet and rest and natural restoratives. In handicraft
and art and architecture the same general change was effected, first
by William Morris, in his rule: "Possess nothing that you do not know
to be useful or believe to be beautiful." Modern architecture, though
it has often been distracted and perverted by technical over-elabora-
tion, can justify its essential innovations as an attempt to simplify the
background of living, so that the poorest member of our society will
have as orderly and harmonious an environment as the richest: it has
discarded complicated forms as a badge of class and conspicuous
waste. Wherever the machine is intelligently adapted to human needs,
it has the effect of simplifying the routine of life and releasing the
human agent from slavish mechanical tasks. It is only where the person abdicates that mechanization presents a threat.

But in order to recover initiative for the person, we must go over
our whole routine of life, as with a surgeon's knife, to eliminate every
element of purposeless materialism, to cut every binding of too-neat
red tape, to remove the fatty tissue that imposes extra burdens on
our organs and slows down all our vital processes. Simplicity itself is
not the aim of this effort: no, the purpose is to use simplicity to promote spontaneity and freedom, so that we may do justice to life's new
occasions and singular moments. For what Ruskin said of the difference between a great painter, like Tintoretto, and a low painter, like
Teniers, holds for every manifestation of life: the inferior painter, not
recognizing the difference between high and low, between what is intensely moving and what is emotionally inert, gives every part of his
painting the same refinement of finish, the same care of detail. The
great painter, on the other hand, knows that life is too short to treat
every part of it with equal care: so he concentrates on the passages of
maximum significance and treats hastily, even contemptuously, the
minor passages: his shortcuts and simplifications are an effort to give
a better account of what matters. This reduction to essentials is the
main art of life.

7: RE-UNION WITH THE GROUP

Withdrawal, detachment, simplification, reflection, liberation from automatism—these are all but preliminary steps in the re-building of the self and the renewal of the society of which we are a part. These initial acts may, and in fact must, be taken by each of us alone: but the purpose of our withdrawal, of our fasting and purgation, is to re-awaken our appetite for life, to make us keen to discriminate between food and poison and ready to exercise choice. Once we have taken the preparatory steps, we must return to the group and re-unite ourselves with those who have been undergoing a like regeneration and are thereby capable of assuming responsibility and taking action. In relatively short order this fellowship may enfold men and women in every country, of every religious faith, of every cultural pattern.

Here the rule is to begin with what lies nearest at hand. Who is our neighbor? He who has need of us whether he lives next door or half-way round the earth. Our best neighbor is he who is ready, for the sake of our common fellowship, to join with us in overcoming the barriers of space and time and culture. Now our first duty today is to secure the continued existence of the human race and to put all more local claims below this paramount condition: before we can have a sound village government, we must have a world government. Families cannot be permanently united with any prospect of a good life together until mankind is united. No household, no village or city, no trade union or chamber of commerce, no church or temple, is performing even its minimum obligation to ensure its own continued existence unless a large part of its activity is actively devoted to the extension of human fellowship and to the institution of a common world law and government, capable of transmuting strife and struggle and frictions and contentions into peaceful forms of conflict and positive co-operations. Universal service is the price of peace; and if we do not undertake it voluntarily, in our daily acts, we shall have it imposed upon ourselves in the negative forms of war, at a far more fearful sacrifice. We cannot escape these obligations and withdraw once more into purely private self-centered lives, individual or national: our only choice is whether we will perform them voluntarily in the name of life, or under strict compulsion in the name of destruction and death.

Our part in the group can no longer be a passive one: it is not enough to belong: one must act and lead; and our achievement of balance will be meaningless unless it makes us ready, on demand, to take our turn at any or all the roles in a group: to command and to think, to emotionalize and energize, to assimilate and obey. Groups become sluggish and automatic in their behavior, incapable of making fresh decisions like persons, just to the extent that their members accept as permanent a stereotyped division of labor and function. Neither democracy nor effective representation is possible until each participant in the group—and this is true equally of a household or a nation —devotes a measurable part of his life to furthering its existence. Our present division of time, whereby forty-odd hours a week is given to work, fifty-odd hours to sleep, and the remaining hours mainly to individual concerns or family affairs and recreation, cannot possibly bring about a balanced life.

The change to be effected in group life is not one that will proceed, like the changes envisaged by earlier forms of revolution, through the agency of political parties; and it is the precise opposite of every form of totalitarian absolutism and single party rule. For just as time and space, for modern man, is multi-dimensional, so likewise are political activities: the new forms of group living and group initiative will become effective at every level: in the family and the neighborhood at one pole, and in a world government, embracing humanity, at the other pole.

Each group, like each person, must become increasingly self-governing and self-developing, with a breaking down of many existing automatic political and economic controls. But in the very act of recovering initiative and extending its proper activities, even the smallest group will, as a constant preoccupation of its existence, work to build up more universal co-operations. No group lives to itself. To create a man of truly human dimensions one needs the co-operation of a universal society; to create a universal society, one must begin and end with men who seek fullness of life: who refuse to be insignificant fractions and seek to become integers. These are two aspects of the same act; and with that act, a new world will come into being.

For the awakened man and woman, life itself is essentially a process of education, through maturation, crisis, and renewal: in that process, the fullest potentialities of the community and the person are realized. Such a philosophy does not segregate learning from living, or knowledge from action. As adult he never leaves the school behind him, for at no point does he believe that his education is completed. When his daily work ceases to be formative and educative, he will make special efforts to restore these qualities, or seek another occupation; for he will regard such a loss of interest as a direct impoverishment of life. The mark of the balanced personality, in the industrial system, will be not higher productivity or higher wages—though both may be possible and necessary—but the integration of work and leisure and social life and education: such a transformation as has taken place during the last decade in France under the Boimondau experiment.*

To achieve unity in the person, the balanced man has need of a community that is equally full and complete; and that, above all, has recovered in every form of organization the human scale and the capacity for intimate knowledge and self-directed action that goes with the human scale. The restoration of the human scale is a matter of utmost importance: till that change takes place no effective regeneration can be brought about. The very extension of the range of community in our time, through national and worldwide organizations, only increases the need for building up, as never before, the intimate cells, the basic tissue, of social life: the family and the home, the neighborhood and the city, the work-group and the factory. Our present civilization lacks the capacity for self-direction because it has committed itself to mass organizations and has built its structures from the top down, on the principle of all dictatorships and absolutisms, rather than from the bottom up: it is efficient in giving orders and compelling obedience and providing one-way communication: but it is in the main still inept in everything that involves reciprocity, mutual aid, two-way communication, give-and-take.

No matter how worldwide and inclusive the province of any association or institution, whether it be a trade union or a church or a bank, there must be, at the central core, an organic form of association: a group small enough for intimacy and for personal evaluation, so that its members can meet frequently as a body and know each other well, not as units but as persons: small enough for rotation in offices and roles, for direct, face-to-face meeting, for discussion and decision on the basis of intimate understanding: the close loyalties of friendship are needed to tide over all conflict and internal opposition. All organic communities of a larger stature should, ideally, be formed by the federation of smaller units: any other method is but a provisional and mechanical solution, destructive of the very purposes of association.

* See All Things Common, by Claire Huchet Bishop in Bibliography.

The perception that every association has a natural limit of growth in its primary units might be called Ebenezer Howard's theorem. Though he set it forth only in relation to cities, it applies to every kind of group organization. By now a succession of sociological studies, from Le Play and Cooley to Homans, re-enforced by an increasing number of practical experiments, has shown that limitation of size is an essential attribute of all organic grouping: the true alternative to big, rigid organizations, cramped by their self-imposed routine, is to limit the number of people in the local group, and to multiply and federate these groups.

In short, balance, even in large organizations and communities, demands a return to the human scale and the personal, I-and-thou relationship. Only by creating such organic self-limited—but not self-centered or self-contained—communities in the school, the factory, the office, the city, can the balanced person have the milieu in which his new powers may be more effectively exercised. There is no upper limit to effective association once these conditions for avoiding over-centralization and congestion and for promoting self-education and self-government are observed.

In an era of balance, the educational and political aspects of life will take precedence over the economic ones: a reversal of nineteenth century practice. As in the Boimondau experiment in France, the development of the worker as person will modify the system of association and technical production; though the latter will often gain in purely physical terms as a result of removing the psychological blockages that have so long impeded full production. What administrators of large enterprises like Mr Chester Barnard have done in analyzing the processes of administration the workers themselves will increasingly do as they take over the tasks of self-government and self-administration.

What possibly gives the Boimondau scheme great significance for the future is the fact that it derives, not from any doctrinaire leadership, but from the inner compulsion on the part of the workers to unify their lives: to make the work process provide the means for re-integrating town and country, education and family life, leisure and systematic effort. These workers, retaining their original ideological identity as Catholics, materialists, humanists, protestants, socialists, conservatives, communists, have nevertheless moved toward a common goal and have laid down the framework for a balanced life. If that method proves viable, it will give a new pattern of development to our whole industrial system: one that will create, for the first time, a balanced work community, on sounder lines than Fourier, even in his best moments, dared to dream.

From this point of view, work and citizenship cannot be divorced: they are co-ordinate phases of a single life-process whose purpose is to create intelligent, animated, and emotionally mature men and women. The first sound steps toward combining these sundered aspects of life were taken by Fourier and Froebel over a century ago: the latter with his conception of the Kindergarten, which started education on the path it has still to follow to its terminus, and the first in his conception of the work army for peace—a proposal later modified by William James in his Moral Equivalent for War.

Once war armies are disbanded, peace armies, on a far larger scale, must be formed. Every young man and woman, at the age of eighteen or thereabouts, should serve perhaps six months in a public work corps. In his own region he will get training and active service, doing a thousand things that need to be done, from planting forests and roadside strips, supervision of school children in nurseries and playgrounds to the active companionship with the aged, the blind, the crippled, from auxiliary work in harvesting to fire-fighting.

Unlike military service, these forms of public work will be carried out with the educational requirements uppermost; and without any justifiably uneasy conscience as to the premature coarsening of the fiber of the tender and the sensitive. No citizen should be exempt from these common work experiences and services. But every effort should be made, for the sake of education, to take the student out of his home environment for a period, introducing him to other regions and other modes of life. Those who show special interest and aptitude should be given the opportunity to perform similar service in an international corps in order to become active participants in the working life and culture of other countries.

In time, these planetary student migrations will, let us hope, take place on an immense scale, comparable to the comings and goings of unskilled labor from Europe to America at the beginning of the twentieth century: but now worldwide in scope and with teachers, not labor bosses, to lead them. The result of such transmigrations would be to enrich every homeland with mature young men and women, who knew the ways and farings of other men, who would bring back treasures with them, songs and dances, technical processes and civic customs, not least, ethical precepts and religious insights, knowledge not taken at third hand from books, but through direct contact and living experience: thus, the young would bring back into every village and city a touch of the universal society of which they form an active part.

Such people would be ready for further study, further travel, further research, for further tasks and adventures, as the harried young people of today, threatened with the horrid compulsions of war, caught in the bureaucratic routine of school, office, and factory, are not. They would no longer live in their present parochial world: that world whose narrow limits are not in fact extended by the vague dribble of information and suggestion that reaches them by way of books or radios, filtered through many political and ideological sieves.

The present trickle of students already passing back and forth between certain parts of Europe and America under the Fulbright Act, are still caught by the routines of conventional education. But in time, their studies, their civic responsibilities, and their vocational interests will be united in a new kind of education; and mighty streams of such students, flowing back and forth along the seaways and skyways, will eventually irrigate the parched cultural soil of many lands.

Though with some misgivings, I have used a concrete but deliberately eutopian illustration of the new doctrines and practices, to bring out the rich potentialities that lie before us, once we rise to the challenge of the present crisis, with positive plans and projects, growing out of an inner renewal. But it would be an error to dismiss this as a mere fantasy. For what have I suggested but a democratic version of the grand tour that the favored classes of Europe gave their young heirs in the seventeenth and eighteenth centuries: a system of education that did much—in purely class terms of course—to promote the true Concert of Europe, and even to bring about a certain humane forbearance in the conduct of war and the settlements of peace that contrasts with our present unseemly practices, due to our isolation, our language barriers, our defective cultural sympathies and our self-righteous harshness.

The comradeship and understanding of such a world fellowship of the young, based on common experience and common purposes carried through together, the stimulus of new interest that would come with foreign service, would turn world co-operation into a working reality; and in time create a true world community. Such a course of education in world citizenship would create seasoned young men and women, awakened to the immense variety and diversity of other cultures, yet more conscious than ever, through the services they have interchanged, of their common humanity. With such young people, a World Constitution, providing positive world government along such firm lines as those laid down by G. A. Borgese and his colleagues in the Chicago group, would be in safe hands.

To submit to a more niggardly and isolated life today, to ask for less from the democratic commitment to universal education than the opportunity to perform such services, engage in such co-operations, enjoy such contacts and adventures, is a sign of our defective life-values, indeed of our barbarized and regressive culture: a culture sunk, for all its advances in health and technology and economic security, far below the level of that which prevailed in 1914 throughout the planet. Even under the very unfavorable conditions of the Second World War, the planetary deployment of military forces gave many young people opportunities for first-hand contacts and co-operations. Unprepared for such intercourse by their education and their provincial habits of life, the majority of Americans got nothing from these opportunities: they turned their backs on them, or perhaps came back with an inflation of self-esteem over American plumbing and iced drinks. But a significant minority, in every country, was deeply moved by these experiences: more than one young man and woman, even when not bound by marriage, has gone back to the far region that awakened his interest or his loyalty—to Burma, China, India, Japan, Italy, or Palestine, or even Germany—to serve as a bridge between Eastern and Western cultures.

By such means, not by books and constitutions and laws and technical devices alone, we will create one world. One of the ultimate aims of our lifetime education will be to make us the sharers in and creators of this universal culture: out of that development will come balanced regions, balanced communities, balanced men. Once the renewal we have pictured begins to work in the person, in a multitude of individuals and groups throughout the world, many projects that now seem as remote as the International Work Corps will become near: many plans for the re-building of cities to human scale, for the re-integration of city and country, for the humanization of industry, for the development of family life, for the general endowment of the workers' new leisure with active opportunities for creation, such as the artist knows, will become feasible.

8: DISCIPLINE FOR DAILY LIFE

Each one of us must find and work out for himself the ways in which he must modify his life, so as to achieve balance and self-direction, make the fullest use of his potentialities, and so contribute to the general renewal of life. There is no single formula for achieving this transformation; for the intellectual, so far from needing a balanced diet of the "hundred best books," often needs rather a stiff turn at manual toil or the assumption of active political responsibilities in his community, or in thought itself intensive study in some neglected domain.

Similarly the manual worker needs to push his mind far harder than he has yet learned: to devote himself to ideas as determinedly as that mid-Victorian British worker who, not being able to buy Ruskin's works, copied them out by hand in order to have them in his own possession. "We went down to the mine," an old miner in England observed to an acquaintance of mine, "with a book of Carlyle's or Mill's in our pocket to read whilst we ate; but the boys today go down with a newspaper and at night they don't wrestle with a book, but go to sleep over the wireless." No one can doubt that the physical conditions among miners have vastly improved in recent years; but their mental attitude has perhaps deteriorated; for they lack the purpose and self-discipline of the older generation. Seebohm Rowntree's second Survey of York confirms this supposition.

The first rule for autonomous development, toward which all education should tend, is to be able in normal health to provide for one's own wants and regulate one's own life, without undue dependence upon others. However ingrained the habits of co-operation in a family, the ideal person should be schooled to self-reliance. To have the habit of making one's own bed, cleaning one's own room, to be able to take turns at cooking meals for oneself or others, and performing whatever other operations are necessary for the maintenance of a household, including care of the sick and minding children, are essential for the development of both sexes: if only because this is the main way of freeing ourselves from claims to service which come down from days of universal slavery.

In this respect, a great advance has been made in many modern communities: not least in the United States where the frontier tradition of self-reliance and self-sufficiency has given the males in particular an unusual willingness to look after themselves and to take on some of the menial burdens of the household. An Italian, self-exiled from Fascism, told me once that he did not know the real meaning of freedom until he was established in a little apartment in New York, and found that since there was no servant to look after him he was expected to make his own breakfast—and actually accomplished this feat. That was both a symbolic and a practical act of liberation. These autonomous activities, bed-making, cooking, dish-washing, cleaning, provide a certain amount of manual labor, bread labor, as Tolstoy called it, essential for a balanced life. Such daily work largely does away with the necessity for special gymnastic exercises. If in addition one cares for a garden, no further routine exercise is necessary to keep the adult body in condition: what one may do by way of walking, swimming, climbing, playing games, will be for relaxation and delight.

Part of the discipline of daily life is to organize one's activities so as to be able to devote a good share of one's time and energy to public service in the community. That service cannot begin too early or be carried on too consistently; for the resorption of government by the citizens of a democratic community is the only safeguard against those bureaucratic interventions that tend to arise in every state through the negligence, irresponsibility, and indifference of its citizens. Many services that are now performed inadequately either because the budget does not provide for them or because they are in the hands of a remote officialdom, should be performed mainly on a voluntary basis by the people of a local community. This includes not merely administrative services too often dodged in a democracy, like service on school boards, library boards, and the like: it should also include other kinds of active public work, like the planting of roadside trees, the care of public gardens and parks, even some of the functions of the police. Through such work, each citizen would not merely become at home in every part of his city and region; he would take over the institutional life of his community as a personal responsibility.

In the new discipline for the daily life, then, public work must receive, along with one's vocation and one's domestic life, its due share of energy, interest, loving care. War tends to over-concentrate such claims, divorcing a soldier from his family, forcing him to abandon completely his vocation: making the claims of the community override all personal desires and preferences. But no form of integration that leaves out the constant need for public service will be capable of redressing the radical unbalance that exists in present-day society. The leisure that has now become possible in advanced societies for workers of all grades must be largely devoted to the tasks of citizenship; for the more world-embracing become the spheres of co-operation, the more essential it is that the local units of government and administration and industrial organization be vigilantly administered, through wide participation in criticism, and through the exercise of democratic initiative: a matter of giving suggestons and making demands from the bottom up, not merely a matter of taking orders from the top down. At the level of the intimate, face-to-face group politics should, as Michael Graham wisely suggests, be a matter for weekly, not quadrennial, consultations.

Finally, the re-building of the family, the assumption of one's role as lover and parent, as son or daughter, is vital to a balanced life. During the last decade, even in countries where little thought has been devoted to the subject, there has been a spontaneous recovery of parental and family values, on the part of children whose parents had taken a more narrowly egotistic attitude toward sex and its domestic responsibilities: in this realm, there have been more spontaneous acts of renewal, perhaps, than in any other department. The violence and evil of our time have been, when viewed collectively, the work of loveless men: impotent men who lust after sadistic power to conceal their failure as lovers: repressed and frustrated men, lamed by unloving parents and seeking revenge by taking refuge in a system of thought or a mode of life into which love cannot intrude: at best, people whose erotic impulses have been cut off from the normal rhythms of life, self-enclosed atoms of erotic exploit, incapable of assuming the manifold responsibilities of lovers and parents through all the stages of life, unwilling to accept the breaks and abstentions of pregnancy, making sexual union itself an obstacle to the other forms of social union that flow out of family life.

Here the way of growth is twofold; for one thing, it consists in giving back to marriage the erotic depth and effulgence that a too-docile bovine acceptance of continuous parenthood, without pause or relief, had once brought with it. To this end, the introduction of relatively safe, though still esthetically unsatisfactory, contraceptives has served a good purpose. But in addition the parental side of marriage needs far greater fostering than it has yet received. With rising national incomes homes must become more generous in space to give full play to family life; social measures must be taken to help families of four or five children from being undue economic burdens to those who choose to have them: more of the functions that have slid into the province of the school must go back to the home, once the domestic environment of house and neighborhood is designed deliberately for the play and education of children under the tutelage of their parents. The loving observation of children's growth, even some systematic habit of observing and recording these transformations, in family books and collections of papers and photographs, brings one of life's most precious rewards: yet in our impoverished urban environments, people devote to bridge or television, to soap operas or to other forms of sodden play, much of the time that they might spend, with far greater reward, in intercourse and play with their young.*

The denial of love here arrests the development of love in every other part of life; whereas the expression of love, through the various stages of attachment and detachment, from infancy through adolescence, is what contributes to human maturity, all the more because the last step in parental love involves the release of the beloved: the willing cutting of the cord that would otherwise keep the child in a state of emotional dependence. At that point in the parents' growth, their love must widen sufficiently to embrace other children besides their own: otherwise they face desolation and bitterness. Meanwhile those who fail to achieve love in marriage and parenthood must be thrice vigilant to compensate that loss in every other relationship by placing it as far as possible within the pattern of the family.

In short, the sharing of work experiences, the sharing of citizen responsibilities, and the sharing of the full cycle of family life, in homes and communities that are themselves re-dedicated to these values—this is part of the constant discipline of daily life for those who seek to transform our civilization. Without this balance in our daily activities, we shall not bring to our larger task the emotional energy and the undistorted love—not crippled by covert hatred and compensatory fanaticism—that it demands.

9: LOVE AND INTEGRATION

Everyone realizes, at least in words, that only through a vast increase of effective love can the mischievous hostilities that now undermine our civilization be overcome. The means are plain enough but

* See The Family Log by Kenneth S. Beam in Bibliography.

the method of application is lacking. Though love could bring regeneration, we have still to discover how to generate love: as with peace, those who call for it loudest often express it least. To make ourselves capable of loving, and ready to receive love, is the paramount problem of integration: indeed, the key to salvation.

Both in the individual personality and in a culture as a whole, the nature of disintegration is to release impulses of aggression and expressions of antagonism that were, during the period of development, sufficiently held in check to be innocuous, indeed, in some degree serviceable to the personality. The transformation of a benign personality into a belligerent one is one of the frequent aspects of senile decay: covered traditionally by humorous references. Though social phenomena are of a quite different order, a parallel deterioration, for parallel social causes, seems to operate there.

The transformation of hate and aggression into kindness, of destructiveness into life-furthering activities, depends upon our discovering the formative principle that prevails during the period of growth and development. Perhaps we can gain a clue to this by looking more attentively at the conditions that accompany senile breakdown. In that unfortunate state there is a curtailment of energies, a deterioration of organic functions, an undercurrent of frustration due to inadequate co-ordination, an increase of uncertainty and anxiety, and a steady shortening of the future: with this goes a shriveling of interest in activities that lie outside the visible present: such a withdrawal as will eventually reduce life to the body's concern with food and evacuation. So the withdrawal of love and the rise of aggression go hand in hand; for love is a capacity for embracing otherness, for widening the circle of interests in which the self may operate, for begetting new forms of life.

Integration proceeds by just the opposite route: a deliberate heightening of every organic function: a release of impulses from circumstances that irrationally thwarted them: richer and more complex patterns of activity: an esthetic heightening of anticipated realizations: a steady lengthening of the future: a faith in cosmic perspectives. Precisely out of this sense of abundance and fullness of life comes the readiness to embrace the divine. Instead of withdrawing from situations it cannot master in order to maintain mere bodily balance, love risks everything, even life itself, for the sake of a more complete engagement with that which lies outside it and beyond it. On this interpretation, the withdrawal of love is the deadliest sin against life; and the unrestricted giving of love and yielding to love are the only effectual means of redeeming its pains, frustrations, and miscarriages. Those who are impotent to love, from Hitler downward, must seek a negative counterpart in hatred and disintegration.

Charles Peirce approvingly quoted Henry James, the elder, on the nature of love: "It is no doubt very tolerable finite or creaturely love to love one's own in another, to love another in conformity to one's self; but nothing can be in more flagrant contrast with creative Love, all whose tenderness *ex vi termini* must be reserved only for what intrinsically is most bitterly hostile and negative to itself." "Everybody can see that the statement of St John," Peirce goes on to say, "is the formula of an evolutionary philosophy, which teaches that growth comes only from love, from—I will not say self-*sacrifice*, but from the ardent impulse to fulfill another's highest impulse."

To extend the domain of love, we must doubtless apply fresh psychological and personal insight toward promoting adventurous courtship, erotic fulfillment, marital harmony, parental nurture, neighborly aid and succor. But while the renewal of all these phases of love is vital to the more general spread of gracious and loving ways throughout society, even this is not enough. Love is concerned, fundamentally, with the nurture of life at every occasion: it is the practice of bestowing life on other creatures and receiving life from them. Love is egocentric and partial until it can also embrace all the dumb creatures who unconsciously participate in the wider scheme of life, until it bestows itself on those who will never thank one, because they are unconscious of our gift or because they are unborn: until it embraces those who would do one injury, prompting us to treat them with dignity and generosity, as warriors in reputedly more barbaric ages often treated the enemy.

So it follows that part of our love must be expressed by our relation to all living organisms and organic structures: some of our love must go to sea and river and soil, restraining careless exploitation and pollution: the trees and wild creatures of the forest, the fish in the rivers, are as subject to our affectionate care as the dogs or the cats who live in closer dependence on us. Consider the systematic wiping out of the natural landscape and the withdrawal from rural occupations and rural ways that took place during the past century: the spread of megalopolitan deserts undercuts love at its very base because it removes man's sense of active partnership and fellowship in the common processes of growth, which bind him to other organisms.

When such habits prevail, love is reduced to a thin verbal precept not a daily practice—a precept to be cynically disregarded on more intimate occasions as well.

For social and personal integration we must develop the small life-promoting occasions for love as well as the grand ones. Not a day, then, without nurturing or furthering life: without repairing some deficiency of love in our homes, our villages, our cities: without caring for a child, visiting the sick, tending a garden, or making at least some token payment of good manners on this common debt. But likewise not a day without some more smiling expression of the delights of love: generous evidence of what William Blake called "the lineaments of satisfied desire." Not just succor and service are the expressions of love: beauty is its oldest witness.

Now beauty, as Plato taught, is the tangible proof of love: both in its incitement and its consummation. Beauty of movement and gesture: beauty of bodily form and costume and manner: beauty that leaps to life in dance or song: beauty as simple people know it in their daily life—the folk of Hawaii, Bali, Mexico, Brazil, or those little islands of farmers and fisherfolk that preserve their old dances and their old songs, full of disciplined passion, in the midst of the drably sophisticated society that envelops them. By all these means, when life is not reduced to a mechanical regimen, we make the love in our souls visible to others, courting their approval and their co-operation, moving them by way of art into a closer union.

When Erasmus came to England he was delighted to find that the Englishwomen of that day habitually saluted the newcomer with a kiss, out of affectionate courtesy; and what could have been a better proof of their sound erotic life?—a life that was to break forth, presently, into such a lyric poetry as only a woodland of mating birds might produce. "Come live with me and be my love!" Though one may not or can not usually carry out that invitation, it ought to hover over the threshold of all human meetings; and where social relations are healthy, and love itself has not become sick with denial, art may honestly serve as surrogate for love: the social blessing bestowed for the personal blessing withheld.

When love takes slow rise in a thousand tiny rivulets, converging from every part of the landscape, even erotic passion will cut a deeper channel, instead of breaking forth, as it now too often does, like a flash flood that spreads ruin to the lovers and in a short while leaves behind the same arid waste it had suddenly overwhelmed. Love is not simply the insidious potion, the almost morbid poison, Tristan and Iseult found it: love, conscious and unconscious, is the daily food of all living creatures: the means of living, the proof of their capacity to live, the ultimate blessing of their life. The final criticism of Western civilization, as it has developed these last four centuries, is that it has produced the sterile, loveless world of the machine: hostile to life and now capable, if modern man's compulsive irrationalities increase, of bringing all life to an end. To open the way to love, by a score of daily acts, is the first step toward integration: not salvation merely through orgasms, but the possibility of creative fulfillment through an ever-widening partnership with life.

10: THE RENEWAL OF LIFE

One phase of civilization does not replace another as a unit, in the way that a guard assigned to sentry duty takes over its post. For a while they mingle confusedly, until a moment comes when one realizes that the entire scene has changed and all the actors are different. So with the internal change that will produce the new person. After a transition period a critical point will come when it will be plain that the new personality has at last matured and that those who wear a different mask look oddly antiquated and are "out of the picture." Though the object of this change is to make possible a new drama of culture, no one who understands the social process would pretend to write the lines or to describe, in any detail, the action and plot; for it is part of the very nature of the living drama that these things must be left to the actors. If here and there, I have ventured to anticipate the next moves, it is only because the first steps have already been taken.

How shall one describe the balanced man and woman, considered as an ideal type? Let me begin with a negative description. He no longer belongs exclusively to a single culture, identifies himself with a single area of the earth, or conceives himself as in possession, through his religion or his science, of an exclusive key to truth; nor does he pride himself on his race or his nationality, as if the accidents of birth were in some way specially laudable: that democratic parody of ancient feudal pride. His roots in his region, his family, his neighborhood will be deep, and that depth itself will be a tie with other men: but one part of his nature stays constantly in touch with the larger world through both his religion and his politics, and remains open to its influences and its demands.

The balanced man has the mobility of the migratory worker of the nineteenth century without his rootlessness: he has the friendliness toward people of other cultures that we see most admirably in the native Hawaiian; and with the habits so engendered goes a lessening of his conceit over what is exclusively indigenous. With respect to his own region, he observes two rules: first he cultivates every part of it to its utmost, not merely because it is near and dear, but because it can thus contribute its specialties and individualities to other places and peoples; and second, when he finds his own region deficient in what is essential for full human growth, he reaches out, to the ends of the earth if need be, to bring into it what is missing—seeking the best and making it his own, as Emerson and Thoreau, in little Concord, reached out for the Hindu and Persian classics.

Into the balance of the new man, accordingly, will go elements that are not native to his race, his culture, his region, even if the place he identifies himself with be as large and multifarious as Europe. The savor of his own idiosyncrasy and individuality will be brought out, rather than lessened, by this inclusiveness. So in him the old divisions between townsman and countryman, between Greek and barbarian, between Christian and pagan, between native and outlander, between Western civilization and Eastern civilization, will be softened and in time effaced. Instead of the harsh and coarse contrasts of the past, there will be rich fusions and blendings, with the strength and individuality that good hybrids so often show: this one-world intermixture will but carry further a process visible in the rise of most earlier civilizations.

The change that will produce the balanced man will perhaps occur first in the minds of the older generation: but it is the young who will have the audacity and courage to carry it through. In any event, the new person is, to begin with, one who has honestly confronted his own life, has digested its failures and been re-activated by his awareness of his sins, and has re-oriented his purposes. If need be, he has made public acknowledgment of such errors as involved any considerable part of his community. What has gone wrong outside himself he accepts as part and parcel of what has gone wrong within himself: but similarly, where in his own life he has had a fresh vision of the good or has given form to truth or beauty, he is eager to share it with his fellows.

The capital act of the new man is an assumption of responsibility: he does not transfer the blame for his personal misfortunes to his parents, his elders, his associates, his circumstances: he refuses to make his own burden lighter by treating himself as a victim of processes over which he could have no control, even when he has innocently suffered: for he knows that in the moral life future intentions are more significant than past causes. On the map that science and objective investigation supply him, he superimposes his own plan of life. So the balanced person treats his own situation, however formidable or threatening, as the raw material he must master and mold. But his humility, born of self-awareness, has another side to it: confidence in his own powers of creation.

Confidence in creation: a sense of the rich potentialities of life and of endless alternatives, beyond those that the immediate moment or the immediate culture offers. Confidence in creation, as opposed to the fixations, the rigidities, the narrow alternatives of the existing economic systems and cultural schemes: yes, here precisely is the deepest difference between the new person and the old, who gave to external conditions and external stimuli the initiative that living organisms and above all living persons must keep for themselves. Those who have this confidence are not afraid to break with the existing patterns, however compulsive and authoritative they may seem; and they are not afraid to make departures on radically different lines, merely because they may meet with rebuff or failure. Such confidence once existed in a high degree among the great industrialists who girdled the planet with railroad lines, steamships, ocean cables, and factories; and those whose task it is to build a new world on the ruins of our disintegrating civilization must have that faith in even fuller measure. The new person, because he has not feared to transform himself, is capable of facing the world in a similar mood of adventurous amelioration.

Only those who have confronted the present crisis in all its dimensions will have the strength to repent of their own sins and those of their community, to confront and overcome the evils that threaten us, and to re-affirm the goods of the past that will serve as foundation for the goods of the future that we have still to create. For those who have undergone these changes, life is good and the expansion and intensification of life is good. To live actively through every organ and still remain whole: to identify oneself loyally with the community and yet to emerge from it, with free choices and new goals: to live fully in the moment and to possess in that moment all that eternity might bring: to re-create in one's consciousness the whole in which man lives and moves and has his being—these are essential parts of the new affirmation of life. The rest lies with God.

Without fullness of experience, length of days is nothing. When fullness of life has been achieved, shortness of days is nothing. That is perhaps why the young, before they have been frustrated and lamed, have usually so little fear of death: they live by intensities that the elderly have forgotten.

This experience of fulfillment through wholeness is the true answer to the brevity of man's days. The awakened person seeks to live so that any day might be good enough to be his last. By the actuarial tables he knows, perhaps, that his expectation of life at birth is almost three score and ten; but he knows something more precious than this: that there are moments of such poignant intensity and fullness, moments when every part of the personality is mobilized into a single act or a single intuition, that they outweigh the contents of a whole tame life-time. Those moments embrace eternity; and if they are fleeting, it is because men remain finite creatures whose days are measured.

When these awakened personalities begin to multiply, the load of anxiety that hangs over the men of our present-day culture will perhaps begin to lift. Instead of gnawing dread, there will be a healthy sense of expectancy, of hope without self-deception, based upon the ability to formulate new plans and purposes: purposes which, because they grow out of a personal reorientation and renewal, will in time lead to the general replenishment of life. Such goals will not lose value through the changes that time and chance and the wills of other men will work on them, in the course of their realization; nor will the prospect of many delays and disappointments keep those who are awakened from putting them into action at the earliest opportunity. Nothing is unthinkable, nothing impossible to the balanced person, provided it arises out of the needs of life and is dedicated to life's further development.

Even in his most rational procedures, the balanced person allows a place for the irrational and the unpredictable: he knows that catastrophe and miracle are both possible. Instead of feeling frustrated by these uncontrollable elements, he counts upon them to quicken the adventure of life by their very unforeseeableness: they are but part of the cosmic weather whose daily challenge enlivens every activity.

Life is itself forever precarious and unstable, and in no manner does it promise a tame idyll or a static eutopia: the new person, no less than the old, will know bafflement, tragedy, sacrifice, and defeat, as well as fulfillment—but even in desperate situations he will be saved from despair by sharing Walt Whitman's consciousness that battles may be lost in the same spirit that they are won, and that a courageous effort consecrates an unhappy end. While the conditions he confronts are formidable, the initiative nevertheless remains with man, once he accepts his own responsibility as a guardian of life. With the knowledge man now possesses, he may control the knowledge that threatens to choke him: with the power he now commands he may control the power that would wipe him out: with the values he has created, he may replace a routine of life based upon a denial of values. Only treason to his own sense of the divine can rob the new person of his creativity.

Harsh days and bitter nights may still lie ahead for each of us in his own person, and for mankind as a whole, before we overcome the present forces of disintegration. But throughout the world, there is a faint glow of color on the topmost twigs, the glow of the swelling buds that announce, despite the frosts and storms to come, the approach of spring: signs of life, signs of integration, signs of a deeper faith for living and of an approaching general renewal of humanity. The day and the hour are at hand when our individual purposes and ideals, re-enforced by our neighbors', will unite in a new drama of life that will serve other men as it serves ourselves.

The way we must follow is untried and heavy with difficulty; it will test to the utmost our faith and our powers. But it is the way toward life, and those who follow it will prevail.

BIBLIOGRAPHY

As with The Condition of Man, the ground covered by this book is almost as large as life; and a reasonably full bibliography might prove as big as the book itself. So in obedience to my own thesis, I have confined the bibliography to a fair sample, aiming at balance rather than exhaustiveness. Though I have occasionally repeated significant books listed in The Condition of Man, many texts are cited only there, since the two books were conceived in 1940 as a unity.

Adams, Henry: *The Education of Henry Adams.* Privately printed: 1907. New York: 1918.
  The Degradation of the Democratic Dogma. New York: 1919.
  The method was faulty; but the intuitions about the approaching age accurate and profound.

Aldrich, Charles Roberts: *The Primitive Mind and Modern Civilization;* with an Introduction by Bronislaw Malinowski and a foreword by C. G. Jung. New York: 1931.
  Though the author sets store by a very doubtful racial unconscious and a gregarious instinct, this is a fruitful discussion of the survival of the primitive in the modern.

Alexander, F. Matthias: *The Use of the Self;* with an Introduction by Professor John Dewey. London: 1932.
  The Universal Constant in Living. London: 1942.

Alexander, S.: *Space, Time, and Deity.* 2 vols. London: 1920.

Ali, A. Yusuf: *The Message of Islam; Being a Résumé of the teachings of the Qur-an; with special reference to the spiritual and moral struggles of the human soul.* London: 1940.
  Sympathetic epitome.

Allport, Gordon Willard: *Attitudes.* In Handbook of Social Psychology, edited by Carl Murchison. Worcester: 1935.
  Personality. New York: 1937.
  Important.

Angyal, Andras: *Foundations for a Science of Personality.* New York: 1941.
  Excellent early part, in which the author attempts a non-dualistic description of the body-mind process, in relation to the implicated environment, though in his definition of autonomy and homonomy as the principal trends of development the dualism implicit in our language limits his analysis.

Anshen, Ruth Nanda (editor): *Science and Man: Twenty-four Original Essays.* New York: 1942.
> Including admirable summaries of their essential positions by Malinowski, Cannon, Niebuhr.

Arendt, Hannah: *The Origins of Totalitarianism.* New York: 1951.

Arnold, Matthew: *Saint Paul and Protestantism.* London: 1883.
> Admirable.

Babbage, Charles: *The Ninth Bridgewater Treatise; a Fragment.* London: 1838.
> Mathematical argument for "miracles" and for design, by the redoubtable mathematician who made the first practical "calculating engine" for handling complex mathematical operations: the Victorian beginning of cybernetics.

Babbitt, Irving: *Rousseau and Romanticism.* New York: 1919.
Democracy and Leadership. New York: 1924.
> The reactionary elements in Babbitt's thought should not obscure his many salutary insights.

Bailey, J. O.: *Pilgrims Through Space and Time; Trends and Patterns in Scientific and Utopian Fiction.* New York: 1947.

Bardet, Gaston: *Polyphonic Organization.* In *News-sheet of the International Federation for Housing and Town Planning.* Amsterdam: Nov. 1950.
> Outline of an organic reorganization of work, as applied to city design. See Bishop.

Barlow, Kenneth E.: *The Discipline of Peace.* London: 1942.
The State of Public Knowledge. London: 1946.
> A physician's original reflections on the processes of thought in our society.

Barnett, L. D.: *The Path of Light; a Manual of Maha-Yana Buddhism.* Wisdom of the East Series. New York: 1909.

Barr, Stringfellow: *The Pilgrimage of Western Man.* New York: 1949.
> Western history since 1500, focused on the emergence of world government. Curiously omits reference to the unifying effects of missionary enterprise, trade, and political imperialism, without which the conditions for world government would hardly have appeared.

Barrows, John Henry (editor): *The World's Parliament of Religions.* 2 vols. Chicago: 1893.
> An epoch-making event, recording the high point of nineteenth century universalism.

Beam, Kenneth S. (Editor): *The Family Log.* With foreword by Lewis Mumford. San Diego, Cal.: 1948.
> A pamphlet setting forth methods and objectives of making family records, on lines suggested in chapter on The Culture of the Family in my Faith for Living.

Bergson, Henri: *Creative Evolution.* New York: 1913.
> An original interpretation. But see Lloyd Morgan.

Bews, John William: *Human Ecology.* New York: 1935.

Bishop, Claire Huchet: *All Things Common.* New York: 1950.
> Description of a new wave of producers' co-operatives in Europe: notably the Boimondau scheme.

Bloch, Oscar: *Vom Tode: Eine Gemeinsverstandliche Darstellung.* 2 vols. Stuttgart: 1909.

Boole, Mary Everest: *Collected Works.* 4 vols. Edited by E. M. Cobham. London: 1931.
> As an educator and a moralist Mrs Boole was worthy to stand alongside those other erratic geniuses, James Hinton and Charles Peirce: minds of high originality. See especially Logic Taught by Love, Vol. II, and The Forging of Passion into Power, Vol. IV.

Borgese, G. A.: *Common Cause.* New York: 1943.
Goliath: the March of Fascism. New York: 1937.
> See Committee to Frame a World Constitution.

Borsodi, Ralph: *Education and Living.* 2 vols. *The School of Living:* Suffern, New York: 1948.
> Attempt to work out in systematic detail the precepts of the philosophy first expressed, as criticism, in This Ugly Civilization: decentralism, household economy, self-help, and soil regeneration.

Bradley, F. H.: *Appearance and Reality.* London: 1893.
> Classic.

Branford, Victor: *Science and Sanctity.* London: 1923.
Living Religions: a Plea for the Larger Modernism. London: 1924.
> An attempt to find working basis of unity between Eastern and Western interpretations of religion. See also Northrop.

Breasted, James H.: *The Dawn of Conscience.* New York: 1939.
> Origins of morality in Egypt: highly relevant.

Brinton, Crane: *The Anatomy of Revolution.* New York: 1938.

Brochmann, Georg: *Humanity and Happiness.* New York: 1950.
> A human document as well as a philosophic inquiry into the paradoxical nature and terms of happiness. Recommended.

Brownell, Baker: *The Philosopher in Chaos.* New York: 1941.
The Human Community. New York: 1950.

Buber, Martin: *I and Thou.* First ed. 1923. Edinburgh: 1937.
> Already something of a classic: on the need for recognizing the intimate and the personal in social relations.
Between Man and Man. London: 1947.
> Further application of the "I-and-Thou" principle: particularly notable in two essays on education, and in the philosophical "anthropology" essay, What Is Man?

Bucke, Richard: *Cosmic Consciousness; a Study in the Evolution of the Human Mind.* New York: 1901.

Burckhardt, Jacob: *Force and Freedom; Reflections on History.* New York: 1943.
> Translation of the *Weltgeschichtliche Betrachtungen,* ably edited by James Nichols. For the depth of his intuitions, as well as for the scope of his thought, Burckhardt stands first among the modern philosophers of history. Even his errors were fertile: witness the effect of his mainly erroneous conception of the Renascence in stirring up scholarly effort in this department. But his truths were too profound to be assimilated by the archivists and historiographers, who dismissed him, in his own lifetime, for not interrupting his original sentences in order to cross his t's. See also Henry Adams and Spengler.

Burrow, Trigant: *The Social Basis of Consciousness; a Study in Organic Psychology Based upon a Synthetic and Societal Concept of the Neuroses.* New York: 1927.

   The Neurosis of Man; an Introduction to the Science of Human Behavior. New York: 1949.

   An attempt to explain the radical defects of civilization as the result of the departure from the natural whole responses of the organism to the partial responses focused in an I-Persona. This thesis is put forward in a private, I-Persona vocabulary which contains some 69 private new terms. An attempt to find an elementalist clue to disorders which must be sought on higher levels. But no one who feels impelled to accept the thesis of The Conduct of Life should avoid testing its weaknesses against Dr Burrow's counter-thesis.

Bury, J. B.: *The Idea of Progress.* London: 1920.

Butler, Samuel: *Life and Habit.* First ed. London: 1877.

   An early statement of the possible relation between habit, instinct, and biological inheritance. Long discredited in conventional scientific circles, because it explains the "simple" in terms of the complex, it will probably rank as a primitive classic in the organic science that is still to emerge. See Schrödinger.

   Unconscious Memory: First ed. London: 1880. Re-issued London: 1922.

   Follows up the trail opened in Life and Habit by reference to work of Hartmann on the Unconscious; anticipates the later concepts of the mneme by Semon. See Marcus Hartog's introduction on the significance of Butler's work to biological science, now acknowledged by many eminent biologists.

Campbell, Lewis and Garnett, W.: *Life of James Clerk Maxwell.* London: 1882.

Cantril, Hadley: *The "Why" of Man's Experience.* New York: 1950.

   Draws heavily on the experiments and interpretations of Adelbert Ames on the nature of sensations and perceptions. See Lawrence.

Cassirer, Ernst: *An Essay on Man; An Introduction to a Philosophy of Human Culture.* New Haven: 1944.

Casson, Stanley: *Progress and Catastrophe; an Anatomy of Human Adventure.* New York: 1937.

   Modest but penetrating.

Channing, William Ellery: *Channing Day by Day.* Boston: 1948.

   Selections from writings of a great Christian universalist, alert to the dangers of statism and nationalism.

Chesterton, Gilbert Keith: *What's Wrong with the World.* London: 1904.

Child, Charles M.: *The Physiological Foundations of Behavior.* New York: 1924.

Chrow, Lawrence B. and Loos, A. William (Editors): *The Nature of Man; His World; His Spiritual Resources; His Destiny.* New York (The Church Peace Union): 1950.

   Synopsis of series of lectures from scholars in many fields, aiming to present a unified view of man.

Chuang Tzu: *Musings of a Chinese Mystic; Selections from the Philosophy of Chuang Tzu.* In Wisdom of the East Series. London: 1906.

   A text, mainly Taoist, at which various hands have been at work. See Hughes, E. R.

Coates, J. B.: *The Crisis of the Human Person; Some Personalist Interpretations*.
London: 1949.
Study of a group of writers, allied to personalism or, like James Burnham, antagonistic
to its principles.

Coghill, G. E. *Anatomy and the Problems of Behavior*. Cambridge: 1929.
Important. Corrective of the simplism of the Watsonian "behaviorists."

Collingwood, Robin George: *Speculum Mentis; or, The Map of Knowledge*.
Oxford: 1924.
An Autobiography. New York: 1939.
Perspicuous on the neutral, self-deflating academicism of British and American
Philosophy.
Religion and Philosophy. London: 1916.
Penetrating: more important than many later books on same theme.

Committee to Frame a World Constitution, The: *Preliminary Draft of a World
Constitution*. Chicago: 1949.
One of several score postwar efforts: probably in every way the most significant,
through the quality of mind at work and the realistic grasp and imaginative insight
shown in attacking some of the most difficult problems: above all, the needful balance
and dispersion of power, for which the Committee presents a striking solution. The
result of two years' effort, and continued application in the current review, Common
Cause. Highly recommended.

Confucius: *The Analects of Confucius*. Translated and annotated by Arthur
Waley. London: 1938.

Conklin, Edwin Grant: *The Direction of Human Evolution*. New York: 1921.
Man, Real and Ideal; Observations and Reflections on Man's Nature, Development and Destiny. New York: 1943.

Cooley, Charles Horton: *Life and the Student; Roadside Notes on Human Nature, Society, and Letters*. New York: 1927.
The life wisdom of a great American sociologist.

Coster, Geraldine: *Yoga and Western Psychology*. London: 1934.

Cranston, Ruth: *World Faith; the Story of the Religions of the United Nations*.
New York: 1949.

Croce, Benedetto: *History as the Story of Liberty*. London: 1921.
The Conduct of Life. New York: 1924.
Vitiated by the author's dualism between the practical and the esthetic. The moral
and the political are not organically reconciled by his Hegelisms.
Politics and Morals. New York: 1945.

Curtis, Lionel: *Civitas Dei*. 3 vols. London: 1934-1937.
A compendium of history seen as the growth of commonwealth. Final hope for world
government via an English-speaking union to begin with.

D'Arcy, M. C., S.J.: *The Mind and Heart of Love; Lion and Unicorn; a Study
in Eros and Agape*. New York: 1947.
Excellent, with a double illumination from analytic psychology and Christian theology.

Das, Bhagavan: *The Essential Unity of All Religions*. Second ed. enlarged.
Benares: 1939.
Significant and useful.

Davies, Blodwen, and Reiser, Oliver L. *Planetary Democracy: an Introduction to Scientific Humanism and Applied Semantics.* New York: 1944.
A little naive, but headed in the right direction.

Dewey, John: *Moral Principles in Education.* New York: 1909.
Rejects teaching about morals in favor of situational moral decisions. Hence it takes for granted the validity of existing conventions and principles so applied. In this little book of an early date both the strength and weakness of Dewey's philosophy are neatly revealed.
Reconstruction in Philosophy. New York: 1920.
Human Nature and Conduct; an Introduction to Philosophy. New York: 1922.
Excellent.
Experience and Nature. Chicago: 1925.
The Quest for Certainty; a Study of the Relation of Knowledge and Action. (Gifford Lectures.) New York: 1929.
A Common Faith. (The Terry Lectures.) New Haven: 1934.
The Problems of Men. New York: 1946.
Collected essays relating to the central themes of Dewey's thought: democracy, education, logic, and value.

Dilthey, Wilhelm: *Gesammelte Schriften.* 11 vols. Leipzig: 1921-1936.
See especially Bde. 2 and 5-6. Cf. Hodges. Though Dilthey had no formative effect on my own thought or that of Ortega y Gasset, our late discovery of him brought the pleasure of confirmation.

Doman, Nicholas: *The Coming Age of World Control.* New York: 1942.

Driesch, Hans: *Man and the Universe.* New York: 1929.
Mind and Body. New York: 1927.

Drummond, Henry: *Natural Law in the Spiritual World.* New York: 1887.

Ellis, Havelock: *The Dance of Life.* New York: 1923.

Emerson, Ralph Waldo: *Essays: First Series.* Boston: 1841.
Essays: Second Series. Boston: 1844.
The Conduct of Life. Boston: 1860.
Society and Solitude. Boston: 1870.
The essay on Domestic Life is classic.
Journals: 10 vols. Boston: 1908.
Among the handful of moralists who have affected Western culture, and who may continue to affect it, I would rank Emerson—*pace* Matthew Arnold!—higher than Epictetus or Marcus Aurelius: for his crystalline vision and his sense of life's capacity for self-renewal. But it is impossible to choose among his works: his best passages are everywhere. There is little that is healthy in Nietzsche that was not first expressed in Emerson, whose influence Nietzsche acknowledged. Not the least important of his thoughts are those that were left over in his Journals.

Farquhar, J. N.: *Modern Religious Movements in India.* New York: 1924.

Fitzpatrick, Edward A. (Editor): *St. Ignatius and the Ratio Studiorum.* New York: 1933.

Flewelling, Ralph Tyler: *The Survival of Western Culture.* New York: 1943.
Recommended. Flewelling used the term "personalism" to characterize his philosophy long before Mounier.

Flügel, J. C.: *Man, Morals and Society.* London: 1945.

Forman, Henry James: *The Story of Prophecy in the Life of Mankind from Early Times to the Present Day.* New York: 1936.

Fouillée, Alfred J. E.: *Morale des Idées Forces.* Paris: 1908.

Frank, Waldo: *The Re-Discovery of America.* New York: 1929.
> Penetrating interpretation and prophecy: a challenge that met no response from the generation it addressed. Almost alone in his generation in America, Waldo Frank understood from the first the mission of religion: not as a genteel archaism that promises salvation from Wasteland, but as a living experience.

Chart for Rough Waters. New York: 1940.

South American Journey. New York: 1944.
> Frank's interpretation of the organic contribution of more "primitive" cultures—often more highly developed in values than our own—is uniquely good.

Freud, Sigmund: *The Interpretation of Dreams.* London: 1913.
> Probably Freud's most original and significant work.

The Future of an Illusion. London: 1928.
> Discussion of what Freud means by religion; so arbitrary that even close disciples, like Dr. Gregory Zilboorg, reject it. See Jung.

Civilization and Its Discontents. New York: 1930.
> Exposition of Freud's theory of an instinct toward destruction and death, to account for the aggressiveness of man and the transposition of that aggressiveness into moral conduct. Suggestive but superficial.

New Introductory Lectures on Psychoanalysis. New York: 1933.
> A re-statement of his whole psychological position.

An Outline of Psychoanalysis. New York: 1949.
> Translation of the 1940 German edition: a final testament that does not alter Freud's original position.

Fromm, Erich. *Escape from Freedom.* New York: 1942.
Man for Himself; an Inquiry into the Psychology of Ethics. New York: 1947.
Psychoanalysis and Religion. New Haven: 1950.

Gandhi, Mohandas Karamchand: *Gandhi's Autobiography.* Washington: 1948.

Gardiner, H. M.: *Feeling and Emotion; a History of Theories.* New York: 1937.

Geddes, Patrick: *The Anatomy of Life.* In Sociological Review. Jan. 1927.

Geddes, Patrick, and Thomson, J. Arthur: *Life; Outlines of Biology.* New York: 1931.
> A rich compendium, both of biological science, and of the authors' fundamental philosophy of life in all its dimensions.

Geisser, Franz: *Mo Ti: Der Künder der Allgemeinen Menschenliebe.* Berne: 1947.
> Excellent study of Mo Ti and affiliated thinkers in the development of a study of the universal ethics of humanity.

Ghose, Aurobindo (Sri Aurobindo): *The Life Divine.* 2 vols. in 3. Calcutta: 1939-1940.

Giedion, Sigfried: *Mechanization Takes Command.* New York: 1948.
> An original study of remarkable scholarly acuity and a wealth of concrete detail never before systematically put together, but with a certain underlying ambiguity of evaluation. See Mumford: Technics and Civilization.

Gillin, John: *The Ways of Men; an Introduction to Anthropology.* New York: 1948.

Particularly good on the biological and psychological side. See Kroeber, Linton, Malinowski.

Goldstein, Kurt: *Human Nature in the Light of Psychopathology.* Cambridge, Mass.: 1940.

An holistic study by an eminent brain specialist, emphasizing abstraction, freedom, and self-restriction as essential characteristics of human conduct at its higher levels.

The Organism. New York: 1939.

Graham, Michael: *Human Needs.* London: 1951.

A biologist's analysis of those long-established habit-patterns that condition man's further development. Full of human insight and sense.

Gratry, A.: *La Morale et la Loi d'histoire.* 2 vols. Paris: 1874.

Logic. Chicago: 1946.

Regarded by Boole as a classic contribution on the subject; particularly notable because of the human insight shown into the actual discipline and hygiene of the mind. Highly recommended.

Gray, Alexander: *The Socialist Tradition; Moses to Lenin.* New York: 1946.

Guérard, Albert Leon: *A Short History of the International Language Movement.* London: 1922.

Best introduction to this subject.

Haldane, J. S.: *Mechanism, Life, and Personality: an Examination of the Mechanistic Theory of Life and Mind.* New York: 1921.

Exposition of the inadequacies of the mechanistic postulates and an excellent statement of a philosophic basis of personalism long before Mounier's school of personalists was heard from. But Haldane's subjective idealism vitiates his statement. The author is not to be confused with his brilliant but less profound—to speak kindly— Marxian son.

The Sciences and Philosophy. New York: 1930.

Gifford lectures elaborating the philosophy set forth in Mechanism, Life, and Personality. Unfortunately, in reacting against the misplaced materialism of conventional science, Haldane espouses an equally indefensible idealism that holds that "the real universe is the spiritual universe in which spiritual values count for everything." If real means "actual" this is nonsense.

Halliday, James L.: *Psychosocial Medicine.* New York: 1948.

Analysis of psychosomatic disorders in contemporary civilization, showing contradictions between rising physical and lowered psycho-social health. Needs further expansion in detail.

Harrison, Jane Ellen: *Ancient Art and Ritual.* New York: 1922.

Brief but important.

Haskell, Edward H., Wade, Burton, and Pergament, Jerome: *Co-Action Compass; A General Conceptual Scheme Based Upon the Independent Systematization of Co-actions Among Plants by Gause, Animals by Haskell, and Men by Moreno, Lundberg, Honing and Others.* New York: 1948.

Compare Geddes's diagrams in *Life; Outlines of Biology.* Vol. II.

Heard, Gerald: *Is God Evident?* New York: 1948.

Essay in Natural Theology: all the better because the author attempts to do justice to Hindu as well as Christian insights. Possibly the best of Heard's books.

Heard, Gerald: *Is God in History? An Inquiry into Human and Prehuman History, in Terms of the Doctrine of Creation, Fall, and Redemption.* New York: 1950.

Unconvincing. For the more classic, Christian view, see the works of Reinhold Niebuhr, especially The Nature and Destiny of Man.

Heidegger, Martin: *Existence and Being.* London: 1949.

Four essays in logomachy, with a long introduction by Werner Brock.

Henderson, Lawrence J.: *The Order of Nature.* Cambridge: 1925.

Contains Clerk-Maxwell's paper on Singular Points.

The Fitness of the Environment. New York: 1924.

Classic.

Herrick, C. Judson: *Neurological Foundations of Animal Behavior.* New York: 1924.

Brains of Rats and Men; a Survey of the Origin and Biological Significance of the Cerebral Cortex. Chicago: 1926.

Hindu Scriptures: Hymns from the Rigveda, Five Upanishads, the Bhagavadgita. Edited by Nicol Macnicol. London: 1938.

One of the most useful editions of the Hindu classics; though I prefer other translations of the Gita.

Hinton, James: *Man and His Dwelling Place; an Essay Towards the Interpretation of Nature.* London: 1861.

Life in Nature. First ed. 1862. London: 1932.

The Mystery of Pain; a Book for the Sorrowful. New York: 1872.

Flashes of great intuitive insight, by a thinker whose central thoughts are closer to our time than they were to his own.

Hobhouse, Leonard T.: *Development and Purpose; an Essay Towards a Philosophy of Evolution.* London: 1913.

Important. Though the argument is not always adequately illustrated and carried through, the main lines of it are admirable and the date is notable. See Urban and Janet.

The Rational Good. London: 1921.

Hocking, William Ernest: *Human Nature and Its Remaking.* First ed. 1918. New Haven: 1923.

Uneven in texture and over-influenced perhaps by the then current psychology of instincts; but remarkably sound in its essentials. Compare with Marxian doctrine that human nature is made and re-made by self-determined economic institutions.

The Self; Its Body and Freedom. New Haven: 1928.

One of the best philosophic discussions of this subject.

Living Religions and a World Faith. New York: 1940.

Excellent discussion of the local and universal tendencies in religion, with an unusual grasp of the significance of the non-Christian faiths. See Söderblom.

Hodges, H. A.: *Wilhelm Dilthey; an Introduction.* London: 1944.

Good.

Höffding, Harald: *The Philosophy of Religion,* London: 1914.

Homans, George C.: *The Human Group.* New York: 1950.

Utilizes case histories and contemporary studies to carry further the original work of Charles Horton Cooley. The perspicuous formulation of theory further validates the direct data.

Hopkins, E. Washburn: *Origin and Evolution of Religion.* New Haven: 1923.
Better than Salomon Reinach's Orpheus.

Hoyle, Fred: *The Nature of the Universe.* Oxford: 1950.
BBC talks by a mathematical physicist giving most recent astronomical picture of the universe. On his interpretation the universe, so far from running down, is in a constant state of creation—out of nothing.

Hughes, E. C.: *Personality Types and The Division of Labor.* In *American Journal of Sociology.* Vol. 33: 1928.

Hughes, E. R. (editor and translator): *Chinese Philosophy in Classical Times.* New York: 1942.
An excellent selection, beginning with the Book of Odes and presenting the very essence of Confucianism and Taoism in a series of generous selections. Indispensable.

Huizinga, Jan: *Homo Ludens; a Study of the Play Element in Culture.* London: 1949.
Philosophic discussion of function of play as an essential characteristic of man.

Hutchins, Robert M. See Committee to Frame a World Constitution.

Huxley, Aldous: *The Perennial Philosophy.* New York: 1945.
Selections and commentary on the religious interpretation of life, mainly from the mystical side.

Huxley, Julian S.: *Evolutionary Ethics.* Oxford: 1943.
Man Stands Alone. New York: 1941.

Jaeger, Werner: *Paideia: the Ideals of Greek Culture.* 3 vols. New York: 1939-1944.
Profound study of education in the most comprehensive sense, derived from the experience and thought of the most educated people in history. Not least valuable because of its presentation of remoter thinkers and poets like Hesiod and Tyrtaeus. Indispensable.

James, William: *Essays in Radical Empiricism.* New York: 1912.
The best of James as philosopher.
Pragmatism. New York: 1909.
And the worst.
The Will to Believe. New York: 1897.
See especially the final pages of the final essay.

Janet, Paul (Alexandre René): *Final Causes.* Edinburgh: 1878.
One of the best nineteenth century discussions, which won the approbation of such a keen thinker as Professor Robert Flint, who wrote an introduction for this translation.
The Theory of Morals. New York: 1892.

Janet, Pierre: *Psychological Healing; a Historical and Clinical Study.* 2 vols. New York: 1925.
A scholarly, many-sided survey of the various contradictory arts for treating mental diseases.

Jennings, Herbert Spencer: *The Universe and Life.* New Haven: 1933.
Philosophic testament of a great biologist. See J. S. Haldane, Lloyd Morgan, Patrick Geddes, et al.

Jespersen, Otto: *Language; Its Nature, Development and Origin.* New York: 1921.
Profound scholarship plus human insight.

Johnson, Martin: *Art and Scientific Thought; Historical Studies Towards a Modern Revision of Their Antagonism.* London: 1944.

Johnson, Wendell: *People in Quandaries; the Semantics of Personal Adjustment.* New York: 1946.
Application of Korzybski's semantic teaching to psychology.

Jung, Carl Gustav: *Psychological Types; or The Psychology of Individuation.* New York: 1923.
Now famous division of types according to attitude and function.
Modern Man in Search of a Soul. London: 1933.
Psychology and Religion. New Haven: 1938.
The Integration of the Personality. New York: 1939.

Kafka, Franz: *The Trial.* New York: 1937.
Fantasy of frustration of individual person in an impersonal and compulsive civilization. Classic expression of the plight of the person today.

Kahler, Erich: *Man the Measure.* New York: 1945.
A distinguished work of interpretation. Dr Kahler is now working on a study that should prove of great importance: on singular and non-repeating events in nature and history.

Kallen, Horace M.: *Why Religion?* New York: 1927.
Anti-church: yet with true insight into the positive role of religion.
The Liberal Spirit. Ithaca, N. Y.: 1948.

Kant, Immanuel: *Perpetual Peace; a Philosophical Essay* (1793). London: 1903.
Fundamental Principles of the Metaphysics of Ethics. (Selections from *The Critique of Practical Reason.*) New York: 1932.

Kidd, Benjamin: *Social Evolution.* New York: 1894.
One of the first sociological studies to weigh the importance and lasting significance of religion in society.

Kierkegaard, Søren: *The Works of Love.* First ed. 1848. Princeton: 1949.
Fear and Trembling. First ed. 1921. Princeton: 1941.

Kluckhohn, Clyde: *Mirror of Man.* New York: 1950.

Kluckhohn, Clyde, and Murray, Henry A. (eds.): *Personality in Nature, Society, and Culture.* New York: 1948.
Excellent collection of recent essays with an important outline chapter on the conception of Personality by the authors. See Murphy, Gardner, and Allport, Gordon.

Koehler, Wolfgang: *Place of Value in a World of Facts.* New York: 1938.
Admirable in intention; but the very title shows how difficult it is for one bred in the scientific tradition to re-state the problem.

Koestler, Arthur: *Insight and Outlook; an Inquiry into the Common Foundations of Science, Art, and Social Ethics.* New York: 1949.
A usually able, sometimes brilliant, improvisation; but still an improvisation.

Kolnai, Aurel: *The War Against the West.* New York: 1938.
The best critical compendium of National Socialist thought, both the relatively sane and the downright insane, to date. Not to be overlooked on the assumption that the physical defeat of Germany brings Nazism to an end.

Korzybski, Alfred: *Manhood of Humanity; the Science and Art of Human Engineering.* New York: 1921.

Once extremely popular; but both naive and dated. The concept of a man as a time-binding animal put into a striking phrase an already familiar sociological concept. But see Science and Sanity.

Science and Sanity: an Introduction to Non-Aristotelian Systems and General Semantics. Science Press, Lancaster: 1941.

Original and important work. The first book I know to do adequate justice to the levels of meaning, including the unspeakable levels, to the multi-ordinal dimensions of every sign and symbol, and to the internal as well as the external aspects of objectivity. Unfortunately, Korzybski, in departing from Aristotelian logic, did not develop his system to a point at which he could include it in a fuller unity.

Kroeber, A. L.: *Configurations of Culture Growth.* Berkeley: 1944.

Significant analysis of the nature of culture growth. All the more valuable because made independent of the findings of Sorokin and Toynbee.

Anthropology—Race; Language; Culture; Psychology; Prehistory. New York: 1948.

Originally written in 1923, the present work has been completely re-written and radically improved. In scholarship, in critical judgment, in philosophical breadth by far the best single study of man and his works that has appeared, with a vein of refreshing originality threading through the descriptions and generalizations. The summation of the life work of a great scholar, endowed with wisdom as well as science.

Kropotkin, Peter: *Memoirs of a Revolutionist.* New York: 1899.

To be put beside Herzen and Gandhi.

Mutual Aid; a Factor of Evolution. First ed. London: 1902.

Written as reply to T. H. Huxley's *Nineteenth Century* article on The Struggle for Existence (1888). Presents evidence of co-operative factors, deplorably absent from Victorian business, but obvious both in human history and animal development. By this classic statement and his equally original Fields, Factories and Workshops, Kropotkin established himself as one of the great seminal thinkers of our time: perhaps capable of counteracting Marx's sinister emphasis on authority, mechanism, and violence.

Ethics; Origin and Development. New York: 1924.

Historical study on which Kropotkin was working at the time of his death. Unfortunately, it lacks his own special contribution to the subject, except by way of criticism of the classical ethical theories.

Krutch, Joseph Wood: *The Modern Temper; a Study and a Confession.* New York: 1929.

A dignified rationalization of the despair and emptiness of our time: itself a classic expression of the Wasteland period. Useful as a balance to those who might take the philosophy of the present book too one-sidedly.

Langer, Suzanne K.: *Philosophy in a New Key; A Study in the Symbolism of Reason, Rite, and Art.* New York: 1942.

Brilliant, penetrating, often original, always provocative. Available now in Mentor edition.

Lao-Tse: *Tao Teh Ching: The Way of Life.* Translated by Witter Bynner. New York: 1944.

Classic statement of life according to nature, with a maximum of spontaneity and freedom. This translation is perhaps over-polished: see E. R. Hughes.

Lawrence, Merle: *Studies in Human Behavior; a Laboratory Manual.* Princeton: 1949.

Attempt to establish basic principles of individual and group behavior with emphasis on perception: so far the most satisfactory exposition and development of Adelbert Ames's far-reaching experiments and interpretation on "sensation," a work which thoroughly undermines the whole conception of a world built up on the basis of "pure" sensation, from Hume onward.

Lecky, William E. H.: *The Map of Life; Conduct and Character*. London: 1899.
Mediocre though well-intentioned. MacDougall drew on it for a somewhat better book on character.

Lee, Vernon (Viola Paget): *Gospels of Anarchy*. London: 1908.
Perspicuous analysis of nineteenth and twentieth century prophets, from Emerson to Wells.
Althea: Dialogues on Aspirations and Duties. London: 1910.

Lenin, Nicolai: *Selected Works*. New York: 1938. Vol. V: *Imperialism and Imperialist War*.
Based on pre-1914 interpretation; and historically inept—despite its wide popularity in communist and even liberal circles—in its inability to interpret the retreat from imperialism into isolationism which characterized the dominant capitalist states during this period. The wide parrot-like acceptance of Lenin's thesis long common even in non-Marxian circles only emphasizes the current need for a revaluation of both the facts and the theories of imperialist enterprise. See Hannah Arendt.
Vol. XI: *Materialism and Empirio-Criticism*.
Upholds orthodox Marxism in interpreting the facts of current science, against Mach and the Neo-sensationists. Though Lenin's metaphysics is of the soapbox variety, which causes him to reject arbitrarily any point of view other than the Marxian, some of his blows against the Machians are well aimed.

Lepley, Ray (Editor): *Value; A Cooperative Inquiry*. New York: 1949.

Lewin, Kurt: *A Dynamic Theory of Personality. Selected Papers*. New York: 1935.

Lewis, C. S.: *The Problem of Pain*. London: 1940.

Linton, Ralph: *The Study of Man; an Introduction*. New York: 1936.
An excellent summary; with a weather eye on the future that has too often been lacking in American sociological analysis. See also Kroeber, Gillin, and Malinowski. (Perspicuously dedicated, incidentally, "To the Next Civilization.")

Loewenthal, Max: *Life and Soul: Outlines of a Future Theoretical Physiology and of a Critical Philosophy*. London: 1934.

MacDougall, William: *Character and the Conduct of Life*. New York: 1927.
Practical counsel from a good psychologist but open to much revision even on medical matters.

Mackail, J. M.: *Life of William Morris*. 2 vols. New York: 1899.

MacMurray, John: *Reason and Emotion*. London: 1935.
Important.
The Structure of Religious Experience. New Haven: 1936.

Maitra, Sushil Kumar: *The Ethics of the Hindus*. Calcutta: 1925.

Major, H. D. A.: *Basic Christianity; the World Religion*. London: 1945.
To arrive at a creed simple enough to unite with other religions Mr Major empties Christianity of its historic meanings.

Malinowski, Bronislaw: *Freedom and Civilization*. New York: 1944.
  Magic, Science and Religion. Boston: 1948.
    Admirable.

Mann, Thomas: *Past Masters and Other Papers*. New York: 1933.

Mannheim, Karl: *Man and Society in an Age of Reconstruction; Studies in Modern Social Structure*. New York: 1940.
  Diagnosis of Our Time. New York: 1944.

Maritain, Jacques: *True Humanism*. London: 1939.
  Ransoming the Time. New York: 1941.
    Includes an excellent series of essays on Bergson's metaphysics.
  The Rights of Man and Natural Law. New York: 1943.
    Application of personalism to constitutional law.
  The Person and the Common Good. New York: 1947.

Marrett, Robert R.: *Faith, Hope and Charity in Primitive Religion*. New York: 1932.
  Head, Heart and Hands in Human Evolution. London: 1935.
    Good.

Marvin, F. S. (Editor): *The Evolution of World Peace*. Oxford: 1921.
    A volume in the well-conceived Unity Series, which uttered some of the best insights and hopes of the twentieth century, without sufficient anticipation of the forces of barbarism whose existence Spengler had already ominously pointed to. As in most other discussions of the subject of unity, neither technology nor imperialism are adequately canvassed, or indeed here canvassed at all. See H. G. Wells.

May, Rollo: *The Springs of Creative Living*. New York: 1940.
  Meaning of Anxiety. New York: 1950.

Mead, George Herbert: *The Philosophy of the Act*. Edited by Charles W. Morris. Chicago: 1938.
    Mead was surely one of the most original thinkers of his generation; but, being an oral communicator, he has been saved from oblivion mainly by the activity of his students. His work on roles, symbols, and forms of communication in development of self is classic.

Melville, Herman: *Moby-Dick*. New York: 1851.
  Pierre; or, The Ambiguities. New York: 1852.
    A badly developed but significant novel, packed with distraught wisdom.

Montague, William Pepperell: *Belief Unbound; a Promethean Religion for the Modern World*. New Haven: 1930.
    Lucid statement of the naturalistic grounds for both religion and ethics, honestly facing the impossibility of reconciling an all-loving with an all-powerful God, yet showing the grounds for believing in an "ascending force, a nisus, a thrust toward concentration, organization, and life." William James's looser statement of this position, and Alexander's more comprehensive but more abstract work on Deity lack the precision and force of Montague's.

Moore, George Edward: *Principia Ethica*. First ed. 1903. Cambridge: 1929.
    Reduces ideal good to esthetic enjoyment, personal affection, and true knowledge. In preface Moore apologized for leaving out all consideration of purpose and end but he never rectified that omission. Influential through its weaknesses: otherwise sterile.

More, Paul Elmer: *The Skeptical Approach to Religion*. Princeton: 1934.

Moreno, Jacob L.: *Who Shall Survive? A New Approach to the Problem of Human Interrelations*. Nervous and Mental Disease Monograph Series, No. 58. Washington: 1934.
An ingenious approach to exact observation in the psychological behavior of men in groups: an attempt to establish an ecology of the psyche.
Psychodrama. Vol. I. New York: 1946.
Original.

Morgan, C. Lloyd: *Habit and Instinct*. New York: 1896.
One of the earliest and happiest works of this philosophic biologist, but without the originality and the epistemological and verbal hurdles of his later volumes. Though there is no indication of his being influenced by Samuel Butler, he shared many of the latter's insights and brought to them the authority of an experimental scientist.
Emergent Evolution. New York: 1923.
Life, Mind, and Spirit. New York: 1926.
The second course of The Gifford Lectures, delivered under the general title of Emergent Evolution; and, with Wheeler's brief exposition, the most satisfactory statement, in strictly natural history terms, of the general doctrine of emergence.
Mind at the Crossways. New York: 1930.
Closely reasoned presentation of the psychological and epistemological problems raised by the author's general philosophy.

Morris, Charles W.: *The Paths of Life*. New York: 1942.
Important in outline if not in development.
The Open Self. New York: 1948.
Re-statement of ideas expressed in Paths of Life, in terms of the self. See Hocking for a more comprehensive and on the whole sounder treatment of the same problem.

Mounier, Emmanuel: *A Personalist Manifesto*. New York: 1938.
Central but not altogether satisfactory exposition.
The Present Tasks of Personalism. Personalist Pamphlets. No. 4. London: n.d.
Existentialist Philosophies: an Introduction. London: 1948.
A useful Baedeker, which should convince the intelligent that there is no reason to take the journey. For those who will not be convinced, see Heidegger, Sartre, Wahl.

Muller, Hermann J.: *Out of the Night: A Biologist's View of the Future*. New York: 1935.

Mumford, Lewis: *The Story of Utopias*. New York: 1926.
The Golden Day; a Study of American Experience and Culture. New York: 1926.
What I Believe. An essay in *Living Philosophies*. New York: 1930.
Faith for Living. New York: 1940.
An attempt to give a debunked and self-devaluated generation an elementary understanding of the things men live and die for; the universal things, like Justice, Liberty, Truth, and the elemental primary things, like family, region, home. See Beam.
Values for Survival; Essays on Politics and Education. New York: 1946.
Includes the controversial essay on The Corruption of Liberalism first published in the New Republic in 1940. The last third of the book consists of a series of Letters to Germans, written originally at the request of the Office of War Information, after Germany had been conquered, and scheduled by them for German publication. When the Army took over, publication in Germany was denied. This singular policy was

doubtless the result of indoctrination in that school of German thought which assumed that Nazism was only a passing episode in German life. This illusion, fostered by those who too often exercised influence over Army education, is in no small part responsible for the radical mistakes the American government has made—and is still making—in relation to Germany.

Mumford, Lewis: *The Social Consequences of Atomic War*. In *Air Affairs*. Washington: March 1947.

Atomic Bomb: Miracle or Catastrophe. In *Air Affairs*. Washington: July 1948.

Alternatives to Catastrophe. In *Air Affairs*. Washington: Spring 1950.

This series of essays on the moral problems raised by the atomic bomb and the commitment to genocide followed Program for Survival, which was written less than a month after the bomb was used to exterminate the inhabitants of Hiroshima. In these essays I endeavored to deflate the grisly romantic flights of the air force strategists, with their irreal concept of a quick cheap victory by universal extermination; and I brought forth a series of concrete proposals for returning to political sanity and human morality. While the hypothetical predictions of 1947 have already been fulfilled to a dismaying degree, their only result was an invitation to lecture at the National War College—though the impression made on our military planners was not sufficient to reverse the disastrous policy on which the United States government had embarked. These essays, taken together, are herewith submitted as pragmatic corroboration of the philosophy set forth in these books.

Green Memories; The Story of Geddes. New York: 1947.

Glimpses of the biographical background and human experience out of which The Conduct of Life was written. To use current slang, this represents the existential side of the present philosophy. More than one page in The Conduct of Life owes a debt to my son—sometimes to his words, sometimes to his example.

Murphy, Gardner: *Personality; a Biosocial Approach to Origins and Structure*. New York: 1948.

An exhaustive study, using the latest findings of the anthropologists as well as the analytical psychologists and the personologists.

Murray, Henry A.: *Explorations in Personality*. New York: 1938.

One of the best attempts to chart the depth and breadth of the human personality, Freudian in background, but deliberately synthetic and comprehensive, not limited to the solutions of a school. See Murphy, Gardner.

Murray, Henry A. (editor). See Clyde Kluckhohn.

Murry, Middleton: *God*. New York: 1929.

Myers, Frederic W. H.: *Human Personality and Its Survival After Bodily Death*. 2 vols. New York: 1908.

Niebuhr, Reinhold: *The Nature and Destiny of Man; a Christian Interpretation*. 2 vols. New York: 1941.

Traditional in its adherence to orthodoxy: original by reason of this adherence, which gives the author a critical fixed point from which to detect the human aberrations of a too guileless liberalism, a too impersonal mechanism and materialism, or a too uncritical Marxism.

Faith and History; a Comparison of Christian and Modern Views of History. New York: 1949.

Assumes that the salvation of man cannot take place in history, since history is full of mysteries that cannot be penetrated and contradictions that cannot be resolved: therefore the meaning of life cannot be found there. The conclusion does not follow from the premises; but as with all Dr Niebuhr's other works he shows great skill in detecting flaws in his opponents' armor. All hangs on the viability of his concept of salvation.

Nietzsche, Friedrich: *The Genealogy of Morals; a Polemic.* London: 1913.
White crystalline blocks of truth, marbled with folly: including in the latter an attempt to derive the notion of moral obligation from the universal practices of a mythical *Urhändlunggesetzmässigkeit.*

Nikhilananda, Swami: *The Gospel of Sri Ramakrishna.* New York: 1942.
Ramakrishna, almost within his own lifetime, was known as the God Man to his followers. He is in many ways a close contemporary of Dostoyevsky's imaginary Holy Man in The Brothers Karamazov.

Nordau, Max: *Degeneration.* New York: 1895.
Appeared in 1893 in German, and caused great scandal in intellectual circles: rightly because of coarse application of half-baked scientific doctrines to ill-observed and maliciously interpreted "facts." But, as with Spengler, the book had merits as intuitive prophecy that it lacked as objective observation: the degeneration that Nordau regarded as mainly physiological, following Lombroso, was in fact a cultural disintegration whose results we have lived to see.

Northrop, F. S. C. (editor): *Ideological Differences and World Order.* New Haven: 1949.
Uneven in value.
The Meeting of East and West. An Inquiry Concerning World Understanding. New York: 1946.
Spirit and purpose excellent: method wooden: results uneven. Despite these reservations an important book.

Noüy, Lecomte du: *Human Destiny.* New York: 1947.
Advocates a doctrine of "telefinalism" as against the improbability of a world governed by chance producing as much order and direction as we find in the biological world and finally in man. Important as an indication of a new wind blowing in science; but unconvincing at many points because of a certain arbitrariness and over-confidence on such difficult matters as the correct way of inculcating morality.

Nyhren, Anders: *Agape and Eros; a Study of the Christian Idea of Love.* 3 vols. London: 1932.
Thoroughgoing study of the ideas contributed by the philosophers and theologians, without any further resolution of the modes of love in human experience.

Ogden, Charles Kay: *The System of Basic English.* New York: 1934.

Ogden, Charles Kay, and Richards, I. A.: *The Meaning of Meaning: a Study of the Influence of Language upon Thought and of the Science of Symbolism.* New York: 1923.

Ortega y Gasset, José: *Toward a Philosophy of History.* New York: 1941.
Ortega's approach to history is similar to that of this series.
Concord and Liberty. New York: 1946.
The Dehumanization of Art. Princeton: 1946.

Otto, Rudolph: *Idea of the Holy.* London: 1923.

Ouspensky, Piotr D.: *A New Model of the Universe.* New York: 1943.
The Psychology of Man's Possible Evolution. New York: 1950.
Pretentiously empty.

Paget, Violet. See Lee, Vernon.

Paley, William: *Natural Theology*. 2 vols. London: 1836.

Attempt to prove the existence of God from the evidence of design in natural history. Weak in science because of the date but generally rejected by naturalists because of a theology far sounder than that of their favorite Victorian Deity, Natural Selection.

Paul, Leslie: *The Annihilation of Man; a Study of the Crisis in the West*. New York: 1945.

Excellent in its diagnosis of fascism; but inadequate, in the same fashion as Toynbee, Sorokin, and Michael Roberts, in its suggestions for Renewal.

The Meaning of Human Existence. New York: 1950.

Pearl, Raymond: *Man the Animal*. Bloomington, Indiana: 1946.

Peirce, Charles: *Chance, Love and Logic*. New York: 1923.

The Philosophy of Peirce. Selected Writings. Edited by Justus Buchler. London: 1940.

Perry, Ralph Barton: *The Moral Economy*. New York: 1909.

General Theory of Value; Its Meaning and Basic Principles Construed in Terms of Interest. New York: 1926.

The Thought and Character of William James. 2 vols. Boston: 1935.

Persoff, Albert Morton: *Sabbatical Years With Pay: a Plan to Create and Maintain Full Employment*. Los Angeles: 1945.

A valid thesis in an age threatened with unusable leisure at the wrong end of life, quite apart from the question of full employment.

Petrie, Maria: *Art and Regeneration*. London: 1946.

Excellent study of the regenerative and formative role of art in education. Cf. Herbert Read.

Plant, James S.: *Personality and the Cultural Pattern*. New York: 1937.

Not merely sound psychology and sociology, but occasionally something more rare: wisdom.

Polanyi, Karl: *The Great Transformation*. New York: 1944.

Analysis of the nature of the modern market economy and its essential impermanence. Important: not least because it offers a satisfactory answer to the notion propounded by Herbert Spencer, Hayek, Lippmann, and others that the free economy disappeared, not because of its weaknesses and its sins, but because of an altogether perverse attack upon it.

Prescott, Daniel A.: *Emotion and the Educational Process*. Washington: 1938.

Rader, Melvin: *Ethics and Society; an Appraisal of Social Ideals*. New York: 1950.

Useful study by a scholar whose integrity and courage give him special qualifications to deal with this field.

Radhakdrishnan, S.: *The Hindu View of Life*. New York: 1927.

Excellent synoptic view of the Hindu religion and philosophy.

Indian Philosophy. 2 vols. New York: 1927.

Particularly useful because it has generous chapters on Patanjali and Sankara.

Read, Herbert: *Education Through Art*. New York: 1949.

Rightly esteemed by the author as his most important book to date.

Education for Peace. London: 1950.

Reich, Wilhelm: *The Discovery of the Orgone*. Vol. I: *The Function of the Orgasm*. First ed. 1927. Second ed. New York: 1948.
What is sound in this work—the belated but perhaps long-suspected discovery that orgasms are important—was not original with Reich, despite his contrary impression. (See Dr Marie Stopes' Married Love.) His originality consists in prescribing the orgasm as a panacea for the ills of mankind: the fallacy of one-dimensional salvation.

Reiser, Oliver L.: *World Philosophy; a Search for Synthesis*. University of Pittsburgh: 1948.

Reiser, Oliver L. See Davies, Blodwen.

Renouvier, Charles. *Le Personnalisme*. Paris: 1903.
Renouvier's mature statement of his own philosophic postulates.

Rhine, J. B.: *The Reach of Mind*. New York: 1947.
Summation of the evidence presented at earlier stages in *Extra-Sensory Perception* and *New Frontiers of the Mind* on the possibilities of clairvoyance, telepathy, and psycho-kinesis. Unless the theory of probability is not as absolute in its workings as mathematicians assume, the work of Dr Rhine and his associates proves that an unknown factor, seemingly human in origin, occasionally modifies some events of a "physical" nature. The most convincing part about the evidence is perhaps the fact that it is so meager in quantity and so hard to interpret.

Riesman, David (assisted by Denney, N., and Glazer, N.): *The Lonely Crowd; a Study of the Changing American Character*. New Haven: 1950.
Perceptive study of ethical sources and current ethical vacuums.

Rignano, Eugenio: *The Aim of Existence; Being a System of Morality Based on the Harmony of Life*. Chicago: 1929.
The Nature of Life. New York: 1930.
Good.

Ritter, William E.: *The Natural History of Our Conduct*. New York: 1927.
Attempt to rectify Huxley's misleading interpretation of discontinuity between man and other organisms in the ethical domain. Not entirely satisfactory; but in the right direction.

Roberts, Michael: *The Modern Mind*. London: 1937.
The Recovery of the West. London: 1941.
One of the best discussions of the intellectual and moral situation today. But see Leslie Paul, L. L. Whyte, and Erich Kahler, and my own book, The Condition of Man.

Roberts, Morley: *Malignancy and Evolution*. London: 1926.

Rocker, Rudolph: *Nationalism and Culture*. New York: 1937.
Important contribution by a distinguished philosophic anarchist. For a more favorable picture, see George Russell's The National Being, likewise Mazzini.

Rorschach, Hermann: *Psychodiagnostics; a Diagnostic Test Based on Perception*. Translated. Berne, Switzerland: 1942.
Theoretic exposition of the famous test, whose remarkable efficacy, in practice, has more than justified its author's original hopes. See Henry A. Murray.

Rosenstock-Huessy, Eugen: *Out of Revolution; Autobiography of Western Man*. New York: 1938.
The Christian Future; or, The Modern Mind Outrun. New York: 1946.
A challenging statement by a highly original mind.

Rosenstock-Huessy, Eugen: *The Multiformity of Man*. Norwich, Vt.: 1948.
Brilliant essay on the dynamics of human relations in work.

Rougemont, Denis de: *The Devil's Share*. New York: 1944.

Royce, Josiah: *The Philosophy of Loyalty*. New York: 1908.
Excellent statement of the higher universal implications of what would be, for Bergson, a static and enclosed morality.
The Problem of Christianity. 2 vols. New York: 1913.
Re-statement of Christianity in terms of human experience, as the religious expression of the "philosophy of loyalty." Penetrating and persuasive.
The Hope of the Great Community. New York: 1916.
One of the earliest and soundest formulations of One World doctrine.

Russell, Bertrand: *Mysticism and Logic*. New York: 1921.
Modern statement of scientific stoicism.
Religion and Science. New York: 1935.

Russell, E. S.: *The Directiveness of Organic Activities*. Cambridge: 1945.
Important, but see Simpson.

Sachs, Curt: *The Commonwealth of Art; Style in the Fine Arts, Music and The Dance*. New York: 1942.
Remarkable pioneer attempt at unification.

Santayana, George: *Realms of Being*. New York: 1942.
One-volume edition of The Realm of Essence, The Realm of Matter, The Realm of Truth and the Realm of Spirit: in some ways the philosophic equivalent of Proust, essentially a soliloquy that subsumes the past, tranquilly hovering over man and the cosmos, without ever wrestling with the present or moving toward the future.
The Idea of Christ in the Gospels or God in Man; a Critical Essay. New York: 1946.
The Life of Reason. 5 vols. New York: 1905.
Pregnant with original thoughts whose significance could not be fully appreciated until the present day.

Sartre, Jean-Paul: *Existentialism*. New York: 1947.
A symptom disguised as a system.

Sayers, Dorothy L.: *The Mind of the Maker*. New York: 1941.
Original conception of both the Christian religion and creativeness, but marred by Miss Sayers' professional assumption, as a writer of detective stories, presumably worked from the final solution forward, that God knew the answers before He began.

Schelling, Friedrich: *The Ages of the World*. Trans. with introductory notes by Frederick DeWulfe Bolman, Jr. New York: 1942.

Schilder, Paul: *Goals and Desires of Man; a Psychological Survey of Life*. New York: 1942.

Schrödinger, Erwin: *Science and the Human Temperament*. New York: 1935.
Brilliant summary of post-mechanistic physics.
What Is Life? New York: 1946.
A physicist's attempt to bridge the gap between the non-organic and the organic, by an extremely interesting application of the theory of probability to the genes of heredity, with their relatively small number of molecules.

Schweitzer, Albert: *The Philosophy of Civilisation*. Vol. I: *The Decay and Restoration of Civilisation*. Vol. II: *Civilisation and Ethics*. London: 1923.

[Vol. III: *The World-View of Reverence for Life.* Vol. IV: *The Civilised State.* In preparation.]

The divorce of his reverence for life from a view of nature partly deprives it of its natural significance and authority.

Out of My Life and Thought; an Autobiography. New York: 1933.

Indian Thought and Its Development. New York: 1936.

Compact and useful study of the life-negating Hindu ideology, by the exponent of a Western life-affirming religiousness.

Schweitzer, Albert: *An Anthology.* Edited by Charles R. Joy. Boston: 1947.

Seidenberg, Roderick: *Post-Historic Man; an Inquiry.* Chapel Hill, N. C.: 1950.

Acute study of the processes that are creating a collective automaton out of the image of God. Puts in rational form the intuitions expressed from Erewhon to *1984.* The author does not allow for human resiliency; or for man's capacity to demolish the machine itself before it takes him so far away from his proper destination. Recommended.

Sellars, Roy Wood: *Evolutionary Naturalism.* Chicago: 1922.

Shaler, Nathaniel Southgate: *The Neighbor; The Natural History of Human Contacts.* Boston: 1904.

The Individual; a Study of Life and Death. Boston: 1901.

Both noteworthy discussions, by a mind that went far beyond its professional province of geology.

Shand, Alexander F.: *The Foundations of Character; Being a Study of the Tendencies of the Emotions and Sentiments.* London: 1920.

Sheldon, William H.: *Psychology and the Promethean Will; a Constructive Study of the Acute Common Problem of Education, Medicine, and Religion.* New York: 1936.

The Varieties of Temperament. New York: 1942.

For an early anticipation of Sheldon's contribution see a paper by Dr J. Lionel Taylor: The Study of Individuals (Individuology) in *Sociological Papers.* London: 1904.

Simpson, George Gaylord. *Tempo and Mode in Evolution.* New York: 1944.

The Meaning of Evolution. New Haven: 1949.

Important.

Söderblom, Nathan: *The Living God; Basal Forms for Personal Religion.* The Gifford Lectures delivered in the University of Edinburgh in the year 1931. London: 1933.

Pure expression of Universalism. See Hocking.

Sombart, Werner: *The Quintessence of Capitalism: a Study of the History and Psychology of the Modern Business Man.* (Translation of *Der Bourgeois.*) New York: 1915.

Though Sombart contrasts this new ideology and psychology with those of a wholly mythical natural man, his characterization is often penetrating. Unlike Weber, he does not overplay the debt of capitalism to Protestantism. Cf. my criticism of Weber's arbitrary interpretation in The Condition of Man.

Somerville, John: *Soviet Philosophy; A Study of Theory and Practice.* New York: 1946.

Sorokin, Pitirim A.: *The Crisis of Our Age*. New York: 1941.

Condensation of thesis on modern civilization set forth in his four-volume Social and Cultural Dynamics (1938). Important because he was one of the first sociologists to recognize the importance of the logico-meaningful element in all social processes.

Society, Culture, and Personality: a System of General Sociology. New York: 1947.

A compendious textbook, which brings together in reasonable order a great deal of material and many bibliographic references.

The Reconstruction of Humanity. Boston: 1948.

Attempt at detailed prescription for overcoming the present disintegration of Western civilization. Full of loose thinking, slipshod generalization, and pseudo-statistical proof, and lacking in an adequate methodology; yet its weaknesses are partly corrected by a wide-ranging scholarship and by a generous recognition of the complicated processes at work in society and the human personality.

Spencer, Herbert: *Education; Intellectual, Moral, and Physical*. First ed., London: 1861.

Classic.

First Principles. London: 1862.

Introduction to Spencer's magistral attempt to unify the physical, biological, and social sciences by means of concept of evolution. The revolt against Spencer's system, led in the United States by William James, was not merely directed against his weaknesses: it was the rejection by an age of chaotic specialization against any attempt at a general order or synthesis.

Spranger, Eduard: *Types of Men; the Psychology and Ethics of Personality*. Trans. From fifth German ed. Halle: 1928.

Stapleton, Laurence: *Justice and World Society*. Chapel Hill, N. C.: 1944.

Attempt to re-establish concept of universal justice.

Steiner, Rudolph: *The Threefold Commonwealth*. New York: 1928.

Steiner's conception of a threefold arrangement of political, economic, and educational life, in which the state would have a minimum to do with economics and education.

Study of Man; General Education Course. New York: 1947.

Theosophical interpretation of the nature of man, by the most influential theosophist after Mrs Annie Besant. Precisely because of the freedom of hypothesis which Steiner gave himself, he has perhaps at times discovered truths, or the beginnings of truths, not admitted as possible by other systems. To preserve an inquiring and open mind, if no more, such books as this, usually contemptuously ignored by scholars, should be kept in view. Even such a flat materialist as Freud was forced, in medical honesty, to take dreams seriously.

Stern, William: *General Psychology*. New York: 1938.

Stevens, Henry Bailey: *The Recovery of Culture*. New York: 1949.

Ingenious interpretation of history and civilization as a perversion on the part of the meat-eating, stock-raising peoples of late neolithic times, which produced butchery and war, supplanting the peaceful plant-raising, tree-worshiping, vegetarian culture that preceded it. Stimulating.

Strömberg, Gustaf. *The Soul of the Universe*. Philadelphia: 1940.

Taylor, Gordon Rattray: *What Is Personalism?* Personalist Pamphlets No. 1. London: n.d.

Thomson, J. Arthur: *The System of Animate Nature*. 2 vols. New York: 1920. *What Is Man?* London: 1924.

BIBLIOGRAPHY

Thoreau, Henry David: *Walden*. Boston: 1854.
  Essay on Civil Disobedience. First published in Aesthetic Papers, edited by Elizabeth Peabody. Boston: 1849.
    Influenced Gandhi: badly needed today, particularly among many of Thoreau's cowed and blindly conformist countrymen.

Thorndike, Edward Lee: *Human Nature and the Social Order*. New York: 1940.
    Copious summation of Thorndike's life work as a psychologist, applied to problems that call for wisdom as well as knowledge. Thorndike's interpretation of purpose in relation to the learning process offers a more radical revision of current psychology than he himself seemed quite aware of.
  Man and His Works. Cambridge, Mass.: 1943.
    Brief summation of some of the data on social institutions in Human Nature and the Social Order. Perhaps most important for the light Thorndike's tests on reward and punishment throw upon penology.

Tillich, Paul: *The Shaking of the Foundations*. New York: 1948.

Tillyard, Aelfrida: *Spiritual Exercises and Their Results; an Essay in Psychology and Comparative Religion*. London: 1927.
    Useful though hardly exhaustive.

Tolman, Edward Chace: *Purposive Behavior in Animals and Men*. New York: 1932.
  Drives Toward War. New York: 1942.

Tolstoy, Leo. *Works*. Vol. XII: *On Life and Essays on Religion*. Vol. XIV: *What Then Must We Do?* Vol. XVIII: *What is Art?* Oxford: 1928-1937.

Toynbee, Arnold: *Civilization on Trial*. New York: 1948.
    Essays which show, perhaps more clearly than the six-volume A Study of History, the limitations of the author's theology and his insight into the nature of human life and destiny.
  A Study of History. Abridgement of Vols. I-VI in one volume by D. C. Somervell.
    This excellent condensation reveals more nakedly Toynbee's essential strength and weakness. He is like a great explorer and colonizer who returns at last to live on a small (spiritual) pension in his ancestral village, next door to the vicarage.

Trueblood, D. Elton: *The Predicament of Modern Man*. New York: 1944.

Tsanoff, Radoslav A.: *The Nature of Evil*. New York: 1931.

Tyrell, G. N. M.: *The Personality of Man*. London: 1946.
    Chiefly on evidence of extra-sensory activities.

Underhill, Evelyn: *Mysticism; a Study in the Nature and Development of Man's Spiritual Consciousness*. London: 1911.

Urban, W. M.: *Valuation; Its Nature and Laws*. New York: 1909.
  The Intelligible World. Metaphysics and Value. New York: 1929.
    Urban's work, with Hobhouse's, stands among the first recent attempts, apart from neo-Thomism, to interpret human experience in terms of value, purpose, and meaning.
  Language and Reality; the Philosophy of Language and the Principles of Symbolism. London: 1939.

Veblen, Thorstein: *An Inquiry into the Nature of Peace and the Terms of Its Perpetuation*. New York: 1917.

Vico, Giambattista: *The Autobiography of Giambattista Vico*. Trans. by Max Harold Fisch and Thomas Goddard Bergin. Ithaca, N. Y.: 1944.
Extremely revealing. Vico was not merely a great humanist in the Renascence tradition; but even more, an early precursor of a more organic and personalist philosophy.

Wallas, Graham: *The Great Society*. New York: 1915.
One of the landmarks that indicate how high the wave of hopeful intelligence and intelligent hope had reached before 1914. Cf. Mannheim's diagnosis almost a generation later.

Our Social Heritage. New Haven: 1921.

Men and Ideas. New York: 1940.
The wisdom of an educator, a civil servant, and a sociologist whose work should be better known to the present generation. See particularly his criticism of Froebelian pedagogy, which is also, incidentally, a criticism of Dewey's too influential little treatise on Interest and Effort in Education.

Wallis, Wilson D.: *Messiahs; Their Role in Civilization*. Washington: 1943.

Ward, James: *The Realm of Ends; or, Pluralism and Theism*. Cambridge: 1911.

Watts, Alan W.: *The Spirit of Zen: a Way of Life, Work, and Art in the Far East*. London: 1936.
Exposition of one of the most elusive forms of Buddhism.

Wells, Herbert George: *A Modern Utopia*. London: 1905.
One of a series of Utopias, all more or less similar in content because of the stress Wells laid on organization, administration and mechanical invention, which express the best of the liberal-socialist nineteenth century ideals though tainted by a tendency toward "scientific" authoritarianism.

The Shape of Things to Come; the Ultimate Revolution. New York: 1933.

The Anatomy of Frustration. New York: 1936.

Mind at the End of Its Tether. London: 1945.
Written when Wells's mind was itself collapsing and projecting its own situation into the world; but significantly fulfilling Chesterton's prediction that Wells's philosophy must end in despair.

West, Rebecca: *Black Lamb and Grey Falcon; a Journey Through Jugoslavia*. 2 vols. New York: 1941.
One of the richest personal interpretations of another culture in our time: a mine of wisdom.

Weyl, Hermann: *The Open World*. New Haven: 1932.
Re-statement in scientific terms of the case for deity as revealed by cosmic law, toward whose elucidation mathematics and physics offer the most useful key.

Wheeler, William Norton: *Emergent Evolution and the Development of Societies*. New York: 1928.
Crystalline statement of doctrine of emergence. But see Lloyd Morgan.

Whitehead, Alfred North: *Science and the Modern World*. New York: 1925.
In a less private language than Process and Reality, and still one of the best expositions of Whitehead's philosophy, though some of the logical weakness of the concept of mechanism applies also to his concept of organism, which is no more ultimate.

Symbolism; Its Meaning and Effect. New York: 1927.
Recommended.

The Aims of Education and Other Essays. New York: 1929.

Whitehead, Alfred North: *The Function of Reason.* Princeton: 1930.
Adventures of Ideas. New York: 1933.

Whitman, Walt: *Democratic Vistas.* New York: 1871.
The best prose exposition of Whitman's doctrine of Personalism which, though philosophically undeveloped, intuitively grasped and anticipated the elements of later personalism. Here and in Leaves of Grass Whitman speaks for a personalism that absorbs science and encloses it, dealing with equal readiness with internal events and the mere show of things: with the innermost recesses of the soul or the outermost reaches of the cosmos: a point of view which the present series of books has consciously expanded, in distinction to the narrower personalism, a variant of orthodox humanism, which is more characteristic of the European personalists.

Whyte, Lancelot Law: *The Next Development in Man.* New York: 1948.
Attempt to develop a unitary philosophy capable of embracing all phenomena; but by founding it on the Heraclitean concept of process and change the author fails to do justice to the static and "eternal" aspects of experience; and is therefore compelled by his logic not only to exclude every form of Platonism but to forgo, by that very act, the unitary goal that he regards as imperative. The concepts that underlie The Conduct of Life seek to escape this weakness and do justice to all the dimensions of experience. See Spencer's *First Principles.*

Wiener, Norbert: *The Human Use of Human Beings; Cybernetics and Society.* Boston: 1950.
Admirable exposition of the social implications of the new thinking machines: their danger and promise.

Willkie, Wendell: *One World.* New York: 1943.
Memorable for its title: the first formulation by a politician of the fundamental truth of our times—that mankind is one, and that the acceptance of its unity has become today a criterion of sanity as well as a goal of statesmanship.

Wilson, Richard A.: *The Miraculous Birth of Language.* New York: 1948.
Sound critique of the Darwinian and behaviorist attempt to minimize the gap between man and the rest of the animal world. Emphasizes the unique role of time and space concepts in language formation. Does belated justice to Kant, but for some reason while treating Rousseau overlooks the more important contributions of Vico; and in our time Cassirer and Langer. Highly recommended.

Wolff, Werner: *The Expression of Personality; Experimental Depth Psychology.* New York: 1943.

Wundt, Wilhelm: *The Facts of the Moral Life.* Trans. from second German ed., 1892. New York: 1897.

Young, J. Z.: *Doubt and Certainty in Science; A Biologist's Reflections on the Human Brain. The Reith Lectures.* In The Listener, Nov. 2, 1950 to Dec 21, 1950.

Younghusband, Francis Edward: *The Living Universe.* London: 1933.

ACKNOWLEDGMENTS

This book is part of a growing body of thought: so my debt to other scholars is properly an extensive one. The bibliography indicates my major sources and occasionally gives some measure of my debts.

In my other volumes I have acknowledged an early obligation to my old master, Patrick Geddes, and to his friend and collaborator, Victor Branford. To make up for the neglect of Geddes's thought by his contemporaries, I have in the past perhaps exaggerated his effect on my own mature thinking, though I have often failed to take full advantage of his most original contributions. While in the present book I have, I trust, pushed beyond the natural limitations of Geddes's period and culture, I should never be surprised to find the blaze of his ax on any trail I thought to have opened alone. To my colleagues and students at Dartmouth College, Columbia University, Stanford University, and the University of North Carolina I owe a debt too voluminous to record in detail. For more strictly personal influences in the conception and gestation of this series I can give no public acknowledgments: enough to recall Whitman's words, "The best is that which must be left unsaid." To this I make one exception, for without the generous understanding, the detached criticism, and the loyal comradeship of my wife, Sophia Wittenberg Mumford, this whole series would never have ripened. That debt crowns every other.—L. M.

INDEX

[*Note: Titles of books and section heads,
as well as foreign words, are italicized.*]